Teaching Adult English Language Learners

Teaching Adult English Language Learners

A Practical Introduction

Betsy Parrish

Hamline University

CAMBRIDGE
UNIVERSITY PRESS

University Printing House, Cambridge CB2 8BS, United Kingdom

One Liberty Plaza, 20th Floor, New York, NY 10006, USA

477 Williamstown Road, Port Melbourne, VIC 3207, Australia

314–321, 3rd Floor, Plot 3, Splendor Forum, Jasola District Centre, New Delhi – 110025, India

79 Anson Road, #06–04/06, Singapore 079906

Cambridge University Press is part of the University of Cambridge.

It furthers the University's mission by disseminating knowledge in the pursuit of education, learning and research at the highest international levels of excellence.

www.cambridge.org
Information on this title: www.cambridge.org/9781108702836

First published 2019

20 19 18 17 16 15 14 13 12 11 10 9 8 7 6 5 4 3 2 1

Printed in Malaysia by Vivar Printing

A catalogue record for this publication is available from the British Library

ISBN   978-1-108-70283-6 Paperback
ISBN   978-1-108-70285-0 Apple iBook
ISBN   978-1-108-70284-3 ebooks.com eBook
ISBN   978-1-108-70287-4 Google eBook
ISBN   978-1-108-70286-7 Kindle eBook

Dedication

To Jonas, Rémy, and Sina. Your genuine excitement for the work that I do in adult education is what encouraged me to take on this new edition.

Contents

3 Teaching Language for Meaningful Purposes

4 Developing Listening and Speaking Skills

5 Developing Reading and Writing Skills

6 Planning for Teaching and Learning

7 Managing Learning in Adult English Language Classes

Foreword

Background: Why did we need this book then?
Why do we need it now?

Sixteen years ago, Erik Gundersen invited reviewers to consider a prospectus for a book designed for novice teachers of adult ESL. It was huge in scope; a book you'd love to read but hate to have to write. The author's proposal addressed classroom practice, skills (speaking, reading, writing, listening), literacy and language development, classroom management, assessment, reporting, and federal accountability guidelines.

I (Janet) responded as thoroughly as I could to the prospectus, thinking all the while of how challenging it would be to develop the book and also wondering, really, do we need another handbook for teachers of adult English language learners?

Betsy Parrish developed and accepted her own challenge to bring such a book to print. The text she wrote, and has subsequently revised, answers my question with an emphatic *yes*. While there are many timeless elements to good teaching practice that may well have been addressed in a text within the past 20 years, there are also many particular things about teaching adults that have changed during that time. By bringing together a guided set of readings and activities addressing sound educational practice, and providing detailed resource lists, all within a solid framework, the author gives new (and not so new) teachers a much-needed overview of what English language instruction for adults looks like, and more importantly, what it looks like when done very well. Betsy brings her work as a teacher educator, her own international experience in learning and teaching languages, and her keen sense of what counts to this text; we hold in our hands a comprehensive introduction to an overview of the work we do when we work with adults learning English.

The original text and this revision are informed by an understanding of the complexities of teaching well, and of the specific issues surrounding instruction for adults possessing a range of prior involvement with education, varied abilities to speak, read, hear, and write in their own languages and in English, and varied expectations of what school looks like in an English-speaking country. The text provides teachers with a thorough overview of what learning looks like from intake to exit, who the stakeholders in the process are, and why it all matters in the first place. Beginning with an overview of who adult language learners might be and how they might learn, the text guides us through both theory and practice of classroom instruction, examining the development of key approaches and their usefulness in different contexts and for different purposes. The text includes a crucial section on assessment, enabling us to engage in critical reflection on how we come to know what adults in our classrooms have learned—and how adults come to understand their own progress as well.

Throughout this book, Betsy draws on examples of classroom practice and interaction gleaned from her own work and from that of other educators around the world. She offers an analysis of techniques and methodologies, describing processes through which to introduce and expand language development activities, considering the different contexts in which the work might occur, and pointing to strengths and drawbacks of methodologies. She consistently credits the reader with the sense to explore, reflect upon, and analyze the choices she or he makes in the classroom.

Betsy brings great integrity to this project. She believes in the primacy of learners' strengths and works against a deficit approach to teaching teachers—believing that English language learners **and** educators possess skills and abilities, if not (yet) experience. Her aim here is to assist teachers in assisting learners as well as they can. She believes that teachers are constantly learning and that they want to know what works for their learners. She believes that learning should occur in a safe and supportive environment and that teachers should care about this learning deeply. With this text she provides both new and more experienced teachers with key points to (re)consider in undertaking teaching, and a wealth of resources for those who so choose, to dig more deeply.

Each chapter contains sufficient information to enable educators to know what questions next to ask, what information next to seek. Betsy amply cites resources for further learning as well, so that the text can function as both a linear guide to teaching adult English language learners as well as a useful reference for regular review and consultation. Each chapter offers an overview of standard terms and practices, resources for further learning, web and print based materials, as well as references to others in the field knowledgeable in a given area. This compilation of resources makes the book especially valuable as knowledge grows; sources are scattered and time for searching, reading, and reviewing is limited. In our roles as instructional leaders, we have often drawn upon the first edition including for a practicum course as well as in planning professional development activities. We can attest to the text's accessibility and usefulness to new teachers. Moreover, as experienced educators ourselves, we have often revisited the text to inform our own practice. This revised edition maintains its predecessor's initial strengths, while adding and incorporating changes that reflect shifts in technology in its uses, as well as contemporary issues facing language learners—immigrants and refugees—living in complicated times.

No work is neutral. As federal, state, and international mandates increasingly drive and limit program possibilities, we need access to voices of reason to remind us of what good **teaching** practice is still all about—and that measurement alone does not improve instruction. Betsy walks readers through mandated frameworks and constraints incurred through those mandates while remaining aware of the realities inherent in daily classroom work. We learn how learners understand progress, how we can understand it, and how we can also translate it to those outside our programs to whom we are accountable. The process is demystified because Betsy has made it transparent. This is no small feat at a time when accountability drives instruction in too many instances.

Audience

We see this book serving multiple audiences. As an overview text for teacher education within higher education, it brings together points that other authors may cover in greater detail, but not always within the broader contexts that this text addresses. It also lends itself quite well to independent reading and exploration, and would be a useful vehicle for program-based, as well as regional-level professional development. For instance, an instructional leader could facilitate a study circle with a small group of teachers based on chapters of interest. Study circles can be conducted face-to-face and online as well as through a blended model. Betsy addresses an ongoing need for educators with a thirst for learning, but limited time and resources for gathering information scattered across various media—print, web-based, and video. She frames her intentions clearly, lays out each chapter carefully, and in the end has created a text that welcomes educators into acknowledging the joys and challenges of the work we do by informing us all of what's come before, what's possible, and what has to be done. The online resources will serve, as well, to keep the book's work current and to engage an ever-broadening community of educators.

This is a text that thoughtfully provides novice English language instructors with the guidance they need to learn how to teach well. However, even educators with extensive experience will be motivated to revisit the text again and again as they seek to enhance the effectiveness of their teaching. The text offers teacher educators and professional developers a well-balanced and theoretically-sound resource to use in courses and training.

This new edition reflects practices grounded in the latest research on language teaching. It also adds relevant and timely guidance on how to meaningfully integrate technology into instruction. Importantly, the text maintains the original version's deep commitment to learner-centered practice. This book is, in our view, the best primer available on the practical aspects of teaching English to adult learners. We believe you will see it that way, too.

Janet Isserlis

Susan Finn Miller

Acknowledgments

Thanks to my editors at Cambridge University Press for bringing this new edition of my book to life. Karen Momber, Teacher Development Publisher, showed tremendous respect, trust, and professionalism throughout this process. She pushed me and was open when I pushed back. Her attention to including other perspectives from the research was particularly helpful, along with her patience and guidance through the writing process. Adult ESL publisher, Bruce Myint at Cambridge in New York, encouraged me to submit the proposal for the new edition of my book to the UK team, and I am grateful for the strong endorsement both he and Jeff Krum, Editorial Director, gave this work as it was going through the proposal process. Senior Editor in Cambridge, Jo Timerick, took the project on with enthusiasm and has provided valuable guidance throughout this process. Finally, thanks to Joanna Garbutt for taking this through the last stages before production, to the permissions team at Cambridge, and to John Contos for that final, very careful edit.

My deepest gratitude goes to my colleague reviewers, Susan Finn Miller, Janet Isserlis, and Kathy Harris, for their insightful feedback, exhaustive recommendations for further research and resources, and tremendous commitment to meeting the needs of both learners and teachers. They have made this a book that is as responsive as possible to the ever-changing needs of the field. They very generously contributed their expertise to the teacher vignettes and voices found in the book as well. Janet worked with me throughout the development of the first edition of this book and her insights and collaboration during that process have left a mark on this edition as well. Thanks to all three of you!

Sylvia Ramirez provided extensive feedback on chapters in the first edition that are still central to this one, and Lynn Savage introduced me to the Cambridge editors in New York. I am grateful for their encouragement as well as everything I have learned from them about effective learning and teaching with adult learners over the past decades. I want to acknowledge the editor of the first edition, Erik Gunderson, for his foresight in identifying back in 2002 the need for this kind of book for teachers working with adult English language learners.

My thanks go to Suzanne McCurdy, Andrea Echelberger, and Julia Reimer for commenting on sections of my chapter drafts. As users of the first edition in their teacher education classes, they all engaged in lengthy conversations about how best to meet the current needs of the field. Thanks to Patsy Egan for sharing her insights on best practices for working with those learners with limited or interrupted prior formal schooling.

Thanks to Ivana Ferguson, Kristin Klas, Celeste Mazur, and Jamie Kreil for welcoming me into their classes as I was working on this new edition. Thanks to Astrid Liden, Brad Hasskamp, Renada Rutmanis, Linda Taylor, MaryAnn Cunningham Florez, Ronna Magy, and Diane Pecoraro for giving so generously of their time and expertise to talk about accountability, assessment, standards, and text selection, and to Jayme Adelson-Goldstein for the many discussions about professional development for teachers. Thanks also to those who responded to surveys and questionnaires, including Margaret Corrigan, Colleen Crossley, Colleen Schmitt, Dan Bruski, Nikki Carson, Lisa Gonzalves, George Schooley, Adrienne Fontenot, Kathleen O'Connor, David Rosen, Jen Vanek, Susan Wetenkamp-Brandt, Donna Price, and Dave Coleman. Also to the many teacher candidates in my classes who have inspired me throughout the years. All of those voices help to bring the book to life!

Many thanks to my colleagues in the School of Education at Hamline University who supported this endeavor.

Betsy Parrish

The authors and publishers acknowledge the following sources of copyright material and are grateful for the permissions granted. While every effort has been made, it has not always been possible to identify the sources of all the material used, or to trace all copyright holders. If any omissions are brought to our notice, we will be happy to include the appropriate acknowledgements on reprinting and in the next update to the digital edition, as applicable.

Key: C = Chapter

Text

C1: Text adapted from "Meeting the Language Needs of Today's Adult English Language Learner" by Betsy Parrish. Copyright © 2015 Washington, DC: U.S. Department of Education, Office of Career, Technical, and Adult Education. Reproduced with kind permission of OCTAE; Text on "Think about it." Reproduced with kind permission of Janet Isserlis; **C2**: Text adapted from "Leisure Time Activities sample instructional task ELPS Module 2: Analyzing Student Tasks in Relation to Content Demands, Thinking Skills, and Language Use." Copyright © 2018 American Institutes for Research; Text on "Problem posing." Reproduced with kind permission of Janet Isserlis; Text adapted from "Integrated Education and Training: Implementing Programs in Diverse Contexts" by Andy Nash and Ellen Hewett. Copyright © 2017 EdTech Center and World Education, Inc. Reproduced with kind permission of Andy Nash and Ellen Hewett; Text adapted from "Defining On-Ramps to Adult Career Pathways." Copyright © 2017 Center for Postsecondary and Economic Success. Reproduced with kind permission of Center for Law and Social Policy; Text taken from "Learning English with Digital Literacy and Community Engagement" by Heide Wrigley. Copyright © 2017 EdTech Center @ World Education, Inc. Reproduced with kind permission of Heide Wrigley; Figure taken from "English Innovations Transforms" by Heide Wrigley. Copyright © 2017 EdTech Center and World Education, Inc. Reproduced with kind permission of Heide Wrigley; Text on "Getting Started Task 2.4." Reproduced with kind permission of Kathleen O'Connor, Margaret Corrigan and Ivana Ferguson; Text on "Retail/Customer Service Certificate." Reproduced with kind permission of Renada Rutmanis; **C3**: Text adapted from "Experiential Learning Theory as a Guide for Experiential Educators in Higher Education, Experiential Learning & Teaching in Higher Education 1 no.1: 7-24" by Alice Y. Kolb & David A. Kolb. Copyright © 2017 Southern Utah University Press. Reproduced with kind permission; Text on "Error Correction." Reproduced with kind permission of Julia Reimer; **C4**: Text and listening lesson based on the interview with Sina Taghavi. Reproduced with kind permission; Screenshots taken from the "Developing Reading Skills for Intermediate/Advanced Learner" by Betsy Parrish. Copyright © New American Horizons. Reproduced with kind permission of Barbara Allaire; Text adapted from *Academic Conversations: Classroom Talk that Fosters Critical Thinking and Content Understandings* by Jeff Zwiers and Marie Crawford. Copyright © 2011 Stenhouse Publishers. Reproduced with permission of Stenhouse Publishers. www.stenhouse.com; Text on "Problem solving." Reproduced with kind permission of Ronna Magy and Donna Price; **C5**: Text taken from the "Research on low-educated second language and literacy acquisition" by Ineke van de Craats, Jeanne Kurvers, Martha Young-Scholten. Copyright © 2006 LOT, Netherlands Graduate School of Linguistics. Reproduced with kind permission; Text on "Whole-Part-Whole." Reproduced with kind permission of Andrea Echelberger; Text on "Literacy level learners." Reproduced with kind permission of Andrea Echelberger; Text on "Sample of student writing." Reproduced with kind permission of Laura Lenz; Text taken from "The Change Agent: Becoming a Paramedic" by Chrishana Burton. Copyright © 2017 The Change Agent. Reproduced with permission; Text on "Dialogue Journals." Reproduced with kind permission of Janet Isserlis; Text on "Responding to Learner Writing." Reproduced with kind permission of Janet Isserlis; **C6**: Text on "Lesson Planning." Reproduced with kind permission of Colleen Schmidt, George Schooley, Nikki Carson and Dan Bruski; Text adapted from "Assessing Success in family literacy and adult ESL" by National Clearing house for ESL Literacy Education. Copyright © 2000 Center for Applied

Linguistics. Reproduced with kind permission; Text on "Lesson planning process." Reproduced with kind permission of Jamie Kreil; Text adapted from "Meeting the Language Needs of Today's Adult English Language Learner" by Betsy Parrish. Copyright © 2015 Washington, DC: U.S. Department of Education, Office of Career, Technical, and Adult Education. Reproduced with kind permission of OCTAE; Quotes from Jamie Kreil and Colleen Schmidt. Reproduced with kind permission; Quotes from Kristen Klas. Reproduced with kind permission; Quotes from Celeste Mazur. Reproduced with kind permission; Text adapted from "Meeting the Language Needs of Today's Adult English Language Learner" by Betsy Parrish. Copyright © 2015 Washington, DC: U.S. Department of Education, Office of Career, Technical, and Adult Education. Reproduced with kind permission of OCTAE; Text adapted from "Meeting the Language Needs of Today's Adult English Language Learner" by Betsy Parrish. Copyright © 2015 Washington, DC: U.S. Department of Education, Office of Career, Technical, and Adult Education. Reproduced with kind permission of OCTAE; Text adapted from "Language Learning Strategies: What Every Teacher Should Know" by Rebecca L. Oxford. Copyright © 1990 Heinle/ELT, a part of Cengage, Inc. Reproduced by permission. www.cengage.com/permissions; Text taken from "Transitions Integration Framework." Copyright © ATLAS (ABE Teaching & Learning Advancement System), 2016, www.atlasABE.org. Reproduced with kind permission; Text on "Vocabulary Lesson." Reproduced with kind permission of Susan Finn Miller; Text on "Vocabulary Workout." Reproduced with kind permission of Jessica Jones; **C7**: Text adapted from "The Translanguaging Project: A Multilingual Pedagogy for Student Advocacy" by Rita Van Dyke-Kao, Christina Yanuaria and Laura Jacob. Copyright © 2017 CATESOL. Reproduced with kind permission of Rita Van Dyke-Kao, Christina Yanuaria and Laura Jacob; Text adapted from "Managed Enrollment: A Process - Not A Product" by Sylvia Ramirez. Copyright © 2001 MiraCosta College. Reproduced with kind permission of Sylvia Ramirez; Text adapted from "Universal Design for Learning graphic." Copyright © 2011 CAST. Reproduced with kind permission of David Gordon; Quote from Laura Kay Prosser. Reproduced with kind permission; **C8**: Text on "Considerations in Selecting Textbooks and Course Materials." Reproduced with kind permission of Lyle Heikes and Renada Rutmanis; Text on "Getting Started Task 8.5." Reproduced with kind permission of Kathy Harris, David Rosen, Susan Wetenkamp-Brandt and Jen Vanek; Text adapted from "DigComp 2.0: The Digital Competence Framework for Citizens and Northstar Digital Literacy Standards (ND)" by Stephanie Carretero, Riina Vuorikari and Yves Punie. Copyright © 2017 European Commission; Text adapted from "DigComp 2.0: The Digital Competence Framework for Citizens and Northstar Digital Literacy Standards (ND)" by Stephanie Carretero, Riina Vuorikari and Yves Punie. Copyright © 2017 European Commission; Text adapted from "Integrating digital literacy into English language instruction: Professional development module" by Kathy Harris. Copyright © 2015 Washington, DC: U.S. Department of Education, Office of Career, Technical, and Adult Education. Reproduced with kind permission of OCTAE; Text on "Digital Learning Tasks." Reproduced with kind permission of Kathy Harris; Text taken from "The 5w's of website evaluation" by Kathy Schrock. Reproduced with permission of Kathy Schrock; Text taken from "Digital Literacy: Consume, Create, Curate!" by Nell Eckersley. Copyright © 2017 World Education, Inc. Reproduced with kind permission of EdTech Center @ World Education, Inc.; Text and table adapted from "Module 9: Information Literacy." Copyright © Northstar Digital Literacy. Reproduced with kind permission; Screenshot taken from "ELL 5/6 class website." Copyright © Kelly A. Ray. Reproduced with kind permission of Alison Shank; **C9**: Text on "A different view of assessment." Reproduced with kind permission of Margaret Corrigan and Diane Pecoraro; Quote from MaryAnn Cunningham Florez. Reproduced with kind permission; Quote from Brad Hasskamp and Astrid Liden. Reproduced with kind permission; Quote and rubric taken from "#IamABE Curriculum." Reproduced with kind permission of Kristin Klas and Jamie Kreil; Text taken from "Learning for LIFE: An ESL Literacy Curriculum Framework." Copyright © 2011 Bow Valley College. Reproduced with kind permission; Quote from Adrienne Fontenot. Reproduced with kind permission; Quote reproduced with kind permission of Jayme Adelson-Goldstein, National Professional

Introduction

This book is a completely revised and updated edition of my 2004 book, *Teaching Adult ESL: A Practical Introduction.* How things have changed in the 15 years since I started writing that book! At that time, the focus of instruction and assessments for adult ESL was primarily on life-skills competencies. Today, we are placing far more emphasis on preparing adults for the demands of work and school in the 21st century, which includes academic language, digital competence, and strategies for accessing complex texts. Of course, development of literacy in all its forms is still central to the work we do, but the field is now acknowledging the need to assist adult English learners to transition to new opportunities at school, work, and in their communities that takes them well beyond survival English. Instruction needs to provide supports that allow all learners to *thrive* in their new communities. So this edition places more emphasis on learning English for professional and academic success, while at the same time providing ideas on working with newcomers with minimal English skills. I have also placed far more emphasis on working with learners who may have limited or interrupted prior formal schooling.

The earlier book was written primarily for teachers working with immigrant and refugee learners in the U.S. This edition has shifted in a very significant way, with far more research, resources, and teacher voices representing global contexts in which adult learners are engaged with learning English in adult education programs, whether in Melbourne, Toronto, or Minneapolis.

I would like you, the reader, to have a sense of what beliefs have shaped my work and then invite you to reflect on your own beliefs about teaching and learning as a means of framing how you read, interact with, and understand the teaching principles and practices presented in the coming chapters.

It is my belief that learning starts from within. Every adult English language learner, as well as every ESL teacher, experiences what we do in the classroom differently. Everything that happens is shaped by experiences, culture, expectations, strengths, and needs. Each of you will experience this text differently. Some of you may have spent a considerable amount of time in an ESL classroom already and will draw on those experiences to shape and understand the principles and practices covered in this book. Those of you who are new to teaching English language learners will draw on your experience learning other things. It is because of this belief that every chapter is interspersed with tasks that allow you to preview content, explore your ideas and practices, and finally, apply what you've learned in your own class, or through observing and collaborating with others.

I also believe that learning is cyclical and that it takes time. While I have chosen to organize the content of this book in a particular order, there may be some topics that you'll revisit as you read the book, particularly those of you who are new to teaching. Chapters 1 and 2 provide a broad context for you as a reader, examining issues of English learner life circumstances, the language demands learners face in today's world, second language acquisition theories, an overview of common teaching approaches, and descriptions of program options. Chapters 3 through 5 focus on the tools of classroom teaching: presenting and practicing language, developing listening, speaking, reading, and writing skills. Chapters 6 through 8 look at planning for teaching, creating optimal learning environments, choosing print and digital materials, and helping learners to develop their digital competence. The last two chapters provide an overview of assessment and accountability principles and practices as well as standards that guide programming. While you may work through these topics in a linear fashion, they should be viewed as interconnected and as a starting point for further exploration.

Finally, I believe that the best learning and teaching are collaborative. Collaboration is what makes my work as teacher, learner, and colleague rich and rewarding. I had the opportunity to collaborate with many people as I developed this book. My collaboration with Susan Finn Miller, Janet Isserlis, and Kathy Harris during the development of this new edition had a tremendous impact on the content of this book. My collaboration with all of those who invited me into their classrooms, and those who shared their expertise for the classroom vignettes and quotes found throughout the book, challenged me to consider many possible contexts, constraints, and beliefs about teaching and learning; they all added much more depth to the text than I could have provided on my own. My collaboration with adult English language learners and teachers throughout my career has given me myriad examples to draw on, which I hope provide you, the reader, with vivid examples of learning and teaching in action. The reflection tasks throughout this book serve to promote collaboration between you and your classmates or colleagues, and the teaching principles presented in these chapters are grounded in the belief that good teaching is based on a genuine collaboration with learners.

Before you begin reading, take some time to think about your own beliefs about teaching and learning. You will be invited to reflect on these beliefs again at the end of the book, but continue to think about how your views evolve and change throughout the process of learning more about teaching English to adult learners.

Looking forward . . .

Complete these statements with your current beliefs about teaching and learning in adult ESL contexts. Work with a group of classmates or colleagues, or write your reflections in a journal.

1. Strengths and challenges adult learners may bring to the classroom are . . .

2. Some common purposes for learning English are . . .

3. Learning a second language involves . . .

4. If I walked into an adult English language classroom, I'd like to see . . .

5. Learners' roles and responsibilities in class are . . .

6. My responsibilities as a teacher are . . .

1 | Working with Adult English Language Learners

To consider before reading this chapter:

- What factors may affect an adult English learner's successful transition to living in a country?
- What does it mean to "know" a language?
- What do you think makes a class "learner-centered?"

Part I: Making the adjustment to a new country

1.1 Introduction

Adult English language learners (ELLs) come to communities and classrooms for a variety of reasons and with a variety of backgrounds. For some, the transition from one country to the other is far easier than it is for others. There are a number of factors that contribute to individuals' abilities to adjust to a new country and to acquire the skills (linguistic and nonlinguistic) to thrive in that new country, where cultural beliefs, practices, and norms may differ greatly from their own. These factors include everything from the reason people emigrate from their country of origin to access to transportation in the new country. In the first part of this chapter, we examine factors that contribute to immigrants' and refugees' successful adjustments to a living in a new country. We also consider principles of learner-centered teaching that are responsive to learners' diverse strengths and needs, and that may help to ease the transition to a new setting and culture. We explore the language and skills needed for access to information and full participation at 21st-century work places and schools as well as in communities. We then turn to the issue of second language acquisition. What do we know about the process of learning a second language? How do age and previous educational experience affect the ability to learn a second language?

Getting Started

 Task 1.1

There is no question that the primary goal of learners in English language classes is to acquire the English skills needed to thrive in a new country, but why does meeting that goal come more easily for some people than for others? Read the following stories of two immigrants and consider the challenges each faces and the strengths they bring to the new setting. Identify the advantages and challenges each may have and complete the table below.

Daris is a 50-year-old Bosnian immigrant who settled in the U.S. with his wife and two children in 2012, joining family members who came to the U.S. as refugees in the 1990s. Daris and his family became U.S. citizens in 2018. He completed an engineering degree in Sarajevo and worked there as an electrical engineer for four years before coming to the U.S. Daris never studied English in school, but he studied German throughout high school and in college. His children were eight and ten when they arrived in the U.S. and acquired English quickly. As a family, they always speak Bosnian at home, and the children are completely bilingual. Daris' first job was as a baggage handler at the airport. Upon completing the highest level of ESL courses in the adult education program in his district, he entered a certification program to become a network engineer and now works for a local telecommunications company. While he is satisfied with his professional situation in the U.S., he misses the professional status he had in Bosnia where he led a team of engineers. Daris and his family take part in sports, go to the YMCA, and spend time with their many extended family members in the area.

Naw is a 39-year-old Karen refugee who is a widow and mother of four. She and her family came to the U.S. in 2009 after spending two years in a refugee camp in Thailand due to turmoil in her home country, Myanmar (formerly known as Burma). She came from a family of rural farmers, and she has no formal education and only basic literacy in her first language. Two of her children were born in Myanmar and the other two were born in the United States. Her husband died after the birth of her fourth child. Her two younger children seem to be learning English and adopting American ways very quickly. Her culture expects extreme respect for elders, which she doesn't see her children extending to her. As a widow, she would like her children to stay with her, but her daughters want to live and work away from home. Naw has held the same job as a line operator in manufacturing for the past three years.

Complete this chart with information from Daris' and Naw's stories:

Daris' Advantages	Daris' Challenges
Came to the U.S. with an advanced degree	
Naw's Advantages	**Naw's Challenges**
Is currently employed	

Follow-up: Compare and discuss your answers with a colleague or classmate. If you are working on your own, you may want to start a journal with responses to the questions in the book. What did you notice about Daris' and Naw's lives? Differences in education, connection to family, and involvement in the community are all factors that would most certainly influence their ability to reach their full potential while operating in a new country and in a new language. These variables have a tremendous impact on teaching and learning, and while you cannot possibly know everything about every learner in class, understanding students' situations can help teachers become more responsive to learner needs and more understanding of what learners are going through as they adjust to a new life. We will return to Daris and Naw after looking at these and other variables in more detail.

1.2 A process for understanding adult English language learners

Many ESL professionals can only imagine what it must be like for adult learners as they come to a new country, which entails learning new systems of education, government, and commerce. At the same time, they may have left behind family, jobs, and the country they probably lived in their entire lives. What can help educators begin to understand the strengths learners bring to the classroom as well as the challenges they face?

There are a number of factors that may influence how successfully one is able to acculturate to a new environment (Dow 2011; Olsen 1988; Scarcella 1990). **Acculturation** describes how members of minority cultures adapt to a dominant culture, a process which involves an understanding of the beliefs, norms, and behaviors of the new culture, without letting go of the first culture (Scarcella 1990). Berry (1997) reminds us that acculturation is, ideally, a reciprocal process where the majority culture makes adjustments as new groups join a community. Schumann (1986) has suggested that acculturation leads to less social distancing and potential marginalization and also leads to more active participation by ELLs in new communities. This, in turn, provides more opportunity to engage with the target language. Acculturation is very different from **assimilation**, which implies complete absorption of the second culture's practices, beliefs, and norms. While some immigrants may be anxious to fit into the new setting, assimilation as such can create both challenges in terms of intergenerational dynamics, and feelings of belonging (or not) to either or both cultures. The following section serves to illustrate that an immigrant or refugee's ability to acculturate is not, for the most part, based on conscious choices, but rather on his or her life circumstances. Understanding those circumstances generally, and the particularities of learners' communities can inform teachers' decisions about classroom materials, activities, and approaches.

Factors affecting cultural adjustment

To help you understand adult English learners' life circumstances, you can consider various factors identified as having an effect on a person's ability to adjust to a new culture, which then contributes to successful language acquisition. Table 1.1 provides an overview of factors you can consider and the questions you can ask yourself about learners in your program.

Table 1.1 Factors Affecting Cultural Adjustment

Factors	Things to Consider / Questions You Need to Ask Yourself
1 Country of origin and country of settlement	Are there any similarities between life in the first and second culture (shared religions, customs)? Have there been waves of immigration from that country at earlier times (Olsen 1988)? Does the country of settlement have a history of welcoming immigrants (Berry 1997)?
2 Reasons for coming to the new country	Has the immigrant come by choice, or due to war or other trauma? Was she or he forced to leave because of political circumstances? In many contexts, refugees represent the smallest percentage of participants in adult education programs overall (Wrigley 2007); however, they may face particular challenges, for example, limited prior formal schooling; coming from a rural area and now adjusting to life in a large, urban area; and feeling "unsettled" in the new country due to hopes of someday returning to their country if the political or social conditions there change.
3 Age at which the person emigrated	As you will see in this chapter, the ability to acquire a second language can be affected by the age at which one begins learning that language. The ability to adjust to differing cultural norms can be easier for younger people as well.
4 Financial resources / Changes in status	Immigration may bring an extreme change in economic conditions or social status, for better or for worse. Does immigration mean improved economic conditions? Many immigrants and refugees come with few resources and find themselves with no work or in low-paying jobs, even after a number of years in the new country (Batalova and Fix 2015). They may not have the English language skills needed to make their intellect visible or to find work commensurate with their years of prior formal education (Wrigley 2007; Scarcella 1990).

5	Difficulties in the journey / Potential life disruption and upheaval during war	Did the learner escape his or her country? Has she or he spent time in a refugee camp? Many learners may have been victims of torture or may have experienced the trauma and atrocities of war. The result may be post-traumatic stress disorder, depression, or at the very least, feelings of insecurity (Dow 2011). It can be extremely difficult for these learners to concentrate and attend to the task of learning language.
6	Immigration status (official refugee, with or without documentation)	If a learner is an undocumented worker, is there fear of arrest? Even those who are documented can be uncertain of immigration laws. A distrust of government and authority may result in immigrants not taking advantage of social and government services from which they could benefit (health, education, etc.). Note that this isn't something you would ask a learner, but it is important be aware of what learners may be experiencing.
7	Education and level of literacy in first language / Types of experiences and attitudes about teaching and learning practices	Does the learner have limited or interrupted prior formal schooling? Are the educational conventions in his/her country similar to or very different from those practiced in the new country? Is the learner pre-literate, meaning she or he can speak a language that does not have a written form, or has a form that is rare or has developed very recently? For those with prior formal schooling, educational practices/ expectations may be very different across cultures, e.g., expectations about teacher/student roles and differing experiences with collaborative learning. Education and level of literacy in the first language has an enormous impact on one's ability to acquire literacy and other skills in the second language. That is not to say that learners without prior formal schooling have less to bring to the classroom. All learners bring **funds of knowledge** (Moll, et al. 1992) or "the historically accumulated and culturally developed bodies of knowledge and skills essential for household or individual functioning and well-being" (p. 133).
8	Previous exposure to English and other languages	Has the learner studied English or other languages before? How many other languages does the learner speak? For many, English will represent a third or fourth (or more) language. Knowledge of English can facilitate the process of cultural adjustment; knowing other languages will facilitate the process of learning English.
9	Opportunities to use the target language	Does the learner have many opportunities to use English outside of class? Learners may be raising a family, working, and attending language classes, giving them little time to use English outside of class. Learners may live in an area where they can secure jobs using their first language (Wrigley 2007).
10	Extent of family separation	Did the learner come alone or with family? Is the extended family in the new country or have they been left behind? Family members' opportunities to reunite or visit one another can have an impact on adjustment to a new country.
11	Experience living in another country	Has the learner been through the experience of navigating new systems (education, government, etc.)?

12 Status of cultural group / Amount of discrimination they face	There may be groups that hold more status, perhaps due to history or familiarity of the immigrants' culture (e.g., North Americans, both in the U.S. and Canada, are more familiar with Chinese culture than they are with Sudanese culture. Is the learner from a group that faces particular discrimination? There may be limited job possibilities due to educational background, literacy, and different life experiences (Scarcella 1990).

Now we can use this list of factors to examine Daris' and Naw's stories. As you will see, this process can lead us to a detailed description of the journey taken by any immigrant.

Table 1.2 Analysis of Daris' and Naw's Journey to a New Country

Daris	Naw
1 Country of origin Daris came from the largest city in Bosnia and has settled in a major city in the U.S. where over 70,000 Bosnians reside. While as a Muslim, he may not be a member of the majority religion in the U.S., he is in a community with many Muslims.	Country of origin The Karen people from Myanmar bring religious and cultural beliefs and practices that may differ from those practiced locally in the U.S. While the Karen are a fairly recent immigrant group, there are many Karen residing in her city in the U.S.
2 Reasons for coming to the U.S. Daris is an immigrant who came through family reunification. He came by choice and then chose to apply for citizenship.	Reasons for coming to the U.S. Naw came as a refugee, as a result of turmoil in her country.
3 Age at which the person emigrated Daris came as an adult. His children came at a young age and acquired language skills quickly. When leaving Bosnia, they experienced separation from friends but the move to the U.S. has brought them closer to extended family they didn't know before.	Age at which the person emigrated Naw came as an adult; two of her children came at a young age and have acquired language skills very quickly and have tried to assimilate into the second culture. This has caused a rift between Naw and her children.
4 Financial resources / Changes in status Daris pursued further training and attained employment related to his original degree. He has been able to support himself and his family. Perhaps some change in his status; he led a team of engineers in Sarajevo.	Financial resources / Changes in status Possible economic deprivation as a single parent. Continued employment in past few years is positive.
5 Difficulties in the journey / Extent of life disruption and trauma during war Daris didn't resettle in the U.S. during the war in Bosnia the way his brother and cousins did in the 1990s, but he may very well have experienced trauma during that conflict as a young man.	Difficulties in the journey / Extent of life disruption and trauma during war Extreme disruption and likely trauma during the turmoil in her country; she has gone from living in a rural setting to living in an urban area.

6 Immigration status Citizen	**Immigration status** As a refugee, she has permanent residency and can eventually apply for citizenship.
7 Education and level of literacy in first language / Types of experiences and attitudes about teaching and learning practices Highly educated with an advanced degree from his country.	**Education and level of literacy in first language / Types of experiences and attitudes about teaching and learning practices** No prior formal education; basic literacy in her first language.
8 Previous exposure to English and other languages Had not studied English formally before coming to the U.S.; has studied German for several years from middle school through university.	**Previous exposure to English and other languages** No previous exposure to English; no experience learning other languages.
9 Experience living in another country Had never lived in another culture, but had traveled extensively in Europe.	**Experience living in another country** None
10 Opportunities to use the target language Considerable opportunities to use the target language (English) in his studies, work, and most likely in activities in the community (e.g., membership at YMCA, interactions with children's teachers).	**Opportunities to use the target language** Opportunities to use English with coworkers, although she may be in a position that doesn't require extensive interactions in English. Opportunities to interact with children's teachers.
11 Extent of family separation The move to the U.S. has brought him closer to extended family. He has left behind some family in Bosnia, but he and his family can return there for visits.	**Extent of family separation** Many of Naw's family members are in the United States. While there may not be physical separation, there appears to be emotional separation with her children.
12 Status of cultural group / Amount of discrimination they face He feels some loss of status here as compared to that which he held in Bosnia. It is difficult to judge the extent to which he experiences discrimination; many immigrants, regardless of their country of origin, feel some degree of discrimination by the majority culture. He and his children may face discrimination as a member of a minority religious group.	**Status of cultural group / Amount of discrimination they face** Naw is part of a group that that may not be well understood by many in the community. For Naw, this may come in the form of discrimination at work because of her limited education.

Through reading and thinking about Daris' and Naw's lives in great detail, we can begin to answer the question: "What *exactly* is it that helps or hinders an immigrant's ability to thrive in the new culture?" Considering language learners' lives in this way deepens opportunities for understanding their circumstances, which in turn can inform classroom practice to address their strengths, needs, circumstances, and abilities.

Some other considerations

Many adult learners may be holding down more than one job or working split shifts due to family needs and obligations. They may not want to leave their children in the care of strangers, preferring to leave them in the care of relatives. This means that they may have to work and take ESL classes at times that allow for other family members to care for their children. This can result in sporadic attendance and fatigue in class, both of which are understandable. Lack of reliable transportation is another factor affecting a learner's ability to access ESL programming.

Another challenge for new immigrants is **intergenerational tension** that may occur within the nuclear family. Children of immigrants may likely adapt to the new culture and acquire the new language very quickly. They may attempt to assimilate in order to fit in with their peer group, resulting in the rejection of their parents' values and beliefs. Parents may experience diminished self-esteem as they rely on their children to translate for them (Foner and Dreby 2011). In cases where the children begin to lose proficiency in the home language while the parents are still acquiring English, the parents' ability to transmit values and provide discipline may be compromised. Potential rifts between parents and children can add to the stress learners are encountering in a new country. At the same time, it should be noted that feelings of closeness often characterize intergenerational relations, which can provide a source of support, both practical and emotional (Swartz 2009).

Unemployment rates can also have an impact on how long students stay with a program. As the unemployment rate fell to record lows in Minnesota, many immigrants and refugees found themselves in the workplace within two weeks of their arrival in the U.S. These realities can have an enormous impact on *what* you need to be teaching students if they manage to attend class while working. Let me share a scenario I encountered in a plant that manufactures plastic containers and screwdriver shafts:

> *Five line workers from Russia had recently been hired at the plant. They had all been here a very short time and had minimal oral language skills. The plant floor was very noisy and hectic, so it was hard to hear people. The workers' job consisted of filling molds and operating presses. One day a supervisor noticed a problem with a piece of equipment that could have caused severe injury to the employee using it. He made a frantic gesture of cutting his throat (meaning that the employee needed to shut off the machine immediately). The employee took great offense interpreting the message to mean: You're fired!*

In a class for newcomer immigrants, you might think of starting with basic introductions and greetings, language needed to find their way around their communities, etc. But were you to have these five newcomers in your class, they may have the more immediate need of understanding gestures used on a noisy shop floor. Finding ways to integrate learners' particular needs and interests is an ongoing challenge in adult ESL classrooms. We look at the process of assessing learners' needs and strengths as well as the most prevalent types of programs in greater detail in Chapter 2. In any event, we need to be mindful of the fact that there are always variables to consider that will differ with any group of learners and these variables will inform and affect the choices you make as a teacher.

1.3 Implications for the ESL classroom

Personal factors (e.g., educational background, financial status, family, and job responsibilities) as well as societal factors (e.g., pressure to move into the workplace before having adequate language skills) have a significant impact on learning and many adult learners have precious little time to attend ESL classes and practice outside of the classroom. That is why it is paramount that adult ESL instruction be highly customized, accessible, and *learner-centered*, giving learners an optimal setting for acquiring the language skills they need to thrive within their communities.

What does learner-centered mean?

Throughout this book, we explore practices that adhere to the following core principles of learner-centered teaching:

- All learners bring to class rich knowledge and experiences that must be acknowledged and incorporated into instruction.
- Learners' first language and culture are resources for learning.
- The content of instruction is relevant to the learners' needs and interests and draws on their experiences and knowledge.
- Learners make choices about/inform content and classroom activities.
- Learners have active roles in the classroom and control the direction of activities.
- Classroom interactions and tasks are authentic, reflecting how language is used in the real world.
- Teachers use authentic language in their interactions with learners.
- Learners acquire strategies that help them learn inside and outside of the classroom without the help of a teacher.
- Classroom tasks challenge learners and promote higher-order thinking skills.
- Teachers listen actively for themes that emerge from learners and build those into instruction.
- Teachers constantly assess teaching and learning in relation to learners' needs and strengths.

A learner-centered view of teaching acknowledges that adult learners come to your class with rich knowledge and experiences, but because of their limited ability to communicate and express themselves in English, that knowledge and experience may feel locked inside of them. Good teaching practice includes designing ongoing means of enabling learners to demonstrate what they know through a range of activities and approaches. As we see in the chapters ahead, learner-centered teaching does not mean leaving learners to their own devices; it entails considerable teacher direction. Teacher-*directed* classes do not necessarily equate to teacher-*centered* classes.

The knowledge and skills teachers need in order to foster truly learner-centered, strengths-based classrooms are the foundation of this book. Examining different program options, as well as approaches and strategies for teaching ESL to adult learners, enables us to consider numerous means of connecting instruction to learners' lives. At the same time, we need to embrace the notion that adult English language learners are capable of meeting rigorous standards that go beyond basic survival skills. Let's turn to what the language demands are for learners in today's world.

1.4　Addressing the language demands of today's world

The needs of adult learners are not always evident to a teacher new to the field, and addressing those needs starts by recognizing the linguistic demands inherent to the tasks all learners must tackle in today's digital-rich, information-dense world.

Think about it

A learner comes to her teacher, Janet, with a very high electric bill. Together they discuss the learner's usage of electricity, ending up at a home repair website with recommendations for simple home repairs that can cut energy costs, for example, products to insulate windows. They also visit an online newsletter from the electric company that shares other tips for saving energy.

Consider the skills that went into this process: analyzing the impact of our actions on energy costs, making use of digital tools to gather information, interpreting infographics at a home repair website and online newsletter, and making decisions after weighing options.

Until not too long ago, many adult ESL curricula focused on basic survival skills, for example, navigating the community, opening a bank account, and making a doctor's appointment. Although these skills are still important for newcomers, this approach does not adequately address the demands of today's world or prepare learners to access information they need for success in all areas of their lives. At home, adult English learners need to read mail selectively, help their children with homework, and communicate using digital tools. They may want to access a parent portal to track their children's grades at school. They need to make decisions about services in their communities, such as healthcare, or the resources available to them from the utility company as above, which require print and digital literacy as well as critical thinking skills.

The jobs and educational opportunities of the 21st century require higher reading levels, understanding of more complex language, stronger communication skills, and more critical thinking skills than ever before (Parrish 2015a). Employees in just about any job are expected to work effectively in teams, understand and produce complex written communications, and use digital tools on the job (Casner-Lotto and Barrington 2006; Trilling and Fabel 2009). Success at the postsecondary level or in work-related trainings requires understanding complex nonfiction texts, writing reports or research papers, note-taking, and synthesizing information from multiple sources, print and digital (Parrish and Johnson 2010). These increased demands (e.g., academic language, digital literacy, interpreting charts or graphs) are reflected in state and national standards where English is taught as a second language to adults (see the Recommended Resources section for examples from the U.S. and Canada).

These increased language demands can be particularly challenging for a student like Naw who has low literacy levels and limited formal schooling. Naw is not alone. In fact, close to half of the immigrants entering the U.S. have limited access to citizenship, jobs, and job training, or other postsecondary education because of limited literacy and language skills (National Commission on Adult Literacy 2008). As we see throughout this book, we need to provide instruction that challenges learners and that mirrors the rigors of language use in the 21st century, thus allowing adult English learners to gain access to opportunities and thrive in their communities. This can start from the very beginning levels of adult ESL.

📋 **Task 1.2**

Read this vignette of a learner who finds herself in what appears to be a primarily "life-skills" class. What is missing for Daniela in this class? What might a more rigorous curriculum that addresses Daniela's needs look like?

Daniela, a mother of three school-aged children, is from Ecuador. She works in housekeeping at a hotel and attends a low-intermediate-level ESL class at a volunteer-run program in her community. The program she attends has a largely life-skills curriculum, covering topics such as shopping, personal finance, and going to the doctor. Daniela feels frustrated because people don't understand her at work. She has a hard time explaining problems to her boss because she can't express herself well in English. She has trouble communicating with her coworkers and patrons at the hotel where she works. Her dream is to get her high school equivalency and then one day become a nurse.

(Adapted from Parrish 2015b)

Work with a partner or on your own and write your ideas here:

Which of Daniela's needs are being met?	Which of Daniela's needs are not being met?	What might a more rigorous curriculum include?

Considering Daniela's personal situation and her long-term goals, she may need help in identifying and implementing the many steps it takes to reach her academic and professional goals. Given her stated frustration with not being understood by her boss and not being able to express herself clearly to her coworkers, Daniela needs practice with effective communication strategies so that she can more easily ask for clarification, state a problem, or interrupt appropriately in work contexts. With her long-term goals of attaining her high school equivalency and one day becoming a nurse, she needs practice with academic reading and listening strategies, and note-taking using a variety of text types, including short prose, charts, and graphs. Her intelligibility (the ability to be understood by others) seems to be an issue for her, so she could benefit from work on areas of her pronunciation that are causing breakdowns in communication. Because of her interest in nursing, she could be working with rich content related to that field. How does this analysis compare to the ideas you generated above? Through this analysis, we can see that Daniela needs far more than English for survival; she needs to develop skills that will allow her to thrive in her new community.

Next, we turn to what the profession has to say about what it means to *know a language* and *how* it is that learners can achieve some level of competence in a second (or, in many cases third, fourth . . .) language.

Part II: What does it mean to know a language?

1.5 Introduction

In order to understand language instruction overall, it's important to first understand what it means to *know* a language. Is it a question of conjugating verbs correctly, using intelligible pronunciation, or knowing how to ask someone for help or offer an opinion? Clearly, the answer to this is dependent on the needs and strengths of the learner. There are, however, a number of areas of *language* that you can draw on when developing your lessons for adult learners.

Getting Started

 Task 1.3

What do the following areas of language have in common and what are the differences? See if you can sort the following examples of language into four categories using the table below.

Grammar	*Appropriate intonation*
Using gestures to demonstrate meaning	*Pronunciation*
Guessing meaning of new words	*Vocabulary*
Writing for different purposes	*Body language*
Formal/informal language	*Asking for definitions*
Language functions (e.g., making complaints, greetings and introductions)	*Reading for different purposes*
Using colloquial language appropriately	*Spelling*
Asking someone to speak more slowly	*Listening only for the information you need*
Interpreting charts and graphs; punctuation	

Four different areas of language: Sort the examples of language into these four categories. If you're doing this in class, work with a partner:

Category 1: Language Forms	Category 2: Social Interaction
Category 3: Language Skills	**Category 4: Learning How to Learn**

Follow-up: Compare your answers with another group. Can you add one more example of your own to each box? Our goal as language teachers is to help learners attain some level of proficiency in *all* of these areas. We want them to attain communicative competence, which goes far beyond a more traditional focus on learning vocabulary and grammar. Consider your own experiences as a language learner. To what degree did your language learning include attention to all four areas of language presented here?

1.6 Helping learners attain communicative competence

Communicative competence describes the ability to use language in a variety settings (at work, at school, at a store, at home) with varying degrees of formality (with a friend vs. with a boss). In order to achieve communicative competence, a learner needs to become proficient in a number of areas, including language forms, social interactions, language skills, and learning strategies. In other words, the ability to convey your intended message and make yourself understood are equally, if not more important, than the ability to produce grammatically correct sentences. The four areas of competence are outlined in Table 1.3.

Table 1.3 Areas of Language That Can Lead to Communicative Competence

Language forms (Linguistic competence)	Knowledge of grammatical forms, spelling, vocabulary, punctuation, and pronunciation
Social interactions (Sociolinguistic competence)	Ability to use language, both verbal and non-verbal, appropriately in social contexts
Language skills (Discourse competence)	Ability to read and write, and the ability to understand and use spoken language
Learning strategies (Strategic competence)	Ability to use strategies to make yourself understood; how to learn on your own outside of the classroom

Regardless of the focus of instruction, for example, English for work or basic literacy development, attaining a degree of competence in all of the areas above should be the goal of any second language instruction. Drawing from all of these areas of language helps shape and inform the choices that adult ESL teachers make about their curricula, materials, and classroom practices.

The chart below represents the four areas of language competence along with the examples that you sorted into categories in Task 1.3. How does this categorization compare to yours?

Category 1: Language forms	Category 2: Social interactions
Grammar	Formal/informal language
Pronunciation	Language functions (e.g., making complaints, greetings and introductions)
Punctuation	
Spelling	Polite intonation
Vocabulary	Using colloquial language appropriately
	Body language

Category 3: Language skills	Category 4: Learning strategies
Writing for different purposes	Using gestures to demonstrate meaning
Reading for different purposes	Asking for definitions
Interpreting charts and graphs	Asking someone to speak more slowly
Listening only for the information you need	Guessing meaning of new words

In order to understand better how these concepts help to shape instruction in ways that are appropriate for learners, look at two teachers' objectives for their lesson plans on "Asking Questions." What areas of language does each teacher include? Which lesson do you think would provide more opportunities to develop some degree of communicative competence in the area of asking questions and why?

Table 1.4 Sample Lesson Plan Objectives for Two Lessons on "Asking Questions"

Teacher	Objectives
Teacher A Question formation	Students will be able to use DO-support correctly in questions. Students will choose the correct question word (who, what, when, where, how). Students will use falling intonation for *wh-* questions; rising intonation for *Yes/No* questions.
Teacher B Asking questions at work	Students will be able to interrupt coworkers politely. Students will be able to ask coworkers for help. Students will explain when and why it's appropriate to ask for help at work. Students will use appropriate polite intonation when asking for assistance. Students will be able to use modal verbs (can, could, would) correctly in polite requests, e.g., "Could you please show me how to . . ."

Everything in Teacher A's lesson focuses on language forms: rules and patterns for question formation, and rising or falling intonation. Teacher B, however, has taken a broader view of the language of questions. She includes the following:

- *Social interaction*: teaching the language function of polite requests; interrupting coworkers politely; using polite intonation when asking for assistance
- *Learning strategies*: learning how to ask for help at work
- *Cultural competence:* When is it advisable or necessary to ask for help at work? What are the consequences of asking/not asking (e.g., many employers would prefer being asked before workers make mistakes, wasting materials/time)?
- *Language forms*: learning appropriate forms for making polite requests

Teacher B's lesson goes farther in addressing a variety of language outcomes and will address a broader range of learner needs, for example, those identified for Daniela in Section 1.4. Lesson B is more authentic as well, including communicative purposes for using language.

1.7 How do learners attain competence in a second language?

Language teaching professionals have long considered how a person becomes a proficient user of a language. What processes underlie second language acquisition? While we may never have an answer to that question, there are many theories about how languages are learned that have been informed by research and observations in second language classrooms. We start with the view of language acquisition that is no longer held by most ESL professionals. **Behaviorism**, a theory that held its ground for many years, shaped much of language instruction throughout the 1950s and 1960s and continues to shape instruction in some venues around the world today.

1.8 Behaviorism

Behaviorism (Skinner 1957) is the theory that human beings learn new behaviors through a stimulus and response cycle. In language learning it holds that language is learned through mimicry and memorization of forms, which leads to habit formation. It suggests that the goal of instruction is to replace bad habits (errors in production) with good ones (grammatical utterances).

This theory resulted in the creation and extensive use of the Audiolingual Method (ALM) for teaching foreign languages. This method of teaching relied heavily on the use of memorization of set dialogues and extensive repetition and drilling. It was developed in the 1950s as a method for teaching foreign languages to military personal very quickly. Its focus on drills and repetition was probably welcomed by that particular student body. However, when used in the public schools and universities throughout the world, it fell short of producing competent users of foreign languages. Why is that? Language production is not based on predictable, set dialogues; language use can be unpredictable and it will vary depending on the contexts in which it is produced.

There is no doubt that human beings have behavioral responses to certain types of input, e.g., we automatically slow down when we see brake lights on the car ahead of us. There may be certain areas of language that are learned through mimicry and memorization, for example, formulaic greetings (*How do you do? Fine, thank you. Nice to meet you.*), or pronunciation of unfamiliar sounds. This theory does not go very far in explaining the complex processes that go into learning a language, however.

1.9 A shift away from behaviorism

Noam Chomsky (1959) was the first noted linguist to refute behaviorism as an explanation for the process of language acquisition. If humans learn though the imitation of forms they have heard, why is it that they create novel utterances and new combinations containing language they have never heard before? Chomsky suggests that as human beings, we are all endowed with the ability to create innumerable forms based on a limited amount of input. We are somehow "hard-wired" to learn language and we use this innate ability to analyze and make guesses about the language. The guesses that we make as language learners often result in ungrammatical production. How many of you have heard children say things like this?

a.   We goed to the zoo today.

b.   We bringed it.

c.   We boughted it last week.

If we can say *looked*, why not *goed*? The last example was spoken by my son, Jonas, when he was about four. He was not imitating anyone; he was making logical guesses about how to form the past tense. He applied the rule of adding the –ed ending, even after learning the irregular past of buy (bought). You've probably heard adult ESL learners make similar overgeneralizations about rules of the language. These errors provide us with evidence that language learning involves far more than imitation and help us see what and how students are learning. Many others have supported Chomsky's view that language learning is an innate process rather than a behavioral one, and a number of the theories that followed have helped to shape the current communicative, learner-centered approaches most prevalent in language teaching today.

1.10 Krashen's model of language acquisition

Stephen Krashen (1985) proposed a model of second language acquisition that includes a number of hypotheses, or proposals as to how a second language is acquired. Like Chomsky, Krashen believes that we have an innate ability to acquire languages through sufficient input and exposure. While many have challenged this model (Lightbown and Spada 2013), its influence on language teaching practices beginning in the 1980s cannot be dismissed. What follows are Krashen's five hypotheses and the implications of each for classroom practice.

1.   *Order of Acquisition:* Learners acquire forms of language in a predictable sequence independent of their first language and of what is taught in the classroom. In the classroom, this means that not all learners are at the same developmental stage and, as a result, may not all be ready to acquire certain areas of language at the same time or rate.

2. *Input Hypothesis:* Learners need abundant **comprehensible input** in order for language acquisition to occur. Language input needs to be at a level just beyond the learner's current level, what Krashen calls **i + 1** ("i" is the learner's current proficiency level and "+ 1" means a step beyond that level). In the classroom, language can be made comprehensible through the use of visuals, realia (real objects such as fruit, tools, etc.) and gestures. Teachers and more proficient peers need to say things in more than one way; students need to see the language, hear the language, and "do things" with the language (sorting pictures, ranking, etc.).

3. *Acquisition vs. Learning:* **Acquisition** refers to language picked up by learners without conscious focus on rules or forms. **Learning** refers to conscious analysis of language. Krashen suggests that acquired language is more permanent. In the classroom, learners should engage in real-life interactions, and the teacher should use authentic materials (books, articles, broadcasts, songs, etc.) and authentic contexts for practicing language. According to the acquisition vs. learning principle, discovery-based learning with little or no emphasis on grammar rules would more likely lead to "acquisition."

4. *Monitor Hypothesis:* The learned language acts as a "monitor," checking and correcting language output. Overuse of the monitor can result in stilted, unnatural speech. We should provide learners with ample opportunities for communicative, spontaneous practice that are not interrupted by heavy use of the "monitor," for example, role plays, information-gap activities (tasks that include a genuine exchange of information), discussions, and skits, which are described in Chapter 3.

5. *Affective Filter Hypothesis:* The affective filter represents barriers to learning such as stress, anxiety, or embarrassment. The teacher can lower the affective filter by providing a classroom that is supportive and free of constraints that can act as a filter:

   • Provide encouragement that is meaningful.
   • Allow for mistakes.
   • Don't spotlight learners.
   • Allow for different learning styles and needs.
   • Show respect for all learners.

Krashen's model had a clear impact on teaching practices as the field moved away from the drill-based approach of the audio-lingual approach. A greater focus was placed on learning for meaningful purposes and on taking the learner's affect into consideration. Can acquisition occur simply through exposure to abundant comprehensible input, as Krashen proposed? Michael Long (1983) suggests that while receiving comprehensible input is a desired element of second language acquisition, it is not enough. In addition to input, there needs to be *interaction,* and it is the interaction itself that helps to make input comprehensible. This theory is called **interactionism.**

1.11 Interactionism

Long (1983) proposes that it is through interactions with competent users of the second language that we move forward in our use of that language. He likens it to the progress children make in their interactions with parents and other sympathetic listeners who modify their language. The modified language has certain features and it is through these modified interactions that language acquisition occurs:

• The listener uses comprehension checks.
• The listener asks for clarification.
• The listener repeats or paraphrases what he/she has understood.
• The listener simplifies his/her speech.

The listener does not need to be a native speaker or the ESL teacher in the classroom. The listener can be another student, but this means that the classroom practices need to allow for ample and meaningful interactions. The teacher needs to make these interaction strategies somewhat explicit to students, i.e., teach them how to ask for clarification or check understanding.

1.12 The Sociocultural Perspective

Central to the **Sociocultural Perspective** is that learning is not an individual process but a social one. Grounded in the work of Lev Vygotsky (1978, 1986), the belief is that understanding of language is co-constructed through collaborative activities, or **collaborative dialogue** (Swain and Lapkin 1998). Vygotsky proposed a zone of proximal development (ZDP) that represents the distance between a learner's current developmental state and potential state the learner can reach provided they have the appropriate supports, or scaffolds, from a more expert listener. Those scaffolds may come from a partner during a language activity, or from teachers when they provide language supports needed to complete a classroom task, simplify tasks in such a way that leads to success, or provide choice and options for the learner (see Sections 3.4, 7.4, and 7.5 for ideas on scaffolding classroom activities and differentiating instruction).

1.13 Taking learners beyond "Basic Interpersonal Communication Skills"

One other theory to look at connects very closely to two of the cultural adjustment factors at the beginning of this chapter: *Education and level of literacy in the first language* and *Previous exposure to English and other languages.* Think about these questions for few minutes:

How long does it take a person to achieve oral skills sufficient to interact and survive in a new culture (language needed to shop, interact with coworkers, make appointments, etc.)?

How long does it take to acquire oral and literacy skills sufficient to function fully in the new culture (read newspapers, manufacturing instructions, or textbooks; listen to a lecture and take notes; follow complex directions; state opinions and elaborate on others' ideas)?

Jim Cummins (2000), a respected scholar of bilingual education, has researched the differences between oral proficiency and level of literacy with learners in academic settings. He suggests that there are two types of language proficiency. The first is **Basic Interpersonal Communication Skills** (**BICS**), and they take about two years to acquire provided the learner is immersed in the second language and has opportunities to use the second language. The second is what he calls **Cognitive Academic Language Proficiency** (**CALP**) skills, which can take anywhere from 7 to 15 years to acquire, depending on a learner's experience with formal education and level of literacy in the first language. Many other scholars have examined the importance of helping *all* learners acquire academic language (Zwiers 2014; Zwiers and Crawford 2011; Gibbons 2009; Snow and Uccelli 2009), which entails an understanding of ". . . the set of words, grammar, and organizational strategies used to describe complex ideas, higher order thinking processes, and abstract concepts." (Zwiers 2014, p. 22)

What are some factors that determine one's ability to acquire this academic language?

- Prior schooling and experience using complex language
- Level of literacy in the first language
- Amount of exposure and practice in the second language
- Amount of experience working with cognitively demanding materials and content

Much of this work on academic language development looks specifically at K-12 learners in school settings. Central to its purpose is developing the understanding that an immigrant child's ability to communicate (to make small talk, follow simple directions, etc.), in and of itself is not an indicator of his/her ability to complete cognitively demanding academic work in the second language. The skills required for navigating academic language need to be developed if they have not already been developed in the first language. Knowledge of and ability with this academic language is connected to completion of higher education, employment with opportunity for professional advancement, and socioeconomic rewards (Scarcella 2003).

So what are the implications of this for those of us working with *adult* learners? As we saw in 1.4, adults need to engage in a variety of complex interactions and tasks at work, in their community, and in school contexts. A learner like Daris already has highly developed academic language in his first language, whereas Naw needs to work on developing that language for the first time in English. Often there is a mismatch between an individual's mastery of basic communication skills and advanced literacy skills, meaning, for example, that one might speak well and clearly but struggle with written communication. This can result in inaccurate assessments and misperceptions about a language learner's abilities in the classroom and in the world at large. Read a supervisor's comments about his employees:

> Sometimes a worker won't mark down that a defective part was thrown out. We have a form to use, but sometimes they won't even know where to mark it down. They don't seem to understand why this is a problem.

This supervisor shared with me that the team is very fluent in English, but as he described other incidents like the one above, it became apparent to me that many of his employees had mastered Basic Interpersonal Communications Skills, but lacked the literacy skills needed to perform tasks that involved completing complex forms or reading technical manuals. Because the employees had highly developed BICS, the employer expected the same level of understanding in completing more complex literacy-related tasks.

The reverse can be true as well, where a supervisor makes the assumption that an advanced education equals advanced oral proficiency in a second language.

> Whenever I ask this one worker to do something, he doesn't seem to understand. It surprises me since I know he was an engineer in Russia and has studied English.

The employee in this second example may have well developed CALP, but if he recently arrived in the English-speaking country, may not have acquired the same degree of BICS. Varying ability in different areas of language is an enormous issue in just about every ESL classroom. Cummins' model helps to give us some understanding of the cause of the discrepancies between basic communication skills and more complex literacy skills.

1.14 Age and the acquisition of a second language

Another area to consider is the effect that age has on one's ability to acquire a second language. If you go back to Daris' and Naw's stories, you may recall that their children acquired the language very quickly. Is this due to age, or do other factors come into play?

It has been suggested that there is a **critical period** for learning a second language, which begins at birth to around puberty (some suggest the period ends as early as five to six). Changes that occur in the brain at or around puberty make it more difficult, if not impossible, to become a native-like speaker of the language. We have all seen that young children pick up a native-like accent with little or no effort, and most of us would agree that far fewer adults attain the same degree of proficiency, at least in terms of accent.

But is accent really an important measure of proficiency or is it about making oneself understood to others? Many times, adolescents and adults can actually acquire other areas of language (literacy, grammar, vocabulary) more quickly than children can (Singleton and Ryan 2004). Older learners can bring the experience of learning other things through formal or informal education to the task of learning a second language. Developed literacy or learning strategies from their first language can be transferred to the second language. Many adults are able to attain very intelligible pronunciation provided they have adequate input and opportunities for interaction in the new language. Other factors such as motivation, identity, and access to adequate input may play a more important role than the age at which one begins learning a language (Muñoz and Singleton 2011).

We need to consider that adults often have far less input and interaction in the second language than children have. Adults may be in a job that does not require extensive use of language and or live in a community where they can get by with limited English. Children, on the other hand, enter regular mainstream classrooms where there are numerous opportunities to hear and use English every day. Some adults may have limited practice of English depending on their work status, mobility within the community, and exposure to and interactions with others in English. All of these factors can have an impact on the adult learner's progress towards learning a language, and these are not related to aptitude or a critical period for learning.

1.15 Identity, investment, agency, and motivation

A final area to consider is the role identity, investment, agency, and motivation play in the language acquisition process. **Identity** refers to ways that learners perceive themselves within their social networks. Norton (2000) defines identity as ". . . how a person understands his or her relationship to the world, how that relationship is constructed across time and space, and how the person understands possibilities for the future" (p. 5). Learner identities change over time and place; they are ever evolving. Identity is closely tied to **investment** on the part of a learner, or the degree to which a learner sees that his or her contributions are valued in a given social context (Norton 2013). Related to identity and investment is learner **agency**, or the ability of individuals to take control of their learning in pursuit of their personal goals and aspirations (Duff 2012). This requires that classrooms are places where learners feel a sense of belonging and empowerment.

Consider the reaction of adult learners whose teacher presents only menial, low-paying jobs as options in a lesson on career explorations. Course content should reflect the actual aspirations of learners, not our perceived aspirations for them; providing multiple entry points for learner input and careful assessment of learner needs is paramount. We revisit these concepts throughout the book as we look at language skills development, lesson planning, and materials selection.

Identity, investment, and agency are all tied to **motivation**, which is highly complex and varies from person to person. Is the learner's motivation primarily extrinsic, or imposed on the learner by an outside force (requirement for a job, citizenship exam), or intrinsic, coming from a desire within the individual for personal growth? Of course, with an adult learning English to survive and thrive in a new environment, those two may be hard to tease apart. Other models of motivation describe instrumental motivation, or a focus on practical goals for learning a language versus integrative motivation, or a desire to become part of a new language community. Dörnyei and Ushioda (2011) remind us that motivation is highly dynamic and dependent on social context and they view motivation as closely linked to the vision learners have of themselves in the new language.

Based on the considerations discussed in Part II of this chapter, it is important to keep the following in mind in your role as a teacher of adult learners:

- Adults **are capable** of acquiring a second (or third or more) language.
- Adult learners need **ample and accessible language input**: provide extensive practice with listening to authentic language in your classroom. Support that language input with visual aids and other tools for making language comprehensible.
- Adult learners need **meaningful and authentic opportunities to interact with others** in order to acquire language: provide scaffolds for success with interactive classroom tasks, help your learners learn beyond the classroom, and help them to become active members of their communities.

- Adults need to **see themselves reflected** in the curriculum, materials, and approaches we take to teaching.
- Adults need practice with **academic language, complex informational texts, digital literacy,** and **critical thinking skills** to access opportunities of the 21st century.

Conclusion

In this chapter, you have been given a glimpse of the strengths adult learners bring to our classrooms as well as the challenges they may face. Their journeys to a new country as well as the contexts in which they are living and working comprise a vast array of needs and expectations in any adult ESL classroom. It is crucial that adult ESL teachers tap into the experiences and knowledge that learners bring into the classroom. It is essential to recognize the increasingly complex language demands of today's digital-rich world. It is also important to understand the complex nature of second language acquisition. Teachers need to provide a classroom environment that is supportive and engages learners in activities that are purposeful and meaningful. We explore teaching principles and strategies that help ESL teachers achieve these goals throughout this book.

On your own, or with a partner, provide an example or brief definition for each concept:

Checklist of Key Terms	
acculturation	
assimilation	
learner-centered	
intergenerational tension	
acquisition versus learning	
comprehensible input	
affective filter	
interactionism	
BICS vs. CALP	
academic language	
critical period	
agency	
investment	

Before doing these activities, revisit your answers to the questions at the beginning of the chapter.

1 Cultural Adjustment and Adult Learners

If you're already teaching, identify a learner in your class who seems to be having particular difficulty with learning English and adjusting to the new culture. What do you need to know about this student? How can you know more? Based on information you have about the student, write a description similar to the ones of Naw and Daris. Try to include as much information as possible about the learner (reason for coming, current situation, family, etc.). Refer to Table 1.1 *Factors Affecting Cultural Adjustment* to examine this learner's journey as I did with Daris and Naw, and then reflect on these questions:

What did this process reveal to you about some of the obstacles this learner might be facing? What are some concrete steps you might take to help this learner in light of what you've learned?

> **NOTE:** It may not be possible to gather all of the information you'd like. Even though you cannot have a complete picture of this learner's life circumstances, this exercise gets you to think about the questions you need to ask yourself about *any* learner.

If you're not teaching, use the following scenario for this task:

> *Ahmed came to the U.S. nine years ago as a refugee when he was 19. Before that, he attended school for three years in a refugee camp after leaving war-torn Somalia. Due to this interrupted schooling, he has minimal literacy skills in his first language. He is married and has four school-aged children. He works as an attendant in a parking garage and attends ESL classes three mornings a week. Due to his limited literacy skills, he has been placed in a beginning-level ESL class. At the same time, he has strong oral skills and is quite confident communicating with teachers and people in his community. His dream is to one day get his high school equivalency. He lives in the city that has the highest number of Somali refugees in the U.S.*

2 Applying Principles of a Learner-centered Classroom

If you are already teaching, give examples of the ways you have incorporated the following principles into your teaching. If you are not teaching, observe a lesson and see whether the teacher seems mindful of any of these principles in the choices she or he makes in the lesson. Provide evidence of any of these principles in action:

1. All learners bring to class rich knowledge and experiences that must be validated.

2. Learners' first language and culture are viewed as a resource for learning.

3. The content of instruction is relevant to the learners' needs and interests and draws on their experiences and knowledge.

4. Learners make choices about content and classroom activities.

5. Learners have active roles in the classroom and control the direction of activities.

6. Classroom interactions and tasks are authentic, representing how language is used in the real world.

7. Teachers use authentic language in their interactions with learners.

8. Learners acquire strategies that help them learn inside and outside of the classroom without the help of a teacher.

9. Classroom tasks challenge learners and promote higher-order thinking skills.

10. Teachers listen actively for themes that emerge from learners and build those into instruction.

11. Teachers constantly assess teaching and learning in relation to learners' needs.

You may also use these questions to observe video-recorded lessons at New American Horizons (newamericanhorizons.org).

3 Teaching Learners to Become Communicatively Competent Users of English

If you're already teaching, look at a lesson you have taught over the past two weeks. What areas of language were included in your lesson?

Areas I covered in my lesson	
Language forms	
Social interactions	
Language skills	
Learning strategies	

How would you assess your inclusion of different areas of language? What would you add or change to make sure you have taken the broadest view possible of the language you are teaching? Do learners practice language purposefully and meaningfully? How responsive is the lesson to the demands of today's world, e.g., incorporation of digital tools or critical thinking?

If you're not teaching, choose a chapter in a textbook used for Adult ESL and evaluate the degree to which it teaches the four areas above. What would you add or change in the unit?

4 Promoting Second Language Acquisition

If you are already teaching, reflect on and write about these questions (if you are not teaching, consider what you would do):

1. What are you doing to make input comprehensible to your learners?

2. What are you already doing that may allow a learner to have agency in your classroom? What are some others ways that you could create a classroom environment that is conducive to learning?

3. In what ways are you promoting purposeful interactions among learners in your classes?

Brookfield, S. (2013). *Powerful Techniques for Teaching Adults.* San Francisco, CA: Jossey-Bass. This text explores the dynamics of power in the adult classroom and provides exercises, stories, and practical teaching tips for empowering the learner both inside and outside the formal classroom.

Dörnyei, Z., and Kubanyiova, M. (2014). *Motivating Learners, Motivating Teachers: Building Vision in the Language Classroom.* Cambridge: Cambridge University Press. An accessible summary of why vision is a principal motivational factor and how it can be enhanced, both in learners and teachers.

Lightbown, P. and N. Spada. (2013). *How Languages Are Learned, 4th edition.* Oxford: Oxford University Press. An introduction to the main theories of first and second language acquisition.

Yang, K. (2008). *The Latehomecomer: A Hmong Family Memoir.* Minneapolis, MN: Coffee House Press. The firsthand account of a family's experience of adapting to a new place and a new language.

WEBSITES AND ONLINE RESOURCES

LINCS Literacy Information and Communication System Here you can join a LINCS community of practice, self-paced online courses, and or use the searchable resources for adult education practitioners. *https://lincs.ed.gov/*

LINCS ESL Pro Each topic-driven suite of resources includes an issue brief, online learning module, and a companion learning resource for educators. The materials focus on advancing the rigor of instruction, integrating digital literacy instruction, and preparing English learners for work and career pathways. *https://lincs.ed.gov/state-resources/federal-initiatives/esl-pro*

Migration Policy Institute MPI provides information on migration and refugee policies at local, national, and international levels. It aims to provide pragmatic and thoughtful responses to the challenges and opportunities that large-scale migration, whether voluntary or forced, presents to communities and institutions in an increasingly integrated world. *https://www.migrationpolicy.org/*

Standards and Frameworks Reflecting 21st-Century Skills

Canadian Language Benchmarks (CLB) National standards used for describing, measuring, and recognizing the English language proficiency of adult immigrants and prospective immigrants for living and working in Canada. *https://www.canada.ca/content/dam/ircc/migration/ircc/english/pdf/pub/language-benchmarks.pdf*

College and Career Readiness Standards for Adult Education;

Office of Career, Technical, and Adult Education / U.S. Department of Education (2013) *https://lincs. ed.gov/publications/pdf/CCRStandardsAdultEd.pdf*

English Language Proficiency Standards for Adult Education;

Office of Career, Technical, and Adult Education / U.S. Department of Education (2016) *https://lincs.ed.gov/publications/pdf/elp-standards-adult-ed.pdf*

Partnership for 21st-Century Skills (P21):

Framework for 21st-Century Learning. Tucson, AZ: 2009. Available online *http://21stcenturyskillsbook. com/resources/*

Transitions Integration Framework, ATLAS (2013; revised version 2016)

The Transitions Integration Framework (TIF) provides guidance to adult basic education (ABE) programs and instructors on the effective integration of transitions skills into instruction at all levels of ABE. The TIF defines the academic, career, and employability skills essential for adult learners to successfully transition to postsecondary education, career training, the workplace, and to enrich community involvement.

2 | Approaches and Program Options for Adult English Language Learners

---

To consider before reading this chapter:

- What does it mean to take a multifaceted and principled approach to teaching English to adult learners?
- What program options are available to adult English learners in your community?
- What factors do you think shape and inform the range of available programming?

Part I: Approaches to teaching

2.1 Introduction

Teachers of adult English language learners find themselves in a variety of settings with a variety of roles. Public school systems, community colleges, community-based programs, correctional facilities, libraries or volunteer organizations provide English language instruction for adult immigrants and refugees. Teachers may work with learners one-on-one, at drop-in centers, at workplace programs, through distance learning, or in classrooms with groups of learners. Each situation will have its unique challenges both in terms of curriculum and teaching approach. What works well in a given situation and contributes to learner progress? No *one* approach will meet the needs of all learners in all situations. As with any teaching, a blending of approaches, methods, and techniques is necessary. This chapter begins with a brief overview of the most common approaches that are particularly well suited for working with adults learning English and from which a teacher can draw ideas and inspiration. In the end, teachers should be able to articulate a principled approach to teaching. Then we turn to descriptions of and purposes for the most common program options offered for adult English language learners. Let's begin by taking a look into Rosie's Adult Basic Education ESL class.

Getting Started

 Task 2.1

Read this class description and talk to your partner or write in your journal about the following questions:

1. What might different learners in this class need to work on in their English?

2. What challenges might Rosie face in working with such a diverse group of learners?

3. What would happen if Rosie used one approach with all of these learners?

   Rosie's beginning-level ESL class is comprised of 24 students ages 17–75 from 14 different countries including Thailand, Iraq, Syria, Vietnam, Russia, the Ukraine, Somalia, Peru, Mexico, and Colombia. Some of the students have professional degrees from their countries, while others have no prior formal education. The level of first and second language literacy varies greatly as well. Very few of the students have had experience in interactive classes (pair or

---

group work) and many of the students rely heavily on writing everything down and checking words in their dictionaries. Some have limited access to computers at home, but many have a smartphone that they use as a resource in class. Rosie has found that a number of her students balk at activities that seem like "fun and games," while others are eager to take part in role-plays and problem-solving activities. Some of the learners are in class to improve their chances of finding employment, some hope to enter higher education, and others want to acquire skills to navigate their communities. One goal they have all expressed is a desire to improve their ability to speak English.

2.2 Taking a multi-faceted approach to teaching

Just as there are varying views on the processes that underlie second language acquisition, there are numerous approaches to teaching ESL from which classroom teachers can draw. Rarely does a teacher or program adhere to *one* method or approach to teaching. The choices we make hinge on a number of factors:

- Who are the learners and how do they learn best?
- Why are they learning English?
- What experience have they had with formal and informal education?
- What are their views of teaching and learning?
- What are your views of teaching and learning?
- What are the overall goals of the program? Who decides or mandates these goals?

When you think about Rosie's class in relation to these questions, you can see that there are many complex issues involved in teaching Adult ESL. How do teachers determine approaches that respond to such varying backgrounds, wants, needs, and learning preferences? Looking at your own experience as a learner can provide a point of reference for you as a teacher as you start exploring approaches that you might adopt in your own classroom, while being mindful of similarities and differences in learners' experiences and expectations.

📋 Task 2.2

Think of recent experiences you have had learning a language, a new skill (cooking, gardening), or how to use a new a computer program or an apparatus at work or home. Reflect on your experiences by answering these questions in your journal or with a partner:

1. What has helped you learn best? Listening to someone describe things to you? Using the language, skills, machine, etc.? Using your hands? Moving around?

2. What has been unhelpful to you as a learner?

3. How have you "figured things out?" Did the teacher give you examples and have you deduce rules, patterns, procedures, or did the teacher just tell you these things?

4. What feedback have teachers given you? Corrections? Praise? What helped you the most?

5. What have you experienced to be more and less effective elements of your own experience?

Follow-up: Share your answers with several other people in your group, or with friends or family if you are on your own. From my experience working with teachers over the past 30 years, there is always tremendous variation in the responses to the questions above. Teachers need to be careful not to approach teaching as they were taught or only in ways that worked for them as learners; all of us learn differently, and what may have worked well for you may not work well for those you find yourself teaching.

The ways in which learners learn best can impact the success they have in a given classroom situation. The theory of **multiple intelligences** (Gardner 1993) suggests that there are at least eight *intelligences* that go beyond traditional definitions of intelligence, to include such intelligences as musical bodily/kinesthetic, interpersonal, and intrapersonal. Formal educational systems and assessments have tended to favor verbal/linguistic and logical mathematic skills, yet there are many other strengths/abilities that contribute to the development and well-being of any community. While criticized in some circles for its lack of empirical support, an approach to teaching that acknowledges multiple learning abilities is more likely to appeal to a broader audience of language learners. The theory suggests that a learner with kinesthetic intelligence who benefits from physical action may not be very successful sitting in a desk for hours at a time. A learner who has strong logical/mathematical intelligence may prefer analyzing grammar over an indirect, inductive approach to grammar teaching and learning. A helpful way to consider this theory may be that *all* learners can benefit from developing multiple means of processing information.

In addition to the theory of multiple intelligences, scholars in education and psychology have proposed a variety of models for describing learning styles, that is, the ways people best acquire and attain knowledge. In some models, learners are classified as visual, auditory, kinesthetic, or tactile. Other models make distinctions between *analytical* (preferring to analyze smaller pieces of information) vs. *global* (preferring to look at the whole) learners. Some people are said to be *random* (they do not process information in a linear fashion) vs. *sequential* (preferring when information is presented in a logical order). Recently, scholars (Kirschner 2017; Newton 2015) have suggested that there is little empirical evidence to support learning style theory. The learning style models imply that we are predisposed to learn a certain way, yet studies suggest that it is more about learners' preferences for *ways* of learning, or the learning strategies that work best for them (An and Carr 2017). Learning preferences are also affected by past experiences with learning and cultural norms within educational settings (Tsui 2009). Labeling someone as "visual" or "auditory" may actually have a limiting effect whereby learners (and teachers) approach learning in very narrow ways (Barry and Egan 2018). Barry and Egan (2018) suggest that learning style inventories may best be used as a means of assessing learner strengths and needs rather than as a tool for identifying a particular learning style. Learners may actually shift preferences based on context and immediate needs (Griffiths 2012). In the end, anyone who has spent time in a classroom knows that not everyone learns the same way; some people *do* prefer lectures while others prefer reading about and discussing the information. The more varied the instruction, the more engaged everyone will be. Since no single approach to teaching is going to be responsive to all learners at all times, drawing on multiple approaches to teaching has become the norm in adult ESL instruction.

In choosing teaching approaches, we can ask ourselves:

- What are learners' and teachers' roles within this approach?
- What types of learning tasks and activities comprise instruction within this approach? Are a variety of potential learning preferences considered?
- What skills are emphasized in this approach (speaking, listening, reading, or writing)?
- To what extent does this approach provide opportunities to develop rich academic language, strategies for accessing complex texts, and critical thinking skills?

2.3 Approaches for teaching adult English learners

The following overview of approaches to teaching English to speakers of other languages provides a range of options from which to shape instruction. While some of them are less commonly used today, it is important to understand how current practice and approaches have evolved. These approaches are used with learners of different ages and in different contexts, but all of those highlighted here have been used extensively with adult immigrant and refugee English learners. Project-based learning, for example, may use activities drawn from a variety of approaches. It is included in this chapter because of its focus on learner participation and the opportunities for highly rigorous outcomes (e.g., poster presentations, development of booklets, web pages) that incorporate language development, digital literacy skills, and engagement around critical issues. The Whole Language Approach and Language Experience Approach are also commonly utilized for literacy development, especially with emergent readers who have very limited literacy skills in their first language. Those approaches are described in detail with illustrations of classroom application in Chapter 5.

Many of these approaches, particularly the Natural Approach and Communicative Language Teaching, emerged as alternatives to the Audiolingual Method (ALM), which grew out of Behaviorism in the 1960s. The Audiolingual Method relies heavily on memorization of largely formulaic dialogues, drill and repetition; there is little room for meaningful use of language in this method. While there are certainly elements of ALM that may be integrated into instruction (more limited use of drills, dialogues), it is generally not used as a stand-alone method among adult ESL practitioners today.

As you read about these approaches, use the chart below to identify the core principles, as well as classroom practices from each. While all of these approaches have merits, see if some are more responsive to the needs of adult English language learners than others.

📋 Task 2.3 (To complete as you read Part I)

Approach	Core Principles	Sample Classroom Practices
Natural Approach		
Competency-Based Education		
Communicative Language Teaching		
Cooperative Learning		
Task-Based Learning		
Content-Based Instruction		
Participatory Approach		
Project-Based Learning		

2.4 Natural approach

Core principles

Stephen Krashen and Tracy Terrell (1983) developed the **Natural Approach** based on Krashen's Input Hypothesis, which holds that language acquisition occurs when learners receive abundant comprehensible input. Designed for learners at the early stages of language acquisition, it shares many of the same principles found in Communicative Language Teaching (2.6); its primary difference is its focus on comprehension first and production later. Based on the belief that all learners will experience a "**silent period**" as part of the language learning process, learners engage in activities that allow them to *demonstrate* understanding of a particular language point before they are expected to produce it orally or in writing. The goal of the Natural Approach is to replicate the conditions under which children acquire their first language.

Classroom practices

The teacher uses frequent comprehension checks, visuals, and gestures to convey meaning to learners. The following example illustrates a typical teacher-student exchange in a class using the Natural Approach.

Lesson Theme: Neighborhood Resources
Level: Beginning

1. Teacher displays a map with places in the neighborhood labeled. She begins by pointing to words and saying place names (students repeat words only if comfortable with language).

2. Teacher removes labels, distributes them, and has each learner affix a label to the correct place on the map (grocery store, park, bank).

3. Teacher removes cards again. Students in class have a set of *Yes/No* cards (*yes* one color, *no* another color). The teacher points to and says a place name, sometimes correctly and sometimes incorrectly. Learners hold up a *Yes/No* card according to whether the teacher said the right or wrong word.

One of the primary goals of the Natural Approach is to allow learners to demonstrate their understanding of language forms and vocabulary before they are necessarily able to produce the language. In later lessons, the learners would take on the teacher's role, directing activities, asking one another questions, and engaging in simple paired activities. These "silent" techniques are not unique to the Natural Approach and are used at any point when the teacher wants to check for learner understanding.

2.5 Competency-Based Education

Core principles

Competency-Based Education (CBE) emerged in the 1970s and focuses on identifying targeted student learning outcomes that are assessed through students' actions and performances of specific tasks (Ford 2014; Malan 2000). CBE, in its early days in the field of adult ESL, emphasized several areas of knowledge needed for adults to function in society: occupational, consumer, health, government and law, and community resources. The skills of listening, speaking, reading, writing, interpersonal relations, problem-solving, and computation were considered requisite to function fully in each of the areas above.

CBE in adult ESL met criticism because of its focus on clearly-defined, often limiting outcomes rather than on learners' actual and more immediate resettlement needs (Auerbach 1986). Nonetheless, it quickly determined content and approach for ESL programs that were welcoming waves of refugees throughout the 1970s and 1980s. Outcomes within each area were identified in terms of performance objectives (learners will be able to . . .), which became the basis for curricula. Most often these outcomes were related to basic "life-skills" competencies, for example, "students will be able to make a doctor's appointment; students will be able to return an item to the store."

There are still many curricula and textbooks that use these life-skills competencies as the core for instruction, especially in those programs welcoming newcomers. With a move toward curricula based on college and career readiness standards, CBE today is most common in career-focused programs (see Section 2.19); it reflects the competencies needed for success in a particular vocational field. A careful analysis of competencies needed for success in a particular job is conducted, and the outcomes of that analysis form the basis of instruction. Learners need to acquire the language functions and skills, grammar, and vocabulary needed to perform competencies as well, so the outcomes of a competency-based lesson in a Certified Nursing Assistants class could look like these:

- Learners will be able to write a patient care report.
- Learners will be able to describe symptoms with sufficient details using simple past tense and descriptive adjectives.

Also central to this approach is the use of carefully designed performance-based assessments and rubrics to determine successful attainment of the competencies being taught (see Chapter 9 for more on these types of assessments).

Classroom practice
The sample below illustrates how this approach could be used in an English course for newcomers; it shows the kind of activity learners could engage in within a competency-based lesson on returning an item to the store.

Competency: Returning an Item to the Store
Learners will be able to:

- Explain reasons for returning an item.
- Demonstrate understanding of return policies: a refund, an exchange or store credit.

Sample activity:
Half of the class assigned the role of store clerk; each clerk is given store policies:

- Must have a receipt for a refund.
- Purchase made less than 30 days ago.
- Must have packaging for a refund.

Each of the other students in class is given an item to return; some are given a receipt; some have item in the box; some have item with no packaging.

Role play:
Students return items to the appropriate store; redistribute items and assign new clerks.

Follow-up:
Did you get a refund, a new item or a store credit? Why? Did you get what you wanted? What were the store policies and how did they affect you?

Assessment:
Teacher assesses students' performance during the role play using a rubric that delineates the expected outcomes.

2.6 Communicative Language Teaching

Core principles
Communicative Language Teaching (CLT) has its origins in a 1970s European movement to make foreign language teaching responsive to the functional communicative demands of people working across cultures, in workplaces, and in international organizations. Likewise, in the U.S., linguists embraced the idea of communicative competence as the goal of instruction

(Hymes 1971). Course curricula included language functions (greetings, making invitations, making requests, etc.) and notions (time, money), a departure from the grammar-based curricula of the previous decades. CLT was also a departure from the rote learning of Audiolingual teaching as it gave primacy to meaningful communication.

CLT is viewed as an approach or philosophy to teaching, not a set method; it sees fluency and the ability to communicate in a variety of settings and in a variety of ways (verbal and non-verbal, oral and written) at the core of teaching and learning. Teachers throughout the world might describe their approach to teaching as CLT, yet their classes could look different from one another in terms of activities, materials, and interactions. What they would share is a belief in the core principles of CLT, which are outlined in 2.1, a belief that teaching should support learners in achieving communicative competence.

Table 2.1 Key Principles of Communicative Language Teaching

- The goal of instruction is learners' ability to communicative effectively and appropriately.
- Instruction is contextualized and meaning-based.
- Authentic materials are incorporated from the start.
- Repetition and drilling are used minimally, and only in service of reinforcing learning.
- Learner interaction is maximized; the teacher acts as a facilitator of learning.
- Fluency is emphasized over accuracy.
- Errors are viewed as evidence of learning and error are addressed judiciously if at all and serve to inform instruction and assessments.

(Richards and Rodgers 2014)

More recently, the field has moved away from CLT as proposed in the 1970s to 1980s to *communicatively-based* approaches, emphasizing the centrality of varying learner backgrounds, strengths, and needs in the classroom as well as an acknowledgment that form-focused instruction has its place within a communicative classroom. Those adhering to a strict view of CLT tended to de-emphasize accuracy and/or the focus on discrete language features. Zoltán Dörnyei (2013) encourages us to take a "principled communicative approach" where instruction has personal significance to learners and is meaning-based, but also acknowledges the need for focus on and understanding of form (Ellis 2008) in order to build the language competence needed to engage in communicative tasks. Dörnyei also notes the need for teaching formulaic language that is pervasive in day-to-day communication as well as time to build automaticity with language through controlled activities. He still emphasizes the importance of language exposure along with abundant opportunities for interaction in the second language and has provided an important update to CLT, making it ever more appropriate for meeting the needs of adult English language learners.

Classroom practice

A communicatively-based view of teaching and learning can be thought of as an umbrella under which an array of approaches and instructional practices can be used. In fact, cooperative learning, task-based learning, content-based instruction, and project-based learning which follow this section all adhere to many of the same communicative principles. Even a competency-based curriculum can be executed using communicative principles.

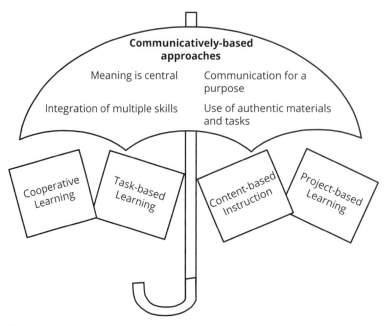

Figure 2.1 Communicatively-Based Approaches to Teaching

In all of these approaches, learners take on very active roles as they engage in problem-solving activities, discussions, or debates. They work with pieces of authentic language, including news reports (online or print), informational texts, or recorded interviews. Both content and classroom activities should represent real-world uses of language that correspond to the strengths, wants, and needs of the students in class. Students develop listening, speaking, reading, and writing skills concurrently. A focus on form along with opportunities for controlled practice are encouraged as needed by learners. The sample lessons presented in Chapters 3, 4, and 5 embody extensive illustrations of how communicatively-based approaches can be applied in adult ESL classes.

2.7 Cooperative learning

Cooperative Language Learning derives from the general education collaborative or cooperative learning approach that emphasizes peer support and learning through carefully planned pair and group activities. It centers around group tasks where each member is held accountable for his or her learning, and where outcomes to activities are dependent on a genuine exchange of information among participants (Olsen and Kagan 1992). Clearly defined roles and outcomes to task are essential. In language teaching, CLL can be considered an offshoot of CLT (Richards and Rogers 2014) and there are many tasks and activities in Chapters 3, 4, and 5 that represent cooperative learning in action, for example jigsaw tasks, group posters, or many of the outcomes in project-based learning. Task-based learning has clear parallels to CLL as well, which we turn to now in our exploration of approaches to language teaching.

2.8 Task-Based Learning

Core principles

Task-Based Learning (TBL) is based on classroom and real-world tasks that learners need to complete in the target language (an information-gap activity or development of a project) rather than on a set of language features that need to be taught. David Nunan (2014) suggests that while CLT is a philosophy of teaching, TBL represents *how* we implement that philosophy in the classroom. The tasks themselves and the language that emerges from them become the focus of instruction. Willis and Willis (2007) suggest a three-step framework to successful task implementation: 1) a pre-task to introduce the topic and the task; 2) the task cycle where learners engage in the task, and 3) language focus where learners analyze and practice further the language generated by the task. TBL is used in conjunction with many other approaches such as content-based instruction or project-based learning.

Classroom practice

Using Willis and Willis's steps as the basis for this example, let's see how a task could unfold in a unit focused on health and wellness. The class has been exploring the dangers of a sedentary lifestyle and the teacher will have learners analyze a pie chart on average time spent on activities among adults in the U.S. The learners' task is to analyze the chart in small groups and make a claim about how healthy these practices are based on evidence in the chart and knowledge they have gained from previous lessons.

Task: Read this chart and answer these questions with your partner:

1. How much time could people spend interacting with others?
2. How much of the time can be spent outdoors?
3. How healthy are these practices? Why?

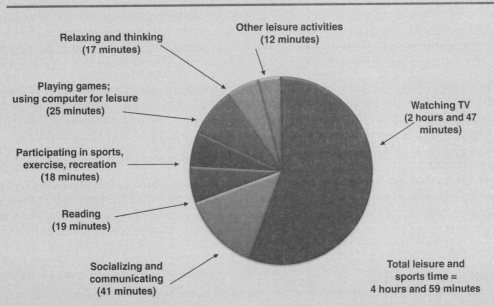

Leisure time on an average day

Relaxing and thinking (17 minutes)

Other leisure activities (12 minutes)

Playing games; using computer for leisure (25 minutes)

Watching TV (2 hours and 47 minutes)

Participating in sports, exercise, recreation (18 minutes)

Reading (19 minutes)

Socializing and communicating (41 minutes)

Total leisure and sports time = 4 hours and 59 minutes

NOTE: Data include all persons age 15 and over. Data include all days of the week and are annual averages for 2015.

From *Bureau of Labor Statistics, American Time Use Survey*

Step 1: Build background knowledge and pre-teach concepts (leisure vs. work/chores)

- Present visuals with photos
- Picture sort/categorizing

Step 2: Answer the questions about activities and health issues related to leisure activities using evidence from the chart to support your claims.

Step 3: Work with the language forms and functions needed to successfully complete the task:

- Pronunciation of vocabulary: word stress matching (words to stress patterns)

- Speculating using language like this:
  - I think people could . . .
  - People can do _____ alone or with others.
- Co-construct language for comparing and contrasting
  - People spend (a little, much, considerably) more time _____ than _____ .

As a final task and outcome, conduct class research on own groups' leisure activities and create their own pie chart. Compare their practices to those depicted in the pie chart.

Figure 2.2 Sample of Task-Based Learning

2.9 Content-Based Instruction

Core principles

Considerable research has been conducted on the benefits of teaching language through content that is meaningful and relevant to students (Brinton, Snow, and Wesche 2003). **Content-Based Instruction** (CBI) is an approach to teaching that makes subject matter such as history, environmental studies, math, or citizenship the basis of the curriculum. CBI is used extensively in university-based ESL programs because it prepares students for the work they need to do when they enter degree programs with other English speakers and faculty who are not language teachers. Some teachers are hesitant to adopt this approach, which requires knowledge of a particular content area; many ESL teachers may not be not as comfortable with a particular content area as they are with teaching language skills.

Within the broader field of English language teaching, there are a variety of models of content-based instruction, from full-immersion in a content course taught in English (e.g., a community college introduction to psychology) with supports from an ESL professional, to a theme-based approach where a teacher uses content (e.g., environmental issues) as the basis of instructional units.

Classroom practice

The career contextualized **Integrated Education and Training (IET)** model (see 2.19) is an example of content-based instruction in action. In a course preparing learners for jobs as personal care assistants, one of the learning outcomes is to identify steps to take when handling client complaints. Learners can engage in a problem-solving task that assesses their content knowledge as well as giving them rich language practice:

What would you do?
Anna, a personal care assistant, is giving her client his daily medication for high blood pressure. The client's family has placed the correct dosage into the weekly dosage container. Anna also has the medication bottle with dosages clearly marked. The client tells Anna he has already taken the medication and is getting agitated. He complains that Anna doesn't know how to do her job. Anna tries to stay calm.

What steps should Anna take?

Figure 2.3 Sample Task from a Personal Care Assistant Integrated Education and Training Class

Citizenship is another example of content-based instruction within adult education. Learning about history and systems of government are both the basis for instruction as well as its primary content. Learners need to read, understand, and answer questions about this content. In such a content-based class, learners take part in language activities that are typical of any communicative classroom: pre-reading, pre-listening, role plays, problem-solving, or discussions. Teachers can focus on language functions, forms, and vocabulary as needed to understand and talk or write about the content.

2.10 Participatory approach

Core principles

Participatory, or Freirean approaches to teaching ESL grew out of Paulo Freire's work in literacy development. Freire, a Brazilian scholar and educator, developed an approach to teaching first language literacy that has been adapted and replicated in developing countries all over the world. His approach has the goal of enabling learners to have and use a voice in their communities. He views education as a means for people "to liberate themselves from the social conditions that oppress them" (Spencer 1993: 77). ESL practitioners have embraced the core principles of Freire's approach, namely that learning must derive from learners' lives and personal issues within their social context so that they can understand options in determining when or how to take action to improve their lives through engaging in problem-posing processes. In the words of Wallerstein and Auerbach (2004):

> *Problem-posing dialogue enables people to connect their personal lives to each other's and to understand the social, political, economic, and historical contexts of their lives. Through personal stories, role plays, and dialogue, we can examine with people the multiple roles they have, sometimes with power and sometimes not. Dialogue enables people to share their strengths and the ways they may resist being labeled in situations where they may have less power (12).*

As such, these participatory approaches do not rely on textbooks, set outcomes, or curricula. Rather, the curricula and outcomes emerge and evolve through learner input and teacher guidance.

Classroom practice

In adult ESL, participatory education can take many forms, but it will share these features:

- Content evolves from learners' real-life issues and concerns, what Auerbach (1997) calls an **emergent curriculum.**
- *Problem posing* (identifying problems) is central to the approach and encompasses looking at causes of problems, exploring additional resources, and possible remedies, gaining tools to deal with these issues; then deciding whether or how to take action to address the given issue (Wallerstein and Auerbach 2004).
- The approach emphasizes dialogue and collaboration among learners and between teacher and students.

Auerbach (1997) proposes a series of steps in the process of problem posing, which are illustrated below through a classroom experience shared by Janet Isserlis. Learners in a basic level literacy class, comprised of refugees and immigrants from Liberia, Haiti, the Dominican Republic, and Russia, noticed and made questioning and disparaging comments about homeless people living on the streets in and around the ESL program site. Learners were hard-pressed to understand how people who appeared to be healthy and could speak English well were unemployed or unwilling to work. They expressed a genuine desire to understand what brought these people to living on the streets.

Table 2.2 Problem Posing Steps

Steps in the Problem-Posing Process	Problem Posing in Action
Describe the content.	Understanding causes of homelessness
Identify: Is there a problem? Define the problem.	The problem of homelessness itself, but this isn't something the class can seek to remedy per se. The objective is to understand the causes of homelessness, a phenomenon that is new to them in the context of the U.S.

Understand the problem in the context of our own lives.	The teacher shared information about jobs available to people with limited education, about costs of housing and about a homeless shelter located within walking distance of the program site. Learners engaged in discussions about how all of these factors could lead to homelessness.
Discuss the problem.	Over a period of several days, the class was invited to think about how it was that people could speak well but still have trouble finding work. They compared what might happen in their country when someone loses a job, suffers from physical or mental illness affecting the ability to work, or lacks the means to pay for housing.
Discuss alternatives to the problem.	Learners decided to raise a bit of money to donate to the shelter. They were invited to tour the shelter and learn for themselves about the challenges of homelessness.

This process enabled the learners in Janet's class to identify the issues and possible causes leading to homelessness, and to arrive at an action that made sense within the contexts of their own lives and situations. While few approaches are so fully anchored in learners' lives, many of the approaches discussed in this chapter and in Chapter 5 are participatory in nature, particularly the project-based learning and language experience approach, and *any* instruction can and should be centered around learners' real-life issues and concerns.

2.11 Project–Based Learning

Core principles
Project-Based Learning (PBL) is an approach that allows for maximum learner involvement and choice in the learning process. Learners choose a topic of interest or concern to them, and then direct their learning through inquiry, research on a topic, and collaboration with others. Teams of learners create projects that showcase their knowledge and then they present their work to others. Heide Wrigley describes PBL in this way: "In its simplest form, project-based learning involves a group of learners taking on an issue close to their hearts, developing a response, and presenting the results to a wider audience" (Wrigley 1998, 1). PBL is an ideal vehicle for building learners' understanding of complex language, developing skills required for accessing and engaging with complex texts and tasks, and for developing critical thinking skills (Vinogradov 2016).

Classroom practice
There are a number of steps a teacher needs to consider in planning and facilitating projects (Alan and Stoller 2005; Wrigley 1998) as outlined in Table 2.3.

Table 2.3 Project-Based Learning: Steps to Consider

Identification of a task to complete, a problem to address, a plan to make	This is determined through a collaborative process with the learners. In some instances, teachers may provide options that are in keeping with the overall program themes and outcomes, but learners should always have a degree of choice in this process.
Determining a final outcome / Product of the project	Will the group create posters and have a gallery walk with others in the school building? Will they create a short video or start a class blog?
Preliminary investigation	Where can we learn more about the topic? What resources are available? What do we already know and what do we want to learn?

Planning and assigning tasks	Who is responsible for each piece of the project? This is determined by the students.
Researching the topic	Different learners take on different responsibilities depending on their interests, strengths, and language abilities. This could include inviting guest speakers, interviews with others outside of class, visits to the library and Internet research. This is a place where learners can leverage all of their linguistic resources (translanguaging), reading materials, or collaborating with others in their first language (Van Dyke-Kao and Yanuaria 2017). (See Chapter 6 for a more complete discussion of "translanguaging.")
Drafting and developing a final product	What language support is needed to finalize the project? Language development activities with the teacher or volunteer are part of the process. Peer editing and feedback are necessary.
Disseminating the product, if there is one / Enjoying the celebration, event, activity	Who is the audience for the project? One teacher had a job fair at the school after students researched job opportunities in their community (Hoose 2017). One school created a school garden and then developed a Garden Movie Project that was disseminated to other classes in the community (see 8.12). Did the class organize a field trip? A graduation event?
Evaluating the project / Outcomes	How is the success of the project evaluated? Audience participation is a measure of success. Self-evaluations on personal and group participation can be conducted. Rubrics aligned to language outcomes and program standards can also be used (clarity of presentation; appropriate register; ability to synthesize information and use appropriate citations). Did they use language, numeracy, and cultural understandings to plan, buy food, supplies, and arrange transportation?

Learners in an integrated English language and civics education class expressed frustration with not being able to interact with their children's school staff and teachers. They also felt invisible in the school community, which resulted in the development of the following project. Their ultimate goal was to develop a booklet about engaging with schools to share with others in their community and also to increase their visibility and make their needs known to the power structure of the school—teachers, leadership, and parents of mainstream learners who led the parent-teacher organization.

Integrated English Language and Civics Education Topic/theme: Engaging with our child's school
Materials and resources needed: online school directory, other parents from school, representative from parent-teacher organization, literature about the school (translated or simplified), list of after-school course offerings, phone cameras
Sample activities to support this project:
1. In-class lessons on telephoning or emailing a teacher; making a request to meet teacher and to organize a school visit.
2. Practice accessing and deciphering online portal with student grades.

3. Guest speaker (other immigrant parent and representative from parent-teacher organization; prepare for visit by developing questions to ask the guest as well as concerns they want to share; provide listening tasks at time of visit (this would be a bilingual process depending on learners' language backgrounds).

4. School visit: prepare questions to ask guide; role-play questions ahead of time.

5. As feasible, take photos of children and parents at the school to include in final booklet; practice creating screenshots of online resources that could also be included.

6. Language experience activity: after the visit, group generates a text about the visit; multiple activities using text.

7. Create a booklet that includes guidelines for making contact with child's teacher, using the online parent portal; list of appropriate free/low-cost after-school activities for children.

Figure 2.4 Sample Activities in Project-Based Learning

Project-based learning need not be used as the sole vehicle of instruction; in fact, projects may be implemented within any teaching approach, as an element of other ongoing skills and language-building work. Colleen Crossley, a teacher in Minnesota, collaborated with a mosaic artist over one term to work with the class to create an "all are welcome here" mosaic for the school entrance. In an ongoing unit on the theme of civil rights, learners explored the critical issue of discrimination many immigrants may face in their communities while also working on the language of following instructions, asking clarifying questions, and explaining a process to others. The project outcome, the mosaic, was shared with other classes and with seniors at an assisted-living facility.

Figure 2.5 Learning Through Mosaic Project: Project Outcome

PBL is ideal for a multilevel class like Rosie's described at the beginning of this section, in which learners' strengths vary. Learners most comfortable with accessing information online may be tasked with gathering information on the Internet; students with stronger verbal abilities may conduct interviews and audio or video record those as part of the project. Finally, due to the multifaceted components of projects, PBL is likely to appeal to a variety of learning styles and multiple intelligences.

Conclusion

A multifaceted approach to teaching means combining elements from different approaches in ways that are most responsive to a particular group of learners. In completing your chart, you may have discovered that some approaches promote more active participation by the learners than others; some may promote development of a wider range of skills. As a teacher, consider which of the principles behind the approaches are most in keeping with your beliefs about teaching and learning, as well with the principles of learner-centered teaching explored in Chapter 1. Now we turn to the program options offered to adult English language learners. As you read about these options, start thinking about the ways these varied approaches might best serve students in these different settings, for example, how can project-based learning be used in a pre-academic Bridge program?

Part II: Program options

2.12 Introduction

Adult ESL programming and curricula can take on many forms, including integrated skills English language development, intergenerational and family literacy, first language literacy, integrated English language and civics, citizenship, vocational English as a second language, and career pathways, or distance learning. All of these options can provide supports for newcomers or for those who have been in country for some years. In all instances, there will likely be a focus on the 21st-century skills outlined in Chapter 1, including problem-solving in digital-rich environments and practice with complex texts encountered at home, school, work or community. What determines the classification of a program largely depends on funding sources, available no/low cost resources (volunteer programs, donated space/materials), and existing community needs, such as an increase in citizenship programs after a shift in government policy or career-contextualized programs based on the employment outlook in a particular community. This section describes goals and focus areas of different program options.

Getting Started

 Task 2.4

With a partner, read the descriptions of four types of classes offering English language support to adult learners and discuss which type of program you think each exemplifies: Integrated skills English language development, intergenerational and family literacy, literacy tutoring, citizenship, Integrated English Literacy/Civics Education, vocational English/workplace/work readiness, or a pre-academic Bridge program.

Group A: *This beginning to intermediate level class consists of ten workers at a large hotel and trade center in Boston. Six participants are stewards with the utility department, tasked with supplying clean dishware and supplies for events, and the others work as room attendants in housekeeping. Many of the units in the multilevel curriculum include reading and using their payroll app, reading workplace email, communicating with supervisors and coworkers, reading workplace documents, and using the hotel's training methods on how to communicate effectively with guests.[1]*

Group B: *This class prepares immigrants to enter a Certified Nursing Assistant Program at a community college in St. Paul. Students work on test-taking strategies and reading skills, as well as job-specific skills such as completing patient in-take interviews and taking patient food orders, all of which the students need to know for the practicum they complete in their training.*

Group C: *Run in partnership with local libraries around Melbourne to increase access to flexible and needs-based literacy education for community members, tutors in this program work one-to-one and with small groups in accessible community spaces, such as libraries and neighborhood houses, to address the immediate literacy and learning needs of adults in their daily lives.[2]*

Group D: *This class meets twice a week in a large adult education center in New York City. There are 30 students from over 18 countries at the high-intermediate/advanced level. Many hold a credential from their country and are computer literate. Within the framework of a theme-based curriculum, they are working on developing their reading, writing, listening, and speaking skills to both feel more confident in an English-speaking community as well as to improve their employment and educational opportunities. Although the topics they are interested in vary, they all want to learn about the U.S. culture and improve their communication skills in ways that are culturally appropriate (i.e., improve their socio-pragmatic skills).[3]*

Follow-up: Compare your answers with another pair in class. What seems to be the dominant emphasis of each program? Are there any that seem to respond to multiple purposes (e.g., life skills and vocational)? What teaching approach might be most responsive to each setting?

[1] This course description is from Kathleen O'Connell, Workplace Education Coordinator and Instructor, World Education, Inc., Boston, MA.
[2] This tutoring program is offered through Carringbush Adult Education, Melbourne, Australia.
[3] This class description is from Ivana Ferguson, ESL teacher in NYC.

2.13 Programming to promote learner persistence and success

Adult English learners come to programs with any number of short and long-range goals and may often underestimate the time it takes to attain those goals (Comings 2007). Studies indicate (Porter, Cuban, and Comings 2005; Sticht 1982; Darkenwald 1986) that a minimum of 100-150 hours of instruction is needed to achieve one grade-level gain in reading for adult learners as a group (this includes those for whom English is their first language). Programs need to attract learners and then provide educational opportunities that motivate learners to persist in that process, giving them the best shot of meeting their goals and transitioning to the new opportunities, either personal or professional.

Programs often refer to student *retention* numbers, but Comings, Parrella, and Soricone (1999) make an important distinction between retention and persistence. **Retention** tends to focus on the program and accountability measures (holding onto students, filling chairs), but **persistence** refers to the intensity of learner participation as well as to ongoing engagement in learning outside of the program; its focus is on understanding and supporting learners' agency and efficacy. This could occur through use of self-study or distance learning, for example. Ideally, learners will find a program option where they feel they have some agency and where they are motivated to persist long enough to attain their goals.

While there's no question adult immigrants need to attain the language, knowledge, and skills in areas that have traditionally been known as life skills—things such as shopping, registering children at school, and opening bank accounts—there is far more one needs to know in order to *thrive* in the new country and in a new language (Parrish 2015a). Community-based or adult education courses for integrated-skills English language development, such as Scenario D above, are places where those life skills can be addressed while also working on pre-employment and academic-readiness skills. Most areas serving large numbers of adult English learners will have leveled integrated-skills English language development[4] programs.

In Task 2.4, Scenario A represents a workplace program, that is, one offered at a worksite for employees. Scenario B reflects a pre-academic Bridge course preparing learners for entry into a postsecondary credentialing program, and Scenario C presents a literacy tutoring program. How does a community or adult education site decide what types of courses or programs to offer? There are a number of factors that determine the types of services provided in any community:

> **Funding:** Most programs rely on government funding, much of which is earmarked for specific program types. Grantors require that programs adhere to specific guidelines and outcomes (See Chapter 10 for a discussion of meeting grantor expectations). It is often the case that the program offerings and outcomes are determined by funding trends and resources, and policy/regulation.

[4] These programs are sometimes called "General English" and in the U.S. under the Workforce Innovation and Opportunity Act (WIOA), they are called "English Language Acquisition" programs.

Employment trends: Jobs in a particular geographic area are in constant flux (Nash and Hewett 2017), so those programs offering career-focused courses need to be highly responsive to those trends.

Resettlement trends: Some communities attract higher numbers of refugees than others based on international or national refugee resettlement agreements, and often an influx of refugees or asylum seekers is sudden due to political strife somewhere in the world.

Community size: Large urban areas with multiple adult education centers are able to offer an array of services, both within large agencies and across entities. Small communities often have one adult education site that must provide everything from basic literacy instruction to career-focused ESL.

Community resources: Are there teachers with expertise in adult ESL in the community? If not, does the state provide training for teachers? Many small, rural communities have experienced sudden and rapid increases of immigrant populations and are ill-prepared to respond to their needs. Are there volunteers available?

Opportunities for collaboration: Are there multiple support services in place to assist learners in entering a particular career pathway (Wrigley 2007)? Are there opportunities to collaborate with other agencies, employers, or community colleges that allow learners opportunities to gain specialized certifications (Nash and Hewett 2017)?

Ideally, learners would enter the type of program that best corresponds to their personal and professional needs: a learner with particular vocational goals chooses an Integrated Education and Training program; a parent of school-age children attends to a family and intergenerational literacy program. Regrettably, this is not always the case since not all of these options may be available where the learner lives. There are a number of factors that determine the type of program learners choose to enter:

Location of the program/transportation: Programs need to be accessible to learners using public transportation.

Personal schedule/work schedule: Employed students have time constraints, especially those living in smaller communities with limited class offerings. If one family member is working, the other may stay home to take care of children, most often the mother (Vesely, Goodman, and Scurlock 2014).

Availability of services: Waiting lists may prevent a learner from attending in his/her neighborhood.

Immigration status: Often state-sponsored programs accept only documented immigrants. Some community-based programs do not check learners' immigration status.

Level of literacy: Ideally, adults with limited or no literacy should attend programs offering "literacy-level" courses. Teaching pre-literate or emergent readers, those without literacy in their first language or who have limited or interrupted prior formal schooling, requires teachers who have specialized knowledge and skills.

Childcare: Some programs, particularly family and intergenerational literacy (FIL) programs, have free on-site childcare. In those places where FIL is offered, parents of small children may choose this option, even if that is not the best program fit for them.

The fact of the matter is that many learners do not have the luxury of researching numerous options and choosing the one that best fits their professional and personal goals. It may be that factors related to location and personal schedule will determine their choice. What does that mean for you as an ESL teacher? Regardless of the type of program within which you teach, more often than not, you need to teach to a wide range of purposes and outcomes. What are those program types and what are the central purposes of each one?

📋 **Task 2.5**

To help you make connections between teaching approaches and program options, use the following grid to identify the purposes for learning in each context as well as approaches from Part I that you think might be particularly suitable within that context.

Program Option	Purposes for Learning	Suitable Approaches to Teaching in This Setting
English Language Acquisition		
Integrated English Language and Civics Education		
Citizenship		
Family / Intergenerational Literacy		
One-on-One Literacy Tutoring		
Workplace		
Career-Contextualized Bridge Integrated Education and Training		
Distance Learning		

While more and more career-focused programs are available in most communities, and all program options tend to include content related to employment and further education, probably the most common type of program for adult English language learners will be English language acquisition programs.

2.14 English language acquisition programs

Many programs within adult education in a variety of settings around the world can be described as English language acquisition programs. The language focus may include literacy development, listening, speaking, functions, and grammar, all in keeping with the needs of the particular group of students and in keeping with current trends in college and career standards and 21st-century skills integration. Unlike content-based programs, for example, citizenship or an Integrated Education and Training culinary arts program where learners have a shared occupational goal for learning English, students in English language acquisition programs may have more divergent wants, needs, and goals for learning English. At the lower levels, learners need to acquire basic skills, or language needed to fulfill basic needs in the community. At the same time, these learners can also be working on digital literacy skills, strategies for accessing complex texts (see Chapters 4 and 5), as well as content that goes beyond survival English. At the beginning levels and particularly with newcomers, instructional themes may revolve around topics such as education, health, community, school, family, and work, but should always be grounded in learners' expressed needs. In all cases, it is important to consider themes that acknowledge an adult learner's intellect (e.g., in a unit about transportation, talk about the benefits of a new light rail system instead of only learning how to read bus schedules).

In past decades, adult basic education programs often offered a "transitions level" to help students with skills and strategies needed in higher education settings (e.g., synthesizing information from multiple sources; listening to lectures and note-taking). Even with those "transitions" levels, a mismatch between the content and goals of those programs and the expectations of higher education settings has been shown (Johnson and Parrish 2010). Current thinking is that those "transition" skills must be embedded throughout instruction and at all levels. For example, a beginning-level learner can listen to an authentic passage and practice note-taking or can gather "data" about classmates, analyze the data to practice numeracy and analytical skills, and create a visual representation of what is learned (a pie chart, graph, or table). **English language acquisition** classes often draw on primary textbooks (see Chapter 8), which include practice in all the skills areas.

Within these programs, there is often a "literacy level" where special attention is paid to literacy-level learners, or reading development for immigrant adult language learners with little or no native language schooling who may be learning the skills of reading for the first time. The **Literacy Education and Second Language Learning for Adults** (LESLLA) professional organization supports research and provides resources into best practices for this learner population. Principles and practices for working with these learners are compatible with family and intergenerational literacy goals outlined below (2.17), with primacy placed on socially-constructed learning. Chapter 5 includes a section on literacy development for learners with interrupted or limited prior schooling.

2.15 Citizenship

Instruction designed to prepare immigrants to pass the citizenship exam has been in existence for well over a century in the U.S. Clearly, the approach to teaching those courses has not always been the same, but governments in many countries have had a long-standing commitment to assisting immigrants in their quest to become citizens. In the U.S., to become a citizen, an immigrant must demonstrate English literacy and knowledge of U.S. history and government systems through an application and interview process. In other countries, for example, the United Kingdom and Australia, learners can meet the language requirements for citizenship through language certifications. Programs focused on citizenship typically include:

- The benefits of citizenship
- The naturalization process
- Preparation for the oral interview and written tests

Citizenship classes sometimes provide referrals to legal advice as well. In many cases, citizenship is included in **Integrated English Literacy/Civics Education** programming.

2.16 Integrated English Literacy and Civics Education

Integrated English Literacy/Civics Education (IEL/CE) programs or courses include instruction in literacy and English language acquisition along with instruction on the rights of citizenship and civic participation. The goal is to promote active citizenship and participation in all aspects of the community including voting and civic involvement, involvement in neighborhood programs, active participation in children's schooling, taking full advantage of community services such as libraries, shelters, or community centers, and job-related skills for pursuing employment. These topics and themes are not unique to Integrated English Literacy/Civics Education; intergenerational and family literacy programs share many of the same goals, and many **English language acquisition** programs draw on the same themes as well and may shift with changes in particular political administrations, parties, and policies.

2.17 Family and intergenerational literacy

Data from the Program for the International Assessment of Adult Competencies (PIAAC), a comprehensive study of educational attainment and employment outcomes globally, indicate that an individual's attainment of literacy and numeracy skills is directly correlated to parents' educational attainment in those areas (Clymer, et al. 2017). **Family and intergenerational literacy** (FIL) programs have long recognized this reality and the goal of these programs is to promote education and prosperity for families. Another central tenet of these programs is to build connections between homes and schools, acknowledging and drawing on the multiple perspectives and experiences of immigrant families.

FIL programs work concurrently with at least two generations within a family: parents or grandparents and children. In the 1970s and 1980s, these programs were primarily focused on parent-school involvement and literacy development. Typically, programs were designed for mothers working on developing literacy as well as basic skills in English. The children spent time playing games, working on art projects, and learning letters, rhymes, and songs. As with other types of programs, FIL has shifted programming to include explicit education and training leading to jobs and/or postsecondary education (Clymer, et al. 2017). First language literacy development is another component found in some FIL programs working with adults who are not literate in their first language.

Whatever the FIL model, it is crucial that educators avoid a **deficit** view of adult learners and their families; programs should not be designed to transmit the school culture and language to immigrant parents (Auerbach 1995). Learners' homes are not linguistically impoverished— parents and children interact and collaborate, they use many forms of literacy, and they educate one another. The interactions and literacy practices used in homes may be different, but no less valid, from those used in institutions. Programs may include what Purcell-Gates, et al. (2012) refer to as "school-only texts" for developing reading and writing skills, but a successful literacy program must also include "real-life texts" (399) and activities, that is, literacy practiced in ways that are situated in the learners' real-world literacy needs and practices (see Chapter 5 for further discussion). Literacy experiences and practices must move from homes to schools as well as from schools to homes. It is important to note that these principles should inform *any* literacy work in *any* program model.

2.18 Literacy tutoring

English language instruction for newcomers is often provided through literacy councils, libraries, faith-based institutions, and other community-based programs with literacy volunteers working one-on-one or in small groups as in scenario C in the warm-up activity 2.4. This is a context where a truly participatory curriculum can evolve as the classes are designed to meet the needs of an individual learner. Volunteers are normally provided with training in literacy skills development and, one hopes, an understanding of the particular challenges of learning literacy as an adult and in an additional language. These classes could integrate components of any of the program types described in this chapter. For example, a tutor may assist the learner with preparing for citizenship, increasing civic participation, retraining for a particular job, or preparation for a part course of study. This is a context where technology integration is essential, providing learners opportunities for additional learning time through self-study and online learning options to increase the intensity of instruction (Porter, Cuban, and Comings 2005).

2.19 Career pathways/career-focused programming

Career pathways refers to a whole host of program options and services intended to educate adult learners about career ladders associated with becoming self-sufficient and earning a family-sustaining wage (Wrigley 2015). This ideally starts with learners identifying their skill sets (at times needing support in recognizing their own strengths and abilities as transferable skills for employment), exploring career options, and eventually enrolling in an occupational training course or attaining a job. Any of the program types above can and should infuse components of career readiness into their curricula. In this section, we look at program models that are career-focused, often leading to a specific certification or job opportunity.

A. Career-contextualized ESL classes

Career-contextualized ESL programs or classes are those that integrate English language skills development with topics such as career awareness and exploration, goal setting, or the language needed for applying for a job (Adelson-Goldstein 2016). Many such programs/courses emphasize general workplace or transferable job skills, such as effective communication with supervisors and coworkers, or problem-solving at work. Learning outcomes for a career-contextualized ESL course could look like this:

Intermediate Career Explorations

- Identify personal skills and strengths.
- Map out a career pathway for a field of interest.
- Identify job requirements and responsibilities.
- Create résumés and cover letters for specific job announcements.
- Engage in effective communication with coworkers and employers.
- Identify safety issues at the workplace
- Identify and know your rights as a worker.
- Use a variety of reading strategies to understand technical materials.
- Compose workplace reports and correspondence.

The example above is not focused on one specific career area, however, courses related to high-demand jobs or industries in a particular geographic area may be offered as well, such as the one below for those interested in customer service jobs. This course leads to a certificate of completion and note the information provided on next steps of a learner's career pathway in this field.

Retail/Customer Service Certificate

Course Description:
This course is designed to prepare students for entry level retail sales positions, concentrating on customer service through sales and service. The course is intended to help participants progress from learning about themselves, to learning how to relate to their classmates as their internal customers, to learning how to relate to actual customers in the workplace. Curriculum is focused on best practices from the National Retail Foundation, supplemented by written practice, vocabulary practice and math skills related to the field. Students will practice handling angry customers, helping customers by describing products benefits and features, phone etiquette, and understanding store policies.

Next Steps and Additional Career Information:
Successful completion will lead to a certificate for 90 hours of classroom preparation from the Hubbs Center. Students may also choose to take the National Retail Federation test for Professional Certification in Customer Service. This exam is offered at multiple sites in the metro area. The fee for the exam is between $70.00 to $80.00.

Ronald M. Hubbs Center for Lifelong Learning; St. Paul Public Schools Adult Education

---

B. Workplace ESL

Workplace ESL programs are those offered at work sites or with a group of learners from the same work site, focusing on the very specific needs of the learners' job. Kathleen's class for hotel employees presented in the warm-up activity represents workplace ESL. In her setting, learners work on the competencies and language needed for their jobs at a hotel. Today's workplace classes often focus heavily on industry-specific technologies as well as language, for example, the app that learners need to use for payroll at the hotel. In a manufacturing company with which I have collaborated, learning outcomes such as "follow instructions for filling drive-shaft molds" are common and demand instruction that is highly focused. This is a setting where competency-based education (2.5) may be particularly suitable.

C. Bridge programs

The primary goal of a **Bridge program** is to prepare students for entry to a post-secondary institution, often to a program for obtaining a certificate such as a Certified Nursing Assistant program as described in Task 2.4. Some of the adult learners in these programs are pursuing their first degree, while others are retraining in the same or similar profession they held in their country. In the context of the U.S., many community and technical colleges and universities offer these pre-academic programs, but they may require students to pay tuition that is beyond their means. The solution to that is to offer Integrated Basic Education and Skills Training (I-BEST) or Integrated Education and Training (IET), which are often offered through publicly-funded adult education systems.

D. Integrated Basic Education and Skills Training /Integrated Education and Training

Integrated Basic Education and Skills Training (I-BEST) or **Integrated Education and Training** (IET) are those programs where the occupational instructor and adult education instructor co-teach in the same classroom or coordinate instruction through **concurrent enrollment** (i.e., enrollment in job-specific content classes along with supports or ESL classes that integrate the field-specific content). IET programs provide basic skills (literacy, math, English language development) alongside the occupational skills needed for a credential. The original I-BEST programs were developed for all adult learners, not specifically for English language learners, but more and more programs are providing integrated options that are targeted to immigrant learners with English language development needs. As with Bridge programs, some learners are pursuing a new credential, while others are retraining in the same or similar field. This example from the Genesis Center in Rhode Island illustrates how an IET program prepares immigrant learners for high-demand jobs in their community. See how they combine language and reasoning skills with the work-specific content.

Culinary Arts Program Genesis Center

- 13-week, full-time training preparing participants to enter the food industry
- Curriculum taught by a professional chef and adult education instructor
- Program is hands-on, with participants preparing daily meals for our students and childcare center.
- Culinary instructor teaches job-specific skills, for example fractions and proportional reasoning for measuring and scaling recipes.
- Adult education instructors use occupational content to teach contextualized reading, writing, or math.
- Participants test for the ServSafe Food Safety Manager Certificate and complete an internship at a local restaurant.

(Nash and Hewett 2017)

Any of these career-focused models can be considered just one component of an on-ramp to a career and need to be part of a systems approach, as illustrated in Figure 2.6.

Figure 2.6 A Systems Approach to Career Pathways (Center for Postsecondary and Economic Success 2017)

Any ESL teacher involved in work-focused English as a second language programming needs to be aware of where they are situated in this broader context and must be willing to collaborate with a variety of players in order to support learner success.

2.20 Distance education

Distance education, often called **distance learning**, has been available to adult learners for decades, but with improvements in technology, greater access by learners to high-speed Internet, and the common use of smartphones, distance learning is an option for just about any adult ESL learner who lacks transportation, has work commitments, or lives in areas where there is limited adult education support. It provides learners added flexibility in choosing the time and place of instruction. Vanek, et al. (2016: 11) define distance education as "all aspects of programming that allow a learner to continue learning beyond the walls of a classroom," so this definition includes programs that are purely distance learning, **blended learning** (a combination of face-to-face and distance learning), and classroom technology integration (see Chapter 8 for a full discussion of classroom technology integration). Distance learning programs may be delivered using any number of materials and resources, including print, audio or video recordings, computer software, or web-based programs or technologies such as webinars and virtual meeting spaces; teachers support learners via telephone, email, or online technologies (U.S. Department of Education 2016a).

Programs may develop their own curricula, use commercially available software, or make use of Open Educational Resources (OERs) such as U.S.A. Learns, which provides free lessons designed to teach English to beginning to intermediate level learners via videos and activities. Web-based software such as LearnerWeb *https://www.learnerweb.org/* can aid tremendously in the implementation of a truly learner-centered, effective distance learning experience. Organized around learning plans, the system allows learners to identify learning goals and then the system structures a plan to help the learner achieve those goals. Each step in the plan is matched to freely accessible online resources and learners can save their work in an e-portfolio (Learner Web 2017).

In the absence of peer support and regular contact with a classroom teacher, learner success in distance learning is greatest for learners who are able to work independently, are self-motivated, and have strong organizational skills (Vanek, et al. 2016). Face-to-face orientation to a distance learning program and ongoing contact are essential for program success. Success will also hinge on the skill set of the teacher, who must possess a level of comfort with the technologies being used. In some instances, adult educators work in tandem with tech educators/facilitators to ensure appropriate and competent content and approach. Distance learning does not necessarily mean self-study for learners, so teachers must provide regular support, guidance, and feedback to learners in any distance education program.

Blended programs are those where the face-to-face courses are complemented with distance learning components. A national model for blended learning in the U.S., English Innovations, provides those with high-beginning literacy levels 100 hours of instruction focused on digital literacy skills development and community engagement. Rooted in the principles of participatory and learner-centered instruction, Heide Wrigley, a leader in adult ESL and collaborator on this project, shares that, "We wanted to create a set of learning experiences for immigrants who had not yet found their way into the formal ESL system and needed opportunities not just to navigate 'technology rich environments' but to express ideas, share their stories, and speak up for themselves and others" (Wrigley 2017). Figure 2.7 illustrates how a blended program such as this one can be used to address the goals of EL civics, family or intergenerational literacy, or integrated-skills English development programs.

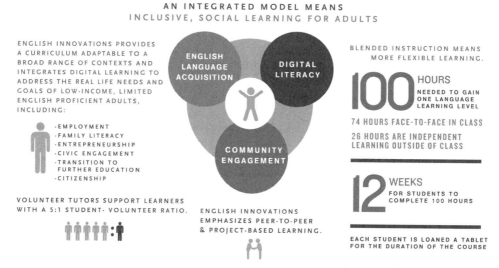

Figure 2.7 English Innovations Blended Learning Model

Any of the program models described in this chapter can be delivered though distance or blended learning, and the outcomes and standards are the same as those for face-to-face instruction. An innovative example of distance learning and workplace instruction is a pilot project called MOBILE UP! which provides industry-specific English instruction leveraging smartphone technologies. The goal of MOBILE UP! is to provide training and accelerate career advancement of long-term care workers, hotel workers, and janitors who cannot attend in-person trainings (Wrigley, 2017). In this model, workers are assigned a coach who provides targeted instruction via text messaging and phone calls, making it "demand-driven vocational training and personalized career coaching to workers entirely by phone" (Wrigley, 2017). Many of the resources developed for distance learning can also be used by students in on-site classrooms, enhancing their educational experience and contributing to persistence as we see in Chapter 8.

Conclusion

In this chapter, we have looked very broadly at some of the most common approaches to teaching adult ESL as well as the program options available. It is essential that teachers new to the field understand that there are many connections between and among all of these approaches and options. There is no recipe for good teaching. What works successfully in one setting may not in another. Through thorough needs assessment, ongoing observation, and abundant opportunities for learners to express their needs and concerns in the classroom, teachers shape their curricula accordingly, drawing from a variety of approaches, techniques, and materials.

In the chapters that follow, teaching techniques and strategies that help learners develop both language and social/cultural knowledge are examined and illustrated through sample lesson plans, activities, and guidelines. The tools and techniques you will learn about can be used within many of the approaches and program options discussed in this chapter.

On your own, or with a partner, provide an example or brief definition for each concept:

Checklist of Key Terms	
receptive skills	
productive skills	
communicatively-based approaches	
participatory education	
emergent curriculum	
problem pose	
civics education	
career pathways	
distance education	

Before doing these activities, revisit your answers to the questions at the beginning of the chapter.

1 Reflecting on Your Own Learning Experience

At the beginning of the chapter, you briefly discussed a learning experience you've had. This activity allows you to examine in greater depth the ways your own learning may shape or inform your teaching. If you have studied a second language, reflect on your own experiences as a language learner as you answer these questions; otherwise, think of a different classroom experience you've had, either for academic or vocational purposes (computer classes, professional training) or for personal growth (piano, gardening, etc.). Write your answers in your journal or discuss them with others in your class:

a. What is your overall recollection of the experience? Was it positive or negative and what made it so? Did you feel you learned something or not?

b. What roles did the students and teacher take in the classroom? Would you describe the class as learner-centered or teacher-centered? Why?

c. What areas of language did you practice (or for non-language classes, what content or skills did you learn—reading, writing, listening, speaking, grammar, language functions, vocabulary?)

d. What was the role of your first language in instruction?

e. What topics and themes were covered? To what extent did you have a say in course content?

f. How do you think your own experiences as a learner can shape and inform the choices you make about approaches to teaching adult English language learners?

g. Do you recognize any of the elements from the approaches in Part I in the approaches used by your own teachers and, if so, which ones?

2 Approaches to Teaching Adult English Language Learners

If you are already teaching, choose one of your classes and answer these questions:

- Who are the learners and what are their goals for learning English?
- What experiences have they had with formal and informal education?
- What are their views of teaching and learning and what is your own view of teaching and learning?
- What program standards are learners expected to meet?

How would you describe the approach you are currently using with this group of learners? How responsive is it to learner needs? What other approaches would you like to try with this group of learners?

If you are not teaching, contact an ESL teacher in your community and ask if you can observe his/her class. **Before class: Interview the teacher using the questions above. After you observe, answer these questions:** How would you describe this teacher's approach to teaching? Is there an approach described in Part I you think might work well with the group you observed?

3 Program Options in Your Community

What program options are offered in your community? Go to your local adult education center or your state Department of Education website to find the following information:

a.   Where are services for adult English language learners provided in your area? Community colleges, public schools, community-based programs, literacy councils, other?

b.   What program options are available? Integrated-skills English language development including emergent literacy, distance learning, Integrated Education and Training (IET), EL civics, or citizenship, etc.?

c.   What are the requirements for teachers of adult English language learners in your state, province, or country?

Adelson-Goldstein, J. (2016) *LINCS ESL Pro Preparing English Learners for Work and Career Pathways: Companion Learning Resource.* U.S. Department of Education (OCTAE). This interactive, digital magazine illustrates current, effective instructional models for integrating career-focused training with academic instruction. Available at: *https://lincs.ed.gov/sites/default/files/LINCS_CLR-1_508_0.pdf*

Auerbach, E. (1992) *Making Meaning, Making Change: A Participatory Curriculum Development for Adult ESL Literacy.* Washington D.C. and McHenry, IL: Delta Systems and Center for Applied Linguistics. The book provides ideas for collaborating with learners to develop relevant curricula that respond to their needs as parents, workers, and community members.

Richards, J. and Rogers, T. (2014) *Approaches and Methods in Language Teaching, 3rd Edition.* Cambridge: Cambridge University Press. This classic overview of approaches and methods to teaching English to speakers of other languages all over the world is now in its third edition and provides details to the approaches in Part I as a comprehensive and historical overview of language teaching.

USEFUL WEBSITES

Ed Tech at World Education and IDEAL Consortium *https://edtech.worlded.org/* This site provides recommendations, research, and resources for quality distance education.

Literacy Education and Second Language Learning for Adults (LESLLA) is an international forum focused on research on the development of second language skills by adult immigrants with little or no schooling prior to entering the country of entry. *http://www.leslla.org/*

New American Horizons (newamericanhorizons.org) Provides authentic classroom videos that demonstrate many of the communicatively-based approaches covered in the chapter.

3 | Teaching Language for Meaningful Purposes

To consider before reading this chapter:

- What does it mean to take an integrated and contextualized approach to presenting and practicing new language?
- What kinds of activities promote meaningful practice of functions, forms, and vocabulary along with higher-order thinking skills?
- How do you decide when and how to give learners corrective feedback?

Part I: Developing integrated and contextualized language lessons

3.1 Introduction

We have looked at a number of approaches to teaching ESL as well as program options offered in most communities. Each program type has a particular focus, but they share the goal of helping learners communicate within their communities more effectively, whether for greater community involvement, to gain or improve employment, to enter a training program, or to engage more fully in their children's education. In this chapter, we explore an approach to teaching language that integrates multiple language skills, is learner-centered, experiential, and that situates learning in real-world contexts. We explore activities that promote natural use of language so that learners gain confidence in using English in the safe environment of the classroom. We also consider how language lessons can be tied to rigorous standards at any level of instruction. As with any type of lesson, teaching begins with understanding your learners' strengths, wants, and needs.

Getting Started

Leslie teaches adult English language learners at the intermediate level in a large adult education center in Tampa, Florida. This integrated-skills English language acquisition class includes instruction in language functions, grammar, and vocabulary, and the four skills of reading, writing, listening, and speaking for the purpose of engaging more fully in their communities and preparing for demands of work or further education. Many of her students have been in the U.S. for over five years and are comfortable with everyday English needed to meet their basic needs. This program has adopted rigorous college and career readiness standards that focus on accessing informational texts, developing critical thinking skills, and interpreting information presented in a variety of formats. She regularly incorporates instruction in digital literacy skills, problem-solving, numeracy, and practice with complex texts, charts, and graphs. She believes that these skills are needed in all areas of life. She wants to make sure that her instruction meets the needs and interests of her learners, so each term she gives her students a survey at the beginning of the session. Here are some of the responses from her students in a recent class:

Talk to my neighbors	Find jobs online
Read in English	People don't understand me
Pronunciation	Get my high school equivalency here
Get a job related to my profession	I want grammar and vocabulary
Understand my child's schoolwork	Get my credentials evaluated
Talk to my landlord about problems	Interview for jobs
I can't understand people	Talk to people at my job
I can't talk to the teachers at my kid's school	Understand when I watch TV
Learn English for college	Make appointments online
Talk to doctors and nurses when my kids are sick	Give my opinion in English

Leslie is struck by the variety of needs and expectations among learners. Her own experience as a language learner in high school and college was to practice grammar and vocabulary, but she knows that her students need much more than that. Some want nothing but grammar, while others want to learn how to communicate in English with their children's teachers. Some have specific college and career goals, and some have needs related to their daily lives. How can she bring all of this together? Look at the list above and see if any themes emerge.

📋 **Task 3.1**

Based on the description of the class and the survey results provided, work with a partner to identify at least three areas of need for this class.

Areas of Need for Leslie's Class
1. _____
2. _____
3. _____

3.2 An integrated approach to language learning and teaching

As discussed in Chapter 2, programs within the U.S. are required to adopt rigorous content standards, which guide program planning and instruction. Communities and jobs across the globe require those same 21st-century skills, including problem-solving, digital literacy, and the ability to access and interpret information presented in a variety of formats. We are still *language* teachers, though, and the focus of this section is on how to help learners develop their *language* abilities while also developing those 21st-century skills. Let's start by looking at some possible themes for Leslie's class. How does this compare to your list above?

Theme 1: **Thriving in communities**

> Managing medical care
>
> Finding housing
>
> Talking to landlords
>
> Interacting with school staff and teachers

Theme 2: **Finding jobs and interacting at work**

> Accessing online job advertisements
>
> Interviewing
>
> Talking to coworkers
>
> Attaining work in an area of expertise

Theme 3: **Accessing and thriving in education**

> Attaining an equivalent credential
>
> Enrolling in a training program or postsecondary education
>
> Obtaining a high school equivalency

As we look at these needs and the many tasks involved for each, we now consider the *language* demands that may be involved in each:

Language competencies: These are real-life skills that enable us to complete the tasks we need to accomplish in our daily lives or at our jobs.

Examples: Making appointments

> Calling or emailing in sick to work
>
> Reporting a problem at work

Social language functions: These represent the ways we use language forms and phrases in social interactions.

Examples: Greetings and introductions

> Making invitations
>
> Making polite requests
>
> Complaints and apologies

Academic language functions: These represent the ways we use language in more formal and academic settings.

Examples: Asking for and giving opinions; expressing agreement or disagreement

> Elaborating on others' ideas
>
> Synthesizing the opinions of group members
>
> Comparing and contrasting ideas

Linguistic competence—grammar, vocabulary, spelling, pronunciation: Learners need to develop their linguistic competence, but it should be done within meaningful and authentic contexts that reflect how language is used for particular purposes.

Cultural competence: Learners need to acquire skills to navigate in a new setting where cultural norms may differ from their own; for example, ways of addressing teachers or supervisors may be less formal.

Language skills: Lessons also need to take into account the modes of communication that we use: speaking, listening, reading and writing. We call those modes of communication the four **language skills,** and listening and reading are considered the **receptive** skills, while speaking and writing are **productive** skills. It is important to note that all of these can be highly **interactive** as well.

Digital literacy skills: The way learners need to complete real-world tasks has drastically changed over the past decades and will continue to change every year. Many tasks that were traditionally done through reading and writing, and even listening and speaking, are now done using technology (Harris 2015b; Leu, et al. 2011).

Examples: Texting in place of many phone calls

Filling out forms online

Email to and from teachers or coworkers

Effective searching for information online

Evaluating the quality of information online

Critical thinking: Lessons also need to support practice with critical thinking skills needed for success in today's world (notice that these overlap with the academic language functions above).

Examples: Organizing and categorizing information

Analyzing and evaluating information

Challenging assumptions

Making decisions and problem-solving

This is not to suggest that learners do not already possess highly developed critical thinking skills. They have made a move to a new country and made their way into your classes and found housing; they can support their families. However, they may come from societies where educational systems are primarily transmission based where learners are not expected to challenge the teacher or ideas presented; where instruction is largely teacher directed (Chowdhury 2003).

Effective language lessons start with identifying the purposes for which learners need to use English. Then, we identify the competencies, functions, grammar, vocabulary, and skills needed to gain confidence and proficiency for those purposes. All of this can come together through integrated language lessons. Figure 3.1 illustrates the variety of components we need to consider while creating an integrated language lesson.

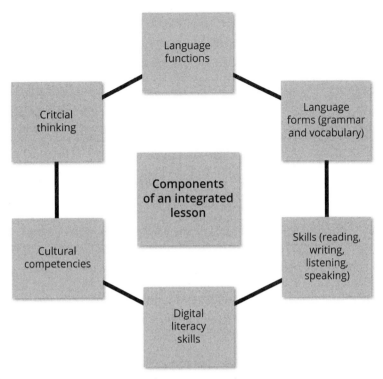

Figure 3.1 Components of an Integrated Lesson

To illustrate what this means, let's take an example that derives from Leslie's list of learner needs at the beginning of the chapter: *Reporting a problem to a landlord*. The multiple components to the task of *making a complaint to a landlord* are shown in Table 3.1.

Table 3.1 Components of an Integrated Lesson: Reporting a Problem to a Landlord

Task or Language Competency	Reporting a problem to a landlord

Language Functions	Introducing the problem:
	    I've had a problem with . . .
	    My _____ is broken . . .
	    The _____ doesn't work.
	Requesting action:
	    Could you please replace . . .?
	    Would you mind sending someone to fix the _____?
	Coming to a resolution to the problem
	    I assure you that . . .
	    So, I expect you to . . .

Grammar	Modal verbs (can, may, could) Question forms Vocabulary for household appliances and items; repair, fix, replace; rooms of the house

Four Skills	Speaking to the landlord on the phone or in person
	Listening to the landlord
	Reading tenant policies, print or online
	Writing a complaint
Digital Literacy	Filling in an online form for reporting problems or filing complaints
	Accessing information online from the housing agency or complex
Cultural Competencies	Using appropriate register, or level of formality based on context
	Knowing how to access consumer advocate offices
	Knowing whom to contact at the housing agency or complex if the problem isn't resolved
Critical Thinking	Problem-solving: determining the best course of action

Reporting a problem to a landlord entails everything from knowing how to make requests appropriately, to knowing the vocabulary for household items. It also involves learning how to access community organizations such as consumer advocates or housing agencies if a problem is unresolved. One aspect of language does not stand alone without the others. In this chapter, you will learn how to bring all of this together by creating *integrated and contextualized* language lessons.

> **Integrated and Contextualized Language Lessons**
> Lessons in which the teacher focuses on a particular language function, grammar point, or a set of vocabulary used in **real-world contexts**: while a lesson may have a particular language focus (e.g., making polite requests or using the simple past tense), many skills and areas of language are integrated into each lesson.

3.3 Teaching language for meaningful purposes

Teachers and researchers have, through the years, proposed a variety of models and procedures for language teaching. After the fall in popularity (in most corners) of the Audiolingual, drill-response approach to teaching, more meaning-based approaches emerged. One such approach to teaching language lessons was called the PPP model:

Presentation: *Show how language is used and formed through a story or dialogue; for example, highlight the target forms; check for learner understanding through accurate reproduction activities*

Practice: *Highly-controlled activities, drills, dialogue repetition (while more meaning-based than the strict mechanical drills, these activities are carry-overs of the Audiolingual approach)*

Production: *Freer activities that allow learners to try the new language more spontaneously—information-gap activities, role plays, for example*

This approach to teaching ESL has come under criticism for a variety of reasons. It implies that, as Jeremy Harmer points out, "students learn in 'straight lines'—that is, starting from no knowledge, through highly restricted sentence-based utterances and on to immediate production" (Harmer 2015: 66). We know that such a linear approach does not represent the complex processes that go into learning a second language. A lesson that focuses too narrowly on a particular language point, and presents and practices it with a set procedure, has the following shortcomings:

- It may not account for the fact that language forms are used in combination with a variety of skills and other language forms. Lessons need to integrate and combine these various skills and forms.

- Language forms are used differently in different settings. A narrowly-focused lesson may result in learners not fully understanding the range of uses a language point might have or how to use it in different settings, e.g., informal vs. formal settings, personal vs. vocational.
- Language learners bring different knowledge and skills to a lesson. Teaching needs to validate and draw on that knowledge, allowing learners to shape the direction of the lesson. Lessons that follow a prescribed set of steps may overlook the role learners can play in shaping the lesson.
- Language use is unpredictable, so highly controlled practice activities won't necessarily replicate real-world use when students leave your classroom.

A number of educators have suggested alternatives to the strict PPP progression. Jim Scrivener (2011) suggests that lessons normally start with restricted exposure to language (i.e., material created for language teaching purposes) or authentic exposure (i.e., language used naturally or authentic materials not designed for native English speakers). In lieu of the "presentation" stage of the PPP model, the teacher leads learners to noticing patterns and clarifying their understanding. Lessons move towards restricted use and authentic use. Restricted use refers to activities that focus on accuracy such as drills and repetition activities. Role plays, information gaps, discussions, or interview tasks are examples of authentic use. Clarification and focus represent those instances in a lesson when the teacher and learners describe or discover rules and patterns of the language, or when corrective feedback is given. Scrivener suggests that all of these elements can exist in a lesson, but that they do not need to happen in a particular order.

Another influential educational model in adult education is the Experiential Learning Cycle (Kolb 1984; Kolb and Kolb 2017), which can also guide the process we take when teaching language. This model starts with a concrete experience such as a group task, moves participants to reflection and analysis of that experience, and ends with putting what is learned through the experience into practice. While not a model for language teaching per se, its central tenet of "experience" in adult learning is in keeping with the learner-centered principles outlined in Chapter 1. Figure 3.2 shows how Kolb's learning cycle can relate to an integrated and contextualized language lesson cycle.

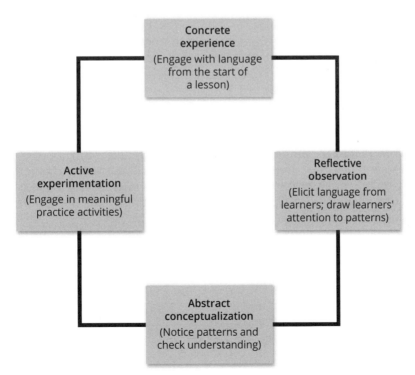

Figure 3.2 Kolb's Experiential Learning Cycle Related to Language Teaching

The samples in this chapter apply these experiential learning principles and also represent many of the principles of communicatively-based teaching discussed in section 2.6. Language is presented in context and for meaningful purposes; learners engage in interactive tasks to practice language. Note the focus on noticing patterns, which acknowledges Zoltán Dörnyei's (2013) recommendations regarding the need for focus on form and formulaic language within meaning-based contexts.

So, what are the benefits to teaching **integrated and contextualized language lessons** that focus on a particular language point (a language function, a grammar point, or a vocabulary set)? Presenting and practicing a targeted language point can have the following benefits, particularly for beginning to intermediate level learners:

- This type of lesson allows the teacher to respond specifically to a language need of a group of learners.
- Working through small chunks of language with a logical progression can be very reassuring to beginning level students; there's a sense of accomplishment in getting it right.
- Many adult learners have had formal instruction in languages and benefit from the opportunity to "notice" and focus on particular language forms.

As you will discover, the key to effective lessons is that they include a variety of practice activities that use language for real-life, meaningful purposes. In addition to that, they need to include a variety of learner options so that, for example, learners with fewer literacy skills can have the same learning opportunities as more literate learners. These lessons also need to address the types of outcomes found in rigorous content standards, for example, these College and Career Readiness Standards for Adult Education (U.S. Department of Education, Office of Vocational and Adult Education 2013):

- CCR Speaking and Listening Anchor Standard 2: prepare for and participate effectively in a range of conversations and collaborations with diverse partners, building on others' ideas and expressing their own clearly and persuasively
- CCR Reading Anchor Standard 7: integrate and evaluate content presented in diverse media and formats, including visually and quantitatively, as well as in words

Perhaps the most important factor is that lessons have learners using language in ways that are as authentic as possible. Authenticity refers to the texts, tasks, and roles learners take on in the classroom. Whenever possible, learners should take on roles in class that replicate the roles that they need to take on outside of the classroom. We can draw on authentic materials (e.g., texts, visuals, videos) in their original form and not simplified for teaching purposes. We have to be careful when determining what is truly "authentic" in language teaching, however. McKay (2013) cautions that use of authentic materials does not necessarily lead to authentic learner voice if they are not used in ways that are authentic for the learner. "By taking a text out of the context for which it was intended and placing it in an entirely different social context with another purpose, educators are using texts in an imaginary way" (2). Also, what we as teachers deem "authentic" may not be for learners in our classes. For example, using menus or labels of foods that learners would never buy is in no way "authentic." Reading a brochure on local farmer's markets might be more authentic. Barnett (2007) defines authenticity as the way learners find their own voice: ". . . at the heart of this particular sense of authenticity is the idea of discovering the world in one's 'own way,' unencumbered by other voices and messages" (43).

Finally, lessons need to take into account the social contexts in which language is used. The language we choose to use is defined by the personal relationships and the social situations of interactions with others (Young 2011). Lessons need to account for socially-accepted norms of formality and politeness, or **register**, which means that we need to include practice of both formal and informal usage:

- Greeting a government official at a citizenship interview as well as greeting friends and neighbors

- Understanding social and cultural norms of communicating on a first-name basis with co-workers, teachers or supervisors; understanding that using first names is not a sign of disrespect

The sample lessons that follow are not intended to be prescriptions of how to teach a language lesson, but rather examples of how experienced teachers each constructed a lesson for a particular group of learners. Each lesson has a different language focus:

Sample 1: Intermediate. Talking about expenses; making comparisons

Sample 2: High-beginning. Sharing life stories using simple past tense

Sample 3: Beginning. Jobs and job responsibilities

Sample 1 focuses on the functional language and grammar needed to make comparisons when discussing expenses. Sample 2 focuses on using the simple past tense to describe milestones in our lives, so it is primarily a grammar lesson. Sample 3 focuses on job vocabulary that could later be used in a variety of lessons, for example, career explorations, describing job skills, reading job advertisements, or completing an application.

This integrated and contextualized approach does not require that you create everything in a lesson from scratch. While none of these sample lessons came out of a textbook, they represent what is commonly found in many current ESL textbooks, which provide similar contexts, stages, and activities (see Chapter 8 for a detailed discussion of using textbooks). In fact, in many cases, teachers have a textbook from which they can develop lessons like these. All three examples contain a lesson progression that is outlined in Table 3.2. Those lessons that focus on a grammar feature are what we call **inductive** grammar lessons, that is, the language is presented in context first and learners deduce or figure out the rules with the teacher's guidance.

Table 3.2 Progression of an Integrated and Contextualized Language Lesson

1 Engage with language in a real-world context	• Provide language exposure in a meaningful context. • Activate prior knowledge about the language feature. • Show how and when the language is used.
2 Draw learners' attention to patterns and check learning	• Get learners to notice patterns and phrases they can use. • Check for learner understanding through checking questions and activities. • Focus on form within meaning-based contexts.
3 Engage in practice for meaningful purposes a. Focus on accuracy b. Focus on fluency	• Practice that may begin with restricted use of the language, for example semi-scripted role plays, chain activities, information-gap activities • Practice that moves to more authentic, spontaneous language practice • Includes extensive student-to-student interaction • The teacher moves back and forth between less controlled and more controlled activities depending on learner ability. These activities will be defined further in Part II of this chapter.
4 Ongoing assessment and evaluation	• Activities and tasks continuously assess achievement of the learning outcomes for the lesson. • The final task serves as a culminating assessment of learning.
5 Application/extension	Application/extension is taking learning out of the classroom and into the real world—interviewing others, collecting information from the community, attending an activity at a child's school.

As you read the following lesson plans, look for answers to the questions below. Write your answers in your journal or discuss them with a partner.

1. How does the teacher connect the lesson to learners' lives?

2. What makes language practice authentic for the learners?

3. When do the teacher and learners focus on language patterns?

4. Which activities help learners to attain accuracy with the target language and which focus on fluency? Which promote critical thinking?

5. When and how are the four skills (reading, writing, listening, speaking) practiced?

6. Identify the techniques used that are particularly suitable for beginning-level students. How do the teachers scaffold learning?

Context for Sample Lesson 1

While working with a community-based program in St. Paul, MN, I taught the following lesson to a group of intermediate-level adult immigrants. This program uses an integrated skills curriculum much like Leslie's. The month I was visiting this program, they were working on financial literacy, for example, managing online banking, using budgeting tools, and learning about Internet fraud. As many of these students, like Leslie's, are working towards the goal of gaining a high-school equivalency, I wanted to work with an informational text—a pie chart on average expenses in the U.S. They also expressed a desire to work on grammar. While there was a focus on comparative forms, the primary objective was for them to gain an understanding of the academic language function of making comparisons. Our state also uses the College and Career Readiness Standards (CCRS) for Adult Education as our state-adopted content standards, so the CCRS addressed are included as well in this example.

Sample Lesson 1: Talking about expenses; comparing and contrasting information
Class Description: 12 adult intermediate-level ESL students

Setting: Community-based Integrated English Language and Civics Education program
Time: 90 minutes

CCR Reading 7 Level C: Interpret information presented visually, orally, or quantitatively (e.g., in charts, graphs, diagrams, time lines, animations, or interactive elements on Web pages) and explain how the information contributes to an understanding of the text in which it appears.

CCR Language 3 Level C: Use knowledge of language and its conventions when writing, speaking, reading, or listening (b. Choose words and phrases to convey ideas precisely).

Lesson Objectives
Learners will be able to:

Functional:
- compare and contrast expenses among residents of the U.S.
- compare and contrast their own spending habits to those presented in a graph

Grammatical:
- make comparisons using "spend *more* on _____ *than* _____"; "*as much on* _____ *as* _____"
- use qualifiers to show degree of differences (considerably, somewhat, a little)

Vocabulary: categorize types of expenses

Speaking/pronunciation: use proper word stress on vocabulary (exPENses; contriBUtion)

Critical thinking:
- compare U.S. Labor and Statistics chart to their own expenses
- categorize expenses
- analyze and question the expenses displayed (surprises they note; explanations for expenses)

> **I. Engage with language in a real-world context.**
> **Purpose:** To establish a context for using the target language; to motivate students by showing real-world use of language; to activate prior knowledge of the target language

Step 1: The teacher briefly shares recent changes with her own expenses using images projected on screen (an auto repair garage; a home natural gas bill). "I was looking at my bank statements online last night and noticed I spent a lot on car repairs in the last six months. I also noticed my gas bill was very high." Elicit possible reasons from the group (drive an old car, the weather is getting colder). "What about you? Have you had a similar experience? What do you spend money on each month?" Elicit examples and write them on board in logical categories (e.g., rent and home repairs; gas and bus fare). "What do we call all of these things?" Establish the theme of *expenses* through shared experiences.

Step 2: "Let's see how people in the U.S. spend their money. The teacher projects a pie chart on screen. "Remember I said I spent a lot on my car. What category would that be?" (transportation) "What about my home natural gas bill? Is that on this chart? What do we call that?" (utilities; maybe "other expenses.") Allow students to speculate about categorizations. To check understanding of categories and personalize instruction: "In pairs, make a list of your expenses for each category. For example, what can go under "transportation"—gas, car repairs, bus or light rail fares? (Give one printout of pie chart per group as needed; giving one per group encourages learners to interact.)

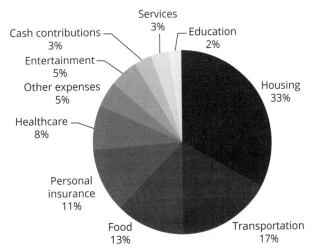

Average Household Expenses in the U.S. 2015

(Pie graph created with information from Bureau of Labor Statistics 2017)

With the pie chart projected on a white board, or on a chart on a white board with columns, learners come to the board to record examples for each category. Use this opportunity to check understanding of any unfamiliar words.

Step 3: Introduce comparative language, eliciting examples from learners:

T: "So, do people in the U.S. spend more on healthcare or housing?" (housing)

T: Let's make a sentence—elicits and waits for student responses; reformulates as needed to create a model:

> People in the U.S. spend more on housing than on healthcare.

Repeat the process to generate two to three more samples. "Let's compare healthcare and transportation. Do they spend a lot more or a little more?" Elicit:

> People spend considerably more on transportation than on healthcare.

How about entertainment compared to apparel and services?

> People spend as much on entertainment as on apparel and services.

II. Draw learners' attention to patterns and check learning.
Purpose: Get learners to notice patterns and phrases they can use. Check for learner understanding through checking questions and activities.

Step 1: T: "Which sentences show similarity and which show differences? What words show that? Talk to your partner for one minute." Then elicit and highlight what they notice.

> (Difference) People in the U.S. spend **more** on housing **than** on healthcare.

> (Difference) People spend **considerably more** on transportation **than** on healthcare.

> (Similarity) People spend **as much** on entertainment **as** on services.

Step 2: In preparation for the practice activities, students now sort the vocabulary words for expenses by stress patterns (knowing how to say the words clearly is as important as knowing the meaning of terms). The teacher says the words and pairs collaborate to fill in the chart like this. The class practices, using clapping or tapping on a stressed syllable.

Pattern 1 O o	Pattern 2 O o o	Pattern 3 o O o	Pattern 4 o o O o
healthcare	personal	expenses	transportation
housing	services	insurance	contributions
		apparel	entertainment
			education

III. Engage in practice for meaningful purposes.
Purpose: Provide opportunities for practice, moving from more to less controlled as appropriate for your learners

---

Practice activity 1
One-question interview: Each student is given a question slip (there should be two to three duplicates of each question slip) like these and they mingle to interview everyone in class for ten

minutes, gathering data about expenses and recording what they find with tally marks. This is highly controlled for language, yet gets learners using the comparative forms in ways that are meaningful. Learners are asked to respond by creating sentences like those modeled above: *I spend more on housing than on transportation.*

1 Do you spend more on housing or transportation each month?	
housing	transportation
JHI III	III
2 Do you spend more on entertainment or food each week?	
entertainment	food
3 Do you spend more on your insurance or apparel and services most months?	
insurance	apparel and services
4 Do you spend more on healthcare or transportation each month?	
healthcare	transportation

Now students are grouped with others with different questions. They analyze their data and make statements like these:

Two thirds of our class spend more on housing than on transportation.

People in our class spend as much on food as on transportation.

Practice activity 2
Create groups with different data sets from above. Small group discussion:

• How do our expenses compare to the expenses shown in the pie chart of average U.S. expenses?
• What factors affect differing expenses (location of job to home; number of children we have; if we live alone or with others)?

> **IV. Assessment**
> **Purpose:** Look for evidence that learners are meeting the lesson objectives or learning outcomes.

Individuals write a paragraph summarizing what they learned about class expenses.

> **V. Application/Extension**
> **Purpose:** To provide learners with opportunities to apply what they learn in class outside of the classroom

Teacher: "If you use online banking, check the expense report and see what they find. Otherwise, make a list of expenses using the categories from the lesson.

• Any surprises? Any place where you could reduce your spending?"

This will serve as a bridge to a later lesson on budgeting. As this information is personal, it would be more appropriate to assign this as an extension to in-class activities.

> **NOTE:** In a career-contextualized class, a similar lesson could start with charts of job numbers in a particular region.

In the lesson above, learners needed to have some degree of literacy in English in order to complete many of the tasks: reading and interpreting the pie chart, reading the interview slips, and writing a paragraph. With this integrated approach, learners practiced the function of making comparisons; they worked on the forms needed to show similarities and differences; they worked on pronunciation and vocabulary associated with expenses. They applied critical thinking skills in speculating about reasons for varying expenses. How can this integrated approach work with beginning-level learners, particularly those with limited literacy skills? In the next section, we turn to sample lessons for beginning-level learners, including those with limited literacy skills in their first language and in English.

3.4 Scaffolding lessons for beginners

The next sample lessons show how to help learners with beginning proficiency acquire basic language skills before moving on to more extensive use of the language. That is not to say that they should be learning small pieces of language, one at a time. What they do need is sufficient input and modeling in order to produce extended spoken or written language. We need to provide scaffolds to make the input accessible to learners and to support language development, such as sentence frames, collaborative learning, first language use, or additional visual aids. Beginners can show understanding by pointing to pictures, ordering pictures or information, or responding with *Yes/No* cards, all of which demonstrate their accomplishments in language development.

Context for Sample Lesson 2

This teacher uses the context of sharing life stories to present and practice the simple past tense. Remember from Chapter 1 that difficulties in the journey and extent of life disruption and trauma during war need to be considered when working with immigrant and refugee students, so this lesson was developed for a group the teacher knew well. While the focus in this lesson is on grammar, you will see that many other areas of language are integrated and the learners also work on transferring information to a timeline. Notice that the grammar is taught **inductively**, that is, the grammar point is presented in context first and the teacher gradually leads learners to notice the patterns.

Sample Lesson 2: Sharing life stories/simple past tense

Class Description: 16 adult high-beginning ESL students

Setting: Community-based adult education center

Time: 90 minutes

Objectives
Learners will be able to:

Functional
• tell others where they're from and share key milestones in their lives

Grammatical
• use simple past tense of regular verbs and irregular *to get* and *to have;* form questions in the simple past tense.

Writing and Speaking
• work together to write short biographical paragraphs or create short videos using cell phone cameras

Reading
• read or retell their stories

Vocabulary
• practice words about education and family

I. Engage with language in a real-world context.
Purpose: To establish a context for using the target language; to motivate students by showing real-world use of language; to activate prior knowledge of the target language

---

Students and teacher around table with photographs (T shares pictures of highlights of her life)

First day of school	High school graduation	First group of ESL students
Wedding	First apartment	First home
First child	Second child	

On table, flashcards with these dates: 1965   1995

Ask students to put pictures in order. Provide nonverbal support with fingers for *first, second,* etc.; model by choosing two pictures and ask: *Which comes first?*

T tapes picture on board; writes dates under pictures

Pairs guess what each picture represents. T confirms guesses and writes phrases by dates:

1965	1978	1983
started school	finished high school	started teaching
1985	1990	1995
got married	returned to the U.S.	had second child
moved to France	had first child	

II. Draw learners' attention to patterns and check learning.
Purpose: Get learners to notice patterns and phrases they can use. Check for learner understanding through checking questions and activities.

T asks appropriate questions of learners based on her knowledge of students, for example: When did you get married? When did you finish high school? When did you move to the U.S.?

T tries to elicit question form by showing a flashcard of a question mark: ?

T writes student answers on the board to use as models for the class and highlights the past tense forms:

When _did_ you start school?

I start_ed_ school in 1970.

Group stands in a circle; each learner chooses a question to ask a classmate. T helps students by reformulating the questions and answers as needed.

When did you start school?

When did you move to the U.S.?

When did you get married?

III. Engage in practice for meaningful purposes.
Purpose: Provide opportunities for practice, moving from more to less controlled as appropriate for your learners.

Practice activity 1: Pairs work together to create visual timelines for their partners. Each is given a blank timeline with some dates:

1970	1975	1980	1985	1990	1995	2000	2005	2010	2015

Students ask questions to complete their timelines with key milestones. Non-literate learners can draw pictures. Provide sample questions:

When did you start school?

When did you move to the U.S.?

When did you get married?

Practice activity 2: Alternative 1—Students help each other write a simple autobiography choosing from the sentence frames below. Learner can use models from teacher's story on board as well. Volunteers or the T can help transcribe the stories.

Alternative 2—Students plan and record a short video autobiography using their phones.

In _____, I started _____.

After that, I _____.

When I was _____, I _____.

Practice activity 3: Pronunciation of –ed endings
Give each student a flashcard with one of the verbs from the lesson and ask the class to move into three groups according to the way the –ed ending sounds in their word. The teacher allows the class do try it without her assistance and then says the words aloud that are causing difficulty.

Teacher elicits: When do we add an extra syllable? Only after /t/ and /d/. (See section 4.13 for a full explanation of this pronunciation feature.)

> ### IV. Assessment
> **Purpose:** Look for evidence that learners are meeting the lesson objectives or learning outcomes.

Read or play story for partner; teacher circulates and listens for use of targeted verbs in past tense. Peers read one another's stories. Underline all the words that show the story is in the past.

> ### V. Application/Extension
> **Purpose:** To provide learners with opportunities to apply what they learn in class outside of the classroom

The teacher takes pictures of each student and the group members collate pictures and autobiographies to create a class book. Students take books home and read (or tell) stories to other family members.

The last sample lesson focuses on teaching vocabulary. Focus on vocabulary happens in many different types of lessons and Dutro and Kinsella (2010) propose the following steps for presenting new vocabulary to English learners:

- Write the word and pronounce it a few times.
- Focus on pronunciation with learners: break long words into syllables and tap or clap out syllables to emphasize the stressed syllable; lead students in quick pronunciation practice.
- Explain words using student-friendly language (learner dictionaries can be helpful).
- Provide a visual representation or have learners create a picture.
- Give two easy to understand examples.
- Engage learners in structured oral and written tasks.

Context for Sample Lesson 3
In this next sample lesson for beginner learners, we see how Dutro and Kinsella's steps are accomplished through the integrated and contextualized lesson model. We also see more ways to scaffold learning for beginners. As you review this lesson, identify the scaffolds used to support learning as well as where you see overlaps between Dutro and Kinsella's recommended steps and the model presented in this chapter. This is an introduction to jobs and job responsibilities, an early step in the career exploration process. In this class, many of these students had jobs in their country and a fair number have jobs now, but they are menial and not where they hope to stay long term.

Sample Lesson 3: Talking about jobs
Class Description: 22 adult beginning-level learners
Setting: Integrated English Language and Civics Education; adult education center
Time: 90 minutes

Objectives
Learners will be able to:

Vocabulary
- Match job titles to visuals
- Match jobs to job responsibilities
- Say job titles with correct word stress
- Categorize types of jobs (e.g., indoor/outdoor; work alone or with others)

Grammar
- Students will be able to use simple present tense to talk about jobs (e.g., a butcher cuts meat)

> **I. Engage with language in a real-world context.**
> **Purpose:** To establish a context for using the target language; to motivate students by showing real-world use of language; to activate prior knowledge of the target language

Warm-up/review current jobs: "What is my job? Right, I am a teacher. I teach at Open Options. I plan lessons and teach English. What about you?"

Students mingle in class to gather information from classmates about where they work and what they now do (this step activates and assesses prior knowledge; there is no expectation of accuracy).

What is your name?	Where do you work?	What do you do?
Aye Lee	at a hotel	housekeeper

Teacher (T): Where does Aye Lee work? What do you do there, Aye Lee?

T elicits from class all jobs they currently have: babysitter, housekeeper, construction work, seamstress.

T shows pictures of other jobs and adds those not already on the list; affixes picture to board and writes name of person doing the job and the name of the job under each picture. This would also be a time where learners could use a picture dictionary[1] or use their smartphones to search for images.

Jobs included: teacher, bus driver, sales clerk, carpenter, florist, nursing assistant, home health aide, butcher, seamstress (these may be determined by learner background, interest, and growth industries in a particular area; we always want to provide instruction that encourages transitions to new opportunities for learners at any proficiency level).

This is Reina.
She is a teacher.

> **II. Draw learners' attention to patterns and check learning.**
> **Purpose:** Get learners to notice patterns and phrases they can use. Check for learner understanding through checking questions and activities.

Remove pictures from board and give one to each student; T points to and says word on board; student with that card puts picture next to that word.

---

[1] *Oxford Picture Dictionary* or the picture dictionary pages often provided within textbook units can be used.

Learners are given words and pictures on small cue cards in envelopes; in pairs, students match picture to word and practice making a sentence: She is a _____.

Whole class: Repeats job names after T. T shows syllables with his/her fingers; claps out stress pattern and students repeat:

TEACH-er

BUS-dri-ver

SALES-clerk

Present question and model response: What does _____ do? _____ is a _____.

Repetition using chain activity—T points to a job and uses the name under the picture:

> T: Angel, what does Reina do?
>
> Angel: She is a teacher.

Now Angel asks another student in class, pointing to another picture on the board.

Angel: Jose, what does Vang do?

Continue until all students have asked and answered a question using the picture prompts on the board. T introduces a job duty and learners find a matching job title from the picture cards at their tables or in a picture dictionary:

- This person cuts meat (use miming and additional images projected on screen).
- This person sews clothing.
- This person sells things at a store.
- This person builds houses.
- This person drives a bus.

III. Engage in practice for meaningful purposes.
Purpose: Provide opportunities for practice, moving from more to less controlled as appropriate for your learners.

With beginning-level learners, especially those emergent readers and writers, we often start with tightly-controlled tasks before moving on to more communicative practice.

Practice activity 1: Spelling practice
Complete missing letters and then copy the whole word.

_____us dri_____   [   ]

tea_____er_____   [   ]

_____rist   [   ]

Now use the technique called *Look, Say, Cover, Write, Check* as a routine to practice spelling any new words (Rudling 2012). Learners can use this routine at home as well to practice their spelling.

Practice activity 2: Bingo
Students are given blank grid and asked to draw or write the name of jobs in each box.

teacher	bus driver	construction worker
electrician	carpenter	sales clerk
butcher	seamstress	home health aide

In the first round, T calls out job names and the first learner to have three in a row calls Bingo. Pairs practice using same Bingo grid.

Second round, T calls out clues:

- This person cuts meat (use miming and project additional images).
- This person fixes clothing.
- This person sells things at a store.
- This person builds houses.
- This person drives a bus.

Pairs practice using clues this time.

Practice activity 3: Categorizing
Each learner is given one picture. T gives categories (signs on wall) and students make groups:

Is this job mostly **INDOORS** or **OUTDOORS**?

Do you do it mostly **ALONE** or **WITH OTHERS?**

Do you like this job? **YES, NO, MAYBE**

Each time they make a group, tell their partners why they are there.

> **IV. Assessment**
> **Purpose:** Look for evidence that learners are meeting the lesson objectives or learning outcomes.

Individually, learners are given a sheet with pictures (or teacher projects pictures); learners write the name of the job.

Yes/No Cards: Hold up card as teacher makes statements such as these:

- A butcher cuts meat.
- A seamstress sells things in a store.
- A sales clerk sells things in a store.
- A carpenter drives a bus.

Or create an online poll to provide practice with tasks and tools, for example: PollEverywhere, Google Forms, Quizlet, or any number of freely accessible online tools for creating quizzes or exit tickets in class (see more on these assessments in Chapter 9).

> **V. Application/Extension**
> **Purpose:** Provide learners with opportunities to apply what they learn in class outside of the classroom.

Have students interview three friends or family members. They can do this in English or their home language. It reviews the vocabulary and leads into the next lesson on job responsibilities.

What is your name?	Where do you work now?	What do you do at your job?

Conclusion

In this section, we have examined an integrated approach to preparing lessons that focus on the development of language competencies, functions, grammar, and vocabulary in meaningful contexts. Learning is made meaningful by:

- Presenting and practicing language that is "real" (authentic information from U.S. Census Bureau; data analysis; teacher and learners sharing their own stories; jobs that learners have expressed an interest in or held in their country)
- Student interaction is maximized (one-question interviews, guided discussions, pair work with timelines, bingo, mingle grids)
- Learning is extended outside of the classroom (investigating their own expenses further, sharing class stories with family, interviewing others about their jobs)

The approach presented is based on the belief that English language teachers need to view learners as active participants who contribute to the direction and content of activities. Teachers still have a prominent role in promoting language acquisition. In fact, many would argue that learner-centered teaching takes more planning and creativity than traditional teacher-centered approaches. Our presence is just as important as ever, but that presence is more evident in the planning stage than in the classroom.

In all of these lessons, the teachers used a variety of practice activities, some which were fairly controlled (chain activities; one-question interviews), and others that promoted more spontaneous use of the target language (analyzing and talking about the data, mingling to interview others, creating a short story). Now we turn to the process of selecting or designing practice activities that generate use of a particular language point in order to build learner confidence with language that is new for them.

Part II: Meaningful and communicative practice activities

3.5 Introduction

In planning integrated and contextualized lessons, teachers need to make choices about practice activities that are most suitable for the ability level and needs of students. These activities may be in an assigned textbook, they may be part of a curriculum that has already been developed by the school, or teachers may need to create their own. In any lesson, there needs to be a balance between fairly controlled activities that help learners attain confidence in using new language as well as authentic, communicative tasks, which allow them to use language spontaneously.

> 📋 **Task 3.3**
>
> **Before you read on**, think about your own experience as a language learner, or as a learner of any new skill. Talk to a partner for a few minutes about the characteristics of good practice activities (or write your ideas down if you're working alone). What helps you remember things? What engages you as a learner?

3.6 Language practice activities

There are several factors to consider in choosing and developing practice activities.

An Appropriate Practice Activity Is One That . . .

involves genuine communication (e.g., an information gap).	Information-gap activities are those where one student has certain information that a partner or other class members do not have. In order to complete the task, students need to find the missing information. This type of activity provides learners with a genuine reason to communicate.
is meaningful, not mechanical.	Mechanical activities involve the pure manipulation of forms with no attention to meaning. Beginning-level learners benefit from repetition and controlled practice, but the activities designed for this purpose need to be meaningful, i.e., allow production of relevant and truthful statements about the learners' lives, the classroom environment, or the world at large. Repeating set dialogues can become meaningful by including names of local stores, companies, or attractions. Personal information about students can be used in place of fictitious information.
is based on a real-life task and authentic use of language.	Activities should, as much as possible, replicate what we actually say and do in the real world. Students should practice emailing a teacher or local service, for example, rather than a family member with whom they normally use their first language.
maximizes student-student interaction.	Activities should be designed in such a way that learners have multiple opportunities to speak, i.e., not just one response and the activity is finished.

integrates a variety of skills.	When possible, choose and design activities that use a variety of skills (listening, speaking, reading, and writing). In multilevel classes, there can be multiple options for the activities. Literate learners can write responses, while pre-literate learners record information with pictures, for example.
promotes higher-order or critical thinking.	Activities prompt students to analyze information, organize and categorize information, explore alternative solutions, or synthesize ideas, for example.

A familiar model of higher-order thinking skills is Bloom's Taxonomy, which originated in the 1950s and was revised by Anderson and Krathwohl in 2001. This model provides a sequence of learning objectives that move beyond simple recall to include understanding, applying, analyzing, evaluating, and creating. Figure 3.3 displays those thinking skills along with examples of corresponding actions. In Sample Lesson 3, learners first showed understanding of information in the pie chart on expenses, then moved to analyzing and comparing expenses. We explore this progression of skills more deeply in Chapters 4 and 5. The examples of controlled language practice activities may be at the lower end of the revised Bloom's Taxonomy.

Thinking Skills	Corresponding Actions
Creating	designing, constructing, producing
Evaluating	hypothesizing, critiquing, evaluating
Analyzing	comparing, organizing, integrating
Applying	implementing, executing, using
Understanding	interpreting, summarizing, inferring, paraphrasing, classifying
Remembering	recognizing, listing, describing, identifying, naming

Figure 3.3 A Progression of Thinking Skills Based on Bloom's Taxonomy (Anderson and Krathwohl 2001)

Practice activities can fulfill different purposes in language development. The continuum below illustrates the key differences between more controlled activities and freer (or authentic, communicative) activities. Activities that fall on the **controlled** end of the continuum can be thought of as language-oriented, i.e., working on mastery of a particular language point. There is a place for both types of activities in your lessons, and you will move back and forth between the two depending on learner level, needs, and outcomes.

Controlled ————————————————————	Free
Focused on use of target language	Spontaneous, unpredictable language
Focused more on accuracy	Focused on fluency
Feedback and correction is often given	Errors noted and handled after task or in later lessons
Build confidence in using target language	Integrate new language with old
Teacher as conductor	Teacher as facilitator, monitor
Check how much has been understood	Check ability to extend language use

Figure 3.4 Practice Activities Continuum

 Task 3.4

The three sample lesson plans in Part I of this chapter included a number of practice activities. Working with a partner or on your own, review each activity and answer the following questions:

- What competencies, function(s), grammar point(s) and skill(s) are being practiced?
- Where does it fall on the continuum of Controlled ———Free?
- To what degree does it promote authentic use of language and promote high-order thinking skills?

In this section, a sampling of activity types is presented, starting with highly-controlled, language-oriented activities, followed by communicative activities.

A. *Highly-controlled, language-oriented activities*

Listen and repeat
At the very beginning of language production, learners need opportunities to say new words and phrases numerous times. While it may seem tedious to us, it will not to your students. Repetition can be an excellent confidence builder as the learners tackle new sounds in the language. That is not to say that repetition activities should be mindless, mechanical drills. Use colorful, interesting photographs from online sources as prompts *https://www.pexels.com/* is a good source for free stock photos); draw on your learners' context for content.

Total Physical Response (TPR) activities
The **Total Physical Response** method has inspired activities that are ideal for initial presentation and practice of language forms and vocabulary before students have sufficient oral proficiency to create extended sentences. TPR is based on the belief that second language acquisition can occur much in the same way that first language acquisition occurs, namely through responding physically to input the way a child responds to parents at a very young age. In a TPR activity, the teacher directs learning through a series of commands, which learners perform. The learners, in turn, take the lead and give commands. TPR is often used to teach grammatical structures, e.g., imperatives ("Stand up." "Sit down." "Point to the window."), prepositions of place or direction, and vocabulary. The following classroom exchange illustrates TPR in action:

> **Samples of TPR in Action:**
>
> **Teaching body parts with beginners** (T performs the action while saying the command)
>> Point to your nose.
>> Touch your shoulder.
>> Shake your head.
>> Pull your ears.
>
> Real-world communication can be limited with TPR, but it can also be used within lessons to provide basic listening practice or to introduce a topic.
>
> **Introduction to a lesson on asking for directions in the community**
>
> T to whole class: Walk to the front of the room (T performs the action as giving the command)
>> Learners respond by walking to the front of the room.
>> Walk to the door.
>> Turn right. Walk to the end of the hall.
>> Go to the room next to the library.
>> T asks individual learners to perform various actions.
>> Students can report where they end up in the building! They could also be asked to gather information (e.g., books, flyers).

In the second exchange, the learners are getting exposure to imperatives (*walk, turn*), prepositions (*to, next to*), and vocabulary (*library*). After abundant practice with following the directives of the teacher, the learners begin to practice the language by taking on the teacher's role, trying new combinations of language: *Walk to the table next to the window.* The physical response appeals to kinesthetic learners, and as with any classroom aid, may enhance memory. Relying on the classroom environment, realia, and visual aids make learning familiar and comprehensible to learners who have had limited exposure to English.

Chain activities

The teacher or student begins a chain by asking a set question (high focus on accuracy). In a lesson on simple present tense and question forms to talk about job routines, prompts can be written on the board from which students choose their answers.

> corrects homework   helps sick people   repairs cars

> T: Raphael, what does a doctor do?

> Raphael: A doctor helps sick people. Min, what does a teacher do?

> Min: A teacher corrects homework. Yoon, what does a mechanic do?

Discourse chains

In a lesson that involves predictable oral exchanges of information, such as calling in sick, making an appointment over the phone, or making a request to a supervisor, a semi-scripted discourse chain can build confidence with the language before a more spontaneous role play.

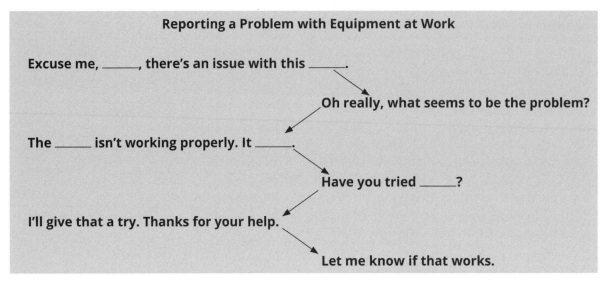

Reporting a Problem with Equipment at Work

Excuse me, _____, there's an issue with this _____.

Oh really, what seems to be the problem?

The _____ isn't working properly. It _____.

Have you tried _____?

I'll give that a try. Thanks for your help.

Let me know if that works.

Using realia—*We need to go shopping for . . .?*
Many of the themes in basic-level ESL curricula involve learning the vocabulary for everyday objects found at home, work, or school. Using realia, or the actual item, makes this chain activity kinesthetic and more meaningful. This activity highlights compound nouns as well as the pronunciation of those words (stress the first word of the compound). This can be done with school/office supplies or items found in the house (furnishings or utensils). Students stand in a circle and each is given an item (see word bank, which is provided on the board).

> ## School Supplies
>
> notebook   backpack
>
> pencil case   pencil sharpener
>
> hand sanitizer   gym shoes
>
> gym shorts   book covers

Teacher: "I know some of you received a school supplies list for your kids and had some questions for me. Let's look at a list and practice saying these words clearly so you are ready when you look for these items at the store. We're going shopping and we need to buy notebooks (T has a notebook in her hand). Elsa, (tosses light ball or hands a talking stick to Elsa), What do we need?" Elsa repeats the first item and adds her item, hand sanitizer, to the list. Continue until all students add to the list (the last one saying all eight items). Ask the class what they notice about these words (two words and the first one is louder and longer (BOOK cover; GYM shorts).

Bingo
Bingo is an excellent vehicle for reviewing and solidifying understanding of new vocabulary. It provides opportunities to repeat the words numerous times, but for a communicative purpose, i.e., playing the game. Bingo can be played with the whole class, with the teacher or a student as the caller, or in pairs. Students can prepare their own grids by copying words from the board, which is very useful for learners with basic literacy skills. As shown in Sample Lesson 3, clues can be called out, not the word itself, which serves to check learning of word meanings.

B. Communicative activities (These activities can fall anywhere on the continuum from controlled to free depending upon the amount of language the teacher provides for the students.)

Find someone who . . .
"Find someone who . . ." activities are common in many classroom contexts. In the language classroom, they can provide learners practice in using the target language in a controlled, yet purposeful and communicative fashion. Completing the activity is highly repetitive, yet production is always meaningful provided that the teacher draws on personal information about the students to design the task. Look at the following example used in a lesson on *Talking about past activities* using "used to":

Find someone who . . .
_____ used to live in Vietnam.

_____ used to ride a bicycle to school every day.

_____ used to work as a teacher.

_____ used to . . .

Interview grids
Interview grid activities are used extensively in English language classes for both controlled and communicative practice. They have the added benefit of giving students practice with interpreting information presented in a variety of formats and the important academic skill of filling in charts and note-taking. The first example shows how beginning-level learners can engage in an interactive task with very limited language. It is scaffolded with visuals and is on a familiar topic.

Question: Do you like to _____ in your free time?

Answer:

☺ Yes, I like to _____.

☹ No, I don't like to _____.

Name	swim	fish	sleep	watch TV	garden	read
	Yes/No	Yes/No	Yes/No	Yes/No	Yes/No	Yes/No
Alex	Yes	No	Yes	Yes	No	Yes

Grid activities can be used at all levels of instruction and are common in adult ESL textbooks, such as this one from *Ventures Student Book Level 3, Third edition* (Bitterlin, et al. 2018: 99) for practicing present perfect continuous with *for* and *since*:

③ Communicate

A **Talk** with your classmates. Find a person who does each activity. Ask how long the person has been doing it. Complete the chart.

> A Do you drive?
> B Yes, I do.

> A How long have you been driving?
> B For about six years. / Since 2012.

Activity	Name	How long?
drive	Josefina	for six years / since 2012
cook for yourself		
attend this school		
work in this country		
speak English		
use a computer		

B **Share** information about your classmates.

Grid activity with extensions

In this sample, learners first gather information about their classmates, which gives practice with a number of language points (simple present to talk about routines, *wh-* question) but then the information can be used to practice other language points as students create a summary, orally or in writing, about the class.

Comparatives: People in Spain stand closer together than people in Vietnam.

Superlatives: Of the countries we represent, the work week in Peru is the shortest.

Comparing Cultures and Customs

Interview at least three people from different countries:

	Interview 1 Name: Country	Interview 2 Name: Country	Interview 3 Name: Country
1 How do people greet one another in your country?			
2 How far apart do people stand when they're talking to one another?			
3 In your country, how much time do teenagers spend with their family?			
4 Where do elderly people usually live?			
5 How many hours do people usually work a week?			
6 How much vacation do they take?			

Information-gap activities

Information-gap activities represent those where one student has information that another needs in order to complete the task. In a lesson comparing geographic features and demographics, half the class has chart A and half has chart B. This teacher uses information about the learners' countries of origin. They interview their partner to complete their chart.

Find the missing information. Ask your partner questions:

What is the population of _____?

How big is _____?

What is the highest point in _____?

Student A

	Population	Area	Highest Point
Ethiopia		435,200 square miles	
Guatemala	16,245,148		4,220 meters 13,845 feet
Mexico		761,600 square miles	
Somalia	10,616,380		2,460 meters 8,071 feet
United States		3,806,00 square miles	

Student B

	Population	Area	Highest Mountain
Ethiopia	86,613,986		4,550 meters 14,928 feet
Guatemala		42,043 square miles	
Mexico	121,736,809		5,636 meters 18,491 feet
Somalia		246,200 square miles	
United States	322,583,006		6,190 meters 20,310 feet

Now write three sentences comparing two of the countries on your chart:

Guatemala is more populated than Somalia.

Other types of activities that fall on the free end of the continuum are role plays, surveys and questionnaires, problem-solving activities, and community tasks. We will look at these kinds of communicative tasks in more detail in Chapter 4 when we turn to teaching the skills of listening and speaking.

Communicative writing practice

Practice activities should not be restricted to oral production of the language. In creating writing activities to practice a particular language point, the same principles of activity choice should apply. Most importantly, writing activities should represent real-life purposes for using written language and should present the most realistic mode of communication. The following practice activity is from a lesson on describing personal skills, qualities, and traits.

Help wanted

(Provide a variety of scenarios from which learners can choose.)

Students are instructed to write a short ad to place on a bulletin board, either asking for help or offering a service. Pairs work together to plan and write the ad.

Help Wanted

Babysitter

Looking for someone who is _____

_____

_____

_____

> ### *Need your car repaired? Car Mechanic Available*
>
> *I am an experienced mechanic. I am* _____
>
> _____
>
> _____
>
> _____

Post ads around the classroom and have the students read the ads and choose one that is of genuine interest to them. Have them respond by role-playing a phone call, text message, or email to the writer of the ad.

In a lesson on making a complaint to a landlord, writing would most likely be done through an online form. The teacher can create a form like the one below, email it to class, and collect learner replies as an assessment of their work.

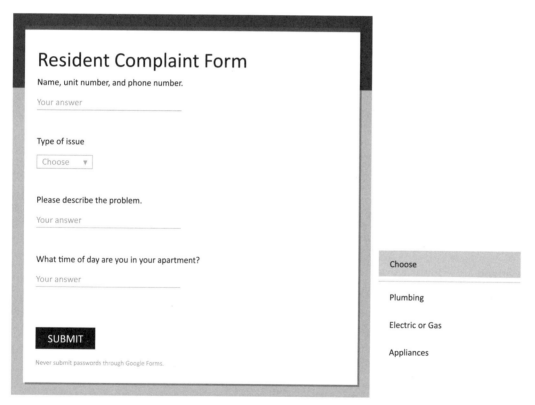

This is only the beginning of the discussion of practice activities and tasks in this book. In Chapter 4, we explore listening and speaking activities that can be used within any curriculum for learners at the beginning, pre-production level, including those with little or no literacy in their first or second language, all the way up to advanced-level students. In Chapter 5, we cover principles and practices for teaching reading and writing skills, but before turning to teaching those skill areas, the place of error correction in these integrated and contextualized lessons is considered.

Part III: Correcting learner language

3.7 Introduction

This chapter has focused on means of presenting and practicing language competencies, functions, grammar, and vocabulary to learners. Many of the activities in section II are form-focused, i.e., they promote accuracy in using the new language. What is the place of correction in these activities? How and when does the teacher intervene? How can the teacher promote self-correction? These questions are the focus of this final section.

Getting Started

Last week I entered my yoga class and found that I didn't have my usual teacher. As I was struggling to move my body into a new pose, this new teacher was calling out my name telling me how to move my thigh muscles and shoulder blades. I couldn't seem to get it right in her class. Had my other teacher been too easy on me? I didn't think so. She had moved around the room working with individuals, coaxing their arms into the right positions. I missed her gentle encouragement. These two teachers had very different styles, and there are undoubtedly many who would appreciate the direct approach of my second teacher.

📋 Task 3.5

What approach to feedback works best for you? Think of a time you were learning something new (a language, a craft, a sport). What kind of feedback did you receive? What feedback was most beneficial to you and motivated you to learn? What discouraged you? Take a few minutes to talk to a partner or write your answer. Now talk to others in class, or to friends or family, and identify any similar themes that arise.

Helpful forms of feedback	Not so helpful forms of feedback

Follow-up: In discussing your answers, did you find a range of preferences? Did some people like being corrected immediately when they were doing something wrong? Was encouragement as important as correction? How did people feel about being spotlighted in class?

Errors are a natural part of language learning. They show us where learners are in their understanding of language structures; they provide evidence of learning as students over-generalize a rule or pattern as in the following example:

> José cans come at 5:00. (adding third-person singular –s to the modal verb *can*)

Learners go through developmental stages of language acquisition, and correct forms tend to emerge over time with increased frequency. Just because learners worked on the past tense over weeks, and the teacher corrected them numerous times does not necessarily mean they will produce the past tense consistently. That does not mean learning has not occurred, however. Over time and with attention to that feature of language, accuracy will most likely increase.

3.8 Considerations in handling learner errors

One of the most important considerations in error correction is learner affect. Constant attention to errors and over-correction only serve to raise what Krashen (1982) refers to as the **affective filter,** or emotional barriers to learning. Imagine the beginning-level learner who can barely construct a complete sentence. Clearly, you would be very careful not to overcorrect. What about an advanced-level student practicing a presentation that she will be giving at work the next day or learners who have expressed a desire to be corrected? In these cases, correction may be more prevalent. In all cases, it is imperative not to interrupt learners while they are speaking and formulating their ideas. Table 3.3 provides an overview of the many considerations teachers should make in deciding how to handle learner errors.

Table 3.3 Considerations in Deciding When to Correct Learner Errors

Who is the learner?	• Consider the learner's level. A beginner will make mistakes all of the time. Correcting every utterance that passes through a learner's lips could be highly demotivating. Always remember to focus on what those learners get right.
	• Consider the learner's confidence level. A more confident learner may be ready for more corrections. A hesitant speaker may become more so if corrected too frequently.
	• Consider learner readiness, or stage in their acquisition of English. All learners make attempts to create utterances using language that is new or difficult for them. Make corrections that correspond to what you believe that student understands about the language.
	• Consider cultural issues. Learners from some cultures may lose face if singled out in class. Find ways to provide feedback individually to those students who you notice seem embarrassed. Older learners may not appreciate being overtly corrected in front of younger learners, particularly those from the same culture.
Might the error cause the student embarrassment?	Most of us who have learned a second language have experienced this type of error, and would agree that a speedy correction can be greatly appreciated. It could be that a mispronunciation results in a word that is inappropriate, or a word in one language means something very different in another (the English-speaker who says *embarrassada* in Spanish, which means pregnant, when they mean *embarrassed*).
Is the learner making a mistake or an error?	A learner who says something incorrectly that she or he has used correctly many times before is just making a mistake, the kind of slip of the tongue we all make. When something is said or written incorrectly numerous times, it is more likely an error that could benefit from correction or further practice.
Does the error cause a breakdown in communication?	Errors that result in a breakdown in communication are worth addressing. This breakdown can be signaled by misinterpretation by a peer during a paired activity or by the response of the listener. Help learners to recognize signals that what they have said is not clear.

What is the stage of the lesson and purpose of the activity?	At the beginning of a lesson, you are assessing what learners do and don't know. Heavy correction is premature at this point. During activities that focus on accuracy (repetition, chain activities, etc.), correction is helpful. During fluency activities such as role plays, mingle activities, discussions, errors can be noted and responded to after the activity individually or as a mini-lesson for the class.
What is the focus of instruction?	If you are teaching a grammar lesson, focus corrections on the structures in question. If you are working on speaking fluency, listen for and record errors that cause breakdowns in communication or are recurrent.

3.9 Providing corrective feedback

Now the question is: *How do I correct students in ways that are sensitive and helpful?* One answer to that question is: *Don't do the corrections for them.* Far too often teachers supply corrections immediately after students make a mistake or error, which ends up being a very passive activity for the students. Students may not even notice that they are being corrected, especially in classes where the teacher tends to echo learner responses.

📋 Task 3.6

Before reading about strategies for responding to learner errors, look at the exchange between a teacher and a learner and identify what the teacher does for each of the following correction strategies:

Strategies Used to Respond to Mira's Language	
Help a learner notice the error	
Trying for the correct form	
Let the student know they have it right (or let it go)	
Let the learner repeat the language	

This low-intermediate class is working on the difference between the simple past and present perfect when talking about the students' new lives in North America. The exchange below is between the teacher and Mira. The class has generated a story about one of the other students, so there are models of the language on the board:

1. T: Mira, how long have you been in Cleveland?
2. Mira: I be here for 6 month.
3. T: Um, Mira, **I've been** (T emphasizes a bit) here for eight years. You....?
4. Mira: I been here for six month.
5. T: Listen: I've been here for six months (points to example on the board).
6. Mira: I've been here for six month.
7. T: Right. Say that again.

8. Mira: I've been here for six month.

9. T: OK, so Mira has been here for six months. Masha, how long have you been here?

Follow-up
In looking back at the considerations in Table 3.3, it seems that the purpose of this activity is to develop accuracy, so that is one of the considerations that is guiding the teacher's decision to help Mira construct an accurate sentence using the present perfect tense. This is what I identified as the strategies used with Mira. How does this compare to your answers?

Help a learner notice the error
"Um, Mira, **I've been** (T emphasizes a bit) here for eight years. You . . .?" The teacher speaks about her own personal history and emphasizes the correct form with the hope that Mira notices the difference between her own language and the teacher's.

Trying for the correct form
T: "You . . .?" Mira: "I been here for six month." The teacher invites Mira to try again, which results in some progress with the form (she uses the past participle *been*). "Listen: I've been here for six months" (points to example on the board). Now the teacher uses a more overt correction, pointing to the model already on the board. This results in Mira getting the present perfect correct: "I have been here for six month."

Let the student know they have it right (or let it go)
T: "Right."

Let the learner repeat the language
T: "Say that again." Mira: "I've been here for 6 month."

Notice in the exchange above that the teacher focused on the correct form of the present perfect (I have been) and did not spend time at that moment on the other error (or perhaps mistake), *six month*. Generally, it is most useful to focus on one language area at a time if accuracy is our goal.

The activity and analysis above represent error correction in accuracy-based activities. During spontaneous conversation with learners, during fluency-based activities, or when learners are presenting information to the class, less obvious means of error correction may be used. Even a raised eyebrow may result in a learner self-correcting. The error correction strategies below move from fairly subtle to more overt.

Help a learner notice the error
As a teacher makes the decision to respond to a learner error, the first thing she or he generally does is help a learner notice that an error has been made. Often the learner will immediately self-correct if the language form is the focus of instruction that day, or if the learner is ready for the correction.

- The least overt and most naturalistic approach is to use **reformulation**, or restating a learner's utterance correctly in as naturalistic a way as possible as in this sample exchange:

  S: Yes, on Saturday I go to St. Paul on trip.

  T: You're going to St. Paul. That'll be nice.

  S: Yes, I'm going to St. Paul, and we see Winter Carnival.

  T: Have you seen the Winter Carnival before?

S: No, this is first time.

T: Really, the first time. So, Sonia's going to the St. Paul Winter Carnival. And what's everyone else doing?

This approach involves responding to the content of what learners say by reformulating errors they have produced in a way that is as natural as possible. Not every learner will notice the correction (Lyster and Saito 2010), but the technique is ideal for those times when a teacher wants to encourage fluency. It also provides the affirmation more proficient learners may desire when they notice their peers' inaccuracies in the language.

- Nonverbal means can be used to help learners notice errors; use a questioning facial expression; use a gesture, for example a motion behind you to indicate that a verb needs to be past tense or a lengthening movement of the hands to indicate present continuous instead of simple present. For word stress errors, clap or tap the correct pattern.
- For recurrent errors, for example the omission of the –s ending on third person singular verbs or with plural nouns or possessives, have a large S sign on the wall and point to it to indicate that kind of errors has been made. For verb tenses, have simple timelines on the wall like the one below for the simple past tense. Point to the time line to indicate an error with that verb tense has been made.

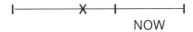
NOW

The choice of signs can be negotiated with or created by the learners, assuring that the representation being used for correction are understood by all.

- Repeat up to the point where the learner made an error:

    Student: People in the States spend more time watching TV from exercising.

    Teacher: More time watching TV...

    At which point the student often "fills in the blank" as she or he notices the error.

- Say the sentence leaving a blank where the error was made (I often hum through the blank):

    Student: People in the U.S. spend more time watching TV from exercising. Teacher: People in the U.S. spend more time watching TV (hum) exercising.

    Or write the same thing on the board leaving a blank.

- If there are samples of the language being practiced on the board or on a chart in room, point to the correct form, as the teacher above did with Mira.

These are only some of the many strategies you can use to help a learner notice an error. Doing so engages the student in the process of thinking about the language and trying to self-correct, which will have a more lasting impact than if the teacher provides the correct form immediately.

Trying for the correct form
In cases where a learner does not notice the error right away and self-corrects, let the student try more than once. In the exchange above between Mira and her teacher, the teacher tried different strategies to help Mira self-correct. If a learner continues to struggle, invite another student to help by asking, for example: *Who can help Mira?* If all else fails, repeat the correct utterance and move on in the lesson.

Let the student know they have it right (or let it go)
Once the student gets it right, affirm the response. Also, focus on and affirm one language form at a time. There are times when a beginning-level learner will not be able to make a correction,

which signals that they are probably not ready for it. Let it go at this point and make note of the fact that this is an area that needs more work for the student.

Let the learner repeat the language
Depending on the circumstances of the class (number of learners, type of activity, time), let the student say the word, phrase, or sentence again. This can help to solidify the language as well as build learner confidence with the language.

Some common pitfalls
In general, it is important not to fall into an initiate-respond-evaluate (IRE) pattern where a teacher immediately evaluates a learner's response. Instead, a teacher can ask the class, "Is that right?" In this way, everyone has to think about the answer before the teacher affirms a correct answer (Finn Miller, personal communication). Learning how to respond appropriately to learner errors takes time and practice for new teachers and comparing different approaches can help new teachers avoid some of the pitfalls. What are the advantages and disadvantages of each of these approaches to providing on-the-spot verbal correction?

Echoing
    S: I am born in Mexico City.

    T: I am born in Mexico City?

    S: Yes, I am born in Mexico.

    T: I was born in Mexico.

When echoing is used for error correction, the learner has no way of knowing if the teacher is confirming what was said, asking for clarification, or making a correction. Also, when a teacher echoes an entire sentence, there is no indication as to what is wrong with it. Generally speaking, echoing is a class routine teachers need to use sparingly, if at all. Think of the times you *would* echo another English speaker in natural conversation.

    Speaker 1: Jan's moving to Brazil.

    Speaker 2: Jan's moving to Brazil?

In this example, speaker 2 is expressing disbelief or maybe excitement about the prospect of Jan's move. Think about the ways you hear teachers echo learners or the way you echo students in your class. Are you echoing language in ways that represent authentic use of language, or is the echoing a teacher routine that does not add anything to learners' understanding of language?

Overt correction (use of grammar terms)
    S: I can to go with you.

    T: You shouldn't use the infinitive with "to" after modal verbs. Use the simple form of the verb.

Unless your student is well-versed in grammar terminology, this technique can be lost on many students. While many students know terms such as infinitive, gerund, and modal verb, you do not want them worrying about those terms as they work on fluency, as this can lead to hesitant, stilted speech. If a teacher senses that a learner appreciates overt corrections, it is preferable to respond this way:

    S: I can to go with you.

    T: Try "go" after can: I can go.

It is important to observe and identify the types of correction learners in your classes benefit from most. Do they know the grammar terms, and if not, do they need to know them? Discuss this with students; find out what their expectations are regarding correction when possible.

Conclusion

Teaching language in context using an integrated, learner-centered approach takes careful planning on the part of the teacher. It also requires careful observation of learners in order to be genuinely responsive to their needs. This is a lot to think about for a new teacher. Whether you are working from a set curriculum, a textbook, or teacher-generated lessons, consistently ask yourself the questions that follow about each lesson you teach. If you answer affirmatively to even some of these questions, you have already come a long way from being the center of attention in your classroom to putting your learners center stage.

Do my learners have active roles in the classroom?

Do they make choices about content and classroom activities and control the direction of activities?

Is the content of instruction relevant to the students' needs and interests? Does it draw on their experiences and knowledge?

Are classroom interactions and tasks authentic?

You will continue to explore more ways to achieve these goals throughout the book.

On your own, or with a partner, provide an example or brief definition for each concept:

Checklist of Key Terms	
competencies	
language functions	
language forms	
four language skills	
register	
authentic language and tasks	
inductive approach	
integrated and contextualized language lessons	
information-gap activity	
critical thinking	

Before doing these activities, revisit your answers to the questions at the beginning of the chapter.

1 Understanding the Components of Integrated Language Lessons

Look at the following competencies/tasks in the left-hand column and identify the functions, forms (grammar, vocabulary, pronunciation), critical thinking, cultural competencies, and likely digital skills needed to successfully complete the task.

Competency or Real-World Task	Functions Needed	Grammar, Vocabulary, Pronunciation	Critical Thinking and Cultural Competencies	Likely Digital Skills Needed
Example: Returning an item to a clothing store	Asking for help/offering help Stating the problem: "I'd like to return this because . . ."	Modal verbs (could, would, may, can) Question forms Clothing items Words that describe problems: Too small, too big Tear, rip	Understanding return policies; choosing the best option when there is more than one; recognizing appropriate register	Reviewing return policies online; verifying store hours (These tasks can happen in class as part of instruction).
Reporting an incident with a coworker to a supervisor (this could be around harassment, unfair treatment, or any issue reported by learners)				
Discussing advantages and disadvantages of career options				

2 The Contextualized Language Lesson

If you are already teaching . . . Think about a lesson you taught last week that did not engage your students as much as you might have liked. Evaluate your lesson using these questions:

a. Did I present and have learners practice language that is "real" (e.g., authentic materials, learners sharing their own stories)? What could I have done differently?

b. What did I do to promote maximum student interaction (e.g., information-gap, role plays, pair work with timelines)?

c. Where did I encourage any higher-order or critical thinking (categorizing, synthesizing, problem-solving, decision-making)?

d. Where did I include practice with digital tools as appropriate?

Based on what you discover, rewrite your plan using the recommended stages in Table 3.2 Progression of an Integrated and Contextualized Language Lesson.

If you aren't teaching yet, choose a language competency, language function, or grammar point and develop an integrated and contextualized language lesson for a group of your choice.

3 Assessing Practice Activities

If you are already teaching, using the checklist of practice activities from Part II, assess three activities you used last week in class. Based on your evaluation, is there anything you would do to make the task more authentic, meaningful, or interactive?

Characteristics of Practice Activities	Activity 1	Activity 2	Activity 3
Involves communication (example: information or opinion gap)			
Is meaningful, not mechanical			
Is based on a real-life task			
Maximizes student-to-student interaction			

Integrates a variety of skills	
Promotes higher-order or critical thinking skills	

If you aren't teaching, choose three activities from an ESL textbook and do the same analysis. Based on your evaluation, how would you implement each activity to make sure it is authentic, meaningful, or interactive?

4 Error Correction

If you are already teaching, audio or video record a segment of your class and complete the task below as you listen to your lesson. **If you are not teaching,** either observe a class or ask someone in class if you can use their recorded segment. Collect samples of student errors and record how the teacher responds to that language. Review the principles in Table 3.3 Considerations in Deciding When to Correct Learner Errors, as well as the recommended steps for error correction that follow. Which error correction strategies helped the students self-correct? At which points in the lesson did the teacher do more error correction? In what other ways did the teacher give feedback to the students about their performance?

Student's language	Teacher's response (correction or praise)	Student's response to correction or praise
Example: "I no have time."	"I no have time?" "I (indicates blank) have time."	Student looks puzzled. "I don't have time."

(Adapted from Reimer 1998)

Coxhead, A. (2014) *New Ways in Teaching Vocabulary*. Alexandria, VA: TESOL Press. Classroom teachers contributed more than 100 step-by-step activities that fit any context, learner, proficiency level, or technology.

Thornbury, S. (2005). *Uncovering Grammar, New Edition*. London: Macmillan Heinemann. This text provides the tools teachers need to help learner uncover and notice the patterns of English grammar.

Ur, P. (2009) *Grammar Practice Activities, 2nd edition*. Cambridge: Cambridge University Press. This book includes principles of grammar teaching and suggestions for designing activities, as well as a collection of nearly 200 interactive activities for practicing a wide range of grammar points.

USEFUL WEBSITES

Academic Wordlist website: *http://www.victoria.ac.nz/lals/resources/academicwordlist/sublists* and for ideas about using AWL in teaching and a highlighter tool to identify AWL words in texts, see *http://www.nottingham.ac.uk/alzsh3/acvocab/*.

New American Horizon videos (newamericanhorizons.org) connected to the topics in Chapter 3:

Teaching Grammar in Real-life Contexts

Tasks to Promote Critical Thinking and Learning Skills

Tasks to Develop Oral Skills: From Accuracy to Fluency

4 | Developing Listening and Speaking Skills

To consider before reading this chapter:

- How do you approach listening differently in various contexts and for various purposes (a conversation with a friend, the news, a lecture)?
- What kinds of classroom activities and tasks promote the development of active listening strategies?
- What kinds of classroom tasks prompt extensive use of language and higher-order thinking skills?
- What is the place of pronunciation instruction with adult English language learners?

Part I: Listening skills and strategies development

4.1 Introduction

In the previous chapter, we examined an integrated approach to teaching language lessons that was both contextualized and learner-centered. While the integration of all four skills (listening, speaking, reading, and writing) was part of the approach, the focus of the lessons was on the acquisition and understanding of specific language competencies, functions, grammar points, and vocabulary. In this chapter, we take a closer look at the development of listening and speaking *skills*. While none of the skills are taught and practiced in isolation, there are many principles to teaching each one that will shape and guide your practice. We begin by examining the nature of oral communication and discourse, particularly different types of communication, informal and formal, that learners may encounter every day.

4.2 The nature of informal and formal communication

Think about it . . .

Hannah receives this voicemail message from her husband:

> *Hey hon, school called and Marcus is sick. I gotta stay here at work. Think you could pick up?*

Hannah sends the following text to her husband: *Sure, no prob!*

Now Hannah needs to ask her boss if she can leave work early. How does the language in this exchange differ from the language her husband used in his message?

> Hannah: *Excuse me, Mary. I just got a call from my husband and my son's sick at school. Would it be possible for me to leave early today?*
>
> Mary: *That should be all right, as long as you get that report in by this evening.*
>
> Hannah: *Of course, I know that's critical. I can finish that from home tonight.*
>
> Mary: *I hope your son feels better soon.*
>
> Hannah: *Thank you so much. I really appreciate this.*

In these two exchanges, spoken language is used in very different ways: everyday English and more formal English.

Informal/Everyday Language	Formal/Academic/Professional Language
• Informal expressions (*Hey; no prob!*) • Extensive use of slang and colloquial expressions (*off the top of my head*) • Non-standard utterances: (*I gotta stay here at work.*) • Reduced speech: *wanna, gonna* • Hesitations and false starts: fillers such as *well, you see, um* . . . • Often in one-on-one interactions with opportunities to interrupt and clarify	• Formal expressions (*Excuse me* . . .) • Longer, complex utterances • More complex vocabulary (appreciate, critical) • More use of polite expressions, *Would it be possible . . .? Do you think I could . . .?* • Fewer opportunities to interrupt or interact with the speaker (may be a lecture or instructional video)

It is essential that learners get practice with both this informal and formal discourse. They need to be able to decipher the meaning of those reductions (*gonna, wanna*). They need to know how to greet a supervisor for the first time. They need to understand and acquire the spoken language used at work, in academic settings, and in the community, for example, with their children's teachers. Acquiring both of these types of language allows learners equal access to opportunities where more formal language is expected (Scarcella 2003).

In past decades with a focus on life-skills competencies in adult ESL, much of the listening and speaking practice found in textbooks and curricula consisted of recorded dialogues or short passages. Today we recognize the need for listening to longer, authentic passages. Speaking was also focused more on short conversations than on extended discussion, presentations, or debates. In a study comparing the skills taught in adult basic education programs to what is deemed essential by community college faculty, gaps were found in the area of listening and note-taking, participation in group projects, and giving presentations as well as listening and synthesizing information from other sources (Johnson and Parrish 2010). In this chapter, we explore how to prepare adult English learners for the communication demands they face in English.

In the first part of this chapter, we look at what goes into teaching listening comprehension skills and strategies. We identify what learners need to listen to and understand in their new English-speaking environment as well as the skills and strategies they need in order to access the meaning of what they hear, both everyday and academic or professional language.

Conducting lessons that focus only on a particular language point will not prepare learners for the communicative demands of spontaneous interactions outside of the classroom. In the second part, we will turn to the topic of teaching speaking, specifically, considering how to help ESL learners become fluent users of the language. Finally, we consider the place of pronunciation in ESL curricula; most importantly, how can we help learners become *intelligible* speakers of English? Let's start with a look into David's plans for a listening lesson on the theme of celebrations around the world.

Getting Started

📋 **Task 4.1**

Working with a partner or on your own, read the following description of David's plans for his lesson and answer the questions that follow:

> David is doing a unit on celebrations around the world with a diverse group of immigrants in his low-intermediate ESL class. He wants to include practice with developing listening skills and strategies with an authentic listening passage. Learners need to be able to listen for the main ideas, but he also wants to give them practice with listening for details and inferring underlying messages. He knows this can be challenging for these low-intermediate level students. He likes the idea of exploring celebrations since it's something all of his learners can relate to whether they are newcomers, are staying at home with family, or already in a job. He'd like to make sure to include some practice with note-taking, as well as a lot of speaking practice, in particular, comparing practices around the world. He has recorded an interview with Farid, an immigrant of French and Iranian descent. David asks Farid about his favorite holidays from the two cultures. The conversation is not scripted. David asks Farid about the origin of the holidays and the various customs, foods, and special clothing for the holidays (see transcript in Appendix at the end of the chapter).
>
> What do you think David could do with this recorded interview in his lesson?
>
> What could students do before they listen to the interview?
>
> What could they do while they're listening?

4.3 Getting students ready to listen

One of the greatest challenges to teaching a diverse group of learners is that everyone comes to class with different experiences and expectations. When a teacher prepares students to listen to a passage, she or he needs to do so in ways that will reach all the students. In David's lesson, he needs to prepare students for the theme of celebrations, but where should he start?

Schema theory

Prior knowledge and expectations that we bring to any situation are based on our cultural background, education, and life experiences. We have "scripts" in our mind about how events in the world unfold, and these scripts are called "**schemata.**" **Schema theory** suggests that prior knowledge shapes our expectations and understanding of what we hear. The closer our schema is to the content of what we hear, the easier it will be for us to understand. In David's lesson, each learner brings different expectations and perceptions about celebrations. Some may have some prior knowledge about Iran and France, while others may have none at all. What they all share is experiences with celebrations, albeit different types. The first thing a language teacher needs to do is to tap into learners' prior knowledge about the theme of the lesson through **pre-listening** activities. Before examining what David could do to activate his learners' prior knowledge, however, we will examine the relationship between schema theory and ESL instruction in more detail.

Much of what learners encounter in a new country may be unfamiliar to them, for example, the ways we enroll kids in school, the ways we communicate with teachers, or practices at a doctor's office. The theme of health and wellness serves as a good example for exploring how prior knowledge affects learning.

Task 4.2

What goes through your mind when you hear the phrase "going to the doctor?" What images and events do you visualize? Write your response in the box below:

Images of Going to the Doctor

Now compare those images with a partner, or with a friend or family member. Do you have the same images? There is a good chance that if you were raised in the same part of the world and live in the same area now, your images are quite similar.

When I lived in France, going to the doctor was a very different experience from what I expected it to be. I walked up to a turn-of-the-century stone apartment building. When I opened the door of the doctor's office, I found myself in a room lavishly decorated with rugs and antiques. The doctor wore a skirt and blouse and sat behind a massive mahogany desk. The examination table was a converted antique dining table. This unfamiliar setting was unsettling for me as a newcomer to France, even though I was sufficiently proficient in French to understand the doctor's questions. Where was the sterile, white table? Why wasn't the doctor wearing a white coat? Why wasn't I given a gown to wear? My script, or schema, for going to the doctor was very different from what I was experiencing in this visit to the doctor.

Now imagine how different the experience of going to the doctor is for many immigrants and refugees as they come to a new country. Here are some of their stories:

In Russia, we go to the clinic and wait. Sometimes we wait for hours to see the doctor.

We sent for the Shaman in Laos, who would rid the house of spirits causing our illness.

The interactions, settings, and routines that we encounter in our daily lives, and at home, work, or school vary greatly from culture to culture. Identifying these differences and familiarizing students with these new routines will help their comprehension tremendously. This does not mean that they need to adopt new practices. If you know what to expect in a given listening situation, you will understand a great deal more of what you hear. So if you ask students to listen to a conversation between a patient and receptionist making a doctor appointment, it is quite possible that they will not share the same perceptions and images of what that conversation will entail. Or if you are playing an informational video on enrolling for a state healthcare program, learners' prior knowledge of such systems may be very limited. The first thing you need to do in a listening lesson is activate your learners' prior knowledge and provide them with crucial background information that will aid them in comprehending what they are going to hear. In a lesson on choosing a healthcare option with intermediate-level learners, for example, the teacher would start with questions like these:

How do you take care of your healthcare needs? When do you see a doctor? For a simple cold or only serious illness? Do you prefer home remedies?

In your home country, if you see a doctor, do you pay for the visit right away? Who covers the costs? You, the government, or someone else?

In a lesson on making appointments with a doctor in a beginning-level class, the teacher may start with questions like these:

What do you do when you are sick?

When do you go to the doctor?

In your country, do you need an appointment to see the doctor?

Now thinking back to David's lesson on celebrations, look at the following **pre-listening** activity. How does this compare to the ideas you generated at the beginning of the chapter when asked how you would prepare learners for the interview with Farid?

Listening Lesson on Celebrations Around the World

Pre-listening:
Teacher: "I interviewed Farid about two holidays his family celebrates. He was raised in Iran, but his mother is French. He had two different cultural experiences growing up: French and Iranian. Look at the activities and customs he talks about in the box below and answer these questions with your partner."

1. What kind of celebrations do you think Farid will tell us about in the interview? Which of the customs, activities, or food do you think are French and which are Iranian?

2. Which of the activities (picnics, visiting family) remind you of celebrations in your culture?

Start of spring	*Fresh fruit*	*White fish*
Rice	*Herbs*	*Visiting family*
Going on picnics	*Jumping over fires*	*New clothes*
French Revolution	*1789*	*Marches*
Dances	*Airplanes*	*Eating outside*
Wearing red, white and blue		

The purpose of this task is to preview the key concepts the learners will encounter in the interview. It allows students to make some educated guesses about the content of what they are about to hear as well as to connect that content to their own lives and experiences. This is also a time to pre-teach any difficult words that are essential to comprehension of the listening passage. Every time you use a listening passage with students, it is helpful to begin with a pre-listening task. Now that students are ready to listen, what will they do *while* they are listening to the interview?

4.4 How do we listen?

Before we think more about David's listening lesson, take a few minutes to reflect on how you listen to language differently depending on your purpose for listening. Talk to a partner or write down your ideas:

📋 **Task 4.3**

How Do You Listen to Each of the Following?	
Voicemail	
A weather report	
The news	
Advertisements	
An announcement at an airport	
Directions from a supervisor	
A lecture	

What did you notice about the way you listen to different types of passages? Do you always listen attentively to the news? What about at the airport? Missing a boarding call would have more dire consequences than missing out on an advertisement on television. When do you listen for the general ideas and when do you listen for more detail? All of this depends on our *purposes* for listening. There are innumerable purposes for listening, but here are some that exemplify my everyday purposes for listening:

- **To seek specific information**: In listening to a weather report, I'll listen for low and high temperatures; chance of rain or snow so that I can dress appropriately.
- **To gain a general idea of the topic**: In listening to news reports on the radio when driving to work, I pay attention to those headlines in the news that interest me or have an impact on my life. I may ignore detailed information.
- **To gain knowledge**: In a workshop or training, I listen more attentively for detail because I am learning something new that is critical for my work.

As we listen for different purposes, we employ a variety of listening strategies, often very consciously, that help us to comprehend what we hear. These listening strategies along with an example of each one in practice are outlined in Table 4.1.

Table 4.1. Listening Strategies and Examples in Practice

Listening Strategies	Examples of Each in Practice
Anticipate content; preview and predict	We approach a listening situation with expectations. At the start of a talk, we expect the speaker to introduce us to the topic; during a meeting, we might expect a supervisor to set expectations for the day or the week. We can anticipate topics based on our past experiences with that type of listening situation.
Listen to confirm predictions	As we listen, we check to see if our predictions are right or wrong.
Listen for gist	In listening to the news, we may filter out many of the details and just zero in on the key concepts of importance or interest to us.
Listen for specific information	In listening to our voicemail messages, we may listen only for the names and phone numbers and write those down.

Listen for details	Listening for detail involves **intensive listening,** or trying to understand the listening passage in its entirety. We may listen intensively to lectures or directions from a supervisor, or to a favorite TV show or movie.
Make inferences	As we listen, we interpret and make inferences about what we hear. After hearing a politician's views on a particular issue, we may be able to make inferences about the way he or she might vote on an upcoming bill.
Use visual or other clues	We pay attention to nonverbal cues such as facial expressions and body language; we may have other visual supports available while listening, such as graphics or pictures in a textbook.
Find evidence to support claims	We listen for examples and evidence to support claims as well as the signal words that go along with that information (*For example . . .; Here are three reasons why . . .*).
Transfer information to other contexts	In work and school contexts, we often need to use the information we have heard to engage in a follow-up discussion, make a decision, or complete a task (create a visual, for example). This is true in our daily lives as well.
Synthesize information we hear with information from other sources	Particularly in work and school contexts, we draw on information from multiple sources, including what we hear in a talk, a lecture, or a meeting. We may do the same when searching the web for practical information (how-to-videos, consumer reports).

4.5 Applying listening strategies instruction in the classroom

Most everyone uses the listening strategies above in their first language, whether they are aware of it or not. If you are already teaching ESL, however, you may have noticed that English language learners do not necessarily transfer those skills as they listen to passages in *English*. They may have a tendency to try to understand every word they hear, and when they are unable to understand, they may become frustrated and overwhelmed. As you will discover, trying to understand every word in a listening passage is not the most productive approach, especially for beginning-level language learners.

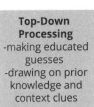

Top-Down Processing
-making educated guesses
-drawing on prior knowledge and context clues

Bottom-up vs. top-down processing

In listening to passages (or in reading, as we'll see in Chapter 5), we can use either **bottom-up processing** or **top-down processing. Bottom-up processing** involves attempts to decode and understand a listening passage word-for-word, whereas **top-down processing** involves listening more globally and trying to understand the overall meaning of what we hear. Top-down processing also involves making educated guesses about content based on prior knowledge and visual clues (facial expressions, context, etc.). Efficient listeners and readers do not rely solely on bottom-up processing in their own language, so why should they in a second language? Many English language learners may not understand a good number of the words in a given text; as a result, they can become overwhelmed by the barrage of new words coming their way as they listen to an authentic dialogue, newscast, or even their teacher's instructions. A listener who manages to connect key words to prior knowledge, and make guesses based on extralinguistic cues

Bottom-Up Processing
-decoding
-attempting to understand every word

(visuals, body language, context), on the other hand, is likely to understand the main ideas or pick out specific information.

Our job as ESL teachers is to help learners practice top-down processing so that they can begin to access the wealth of language coming their way day to day, much of which is highly colloquial, full of reduced speech, and delivered at a rapid pace. In order to do this, we need to develop listening tasks that allow learners to draw on prior knowledge, make guesses, and listen selectively, i.e., focusing on the information they need. In other words, the goal of listening instruction is to help learners develop effective listening strategies that they can use inside and outside of the classroom. Now let's return to David's lesson on celebrations. He has developed a series of listening tasks that promote selective listening, as well as opportunities to connect the ideas generated in the pre-listening portion of the lesson to what they understand from the interview.

📋 **Task 4.4**

Look at the listening tasks David has created and identify the listening strategies from Table 4.1 that learners practice while completing each task.

Listening tasks for celebrations interview
Listening task A: Listen and check predictions from pre-listening: What holidays does Farid share? Which of the customs relate to Iran and which to France?

Listening task B: Students are assigned an A grid or a B grid; they complete their grid as they listen to the interview again.

Complete the table with the missing information.

GROUP A	Nowruz in Iran	Bastille Day in France
History/origin of holiday		Freeing of Bastille Prison French Revolution 1789
Special food	Fresh fruit White fish	
Activities		Marches Military marches Dances and music
Clothes	New clothes	

GROUP B	Nowruz in Iran	Bastille Day in France
History/origin of holiday	Celebrates start of spring	
Special food		Eating outside
Activities	Visiting family Going on picnics Jumping over fire	
Clothes		Anything red, white, and blue

Task C: A's get together and B's get together to check their answers. Play the interview again to fill in or clarify anything they missed. Then students work in A-B pairs and share the information from their grids (not reading from one another's grid, but sharing orally what they understood). Notice that this activity is designed so that peers can provide feedback and correction.

Task D: Listen one more time to answer these final questions:

1. Which of the two holidays has a longer history?

2. Why do you think kids wear brand new clothes for Nowruz?

3. Why is Bastille Day a national holiday? Do you believe that Nowruz is as well? Why or why not?

4. What does Farid mean when he says, "Anything red, white, and blue is in order"?

In completing these listening tasks in David's lesson, learners make predictions and then listen to confirm their predictions; they listen for specific information as they fill in their grid. They are also asked to make inferences with the questions in Task D (spring brings good weather, so new clothes; "goes back to antiquity" implies that Nowruz is much older; Bastille Day was a military conquest; red, white, and blue must be the color of the French flag). Finally, they also get practice with information transfer as they end up with a complete chart representing the information from the interview, just as we may see in a more academic or work setting. Additionally, students are working on effective communication skills as they exchange information between their A and B grids and they practice note-taking skills.

Remember that we generally listen for a particular purpose, which often entails acting on what we listen to in some way: discussing what we have listened to with a friend; acting on the request of a supervisor; making a decision or choice based on what we learned. What would be a logical response to the interview for David's learners? To complete the listening lesson in the celebrations unit, David includes **follow-up** or **post-listening** activities. The purpose of this stage in the lesson is to extend learners' understanding of the content of what they heard, respond to it in an authentic manner, and apply it to their own lives.

Follow-up tasks for lesson on celebrations around the world

Follow-up/post-listening: Ask students to think of a significant holiday their family celebrates and write or draw the origin, foods, activities, and clothes for that holiday (students from the same the country could work together on this stage). The mind maps serve as a tool for organizing their ideas.

Holiday: _____

Origin: _____

Now students mingle and interview at least five other students in class:

Classmate's name and holiday	Origin	Foods	Activities	Clothes

Finally, students analyze the information they have gathered and, working in teams of three, identify three common themes that emerge regarding celebrations around the world along with evidence to support their claims. This last step allows them to synthesize information they have gathered from their classmates. The teacher can provide sentence frames like these to help them formulate their ideas:

It seems that . . . because . . .

We found that . . . for example, . . .

It seems that many celebrations are connected to harvests because over half the group talked about their harvest festivals.

4.6 Summary of listening skills and activities

There were three stages in David's listening lesson: **pre-listening**, **listening**, and **follow-up**. Each listening lesson can include a number of different activities, each one practicing a different listening strategy (confirming predictions, listening for gist, listening for specific information). The number of listening strategies practiced would depend on the nature of the listening passage, the level of the learners, and the purposes for listening. Table 4.2 provides a summary of the stages that can be included in a listening lesson, along with suggested activity types for each stage. Not every lesson will include all the steps; however, every lesson should begin with pre-listening activities and end with a follow-up activity.

Table 4.2 Recommended Stages of Listening Lessons and Suggested Tasks

Lesson Stage/Purpose	Possible Activities and Tasks
1 Pre-listening Generate the learners' schemata; get the learners thinking about and talking about the content of what they are about to hear.	• Questionnaires or one-question interviews • *True/False* predictive questions • Discussions • Look at words from the passage and guess what it will be about. • Pictures that set the scene • Pre-teach vocabulary

2 Listening to confirm predictions Enable learners to confirm predictions made during pre-listening.	• Match predictions with what is heard. • Check answers to pre-listening activities. • Cite evidence from the listening text to support predictions.
3 Listening for gist (main ideas) Determine the main ideas of a passage; discriminate the main ideas from details of a passage.	• Listen and answer *True/False, Yes/No*, multiple choice or open-ended questions about the main ideas of the passage. • Provide a list of statements and check off those that reflect the main ideas. • Choose a picture that corresponds to the main idea of the text.
4 Listening for specific information Pick out specific information in a listening passage.	• Listen and point to pictures/words as they appear in the passage. • Order information as it appears in the text using pictures or words. • Choose the correct word, number, etc. (multiple choice). • Provide a list of specific information and check off those ideas that are heard. • Fill in missing words/numbers in a text or fill in a grid/table with words or draw pictures. • Jigsaw tasks: different groups listen for different information; exchange info in new groups. • Correct misinformation in a text. • Listen and fill in a graphic organizer (e.g., a timeline as they listen to a narrative).
5 Listening for details Listen intensively for details of the text; move from identifying short, factual information, to interpreting the meaning more deeply.	The types of activities are similar to those listed in Parts 3 and 4 above. The *content* of the questions will differ. Listening for specific information with a short news report might entail simply identifying the countries mentioned and the event that occurred in each one. A more detailed listening could require learners to identify the players, the time, and exact location of the events. You can use the same news report with a variety of levels, but simply change the nature of the task you assign.
6 Making inferences Analyze, interpret, and evaluate the meaning of a listening passage. Beginning-level learners may be challenged enough by determining the gist and specific information from a listening passage, but it is important to go beyond the factual information presented to them.	• Discuss underlying messages, e.g., view advertisements and determine the target audience for the advertisement. • Choosing statements that could be inferred from the listening passage (this could be with *True/False* statements or multiple choice). • Cite evidence in the passage to support claims.

7 Follow-up / Post-listening	• Discussion questions
Extend learners' understanding of the content of what they heard; respond to it in an authentic manner.	• Questionnaires or one-question interviews • Role plays • Writing tasks: reports, summaries, journal entries • Interviews and surveys conducted in or out of class • Community research and reports back to class • Problem-solving or decision-making activities

Students completely new to English may do nothing more than listen and point to a picture of what they have understood or identify how a speaker feels (e.g., happy, angry). All learners, especially intermediate to advanced, need to practice listening for detail, opinion, and attitude, making inferences about the meaning of the listening passage, and synthesizing information from multiple sources. As with everything we have talked about in the book, always remember the interrelatedness of language skills, particularly listening and speaking. Further ideas for pre-listening and follow-up activities are presented later in this chapter (see section 4.9).

4.7 Sources of listening passages

For the sample listening lesson in this chapter, David conducted and recorded an interview. There are many other types of listening passages that you can use.

📋 **Task 4.5**

Sources for Listening Passages

Work with a partner or on your own and brainstorm sources for listening passages.

Sources for listening passages will generally fall into one of these categories:

Authentic texts: news broadcasts, how-to videos, TED Talks, podcasts, interviews, songs, advertisements, TV shows, movies, sports broadcasts, or anything that was produced for public use that is unmodified.

Teacher-generated:
- Recorded conversations/dialogues, preferably unscripted: scripted dialogues are useful when presenting particular language points. When teaching listening strategies, however, we want to expose learners to language as actually spoken with false starts and hesitations.
- Story-telling: teachers can use themselves as an invaluable source for listening practice. This has the benefit of allowing students to pick up on visual clues such as gestures and facial expressions. Students can also ask for clarification, as they would in real-life interactions.
- Video recorded real-life scenarios: teachers can record everyday interactions at stores, banks, restaurants, schools, or home and use them as the basis for listening practice. These have the added benefit of visual support.

The interview with Farid falls into this last category. There are also online sources produced for ESL, for example elllo.org, which includes hundreds of short recordings and lessons on an array of topics for classroom use or self-access.

ESL textbooks: commercially-produced ESL texts are full of listening passages and activities from which you can draw. Now look at your list above and decide which you would consider teacher-generated, and which you would consider truly authentic.

📋 **Task 4.6**

Teacher-Generated	Authentic Texts

Integrating various technologies into your lessons, along with choosing and developing classroom materials are covered in more detail in Chapter 8. For now, we have taken a brief look at the array of sources from which you can draw when developing listening lessons. We have also examined the importance of connecting learners' prior knowledge to the content of the listening passages we choose. As noted throughout this book, no language point or skill is taught or learned in isolation. Learners in David's class interacted with one another throughout, using speaking as well as some writing skills. Now let's turn to what you need to consider in order to engage learners in speaking and fluency development.

Part II: Developing speaking skills

4.8 Fluency as the goal of instruction

In a learner-centered, communicative classroom, just about anything you do, provided the learners are communicating with one another, serves to develop their speaking skills. There is much more to teaching speaking than simply getting students to talk, however. As with listening, we normally have specific purposes for communicating with others, such as asking for help at a store or describing a problem to a supervisor. These are examples of **transactional dialogue**, the purpose for which is to transmit factual information. We also take part in **interpersonal dialogue**, for example, making small talk with a coworker or talking to a friend about a concern at home (Brown and Lee 2015). Finally, we engage in **academic conversations** (Zwiers and Crawford 2011), where we express opinions, elaborate on others' ideas, or synthesize ideas as we come to consensus. The language we encounter can be more or less predictable depending on our shared knowledge and experience with our interlocutors (Brown and Lee 2015). We need to be fluent users of language in order to handle the communicative demands of day-to-day interactions outside of the classroom. What does it mean to become a fluent user of the language?

- The ability to handle unpredictable language
- The ability to pick up on and use visual cues from the environment and other speakers/listeners
- The ability to anticipate the direction a conversation or discussion will take
- The ability to make oneself understood and negotiate meaning (e.g., ask for clarification, check to assure others understand us, paraphrase what one understands); use compensation strategies (point to something when you don't know the word for it, describe an object for which you don't know the name)
- The ability to convey meaning and "get things done" with the language, even with limited words or accuracy
- The ability to engage in and sustain discussions; support our arguments with details

As we looked at language lessons that focused on a particular competency, function, or language point in Chapter 3, practice activities fell on a continuum from controlled (with more emphasis on accuracy) to free (with a focus on fluency). All of the activities were designed to generate use of particular language points. For example, in a lesson on "calling in sick to work," the teacher would develop activities that include greetings, stating the problem, asking permission for time off, and closures. Of course, the goal of such a lesson would be the ability to communicate effectively, and success with the language would be measured by the ability to complete the task of calling in sick (even though the learner may make some errors in production). In a grammar lesson, the teacher would be looking for some degree of accuracy with the language as well as the ability to integrate grammar use in meaningful, real-world contexts, e.g., using the past tense to talk about work experience in a job interview. In order for learners to become fluent users of the language, they need time to develop the traits highlighted above. Lessons need to include activities during which learners communicate ideas and negotiate meaning as they need to do outside of the classroom. How can we facilitate that in our classes?

4.9 Developing interactive speaking activities

📋 **Task 4.7**

Look at these two speaking activities and discuss the following question with a partner: Which activity will generate more language production and why?

Activity 1

Talk about your hobbies and interests in small groups. You have 15 minutes.

Activity 2

How do you like to spend your time after work or on the weekend? Circle three things you like to do. Cross out three that you never do. Write three other things you like to do in your free time.

swim	visit family	listen to music
go to the library	garden	cook for friends and family
visit friends	sew	watch television
take walks	exercise	read

Three other things you like to do: _____

Now talk to the other students in class and find the person who has the most things in common with you. Ask that person the following questions:

How often do you do that activity?

What do you like about that activity?

What are some things you did in your country that you can't do in the U.S.?

Simply telling students to talk to a partner about a particular topic for 15 minutes will not necessarily generate much production. With Activity 1, more verbal students are likely to monopolize the discussion since there are no clear roles assigned to participants. There is no specific direction or outcome to the task. While Activity 2 might appear quite controlled, the structure of the task allows all students an equal opportunity to participate. It also has a concrete outcome, which gives the task a clear purpose or goal. It allows for multiple interactions as the students mingle around the classroom and talk to everyone, rather than just the two or three people in the small group.

There can be challenges to dedicating substantial amounts of class time to fluency development. Some learners will come to class with the expectation that the teacher should be teaching grammar lessons and leading the class through repetition activities. While providing learners with extensive opportunities to speak in your classes should be your goal, it is important to make the outcomes and purpose for doing communicative speaking activities clear to adult learners:

- Explicitly state how the fluency activity will help them outside of the classroom, for example, that the activity will give them practice in making small talk with neighbors or coworkers, or build their confidence when talking to their children's teachers.

- Use content that is generated from students, is connected to their life circumstances and needs, or is a timely, high-interest topic (e.g., an upcoming election).
- Balance fluency practice with lessons that are more language-oriented and focused on accuracy.
- Include mini-grammar lessons or more controlled practice in preparation for a fluency activity. For example, in preparation for an interview task, work on question formation as a class.
- Provide language frames needed to engage meaningfully in a task. For example, if learners are asked to express opinions, agree or disagree, provide supports like these:

Asking for Opinions

What do you think about . . .?

What's your opinion of . . .?

Disagreeing Politely

You have a point, but . . .

I don't think so. Have you considered . . .?

For example, . . .

Showing Agreement

Exactly, that's what I think.

I couldn't agree more.

For example, . . .

For fluency to develop, learners need genuine reasons to communicate with one another. The activities that follow demonstrate a variety of ways you can promote this kind of purposeful communication among students. Learners at all levels need practice developing their speaking fluency, but this can be challenging with learners at the pre-production level. A number of the activity types that follow can be used even with level 1 learners. As you review these activities, consider the degree to which the activities foster practice with these characteristics of a fluent speaker:

- Make oneself understood and negotiate meaning (e.g., ask for clarification); use compensation strategies (e.g., paraphrase what one understands)
- Engage in and sustain discussions; support our arguments with details

Also consider the degree to which the tasks promote higher-order thinking (3.6) as well as the topics you could use for that type of task in your setting.

A. Picture stories
Picture stories can be used with all students, particularly those with limited literacy skills. Learners can interpret a story based on a picture sequence. Alternatively, each student is given a picture of a story sequence. Students work collaboratively to put the story in the correct order and once they have done so, they stand in a circle and tell the story. Teachers can easily create picture stories using clip art visuals or photos they have taken themselves.

B. Information-gap activities
As noted in Chapter 3 (3.6), **information-gap** activities require that students exchange information in order to complete a task. There are many activities that fall into this category (and many texts with ideas for activities in the resource section at the end of the Chapters 3 and 4). Information-gap activities are often used to practice specific language points as we saw in 3.6, and they are also ideal for general fluency practice. While not all the sample activities that follow are appropriate for all learners, they serve to illustrate what constitutes an information-gap activity.

Find the other half
Each student is given half of a picture.

Mingle and ask questions:

What is in the middle of your picture? Is it of a place or a person? Does the person look worried?

Once students find the other half, they imagine what happened right before the picture was taken and then present that to the class. Classmates may offer alternate interpretations. Even very beginning-level students could use one-word utterances to complete the task.

Find the difference (simple to more complex)

Similar to *find the other half*, students are given two similar drawings or pictures with several small differences. They must ask one another questions to find the differences. This sample could be in a lesson on describing problems to a landlord.

Is there a stain on the carpet?

Is the sink leaking?

This task can be used for general fluency practice and the complexity of the images used affects the complexity of the language produced.

Calendars/schedules/grids

Give each student a schedule for the week to fill in with all appointments, classes, etc. they have for that week. Tell the students they need to talk to other students in class to find a time they would all be free to form a study group before or after class. In a work-readiness program, you can create scenarios like this one:

Student A: You are calling in sick to work today, but you need to know your schedule for next week. Ask you supervisor over the phone and fill in the schedule below:

Schedule Week of _____	
Monday	
Tuesday, etc.	

Student B: _____ is calling in sick and needs his/her schedule for next week.

(Student B is given the completed schedule)

Prepare two schedules so that students can repeat the task taking on new roles.

C. Groupings

Finding connections among objects, concepts, and ideas is a good way to enhance understanding and remember new words or concepts in a second language. It also promotes higher-order thinking skills such as categorizing, comparing, and contrasting, or justifying answers. This activity can be done around any theme and with any set of words students have been working with. It is ideal for review or for previewing a theme and can be done with any level.

We'll use the theme of *jobs* to illustrate how this works. Give each student a picture depicting a particular job: carpenter, doctor, nurse, server, mechanic, beautician, etc. Ask students to create job groups based on different criteria for the picture they are holding, for example:

Indoor vs. outdoor jobs

Jobs traditionally held by men/women

Jobs that require specific training (group by type of training needed)

Have students group based on criteria of their choosing.

In creating groups, learners need to negotiate, justify their choices, and describe the job depicted in the picture they are holding. The task generates language production of varying degrees depending on the learners' oral proficiency, making it ideal for multilevel classes.

This same task can be done with more advanced vocabulary. In a lesson on personality and birth-order theory where learners have read articles and watched short videos on conflicting theories, the teacher decides to focus on the personality traits that were included in the lesson, sorting them according to whether the traits are positive, negative, or either. The learners must analyze the words and justify their categorization.

(New American Horizons 2012)

D. Mingle activities

A mingle activity involves learners milling around and gathering information from other students in the class on a given topic. Mingle activities have the benefit of maximizing student participation for learners at all levels. The most proficient students may talk to everyone in class within the assigned time frame, while the students who are less proficient can be equally engaged through talking to just a few students. This sample **interview grid** activity could be used in a lesson on health and wellness.

Home Remedies		
Many of us choose NOT to go to the doctor when we have a minor illness. What are some home remedies in your culture for common illnesses? Talk to the other students in class and find out what they do in their cultures?		
Student/Country	**Illness**	**Remedy**
Mira/El Salvador	*Cold/fever*	*Hot tea*

Mingle activities can be continued outside of class by having students interview family, neighbors, or friends as homework. They can report their findings during the next class period (see 3.6 for additional examples).

E. Data collection and analysis with one-question interview

A one-question interview provides opportunities for learners to collect data on a topic, analyze the data, and engage with a series of tasks that also develop their academic and work skills. It can be used for virtually any topic (we saw this task type in Sample Lesson 1 in Chapter 3 on expenses). Here is another example on the theme of sustainability and our environmental footprint. Students are given questions such as these:

> What topics would work well for learners in your classes?

1. Do you try to buy products that are as environmentally friendly as possible?

    All of the time   Some of the time   Not sure   I don't think about it.

2. Do you bring your own bags to the supermarket?

    All of the time   Some of the time   Not sure   I don't think about it.

3. Do you take advantage of your city's recycling program?

    All of the time   Some of the time   Not sure   I don't think about it.

4. Do you choose paper over plastic bags when given the option?

    All of the time   Some of the time   Not sure   I don't think about it.

After mingling and tallying results, students with the same question get together in groups to analyze their data. As an alternative, to ensure that the data students collect is accurate, students fill out a data collection sheet with the names of all students present. Pairs are assigned the same question. After collecting their data, pairs then have to check to make sure their information is the same; if there are discrepancies, they need to go back and ask again.

Students are provided with useful language to talk about the data, for example:

- *Most people in class . . .*
- *Some people . . .*
- *Half the class . . .*
- *Three quarters of the class . . .*

Next, learners create a bar graph depicting the results of their question, which they use in presentations to others in class. For that stage, they can be given more useful language frames such as:

- *We found that . . .*
- *Our data indicate that . . .*

E. Presentations and gallery walks
As the result of an extended inquiry or project-based learning (2.11), learners prepare posters, presentations, or videos as a culminating product. Students in a class then present their work through a gallery walk, allowing class colleagues to actively engage with one another as they view each other's work. They are expected to ask and respond to questions about the information, images, and any documents presented. The presenter can prepare questions for the audience to listen for during the presentation. In a gallery walk with posters, students can add comments and questions with sticky notes, which can then be used for discussion.

F. Discussion activities
All learners can take part in a discussion, but beginning to low-intermediate level learners may need more supports and scaffolds to engage in sustained discussions in English. Successful discussion activities have the following features:

- An identified purpose and outcome
- Clear roles for all participants, for example, facilitator, scribe, time keeper.
- A clear time frame
- A genuine reason to communicate, for example, the group needs to make a decision, reach consensus, or generate a list.

Discussions can be about current events, cultural issues, education, work, or anything that is of relevance in your learners' lives. Zwiers and Crawford (2011, 32–33) emphasize the importance of teaching learners the *language* they need to sustain these conversations, highlighting these language functions:

Elaborate and Clarify

How so?

What do you mean by . . .?

What makes you think that?

Why is that important?

Build on a Partner's Idea

I would add that . . .

I want to add to your idea . . .

Challenge a Partner's Idea

Well, I think that . . .

Another way to look at it is . . .

Support Ideas with Examples

An example from my life is . . .

It says in the reading that . . .

Paraphrase Ideas

It sounds like . . .

In other words . . .

Synthesize Conversations

We can say that . . .

We all agree that . . .

Teachers can give these language frames to students on small cards, as a poster in the classroom, or as a handout for a group as they are engaging in a discussion. Notice that this language also promotes critical thinking skills.

Another scaffold that can be particularly useful for beginners is a discussion planner (Kinsella 2012). Give learners a chart or graphic organizer where they can record ideas for these four steps:

Think: Brainstorm ideas on the topic.

Record: Write ideas before the discussion starts.

Discuss: Interact and engage in the discussion. This is where the discussion language frames can be particularly helpful for learners.

Report: Be prepared to report the outcome of the discussion. It's often best that this be in the form of a summary or synthesis of the group's ideas.

G. Problem-posing/problem-solving

Problem-posing/problem-solving tasks revolve around particular problems learners have encountered or may encounter in their lives, for example, a conflict between an immigrant and her U.S. born in-laws regarding child-rearing, a child who spends too much time on video games, or issues of harassment at work. Teachers can provide representative scenarios like the one below, or learners can pose their own.

> Last year, Juan gave his teenage son a computer for his birthday. It is in his bedroom. Now he spends a lot of time in his room playing games online. His grades are not good, and his teachers report that he doesn't turn in his homework. What should Juan do?
>
> From *Ventures* 3rd edition, *Student Book* 4 (Bitterlin, et al. 2018: 80)

Learners work together to identify the issues and discuss the possible solutions. Magy and Price (2011) suggest these templates for organizing ideas and looking at the pros and cons of possible solutions:

Step 1	Step 2	
What is the problem? What can Juan do?	What will happen?	
	Good	Bad
1. _____	1. _____	1. _____
2. _____	2. _____	2. _____
3. _____	3. _____	3. _____

They also suggest providing possible solutions to get the conversation started as well as these language frames:

I think Juan should _____ because _____.

The problem is _____, so I think that _____.

What will happen if Juan _____? What if he _____?

If Juan _____, then _____.

Providing scaffolds like these makes problem-solving a task type that can work at all levels of instruction.

H. Decision-making

In a class exploring entrepreneurship in their community, learners explore a variety of options for starting their own businesses. The types of businesses should reflect what could realistically interest learners in the class.

> Think of other topics you could use.

Task: Look at these three types of businesses and discuss which you have the skills and expertise to develop.

Restaurant   *Food truck*   *Small market*

Start with online research in teams.

- Create groups based on which type of small business interests you most.
- Choose a targeted neighborhood.
- Research the number of similar businesses in the area.
- Research spaces available for rent or lease, or the cost of purchasing a food truck.

Discuss the pros and cons of starting this type of business for the targeted area based on the information you gathered. Present findings to the class either at the board, with a PowerPoint presentation or a poster.

I. Role play

Role plays are used with any level of learner for a variety of purposes. They can be used to practice particular language points or for general fluency practice. Because learners are taking on a different persona to a degree, they sometimes are less inhibited than they might be with other fluency activities. On the other hand, role playing is new for many learners and may appear frivolous. Therefore, careful planning and implementation are crucial. Here are some tips that will help make role plays successful:

- Model the role play with a student.
- Provide language support to successfully complete the role play (place samples of language needed on the board or project them on a screen; use familiar language in role descriptions).
- Include an incentive to communicate (shopkeeper is out of a particular item, so the shopper has to make another choice when doing an exchange at a store).
- Assign roles that are achievable for students of varying ability levels.
- Use realistic scenarios.
- Incorporate realia and visual aids (e.g., workplace informational charts, items to return to a grocery store).

Conclusion

This section has included a variety of examples of speaking activities that you can use with students at different levels with the goal of promoting fluency in English. Keep in mind that the activities presented in this chapter can also be used in the following ways:

- Pre-listening, pre-reading, or pre-writing activities (the last two are covered in Chapter 5)
- Warm-up or review activities
- Follow-up activities
- Fluency-focused practice activities in integrated and contextualized language lessons like those explored in Chapter 3

It is important that you keep the following in mind as you choose and develop tasks for your students:

- Assure that there is a true communicative purpose to the activity.
- Provide clear guidelines and outcomes for the activity.
- Provide language supports needed to sustain conversations.
- Assign roles according to learners' strengths and abilities. As learners become more familiar with one another and comfortable with fluency activities, they can self-assign roles.
- Use visuals and realia to provide context and add authenticity (e.g., real menus in a restaurant role play; real maps for an information-gap activity).

An aspect of speaking that is often of utmost importance to your students is pronunciation. We complete this chapter with a discussion of the place of pronunciation instruction in ESL classes as well as techniques for promoting awareness of and intelligibility in pronunciation with students.

4.10 Making a case for pronunciation in your curriculum

There has been extensive debate over the past decades about the role pronunciation should play in English language acquisition curricula (Derwing and Munro 2005). Some have argued that within a communicative approach to teaching, attention to discrete phonemic features of the language is counter to meaning-based approaches to teaching. Many favor the integration of pronunciation throughout instruction. What are your own views about pronunciation and adult ESL instruction?

📋 **Task 4.8**

Take a few minutes to complete this questionnaire and, if you're working in a group, discuss your answers with a partner.

Rate yourself from 5 (strongly agree) to 1 (strongly disagree):

1. It's important that adult English language learners attain a "near-native" accent.

2. A pronunciation component should be included in most any curriculum.

3. Heavily accented English can lead to negative judgments about people and to discrimination.

4. Pronunciation drills are the best way to help learners acquire intelligible pronunciation.

In the 1980s and 1990s, explicit pronunciation instruction took a backseat to other areas of language with the advent of communicative teaching approaches. One reason for this is that early approaches to pronunciation instruction focused heavily on mechanical drills and practice of sounds in isolation, which do not necessarily transfer to accurate production in real-life communication. Current approaches have thought of pronunciation as only one small piece of the language puzzle, and one that develops through exposure to language and practice. The fact is that many adult learners who receive no formal instruction or feedback on pronunciation may be highly unintelligible, even those who have been in an English-speaking environment for many years (Derwing and Munro 2014).

Jobs and educational opportunities in today's world require strong communication skills and a command of language for engaging meaningfully while sharing opinions, elaborating on others' ideas, or clarifying to overcome breakdowns in communication (Pimentel 2013). Central to successful communication is being understood by others, and that means acquiring *intelligible* pronunciation, or pronunciation that does not cause frequent breakdowns in communication. The extent to which pronunciation instruction becomes part of your curriculum, therefore, depends on the needs and expectations of your students. Does their intelligibility frequently affect their ability to communicate effectively? If they are working, how important is intelligible pronunciation? Unintelligible pronunciation can affect one's ability to thrive or be promoted professionally, and immigrants and refugees can face discrimination on the job because of native speakers' unwillingness to adjust to a variety of accents (Akomolafe 2013). Sadly, some listeners even ascribe pronunciation issues to non-native speakers that are not even there based on negative assumptions they hold (Rubin 2012).

Learners themselves often report that native English speakers judge their credibility, intelligence, and competence based on accent (Derwing 2003), and studies have confirmed this (Munro 2003).

It would be wonderful if, as ESL professionals, we could be sensitize and educate employers, landlords, and other speakers of English in our learners' lives. Given the uncertainty of achieving that goal, we owe it to learners to help them achieve their highest level of intelligibility so that they can access a whole array of positions.

Some professions have higher linguistic demands than others and an employee who is highly unintelligible may not have adequate skills to meet those demands. The Equal Employment Opportunity Commission (EEOC 2016) has published guidelines that are used to determine whether or not a non-native English-speaking employee has been discriminated against because of accent. The commission states that:

> "An employment decision may legitimately be based on an individual's accent if the accent 'interferes materially with job performance.' To meet this standard, an employer must provide evidence showing that: (1) effective spoken communication in English is required to perform job duties; and (2) the individual's accent materially interferes with his or her ability to communicate in spoken English" (EEOC Notice 915.005).

Case law has defined communication demands of a particular job in the following ways:

a. the frequency and complexity of oral communication demanded by the job;

b. the relative gravity of an episode of miscommunication;

c. whether speaking is done under high stress circumstances where time is of the essence; and

d. whether communicative encounters typically exist with one-time listeners or, in contrast, listeners who will have further contact with the employee so as to adjust to listening and comprehension patterns.

These criteria are useful for ESL teachers because they help us and our learners assess the language demands of a particular job.

📋 **Task 4.9**

Using the criteria above, let's look at the job of nurse. How frequently does a nurse use English? How complex is the language? Would miscommunication have grave results? Is communication done under high-stress conditions? Is communication with one-time listeners, or would a listener have the time to become accustomed to the speaker's accent? From the answers to these questions, we can see that being a nurse has very high linguistic demands and one would need highly comprehensible language skills in order to succeed in that job. Now ask yourself these same questions for each of the jobs below and see what you notice. Work with a partner or write down your answers if you are working alone.

Restaurant server	Nursing assistant	Manufacturing line operator
Supervisor in manufacturing	Doctor	Nurse
Dental hygienist	Dishwasher	Housekeeper
Teacher	Landscaper	Truck driver
Receptionist		

Which of the jobs have the highest linguistic demands based on the EEOC criteria? What types of jobs do many of your students hold? Did you discover that those jobs with the most minimal linguistic demands are also the least stable and low paying? Helping learners achieve intelligibility is a way of advocating for them; it's helping them access the jobs they may very well be trained for already, or have the potential to attain.

4.11 Factors affecting pronunciation

There are a number of factors that can have an impact on one's ability to achieve intelligible pronunciation (Celce-Murcia, et al. 2010).

First language: How phonemically different are the first and second language? For example, there are several English consonants that do not exist in Korean. While this might seem like the most obvious factor, it is by no means the most important one. Learners whose first language is more phonetically similar to English will not necessarily have the most ease in acquiring the sounds of the new language. Other factors are equally important to consider.

Age: The assumption that the younger you are, the more likely you are to acquire a second language without an accent has come under increasing question. Studies on the effect of age on pronunciation in a second language have produced conflicting results (Flege 1981; Jacobs 1988). Generally speaking, however, learners exposed to English at an early age are more likely to achieve a native-like accent in a second language than adults who start learning English later in life (Ioup 2008). Adult learners *are* capable of achieving comprehensible pronunciation, however.

Motivation: Studies indicate that there is a positive correlation between clear professional goals and attainment of intelligible pronunciation (Bernaus, et al. 2004; Gatbonton, Trofimovich, and Magid 2005; Moyer 1999). It is often the case that adult English language learners live in an environment where they can get by with limited English, but as adult ESL curricula more realistically represent the language demands learners face in today's world, learners may see the need for more intelligible speech.

Expectations: Along with motivation comes expectations about how one wants to sound in a second language, which are sometimes unrealistic (Parrino 2001). Few adults ever attain a native-like accent in a second language, but some learners hold this as a goal of instruction. As teachers, we can help learners to manage those expectations, emphasizing their successes with attaining intelligible speech.

Exposure to English: While adult English language learners may be living in an English-speaking country, they may not be immersed in English at home or work. It is imperative that teachers provide abundant exposure of spoken English in ESL classes, and encourage learners to seek opportunities to listen to spoken language outside of class as well (Celce-Murcia, et al. 2010). Moyer (2007) found in her study that more experience with the target language community can lead to more intelligible speech.

Attitude and identity: Accent has a strong impact on our identity as first or second language speakers. Learners may have a stronger desire to sound like peers than to sound like the native-speaking population; this can result in a resistance to work on pronunciation in English.

Innate phonetic ability: Some learners may be better than others at discriminating between sounds or mimicking sounds.

These factors come into play in different ways and to different degrees for each learner. Recognizing these variables helps us to remember how complex the process of acquiring language really is. Understanding this complexity can help us to keep the goals of pronunciation instruction realistic.

4.12 | What should we teach?

It is important to understand that the goal of pronunciation instruction is not accent-free English—that's neither realistic nor a necessity. Morley (1991) makes a distinction between pronunciation production and performance, suggesting that both have a place in ESL curricula, the latter being more important. Production refers to the understanding of discrete sounds as well as stress, intonation and rhythm patterns, the traditional view of pronunciation. Performance refers to overall **intelligibility** (the ability to make oneself understood) and **communicability** (the ability to meet communicative demands). This view gives pronunciation a place within a communicative approach to teaching.

As English language teachers, you need a basic understanding of the pronunciation features of English. Pronunciation is broken down into two areas: segmentals, or the sounds of the language, and suprasegmentals, or the stress, rhythm, and intonation patterns of the language. Segmentals consist of the phonemes of the language, or its smallest meaningful units. In English, /b/ and /v/ are phonemes because when one replaces the other in a word, the meaning changes:

bat/vat   veil/bail

If two sounds are not phonemic in a learner's language, they may have difficulty differentiating between the two sounds in English. If a native Spanish speaker uses English /b/ and /v/ interchangeably, which is possible in Spanish, the results can be problematic (bowel for vowel, for example).

There is more to English pronunciation than the individual sounds. In fact, various sounds used in combination, or sounds used in particular environments, are often more problematic for students learning English. Two examples of learner problems you may encounter in the production of English are the deletion and insertion of sounds. Many languages do not have consonant clusters (split, prompt). In attempting to produce the cluster, speakers might delete one of the consonants to make the cluster more manageable, or, as with many Japanese speakers, they may insert a vowel (usually a schwa /ə/ sound) between the consonants: action /ǽkəʃən/[1]. Spanish and Farsi words do not begin with /s/ + another consonant, so it's not uncommon for speakers of those languages to insert a vowel sound "/ɛ /-Spanish," "/ɛ/-special" (/ɛ/ represents the vowel sound in "met"). Learners whose first language does not have final consonants may omit final consonants in English. This can result in misinterpretations of the causes of particular learner errors, for example, plural endings and the –s in the third person singular of simple present verbs (She lives next door). Some learners omit final –s in speaking, but not in writing, which may indicate that the omission is an issue of pronunciation rather than understanding of a grammar point. A complete overview of phonetics is beyond the goals and scope of this book. There are a number of resources to guide you, however (see Recommended Reading). Your job is to identify those areas that affect intelligibility the most and find ways to integrate practice of those pronunciation features into your lessons, which we explore in section 4.13.

Stress, intonation, and rhythm

Depending on your learners' first language, inability to employ English-like stress, intonation, and rhythm can have an even greater impact on intelligibility than the mispronunciation of sounds (Hanh 2004). In fact, we can often derive a speaker's intended meaning from context when phonemic errors occur. What does the speaker mean in each of these utterances?

---

[1] The symbols used here are from the International Phonetic Alphabet, or IPA. Each symbol represents the sound found in the word, regardless of spelling. *Met* and *meant* both contain the vowel phoneme represented as /ɛ/. It is very helpful for ESL teachers to learn the IPA in order to decipher phonetic transcriptions in ESL handbooks, articles, and textbooks. Some ESL students have learned the IPA in their country (Korean, Japanese, and Chinese students, in particular). I am not suggesting that you necessarily teach the IPA to students, but some teachers do teach certain symbols depending on the focus on instruction.

I have "lice" with all meals. (/lays/ in place of /rays/)

This shirt "feets" me well. (/fiyts/ in place of /fɪts/)

I "leave" in Gainesville. (/liyv/ in place of /lɪv/)

In each of these instances, the speaker is understandable through contextual clues. Now think of how intelligibility would be affected if a speaker used the wrong word stress on *committee* or *comedy* in these sentences:

What did you think of the **co**medy?

What did you think of the com**mit**tee? (Gilbert 2012: 166)

What often affects intelligibility more is a speaker's inability to stress the right syllable within a word (word stress), the right words in a sentence (sentence stress), or use intonation (changes in pitch) appropriately. These features of spoken language can be very difficult for speakers of other languages to perceive. Below are examples that illustrate some ways in which suprasegmental features affect meaning:

1. Word stress:

    a. Now you need to add cold **cream.**

        What would happen to the meaning of the sentence if you said "**cold** cream?"

        The first word of a compound noun is stressed: <u>book</u>case, <u>coff</u>ee table. Compound nouns are those combinations of two words referring to a specific item. "<u>Cold</u> cream" is a compound noun, whereas "cold <u>**cream**</u>" is not.

    b. The pronunciation of teens/tens 13/30, 14/40, 15/50, etc.: In natural discourse the prominent difference between each is that the second syllable is stressed on the teens (thir<u>**teen**</u>) and the first syllable is stressed on the tens (<u>**thir**</u>ty).

2. Sentence stress:

    I lost my **red** scarf. (not the blue one)

    I lost my red **scarf**. (not my red hat)

3. The following examples illustrate how intonation affects meaning (Levis 1999: 48):

    She's my sister, Marcia. (Marcia is my sister.)

    She's my sister, Marcia. (You're identifying your sister for someone else named Marcia.)

4. Another important feature of English is the use of thought groups, or semantically related groups of words within a sentence that are produced as chunks. These examples from Gilbert (2012: 137) demonstrate the importance of developing an awareness of this feature of English. Were it not for changes in word groups and pauses, the pairs of sentences would sound the same:

    Would you like the Super Salad? Would you like the soup or salad?

    They have a house, boat, and trailer. They have a houseboat and trailer.

English is a stress-timed language: that means the time it takes to say an utterance depends on the number of stresses in that utterance:

I like movies. = 3 beats

I **went** to the **movie** with **Jane.** = 3 beats

Many learners will come from languages that are syllable-timed: the length of the utterance depends on the number syllables. When speaking English, those learners may have a tendency to stress every word in a sentence. Helping learners to recognize what kinds of words are stressed in English can improve their intelligibility (it also aids in their ability to understand key words when listening since those are the ones that are stressed). Table 4.3 illustrates those words that tend to be stressed in a sentence (called content words), and those that are unstressed (called function words). Of course, we can choose to stress any word for emphasis, contrast, or clarification: Are you coming to the party? No, I'm going to the **movies.**

Table 4.3 Content vs. Function Words

Content Words	Function Words
These are the words that carry the most meaning in the sentence. We tend to stress these in natural discourse.	These are the small words that are the glue of the sentences. We tend not to stress these words.
Nouns	Articles
Verbs	Prepositions
Adjectives	Short conjunctions (and, but, so)
Adverbs	Auxiliary verbs
Conjunctions (however, therefore)	Pronouns

4.13 Approaches to teaching pronunciation

As the tide has turned back to including pronunciation instruction within learner-centered, communicative approaches to teaching, emphasis has been put on making that instruction meaningful, i.e., teaching features of pronunciation in context and for communicative purposes. In the past, a good deal of instruction relied on repetition of minimal pairs (words with only one phonemic difference). So, a student who had difficulty differentiating between the sounds /l/ and /r/ would practice pairs like the following: lice/rice; long/wrong; late/rate. Limericks, tongue twisters, and other texts that included multiple instances of the target sounds were also common. Anyone who spent time learning a foreign language in a language lab undoubtedly recalls hours of listen-and-repeat drills. While there is still a place for this focus on pronunciation production, and these kinds of exercises might give some immediate accuracy of sounds, that accuracy in these kinds of activities rarely transfers to extended, spontaneous speech produced outside of the classroom. That's where the need for a focus on pronunciation performance comes into play.

Celce-Murcia, et al. (2010: 45) recommend the following progression in a pronunciation lesson: *Description and Analysis, Listening Discrimination, Controlled Practice, Guided Practice, Communicative Practice.*

1. Description and Analysis/Discrimination
The goal of these steps is to raise learners' awareness of segmental and suprasegmental features through the use of visual charts, drawings, hand gestures, whatever means are within your learners' language abilities. Learners then need to take part in **listening discrimination** activities that allow them to demonstrate their ability to perceive sounds or patterns of the language. If learners are unable to hear sounds or patterns of stress, intonation and rhythm, they will have tremendous difficulty producing them. In the sample discrimination activities that follow, learners need to listen to the teacher or fellow student and make choices about what they have heard. Completion of the task demonstrates their ability (or possible inability) to differentiate between sounds or among pronunciation patterns.

a. Discriminating between /l/ and /r/: word search

In this activity, only student A is given the word search handout below. Student B is given the list of words to call out to student A. Instruct both students not to look at the other's sheet.

Student A: Circle the words that you hear from your partner. Words can go across or up and down.

			R	I	C	K								
			O						L	I	C	K		
			C										F	
L	A	C	K		R			L	O	W			I	
				L	I	G	H	T		R			L	
					G				P	A	I	L	E	
R	A	C	K		H					P				
O					T		L	A	P			N		
W	W						O		A			K		
	R	I	N	K			N		I	F				
	O						G		R	I	D	E		
F	N								R					
A	G				L	I	E	D	E					
I									L	O	C	K		
L				F	A	I	R							

Student B: Your partner needs to find these words. Do not show your list to your partner. Read each word aloud clearly so that your partner can find it on the Word Search sheet:

light	rack	lick	low	file	wrong
ride	rink	pail	fair	lap	rock

b. Connecting vowel sounds to color

The Color Vowel Approach (Taylor and Thompson 1999), which associates colors to the vowel phonemes of English, is widely used in English as a second and foreign language teaching. Each vowel phoneme is associated with a color, for example:

GREEN is the high front vowel /iy/ (as in "me," "three").

BLUE represents the high back vowel /uw/ (as in "you," "through," "news").

For discrimination practice, learners can point to or call out the correct color on the chart as they hear a new word (see the Color Vowel Chart link in Resources). The color chart is also a powerful means of helping learners make sense of the sound-spelling correspondences of English, for example, consider all the ways the first vowel sound in "silver" /I/ can be spelled: hit, women, pretty, build, symbol. Words with a confusing spelling pattern can be written using the corresponding color sound.

c. Recognizing word stress

Learning the word stress patterns of new words begins with perceiving the patterns. In a lesson on jobs and places of work, learners listen to a list of words spoken by the teacher and sort them into the correct stress pattern.

Listen to these words and place them under the correct pattern below:

beautician	carpenter	plumber
line worker	teacher	server
mechanic	doctor	

O o o	o O o	O o
	beautician	

2. Controlled Practice

Once learners begin to perceive patterns, your instruction can turn to activities that provide opportunity to say the target sounds repeatedly, but in a meaningful context. The table below includes sample activities that provide this kind of practice.

Table 4.4 Sample Controlled Practice Pronunciation Activities

Strip stories: Write a story or dialogue that contains numerous instances of the target sound or stress, intonation, or rhythmic pattern. Each learner receives a line of the story, which is practiced and recited for the group. As a class, students put the story in the correct order without looking at one another's strips. The stories can be generated by the class using picture prompts or realia, and they can be related to any theme. For example, in an Integrated Education and Training class, a dialogue between a home health aide and patient could be used, or a conversation between a head chef and a sous-chef.

Picture stories: Collect pictures of places and items that include the target sound(s). Tell the class the story and them have them recall the order and tell the story, shuffle the cards, and change the story. Have learners use online photos or clip art that use the sound and make up a new story to tell a partner.

Semi-scripted skits/role plays: In working on sentence stress and intonation, use semi-scripted skits or role plays (learners have to fill in some of the words). The context for these should relate to the content of the overall curriculum you are teaching: a job interview for work-readiness program; a mock interview with a government agent for a citizenship class.

Chain activities: For sounds or word-stress patterns, collect a set of words or pictures around a theme. S1: *We're going to garage sales and we need* _____. Choose another student, who repeats the first item and their own. Compound nouns: *bookcase, coffee table, ironing board, light fixture, area rug*. This provides practice of stressing the first word of the compound noun.

Word search: The word search above done in pairs provides controlled practice of the sounds. Different Word Search grids can be created for different learners in the same class. Minimal pairs are included in the activity, but because of the interactive format of the task, learners work on other communication strategies:

Did you say light (pointing to the light on the ceiling)?

Did you say wrong, as in incorrect?

Reader's theater: This involves reading and rehearsing poetry, excerpts from plays, or scripts with expression. This is an ideal controlled practice activity for working on features such as prominence on key words in thought groups, intonation, or contrastive sentence stress (Daly 2009). Learners can also apply different emotions as they read (excited, angry) and reflect on how these suprasegmental features may need to be adjusted.

3. Guided Practice/Communicative Practice

Finally, it is important that learners practice pronunciation patterns in unplanned, extended speech (much like "authentic use" activities mentioned in Chapter 3). The activities will not be completely spontaneous because you are guiding the students to use particular pronunciation patterns. The table below includes samples that move from *guided* to *communicative practice*.

Table 4.5 From Guided to Communicative Pronunciation Practice

Information-gap activities: To work on the stress difference with the tens and teens, thirTEEN vs. THIRty, students have to ask each other questions to complete a chart as in this example:

Student A				Student B		
Flight #	Leaves New York	Arrives in Miami		Flight #	Leaves New York	Arrives in Miami
790				790	4:50 p.m.	
380	7:13 a.m.			380		10:30 a.m.
618		1:50 p.m.		618	1:40 a.m.	
413	11:14 a.m.			413		

Celce-Murcia, et al. (2010: 205)

Word association: Write a set of words that represent the pattern being taught. One student gives clues for the word and the rest of the class guesses which word it is. For example, a class working on a word stress rule for words ending with suffixes: tion/sion: stress the syllable before the suffix.

Sample words: education   tradition   decision

Student might say: *"All the things my family has done for years. Different practices from my culture."* (tradition)

Discussions or problem-solving activities: Create a task that includes the targeted feature, but also has a clear communicative outcome. Here is an example that you might use in a career/job exploration class: small groups of learners discuss (with one acting as a scribe with this sheet) the pros, cons, and training needed for these jobs. They share which jobs they would consider and write their names in the final column. Groups report on their top three job choices and why. This example is targeting the /b/ vs. /v/ sounds in English, but the same task could be used to practice word stress on multisyllable words or for contrastive stress: I'd rather be a SERver than a BANker.

	Pros of this job	Cons of this job	Training needed	Why I might or might not consider this job
Banker				
Server in a restaurant				
Customer service representative				
Bus driver				
Executive				
Veterinarian				
Postal service worker				
Bartender				
Police detective				
Civil engineer				

Making pronunciation a routine

In all lessons, it is essential to integrate pronunciation instruction along with other skills and areas of language. In a lesson on the simple past tense (*I moved here in 2009*) or present perfect (*I have lived here for 10 years*), you could use the following task for recognizing –ed ending variations with regular simple past tense (or regular past participles). This activity helps learners discriminate among the three different pronunciations of –ed endings in the past tense as well as recognize the rules that govern those variations:

Give each student a flashcard with one of these words on it and ask the class to move into three groups according to the way the –ed ending sounds in their word. The teacher allows the class to try it without her assistance and then says the words aloud that are causing difficulty:

studied	graduated	worked	lived	learned
helped	decided	completed	stayed	hoped

Students tape their cards to the board in the three categories they have chosen and the teacher elicits what they notice: endings /t/, /d/, /ld/. When do we add an extra syllable? Only after /t/ and /d/.[2] (Depending on the learners' interest in or knowledge of phonetics, you can help them notice that we say /t/ after voiceless consonants and /d/ after vowels and voiced consonants).

Sample Lesson 1 on comparing expenses in Chapter 3 included a segment on categorizing the vocabulary according to the word stress patterns. These examples show the importance of routinely integrating pronunciation into any type of lesson.

---

[2] The three groupings are: /t/: helped, worked; /d/: studied, lived, learned; /ld/: graduated, decided. /p/ and /k/ are voiceless sounds and are followed by voiceless /t/. Voiceless which means that there is no vibration of the vocal chords as the sounds are produced. /iy/, /v/ and /n/ are all voiced and are followed by voiced /d/. Only those words ending in /t/ or /d/ add the extra /ld/ or /əd/.

Conclusion

This chapter has explored the areas of listening, speaking, and pronunciation within meaning-based, communicatively-based approaches to teaching. Competent users of English employ a variety of skills and strategies to access spoken texts, interact with others, and make themselves understood. It takes time and practice to acquire these skills, and it is our job as English language teachers to provide ample time and opportunities for these skills to develop.

On your own, or with a partner, provide an example or brief definition for each concept:

Checklist of Key Terms	
schema theory	
bottom-up processing	
top-down processing	
pre-listening	
follow-up	
listening for different purposes	
fluency	
information-gap activity	
intelligibility	
communicability	
phoneme	
discrimination task	
minimal pair	
word stress	
sentence stress	

Before doing these activities, revisit your answers to the questions at the beginning of the chapter.

1 Listening skills development

If you are already teaching, choose an up-coming unit for which you haven't yet planned any authentic listening practice. Select an authentic audio segment related to the theme of your unit:

- news report, how-to video, or check elllo.org
- record a brief interview of someone on that theme of your lesson

Using this listening passage, design a listening lesson. Include a pre-listening activity, two listening activities (these could be listening for gist, specific information, etc.), and one follow-up activity.

Classroom application

Now implement the lesson and answer the following questions:

> How successful were students at achieving the tasks you prepared?
>
> How well did your pre-listening activity prepare them for the listening activities?
>
> How did you know?
>
> Is there anything you would do differently the next time you teach this lesson?

If you are not teaching, choose a theme (e.g., health, accessing community resources, getting ready for job interviews) and prepare a lesson as described in 1. Show it to a partner and discuss these questions:

> How well will the pre-listening activity activate prior knowledge about the content of the lesson?
>
> What listening skills do your activities enable students to practice?

2 Evaluating fluency activities

Choose three texts that your program uses for developing speaking skills, or integrated-skills texts (if you are not teaching, find three texts to evaluate). Identify the activities that you think are designed to develop speaking fluency and evaluate those activities using this checklist.

	Yes/No Strengths and Weaknesses of the Activity
Is there a true communicative purpose to the activity?	
Are there clear guidelines and outcomes for the activity?	
Does the activity allow for different learner strengths and abilities?	
Are there visuals that provide context and add authenticity?	

Does the activity allow for sustained interaction among students?	
Are there other things you're looking for in a fluency activity?	

3a Your views about pronunciation

Respond to the questionnaire from Task 4.8 again and discuss, with specific examples, how your views have changed after reading Part III of this chapter.

1. It's important that adult English language learners attain a "near-native" accent.

2. A pronunciation component should be included in most any curriculum.

3. Heavily accented English can lead to negative judgments about people and to discrimination.

4. Pronunciation drills are the best way to help learners acquire intelligible pronunciation.

3b Developing an awareness of intelligibility

The purpose of this activity is to raise your own awareness of what has the greatest impact on intelligibility.

If you are teaching . . . For one week, complete the following learner pronunciation log for one of your classes. Listen for errors in the production of sounds, as well as stress, intonation, and rhythm that you believe cause breakdowns in communication (intelligibility). Also notice any compensation strategies your learners use (e.g., paraphrasing when they know they haven't been understood, using gestures, etc.).

Learner Pronunciation Log	
Sounds (individual sounds, clusters (spl), insertions, deletions)	
Word stress (syllable stressed in a word)	
Sentence stress (words stressed in sentences)	
Intonation (rising and falling pitch)	
Rhythm (natural thought groups)	

After that week, prioritize the pronunciation problems affecting intelligibility that seem most prevalent for this group of students. This will help guide the choices you make about what are areas of pronunciation to include in your curriculum.

If you are not teaching, use the pronunciation log as you observe a class and as you interact with those for whom English is not their first language. What areas of pronunciation seem to have the greatest impact on intelligibility? From what you've observed, choose two to three areas you would most likely include in any ESL curriculum.

Listening

Nation, I. and Newton, J. (2009) *Teaching ESL/EFL Listening and Speaking.* New York, NY: Routledge. An in-depth overview of principles and practices for teaching listening and speaking to ELLs.

Speaking

Klippel, F. (1985) *Keep Talking.* Cambridge: Cambridge University Press. A collection of highly interactive and personalized speaking activities including surveys, discussions, and games.

Lewis, M. and Reinders, H. (Eds.) (2015) *New Ways in Teaching Adults.* Alexandria, VA: TESOL. A collection of activities compiled from practicing ESL/EFL teachers for all stages of the learning process. They encourage discovery learning, provide practice, and extend students' learning beyond the classroom.

Wright, A., Betteridge, D. and Buckby, M. (2006) *Games for Language Teaching.* Cambridge: Cambridge University Press. This book contains enjoyable games to practice language at any stage of the learning process, ideal for practicing particular language points, as ice breakers or warm-ups, or for supplementing a course book.

Pronunciation

Brown, J. (2012) *New Ways in Teaching Connected Speech.* Alexandria, VA: TESOL Press. This book has ideas that lead learners to recognize rules of and get practice with connected speech in English.

Celce-Murcia, M., Brinton, D. and Goodwin, J. (2010). *Teaching Pronunciation.* Cambridge: Cambridge University Press. This comprehensive overview of English pronunciation is highly accessible to new teachers and contains myriad suggestions for classroom application.

Grant, L. (2014) *Pronunciation Myths.* Ann Arbor, MI: University of Michigan Press. The book provides a review of the last four decades of pronunciation teaching, the differences between accent and intelligibility, the rudiments of the English sound system, and other factors related to the ways that pronunciation is learned and taught.

Hewings, M. (2004) *Pronunciation Practice Activities.* Cambridge: Cambridge University Press. This resource book for teachers provides ideas on how they can make pronunciation teaching more interesting. It contains a collection of pronunciation practice activities for a wide range of levels, using a variety of methods.

Levis, J. (2018) *Intelligibility, Oral Communication, and the Teaching of Pronunciation.* Cambridge: Cambridge University Press. The book shows teachers how intelligibility research can be practically used in the classroom.

These texts are for learners, but are great resources for guiding pronunciation instruction with adult learners:

Gilbert, J. (2012). *Clear Speech: Pronunciation and Listening Comprehension in North American English, 4th edition.* Cambridge: Cambridge University Press.

Grant, L. (2017). *Well Said: Pronunciation for Clear Communication 4th ed.* and *Well Said, introduction 2nd edition. (2016).* Boston, MA: National Geographic/Cengage Learning

RECOMMENDED WEB RESOURCES:

Elllo provides over 25000 free listening lessons with audio or video. *http://www.elllo.org/*

Rachel's English provides a large number of videos targeting specific aspects of the English sound system *http://rachelsenglish.com/*

Sounds of Speech, University of Iowa *(http://soundsofspeech.uiowa.edu/index.html#english)*

Sounds of Speech™ demonstrates how each of the speech sounds of American English is formed. It includes animations, videos, and audio samples that describe the essential features of each of the consonants and vowels of American English. Sounds of Speech is useful for students studying English as a second language.

Appendix
Transcript of interview

David: Hi Farid. I wanted to ask you about the holidays you celebrate from France and Iran. I know you grew up in Iran, but I know your mother's French. What's your favorite holiday in Iran?

Farid: My favorite holiday in Iran is called Nowruz, which is...celebrates the Persian New Year.

David: Uh huh. What's the history of that holiday?

Farid: It's an old holiday that dates back to antiquity and...uh...it's the official start of spring. It's exactly at the equinox of spring.

David: What are some of the foods you eat at Nowruz?

Farid: A variety of food. Fresh fruits that celebrate spring. But in particular a dish that is made of rice, herbs, and white fish.

David: What are some of the activities you do that day?

Farid: Typical activities that you do on New Years...visiting families, eating out, and going on picnics.

David: Isn't there a special holiday a few days before Nowruz, where you jump over a fire?

Farid: Ah, yeah, it's called the Holiday of Fire Wednesday and in that holiday, people make fires and jump over the fire. They say they would like to get good health from the fire and give their bad health to the fire.

David: What about clothing? Are there any special clothes for Nowruz?

Farid: Nothing in particular except all the kids wear their brand new clothes.

David: OK, what about France? What's your favorite holiday in France?

Farid: One of my favorite holidays is the 14th of July, which is Bastille Day.

David: What's the history of that holiday?

Farid: That holiday celebrates the freeing of the prisoners of the Bastille prison, on the occasion of the French revolution in 1789.

David: What are the special activities for that day?

Farid: It's a national holiday and there are some official celebrations…marches on the Champs Elysee, airplanes, and military marches. At night there's music and dances in the street.

David: Are there any special foods?

Farid: You know, I don't know in particular, but I think people just like to eat outside because it's during the summer and people enjoy being outside.

David: Are there special clothes?

Farid: Not really. I'd just say anything red, white, and blue might be in order.

5 | Developing Reading and Writing Skills

> **To consider before reading this chapter:**
> - How are reading and writing situated in our daily lives?
> - What strategies do readers employ with different types of texts? How do you approach writing for different purposes?
> - How can we address the literacy needs of learners with limited prior formal schooling and limited literacy skills in their first language and in English?

Part I: Situated reading and writing skills development

5.1 Introduction

Consider how much written material (print and digital) comes your way every day: bills, junk mail, school materials, or work instructions. Print is everywhere in signage, advertisements, phones, ATM machines, and packaging. As a reader, you scan through some things quickly, while taking the time to digest others more carefully. As a writer, you employ different practices as well, depending on your purpose for writing and your audience. In this chapter, we turn to the issue of literacy development. We explore how literacy is situated in our lives. We look at varying purposes for reading and writing, the needs of learners with little or no literacy in their first language, and common approaches to teaching reading and writing to adult learners.

Literacy levels are closely linked to the ability to attain gainful employment, to participation in ongoing learning, and to improved health outcomes (Batalova and Fix 2015). In a print dense society, literacy enables adults to gain access to information and opportunities in their communities. Research also suggests that the ability to read and understand complex texts is linked to success in college and careers (Pimentel 2013). Whether you are working with learners with print literacy in their first language or a learner who is learning to read for the first time, literacy development matters!

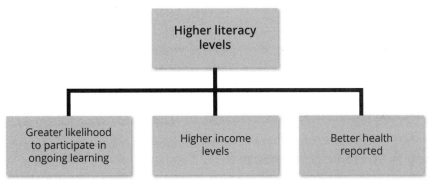

(Batalova and Fix 2015)

How do we define literacy? As we see in this chapter, literacy entails far more than a set of discrete skills and strategies to develop and hone. Literacy is socially constructed and dimensions of personal background, power, and identity are all at play in the process of deriving meaning from print (Street 1995).

> *This means that knowledge of the learner and the sociocultural context in which literacy is practiced is just as crucial to successful literacy instruction as is knowledge of tools and techniques grounded in empirical research about best practices (Belzer and Pickard 2015: 252).*

Let's start by thinking about what we read and what is involved in reading for different purposes.

Getting Started

 Task 5.1

Working with a partner or on your own, think of everything you read in a given day. Write your answers in this box:

Daily Reading

Now look at your list of items and put them into one of these two categories: **everyday reading texts or extended reading texts**. I've included some examples to get you started.

Types of Reading Material	
Everyday reading texts	**Extended reading texts**
menus	*novels*
text messages	*poetry*
online forms	*articles (print or online)*
billboards	
packaging	

1. What types of reading texts do you encounter most often?
2. Which texts do you tend to read digitally and which in print?
3. How are those texts connected to your daily activities?
4. How do we approach reading these types of texts differently?

Follow-up: As you read about reading principles and practices in the chapter, reflect on how learners in your classes might complete the chart. What are their reading needs and abilities and what kinds of texts should you incorporate into your classes? What prior knowledge, understanding, and experience do students bring to these different types of texts? What reading skills and strategies does a reader employ when reading these different types of texts?

5.2 Literacy is socially constructed

Literacy is situated in different contexts or domains in our lives, for example home, work, or school (Dyck, et al. 1996; Purcell-Gates, et al. 2002, 2012), and the skills we use to access print in these different contexts vary. Also, activities that involve literacy do not occur in isolation. Look at the following daily tasks in the domains of home, work, and school that learners may encounter along with the literacy skills that may be used for each one:

Daily Tasks	Literacy Activities
Preparing meals	Reading packaging; measurement/numeracy
Food shopping	Making lists; reading labels and pricing; searching for online coupons; reading signs in the store
Getting to work	Reading bus schedules and street signs; using a phone app for planning bus routes; refilling a bus card online or at a kiosk
Interacting with coworkers or classmates	Writing emails; contributing to shared documents
Enrolling in a class in the community	Reading course offerings (print or online); filling in registration forms

With this task analysis, we can see the ways in which literacy is situated in everyday tasks, and how its uses combine with other language and life skills, including digital literacy skills. Educators need to look beyond reading and writing as a skill set taught in a classroom to the actual contextualized uses of the varied forms of literacy used in learners' lives.

Teachers need to have a view of literacy that encompasses multiple purposes for reading and writing; there are reasons other than survival and work that motivate adult English language learners to attain literacy in English or in their first language. Parents want to understand and help their children with homework, and correspond with school administrators and teachers. Literacy is also a vehicle for recording and passing on culture and traditions from one generation to the next (UNESCO 2005).

5.3 Types of literacy

A variety of terms describe the different types of texts we encounter and the ways we read them. Everyday reading includes **environmental print**: billboards, signs, packaging, menus, etc. It also includes **functional texts** (forms, applications, bills, etc.) that we access in print, online, or with phone apps. We look a number up online or in a phonebook when we need to call a store; we read a menu in order to make a choice at a restaurant.

In academic and work settings, we may encounter these kinds of functional texts (class registration forms; work schedules), but we also encounter more extensive texts, such as textbooks, articles, or instructional manuals, where we employ a more intensive approach to reading. Reading functional texts often involves reading very selectively, for example, when we receive a phone bill, we likely look directly at the amount due and due date; we **scan** the text, or read for specific information; we probably do not read all of the fine print. On the other hand, when approaching an article, we may preview the headings, take notes in the margins, read and interpret tables and charts included in the text; we employ a variety of complex reading strategies. We also take part in extensive reading for pleasure, not necessarily for a functional or academic purpose.

In competency-based literacy instruction in the 1980s and 1990s, four types of reading were identified as critical for success for newcomers in English language programs (Savage 1993) and these still characterize literacy needs of adults learning English. **Survival literacy** revolves around learners' immediate day-to-day needs, e.g., recognizing prices, forms of identification. **Document literacy** is needed to decipher charts and tables, labels, bills, and advertisements. **Quantitative literacy** is needed to use and understand texts with numeric information, e.g., pay slips, schedules. **Prose literacy** represents an ability to understand more extensive texts, e.g., manuals, rental agreements, textbooks, articles, novels, etc. This classification aligns well with a competency-based approach, especially in curricula focused more on functional texts. To this list, we need to add:

Digital literacy: This represents using current technologies (which are ever-evolving) to evaluate, organize, communicate, solve problems, and create information in our technology-rich world (Leu, Kinzer, et al. 2013; U.S. Department of Education 2015).

Visual/graphic literacy: This represents the ability to process and represent knowledge through images. Visual literacy will often represent a literacy strength for learners who don't have print literacy. Consider the literacy skills a Hmong learner brings to "reading" this Pandau:

(Photo by Mark Eifert. Reproduction courtesy of Michigan State University Museum.)

What story does this tell? (See the story in the Appendix.) Considering learners' varied backgrounds with various literacies is a way to draw on their strengths. Visual literacy is also concerned with the relationships between information presented visually (e.g., in a flow chart, bar graph, or as a timeline) and the same information represented orally or in writing.

Financial literacy: More than just understanding and using texts with numerical information, learners need to navigate financial systems, learn about online phishing and identify theft, and acquire skills for meeting their financial needs and goals.

These descriptions of various literacies illustrate the enormous range of text types learners need to access. In the process of conducting a needs assessment at a company concerned about cross-cultural issues, I noticed that many of the concerns supervisors cited were related to issues of literacy. The examples below illustrate the different types of literacy identified above:

1. *Some of our workers don't punch out on the new computer system we use for that, even though we've shown it to them again and again.* (**document, quantitative, and digital**)

2. *I requested a schedule (verbal request), and the schedule was provided, but not in the format I expected.* (**document, quantitative, and visual**)

3. *Sometimes a worker won't mark down that a defective part was thrown out. We have an online form to use, but sometimes they won't even know where to mark it down.* (**document, visual, and digital**)

In these workplace examples, literacy involved reading and writing schedules, knowing the conventions of a particular workplace, reading and using online time cards, and reading and completing forms. Literacy involved the ability to perform these tasks as well as the ability to use technologies to complete the tasks.

5.4 How do we read?

Reading and listening have many parallels and are referred to as the **receptive skills** (writing and speaking the **productive skills**). There are, of course, many differences as well, one being the permanence of written text, allowing the reader time to go back to reread as needed. In real-world listening situations (i.e. the teacher is not replaying a recording), the listener has one opportunity to access the information or seek clarification. One of the key similarities between reading and listening is the important role **prior knowledge** plays in order to understand and use written or oral texts, or what is called **schema theory** (for a complete discussion, see 4.3). As with listening, an efficient reader is one who can draw the information they need from the whole text, using **top-down processing**. Task 5.2 illustrates the powerful role prior knowledge plays in helping us access the meaning of written and visual texts.

📋 **Task 5.2**

Look at the following text and images below and answer these questions:

What is the purpose of this text?

How would you use this text?

What information is given?

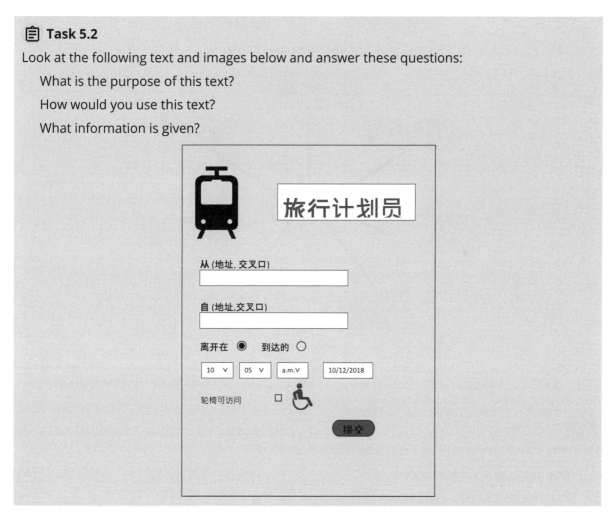

Even if you do not know how to read Chinese, what could you decipher from this text? Could you determine that this is a trip planner for a light-rail system? Could you "read" the words? No, but if you have used a planner like this one in your own language, you could probably gain a preliminary understanding of what the text was about, what it would be used for, and the places in the text where you would find certain types of information, for example, start and end points or arrival and departure times. **Top-down** approaches to teaching literacy are based on the premise that any reader brings knowledge and life experiences to a text and that is where literacy development needs to begin. Had I asked you to decipher individual characters in the text, you would have gotten nowhere in your understanding. Starting with a **bottom-up** approach to reading, or attempting to decode each word, with adult English learners may have the same effect. That is not to say that working on letter/sounds, word and sentence level decoding is not a large part of what we do as readers; it is just *one* part of the picture.

Reading, like listening and speaking, is interactive in nature and open to various interpretations. A text does not just transmit information, as shown in Figure 5.1. It involves information going from the text to the reader and back; it may be used collaboratively with others. A text means something different to each of us because of what we bring to it. The ways we read a text depend on prior knowledge, our needs, expectations, and the context in which we are reading, as well as our own interpretations, experiences, and culture, which is depicted in Figure 5.2.

Figure 5.1 A One-Way View of Reading

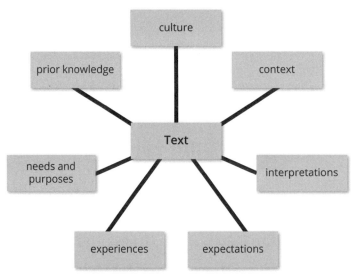

Figure 5.2 An Interactive View of Reading

Bottom-up approaches that rely heavily on decoding letters, words and sentences are one-way approaches to reading. Holistic, top-down approaches allow for these multiple interpretations and experiences that a reader brings to a reading text.

5.5 Teaching literacy skills: working with learners with limited literacy

Read the following vignette and consider these questions:

1. What are Choua's literacy needs?

2. What unique challenges does she face?

> Paseng goes to a university in Eau Clare, WI, about a five-hour drive from his mother Choua's home in Milwaukee. He returns to his mother's home every weekend. Aside from his desire to see his mother, his primary reason for returning home each week is to help her go through all of the mail she received the previous week. Choua is not literate in English or in her first language. She can't tell the difference between the Publisher's Clearinghouse ad and a request to visit the Social Security office to go over her benefits. When Paseng speaks to her on the phone before each week's visit, he can hear the panic in her voice.

This is a common scenario for many immigrant families. Choua recently enrolled in a literacy-level English class, but it will take some time for her to acquire the literacy needed to maneuver independently through the barrage of text coming her way. Approaches to working with learners like Choua look quite different from those we use with learners who have already acquired print literacy in their first language. You learn to read once, and reading skills and strategies learned in the first language transfer to reading in a second language (Ediger 2014). Classes that focus on the needs of these emergent readers are often called literacy-level classes[1] and serve different types of emergent readers, as depicted in Table 5.1.

Table 5.1 Types of Emergent Readers

1. **Preliterate**: Students speak a language that does not have a written form, or has a form that is rare or has developed very recently.

2. **Nonliterate:** Students who never went to school and cannot read or write in the first language, the standard language of the country of origin, or the second language.

3. **Low-literate**: An adult who has attended school, but who has a reading level below the average primary school level.

4. **Low-educated**: Adult learners who have at most ten years of education in the country of origin. For many adult immigrants and refugees, this means at most primary education.

(2., 3., and 4. from Van de Craats, Kurvers, and Young-Scholten 2006: 8)

In this section, we explore approaches for working with emergent readers, starting with the Language Experience Approach (LEA) which begins with language that the learners are able to produce orally, and uses that language as the basis for creating written texts.

A. Language Experience Approach
The Language Experience Approach (LEA) has been used for decades in elementary schools for first-language literacy development. Because the texts used in this approach are student-generated, it is ideal for any age learner and is highly useful as an approach for adult emergent readers and writers. LEA is based on the assumption that if the words we generate describe our experiences, we are far more likely to be able to read and understand them. Far too often, the reading texts found in even beginning-level ESL materials are beyond the level of the learner audience; often the content is disconnected from their life experiences and is outside their frame of reference.

So how does LEA work? A teacher who uses LEA can begin by having the class take part in a group experience; this may be a field trip or a hands-on activity such as cooking, planting, etc. Many times a field trip or other joint activity is impractical, so teachers commonly have students describe something they've done over the weekend or before school, retell an event from their lives, or describe a sequence of events using a picture sequence. In all of these cases, an oral account is generated as the starting point for creating a core text. The teacher elicits orally from the class what happened during the experience and transcribes the story on the board, or types and projects it for the group.

There are divergent views on what the teacher transcribes. Many educators transcribe the text verbatim, with all of the learners' errors. This is based on the idea that in order for learners to make meaning of the written word, it needs to be connected to what we know they can already say and understand orally. Teachers can make corrections offered by other classmates as

---

[1] With the establishment of the international organization dedicated to working with adults and adolescents with interrupted or limited prior formal schooling and limited literacy (LESLLA), more and more programs are referring to these as LESLLA learners or programs.

they are recording the story on the board, but other corrections to the text become part of an extension activity in a later lesson. Some educators are hesitant to send an imperfect text home with students. The other approach is to make corrections to the text as it is being written, but those corrections need to be accessible to the students in class, i.e., no changes in vocabulary or addition of complex grammar forms. The teacher taking this approach would add a plural –s, perhaps, or –ed verb endings, for example. Once the class has created the text, the students can take part in any number of activities, many of which are used in any reading lesson.

Table 5.2 Language Experience Activities

- Give the story a title.
- Copy the story for writing practice (handwritten or typed and printed on the spot to take home).
- Illustrate the story or match lines from the story with a visual representation.
- Cut words in sentences up and have student reorder them; cut the sentences up and have student reorder them.
- Generate comprehension questions to ask a partner.
- Make a **cloze text** (leave out all the verbs, or every fifth word, for example, which learners fill in).
- Collect stories and create a class text for other groups at school to use as their reading text.
- Do phonics work (see 5.4 C).

The Language Experience Approach by no means needs to be used as a stand-alone approach to teaching literacy. The principles of LEA have become standard practice as part of many English language classrooms. This may take the form of learners with limited literacy reporting to a fellow student what they did over the weekend, and having the more capable writer transcribe the story. In project-based learning (2.10), a language experience may be part of a project, for example a book of folktales told by students in class and transcribed by the teacher, students with more literacy skills, or volunteers.

B. Whole Language

Whole Language is an overall philosophy to learning, which views language as something that should be taught in its entirety—not broken up into small pieces to be decoded. It is often thought of as an approach to literacy development, particularly because it replaced phonics-based, bottom-up approaches in many school systems. Whole Language principles related to literacy development are the following:

- It is a top-down approach and works with whole, authentic texts (not adapted, simplified books).
- It encourages the use of inventive spelling so that learners can begin to write without worrying about mechanics at first.
- It is process oriented; learners create texts in steps including pre-writing and multiple drafts.

Whole Language represents much of what we know to be "best practice" with adult learners, namely, a focus on meaningful and relevant material, a valuing of prior knowledge and experience, and an emphasis on using reading and writing skills and strategies to understand texts (predicting, using contextual clues, etc.). What it may not fully address are the needs of learners who are learning to decode print for the first time.

C. The place of phonics

Phonics instruction is the direct teaching of alphabetic skills such as phonological awareness, or the ability to notice individual sounds in spoken words, and decoding, for example, recognizing **sound/letter** (or sound/symbol) **correspondences**. On its own, phonics instruction represents a linear process whereby learners first acquire sound/letter correspondences, with which they create words and then sentences. It is based on the assumption that the learner has acquired oral language, which is the case for children learning to read in their first language. This is not necessarily the case for adult English language learners, however. In cases where adults have minimal or no oral skills in English, this bottom-up approach can be problematic for ESL literacy development. Phonics by itself does not encourage readers to make meaning of what they are reading, or to use contextual clues, predicting, or other top-down, holistic processes that are all used by efficient readers. There is no question that we use both top-down and bottom-up processing as we read, but the two are best used in combination, and always with the goal of creating meaning out of what we read (Anderson 2014; Grabe and Stoller 2014). Proponents of Whole Language principles have proposed an approach to working with emergent readers that combines elements of LEA and bottom-up decoding skills needed when learning to read for the first time called the **whole-part-whole** approach (Trupke-Bastidas and Poulos 2007).

D. *Whole-part-whole: a balanced literacy approach*

This approach encompasses Whole Language principles while acknowledging the need for developing phonological decoding and phonemic awareness, or with some adult learners, the ability to hold a pencil or write the alphabet. Proposed by Trupke-Bastidas and Poulos (2007), which they adapted from Moustafa and Maldonado-Colon (1999), the approach begins with a whole text that learners understand and then moves on to phonics instruction.

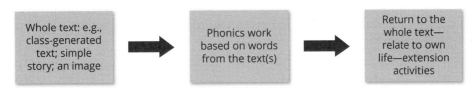

Figure 5.3 The Whole-Part-Whole Approach

The "whole" text may be generated using LEA as described above, or it may come sources such as these:

- Responses to a photograph or visual, picture stories, or photo books
- Transcribed recorded conversations
- Journal entries
- An instructional unit from your curriculum, for example, family relationships or job explorations

(Liden, Poulos, and Vinogradov 2008; Vinogradov 2008)

Andrea Echelberger's whole curriculum is based on learner-generated texts and the whole-part-whole approach using topics related to learners' personal needs. For this example, learners in her literacy-level class were experiencing problems with pests in their building. Andrea wanted to empower learners to acquire the language they needed to talk to their landlord about the problems and she wanted to provide them with practical tools and language needed for buying products they needed to control pests. This example showcases the steps that could be applied to any whole-part-whole lesson. By the end of a one-week instructional cycle, the emergent readers in her class can retell their story fluently in English.[2]

---

[2] A video of this lesson can be viewed at New American Horizons (newamericanhorizons.org)

The Whole
- The class takes a field trip to a hardware store; pictures are taken during the field trip.
- Next class, show the pictures—"What do you see? What did we do?"
- Teacher records what learners say to create a story about the field trip.
- Learners copy the story in their notebooks.
- Learners read and follow along as Andrea reads; helps connect oral language to print, then read chorally to reinforce the connections between spoken language and written word.

The Parts
- Focus on individual words in the story: pronunciation of more difficult sounds.
- Work on onset/rime (different from rhyme); onset refers to the initial phonological unit of any word (e.g., /w/ is will) and the term "rime" refers to the string of letters that follow, usually a vowel and final consonants (e.g., "ill").
- What other words do you know with that same sound? Knowing one word in a set (or word family) helps to spell other words (in this lesson, will/bill/kill/).
- Sentence ordering: each learner is given a word from the story. Andrea reads a sentence and students stand in order. Do they recognize their words and where they go in the sentences in the story? Class recites sentences, placing emphasis on the key words to practice sentence stress. This process also addresses word order, upper and lower case letters, and punctuation.
- Sight words: a fluent reader can recognize sight words without sounding them out. Learners do a flyswatter game to identify words quickly.
- Spelling with letter tiles: focused on words with diagraphs -ch (change; cockroach); th/ (with); sh (dish soap)—she says a word from their story and learners spell the words collaboratively.

Returning to the Whole
- Making a complaint to the landlord: interview activity that draws from the whole text as well as earlier lessons.
- Co-constructed dialogue: "What is your name? My name is _____. What is your address? What is the problem? My _____ is (broken, leaking, etc.). I have _____ in my apartment." Choral practice of dialogue
- Mingle activity with grid: name, address, phone number, problem

5.6 Other strategies and techniques for emergent readers and writers

In addition to the approaches outlined so far in this chapter, there are other practices and techniques for working with literacy-level learners that can be incorporated into any type of lesson. Lisa Gonzalvez shared these recommendations from her practice with literacy-level learners:

For literacy level learners, I consider what other language elements I can sprinkle into the lesson to foster metalinguistic understanding. For example, in a lesson focused on building a new vocabulary set, aside from simply concentrating on the new words and their meaning, I can also focus on orthographic and phonemic level structures as well—for example, taking the time to spell out the words letter by letter to reinforce letter-graph correspondences, calling attention to how many letters and syllables a word has to highlight "parts" of a word, having students identify the first sound of words and brainstorm other words with the same initial sound to emphasize phonemic awareness, etc. In other words, I try to get a lot of mileage out of a seemingly simple activity, hitting on many skills at once!

Table 5.3 outlines considerations and practices that make instruction responsive to the needs of literacy-level learners with limited prior formal schooling.

Table 5.3 Working with Low-Literacy, Non-Formally Educated Learners

Principles	Examples
Teach within a context; focus on meaning and communication	• Find out about learners' families, homes, hobbies, interests, prior work experiences, and teach language skills around a central theme.
Draw on learners' funds of knowledge, creating lessons that leverage their prior knowledge and skills	• If you have a former farmer or mechanic in class, build units about gardening or cars; consider cooking, sewing, and other skills learners have. • Extend textbook readings by having students talk and write about their own similar experiences.
Teach to a variety of learning strengths and backgrounds	• Use graphics, pictures, and realia (i.e., real objects such as tools, food items or real texts such as flyers, junk mail) • Use hands-on activities; get students moving around the room; use music, rhythms, and chants.
Make the connection between oral and written language meaningful	• Focus on oral language before moving to print. • Make sure that students understand a word before they read it.
Integrate instruction in basic alphabetics as well as numerical literacy and numeracy[3]	• Practice tracing shapes, letters, and numbers. • Display alphabet in room; practice copying the alphabet; play concentration with letter flash cards. • Work on alphabetization, e.g., learners stand in alphabetical order by first letter of name and gradually go to second and third letters of names. • Listen and respond to simple addition facts, e.g., "How many children do you have? How many does Elena have? How many do you have all together?"
Use learners' first language for clarification	• Allow learners to attend to the task at hand. • Learners clarify among themselves.
Build in frequent breaks and don't be afraid of repetition	• Learning to read can be exhausting. • Learners need to see, say, and read words multiple times and in multiple ways.

(Bigelow and Vinogradov 2011; Vinogradov 2009; Tarone and Bigelow 2005; Condelli and Wrigley 2004)

---

[3] Visit the Project TIAN (Teachers Investigating Adult Numeracy) website for ideas and resources for addressing numeracy in adult English language classrooms— *https://external-wiki.terc.edu/pages/viewpage. action?pageId=39846228.*

Conclusion

This section has focused on approaches that integrate reading and writing instruction for those students with very limited literacy or who may be learning to read for the first time. Next, we turn to activities and lessons for working with longer texts, focusing on the development of reading strategies that help learners access the print they encounter at school, work, home, and in their communities.

Part II: Accessing a variety of text types

5.7 Preparing students for functional reading texts

Learners new to a country often need practice in understanding environmental print (labels, signs) and functional texts (forms, applications, IDs), which typically follow set conventions. The nutritional value of a food item is displayed in a format that is consistent from one product to the next; medication labels are presented in consistent formats as well. These conventions are not universal, however, so teaching functional reading goes beyond reading words; it includes helping learners know where to find information, knowing which information is helpful and necessary to the reader, and is driven by the assumption and understanding that information *can* be gleaned from text in particular ways. Within an integrated curriculum, functional reading tasks are commonly incorporated within thematic units, or situated in contexts that relate to what learners need to do outside of the classroom, and they include both print and digital texts.

The theme of health and wellness is found in many adult ESL curricula. In the following example from an intermediate-level integrated-skills English class, the teacher brings in over-the-counter medications students may need to use, which are distributed to each class member. The purpose of this task is to give learners practice in finding key information on medicine labels. Each student has the grid below and mingles to gather information from classmates to fill in the instructions for each product.

Gathering Information About Medicine

Product	Directions: Frequency and Amount of Dose	Helps the Following Symptoms:	Warnings:
Aspirin			
Antacid			
Cough syrup			
Decongestant			
Non-aspirin pain relief			

Functional reading tasks can be developed for any type of functional reading text (e.g., washing instructions in clothing labels, directions for assembling a piece of furniture) or environmental print (e.g., advertisements, signs). If you are in a career-contextualized or Integrated Education and Training program, look for the functional reading tasks associated with that type of job or career. It is important that you identify the types of texts that follow set conventions within a particular society or career context so that learners gain the skill of reading selectively to find the information they need within a text (print or digital). Here are some examples of those types of texts. Can you think of any others? Look back to your list of reading texts that you generated in task 5.1 for ideas.

- Unit pricing at the grocery store
- Product quantity and measurements
- Online forms from child's school, e.g., grading portal
- Work schedules
- Warning signs

- Work forms for reporting task completion
- Pay slips, print or electronic
- Classified ads, print or online
- _____
- _____

Learning about learners' daily activities and analyzing the reading tasks associated with those daily activities can help identify learners' literacy needs and should inform the content you choose and lessons you develop.

5.8 Lessons to promote strategies development

Learners at every level encounter extended texts, for example, articles, short stories, or work manuals in their daily lives (remember the list generated in column 2 of Task 5.1). In this section, we turn to the strategies learners can employ to access more complex texts, print or digital, and prose or visual.

Think about it . . .
Take a moment to go back to the ideas you generated in task 5.1, particularly the extended texts. What strategies do you employ as you read those types of texts? For example, do you anticipate content and make predictions? When do you skim for the general idea or scan for specific information? As with listening, we employ a variety of reading strategies depending on our purpose for reading and the type of text we need to comprehend. Table 5.4 provides an overview of reading strategies along with the purpose and some practices of each.

Table 5.4 Reading Strategies, Purposes, and Practices

Reading Strategy	Purpose and Practices Readers . . .
Anticipate content; preview and predict	approach a reading text with expectations; they look at pictures, the title, subheadings, and captions and make guesses about what the text will tell us.
Read to confirm predictions	check to see if predictions are right or wrong.
Skim	read quickly to get a general idea (gist) of a text.
Scan	read only for the information they need, for example, the total amount due and the due date on a bill; our name and assigned hours on a work schedule posted in a break room.
Read for details	employ **intensive reading,** or try to understand the text in its entirety.
Make inferences	interpret and make inferences about what they have read; "read between the lines."
Recognize the structure of a text	recognize how specific sentences, paragraphs, and larger portions of the text relate to each other and the whole. Does the text represent a narrative, a process, or a chronology?
Find evidence to support claims	identify the main points and claims made in a text and then identify evidence that supports those claims.

Transfer information to other contexts	recognize the connections between what is presented in a text with an accompanying visual (chart of graph); transfer information from the text to a visual representation.
Interpret information presented in variety of forms	recognize what informational charts, tables, or graphs represent. Is it showing comparisons, cause-effect relationships, or categorization?
Summarize text and synthesize information from multiple texts	determine central ideas or themes of a text and analyze their development; summarize the key supporting details and ideas.
Analyze relationships within a text	analyze how and why individuals, events, and ideas develop and interact during the course of a text.

A reading lesson unfolds in a series of stages, similar to those described for listening lessons in Chapter 4 (see Table 4.1), beginning with pre-reading to activate learners' schema. This is followed by during-reading tasks to promote practice with a range of reading strategies. The lesson ends with follow-up/post-reading activities that allow learners to make use of the knowledge gained from the reading text and apply it to their own lives or to a new situation. While lessons should always begin with pre-reading and end with follow-up, the number of activities in between will vary depending on the level of the learners and type of text used. Let's see what kinds of reading tasks will provide practice with some of the strategies in Table 5.4 using a short biographical passage about President Barack Obama in a class for high-beginning English learners.

Sample Reading Lesson 1

Class description: 20 high-beginning adult ELs from a variety of backgrounds

Reading objectives:

- make and confirm predictions about a text
- scan for specific information; transfer key facts to a graphic representation
- find evidence to support claims

Assumptions: The students have print literacy in their L1 and need continued practice developing strategies for comprehending texts in English.

Pre-reading anticipate content; preview and predict:
Students look at a photo of President Barack Obama and work with a partner in small groups to complete a KWL chart.

K What do you know about President Barack Obama?	W What do you want to learn?	L What did you learn?

- Using a KWL chart allows students to explore their prior knowledge about a topic.
- The accompanying visual provides a prompt for sharing what they already know and would like to learn.

Reading Task 1: Read to confirm predictions

Next, learners read the passage one time to check their predictions (K) and to see if they can find answers to any of their questions (W).

> Barack Hussein Obama was born on August 4, 1961. He finished high school in 1979. He earned his bachelor's degree in 1983 and went to law school from 1988 to 1991. He met Michelle in 1989. He married Michelle in 1992. He became a state senator in Illinois in 1996. His first daughter, Malia, was born in 1998, and Sasha was born in 2001. He became a United States senator in 2004 and became the 44th president of the United States in 2008, the first African American to hold that office, and served two terms until January 2016.

- The K column directs student reading; students may read more selectively, looking only for information to confirm predictions.
- The W column helps personalize the reading task, which can lead to higher levels of engagement.

Reading Task 2: Scan for specific information

Learners read the text again and fill in this graphic organizer:

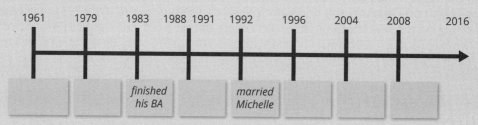

In doing so, learners now practice these reading strategies:

Recognize the structure of a text: The timeline signals to the reader that this is a chronology.

Transfer information to other contexts: Reading and filling in the timeline demonstrates that there is a connection between the text and a visual representation.

Interpret information presented in variety of forms: Transferring information from a text to a visual representation gives direct practice in interpreting information in a variety of forms.

Reading Task 3: Close reading

Learners read again and answer these questions:

1. True or False: President Obama started a family right after getting married.

   Why: _____

2. True or False: He met Michelle when he was still a student.

   Why: _____

3. True or False: He and Michelle started a family before he worked in state politics.

   Why: _____

4. True or False: President Obama's election made history in the United States.

   Why: _____

These questions give learners practice with finding evidence to support claims:
- A reader must analyze the meaning of "right after." He married in 1992 and started a family in 1998, which is not "right after."
- These questions prompt students to analyze the information, not simply repeat facts as they are presented (e.g., When did he meet Michelle?). If he was in law school from 1988 to 1991, he had to be a student when he met Michelle in 1989. The reading doesn't state directly that he made history, but the reader can recognize the significance of being the first African American elected president of the U.S.

Follow-up/post-reading: Learners identify an important figure they would like to learn more about or share about with others in class. They may do web research, visit their local library, or interview (and audio record) someone they consider knowledgeable on the subject. For the next class, they write or audio record a short biography and a partner listens or reads and completes a timeline graphic organizer.

5.9 Reading and the development of academic language skills

The following sample lesson demonstrates a variety of ways to work with longer texts that reflect what a learner may encounter in an academic setting. Here we see how to use a **jigsaw approach,** which is where groups are assigned to work with one portion of a reading and then they present what they have learned in new groups to bring the pieces of the reading together. When sharing what they have read, there is a genuine information gap among students since each group member has read something different and everyone has something new to learn. In Sample Reading Lesson 2, we also see how to weave in practice with a variety skills deemed essential in academic settings (Bunch and Kibler 2015):

- Using graphic organizers to help learners organize ideas and recognize text structure
- Highlighting academic language frames to talk about the reading
- Interviewing others, collecting and analyzing data, and developing a visual representation (bar graphs)
- Synthesizing information from multiple sources (the reading and their class research)

As you review this sample lesson, note which reading strategies from Table 5.4 are promoted through the reading activities in this lesson. The topic, the science of happiness, was chosen to represent what learners might encounter in an introductory psychology course and is also a topic that could have universal appeal. It also opens up the opportunity to reflect critically on what might be considered a "first-world" concern.

Sample Reading Lesson 2: The Science of Happiness (see reading text in appendix)

Class Description: 22 high-intermediate/advanced level learners from a variety of countries in a pre-academic Bridge program

Objectives
Reading:

- Read for specific information to define terms and identify research findings in an article
- Transfer information from a reading to a visual representation

Speaking:

- Report on the findings of one study
- Interview others and summarize findings

Academic language:

- Use language for reporting: e.g., *it was found that, the study showed that* . . .
- Use language for defining terms in academic writing: e.g., *it is, which is, means* . . .
- Use language to describe results: e.g., *the majority of the class, two thirds of the class*, etc.

Critical thinking:

- Compare and contrast views on happiness
- Analyze results

Assumptions/anticipated problems: Although students have an advanced level of reading and writing, there is a wide range of oral language skills represented in the class. Anticipate that some students may need additional scaffolding. Students may struggle with interacting/sharing openly about this topic.

Stage I (pre-reading): *Talk to a partner, someone from a different culture, if possible, and compare your definitions of happiness. Write anything that is similar in the center of this Venn diagram. Write what is unique for each of you on either side.*

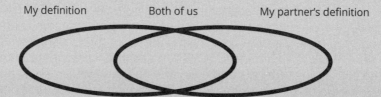

My definition   Both of us   My partner's definition

Discussion
Now, consider what makes you genuinely happy. Does the society we live in affect our measures of happiness? Take a few minutes to note some of your ideas and then discuss these questions in small groups:

1. Are those living in a developed society with everything they need to meet their daily needs happier than someone living with very little in a rural area of a developing country?

2. In what ways do the following factors affect our sense of well-being or happiness: age, wealth, political climate, marital status?

Jigsaw reading part 1 T: *Psychologists have conducted research on a variety of tools to help us enhance our feelings of happiness. Complete your assigned section of this chart. Write a definition of your assigned technique in the left-hand column and the effect of the technique on the right. Notice the <u>underlined words</u> help you find the definitions and the **bold words** direct you to the results, or effect of each technique in the studies.*

(Make four groups and assign each group one technique to learn about: A, B, C, or D.)

The Science of Happiness

Technique	Results
Technique A: Gratitude Journal	➡
Technique B: Acts of Kindness	➡
Technique C: Gratitude Visit	➡
Technique D: Three Blessings	➡

Jigsaw reading part 2 T: *Now mingle to complete your chart. Find classmates who have read the other sections and learn about the happiness enhancers and the results of the studies. As you present to your classmates, notice words that you can use to describe the results.*

It was found that...

The study showed that...

The researcher found that...

When people tried _____, they _____

Close reading: notice that these are what are called **text-dependent questions**, that is, the learner needs to go back to the text and read carefully to find the information. This gives them valuable practice in finding evidence in a reading to support claims.

Now look at the entire reading. Answer these questions and then compare your answers with a partner.

1. What changes have there been regarding the types of psychological research conducted?
2. What approach to using the gratitude journal has the greatest impact?
3. Why might "three blessings" be a more promising technique to use for boosting happiness?
4. What does it mean to have a "control group" in these studies? Why is having a control group important?
5. Why might these studies not be generalizable to other populations?

Post-reading/follow-up T: *Let's do our own research. Which of the happiness enhancers are people in class most likely to try? Interview everyone in class with your assigned question and tally your results.*

1. How likely are you to try the Gratitude Journal?

Very Likely to Try It	Likely to Try It	Somewhat Likely to Try It	Not at All Likely to Try It

2. How likely are you to try Performing Acts of Kindness?

Very Likely to Try It	Likely to Try It	Somewhat Likely to Try It	Not at All Likely to Try It

3. How likely are you to try the Gratitude Visits?

Very Likely to Try It	Likely to Try It	Somewhat Likely to Try It	Not at All Likely to Try It

4. How likely are you to try the Three Blessings?

Very Likely to Try It	Likely to Try It	Somewhat Likely to Try It	Not at All Likely to Try It

Once the students have interviewed everyone, place those students with the same question together to analyze their data. Give useful language frames to talk about the data:

Most people . . .   *Some people . . .*

Two-thirds of the class . . .   *Half the class . . .*

More people _____ than _____.   *A considerable number of people . . .*

The vast majority of the class . . .

Students now create bar graphs for their question and present their findings to others in class.

Summarizing the results T: *Working in groups, compare your results. Be ready to report at least two generalizations you can make about this group and their likelihood to try the different techniques.*

5.10 Paired reading

Similar to jigsaw reading, **paired reading** involves working with two texts on the same topic. Pairs of learners read one of two assigned texts and then work with another pair of learners to combine the key concepts from their texts. They then use their shared knowledge to complete a team task, for example, a Venn diagram comparing and contrasting the information that was presented on the same topic but from two different perspectives (Adelson Goldstein 2016). Jayme Adelson Goldstein enumerates the myriad skills this approach generates:

> While relating the key points of their texts, learners are employing the language skills of summarizing and paraphrasing and working on communicating clearly and checking their listeners' understanding. Likewise, learners listening to their peers are listening for key details by using active listening skills and self-monitoring to ensure they get the information they need (2016: 25).

Working with two or more readings on one topic allows learners to explore multiple perspectives on a topic and promotes an authentic purpose for a reader to engage with others. Also, working in teams and drawing on a variety of sources represents what we might do while collaborating with others in work, community, or school settings.

5.11 Using learner-produced texts

Students who publish their writings within and beyond the classroom experience many benefits. They discover that the realities of their own lives are worth thinking about, getting down on paper, and sharing with others. When they see their thoughts and concerns and those of others like them in print, they find they have a powerful voice and play a vital role in their new culture (Peyton 1993: 60).

Joy Peyton, a specialist in adult literacy for English learners, makes a strong case for using student-generated texts in the ESL classroom. Doing so has many advantages:

- The texts are simply written and easy to understand.
- The content is relevant to new immigrants as the themes are those chosen by other new immigrants.
- Using stories written by other immigrants, especially those that have been published, is very motivating for English language learners.

In her family literacy program, Laura Lenz used project-based learning to create a world travel book. Students from the same country took responsibility for writing about different topics. Three different students from Liberia wrote these excerpts from the world travel book.

Liberia

People
In Liberia people don't have money, clothes, food, or good water. People make farms before they eat and sell some food at market. They buy clothes at market. In Monrovia our people have businesses and electricity and rent refrigerators. There are different languages like Mano, Gio, Bassa, Kpelle, Vai, Kru, Grebo, Kissi, Loma, and English.
History
Liberia is in west Africa near the Atlantic Ocean. Guinea, Ivory Coast, and Sierra Leone are next to Liberia. Liberia was named by slaves from America who returned to Liberia in 1816. Monrovia is the capitol of Liberia. Monrovia is a city on the west coast of Liberia.
Food
In Liberia in the morning we eat potatoes, cassava with gravy, or doughnuts. Cassava grows on the ground and is big and long. You take off the peeling and boil it or eat it raw. For lunch or dinner we eat rice with meat. We eat goat, chicken or beef. We also eat fufu with palm butter. Fufu is made out of cassava.
Some types of food that grow in Liberia are plantains, potatoes, eddoes, plums, oranges, coffee, and cocoa. Many people grow their own gardens. They plant potatoes, greens, cabbage, bananas, eggplants, rice, and cassava. When the food is grown, people eat it or sell it.

In producing these texts, Laura took learners through multiple activities and learners created numerous drafts before publishing their work (See sections 5.14 and 5.15 for more ideas on developing written texts like these). The results show the care students take in completing their work as well as the rich content of learner-generated texts; they are authentic, yet the level of language in the stories is accessible for other learners with beginning-level literacy skills. Now these texts can be used as the basis for a reading lesson like the one that follows.

Sample Reading Lesson with Learner-Generated Texts

I. Pre-reading

Task 1 Teacher asks class these questions: *Where is Liberia? Who can find it on this map? Do you know anyone from Liberia?*

Task 2 Teacher: *Let's see how much you know about Liberia. Don't worry if you are not sure. You will read what other students wrote about this country later in the lesson.*

Are these sentences true or false? Circle True or False.

True False	Most people in Liberia have electricity.
True False	People speak many languages in Liberia.
True False	Liberia is on the East coast of Africa.
True False	Many people buy and sell food at the market.
True False	Liberia was named by slaves who returned to Africa.

Compare your answers with a partner.

II. Reading Activities

The reading on Liberia with the multiple sections makes it ideal for **jigsaw reading.**

Teacher: *Now you can learn more about Liberia. Some of you will learn about food, some about people, and some about the history.*

- Three groups (A, B, and C) are created and each one is given only one section of the reading about Liberia (A: People, B: History, C: Food).
- Each group (A group, B group, C group) is given the worksheet below and must work together to find answers to only their questions.

Work with your group to find answers to these questions.

Group A People	How do people make money? Where do they get clothing? What languages do they speak? How is life in Monrovia?
Group B History	Where is Liberia? How was it named? What is the capital?
Group C Food	What do people eat in the morning? What do people eat for lunch and dinner? What foods grow in Liberia?

- Once each group has answered the questions for their section, the teacher creates new groups made up of one member from each of the original groups (ABC, ABC, etc.).
- Students in the new groups present the information found in their section on people, history, or food.

As students listen to their classmates, they write answers to the questions for the sections they did not read.

Teacher: *Now go back to the true and false questions and see if your responses were correct.*

Follow-up/post-reading: *Now interview your classmates to learn some things about the history, people, and foods from their countries. Use the same questions you used for the reading activity.*

	People	History	Food
Name **Country**			
Name **Country**			
Name **Country**			

This lesson contained the same stages as the advanced-level reading lesson using a longer informational text. The activities for beginning-level reading lessons serve the same purposes: activate prior knowledge, read for a purpose (any number of strategies outlined in the chapter), and apply the knowledge gained in other contexts.

An excellent source for learner-generated texts is the World Education publication, *The Change Agent*, which has as its mission to "to promote social action as an important part of the adult learning experience" (*The Change Agent* web page). The magazine is comprised of articles written and submitted for publication by adult learners. Each issue revolves around a theme, making it ideal for developing paired reading lessons. The accompanying web page provides sample lessons for some of the articles along with audio, alignment to standards, and the opportunity for readers to respond to the articles. This example below focuses on the steps toward a career pathway, which could be highly relevant in a career-contextualized English class or an integrated skills class. Reading about other learners' career paths can be highly motivating for adult English language learners.

Career Pathways

Becoming a Paramedic

Chrishana Burton

I've always wanted to explore the medical field, but I wasn't sure where to start. I've done some research and decided I'd like to start out as an Emergency Medical Technician (EMT) and then work my way up to paramedic.

There are many reasons I am excited about becoming a paramedic. I will be able to read heart monitoring machines, run IVs, and give medication. To me, this is very exciting. I like being in a fast-paced environment, and this has "me" written all over it. Also, the opportunity to save someone's life: what's better than that?

The opportunity to save someone's life: what's better than that?

Despite all this career excitement, I've also discovered some cons to this field: like possibly being exposed to contagious diseases and viruses. There is also the risk of being injured by combative patients, as paramedics often arrive at the scene before the police. Also, being a paramedic, you are always on call. Some paramedics work more than 40 hours a week. This leads to less family time which is very important to me. I want to be there for my daughter while she is growing up. I don't want to miss the little things, like who her friends are, where they like to hang out, and what hobbies she is interested in.

However, what matters most to me is being able to provide a childhood for my daughter that is better than the one I had. I want her to be proud of me. So I am willing to take on this very demanding career. I will have to prepare myself mentally and physically. I really cannot see myself staying in the dead-end retail world that I'm currently in. I demand to make a difference in this world by doing something that's beneficial to both my family and me.

I cannot see myself staying in the dead-end retail world that I'm currently in.

Chrishana Burton is a student at the Mid-Manhattan Learning Center in New York City.

Emergency Responder Pathway

Title	Work	Credential
EMT Basic	EMTs take care of patients at the scene of an incident and transport them to the hospital. They can assess a patient's condition and manage respiratory, cardiac, and trauma emergencies.	Certification, which takes about 6 months of part-time classes.
Advanced EMT	In addition to the above, Advanced EMTs can administer intravenous fluids and give some medications.	Certification as an EMT plus 188 additional hours of training.
Paramedic	In addition to the above, Paramedics can give more medications, perform endotracheal intubation, interpret EKGs, and use other monitors and complex equipment.	Technical certificate or Associate's Degree, which takes 1-2 years.

5.12 Extensive reading: book groups and reading circles

A final consideration in this section is the benefits of reading extensively and for pleasure. As William Grabe notes: "There is no escaping the simple fact that one learns to read by reading (and by reading a lot)" (Grabe 2009: 28). Providing time for extensive reading in class and promoting practice for extensive reading outside of class (e.g., reading logs) have shown to increase adult learner interest, motivation, and confidence in reading (Ewert 2013, Garvey 2018). Texts used for this purpose need to be highly accessible (95-98% of words are known) and on topics that are of interest to learners (Nation 2007). Teachers can do any of the following to promote practice with extensive reading:

- Establish book clubs within a class or at the program level.
- Create a leveled reading library with a range of texts (fiction, non-fiction, informational)[4].
- Provide class time for sustained silent reading.
- Assign reading logs and reading journals; use that information as the basis for in-class discussions.

Conclusion

Whether a teacher is working with preliterate students or learners with highly developed literacy skills, all instruction should have some key elements in common. Activities need to reflect the ways in which literacy is situated in learners' lives and teachers need to draw on learners' prior knowledge about the content of the lesson. Learners should be given opportunities to go beyond the information provided in the text and interpret it through their unique experiences, knowledge, and interests. They should also be afforded the opportunity to work on higher-order reading and thinking skills such as interpreting information presented in multiple formats (tables, graphs) or extracting evidence to support claims in a reading.

---

[4] Grass Roots Press and Peppercorn provide extensive lists of easy-to-read biographies *http://www. grassrootsbooks.net/us/biographies; http://www.peppercornbooks.com/catalog/*

Part III: Teaching writing to English language learners

5.13 Introduction

The Language Experience Approach as well as Whole Language and Balanced Literacy Approaches outlined in Part I of this chapter all integrate reading and writing instruction. Regardless of learners' level, literacy development is, ideally, always integrated with other language skills and taught in rich, meaningful contexts. That said, there are specific instructional strategies for teaching writing that are the focus of this section. We explore practices for developing writing skills for both everyday and academic purposes. We also need to remember that we compose with pen and paper as well as with computers or other digital tools. Consider how the examples we explore would apply using either one.

While life-skills, product-oriented approaches common in adult ESL classes (e.g., writing to meet basic functional needs such as filling in forms) may still have a place for newcomers, they do not adequately prepare learners for the demands of work or further education (Fernandez, Peyton, and Schaetzel 2017; Johnson and Parrish 2010). In this section, we look at the types of writing we encounter in our daily lives, at work, and post-secondary settings.

Getting Started

 Task 5.3

Take a few minutes to brainstorm what you have written in the past two days. Work with a partner or on your own.

What have you written in the past two days?
an email to a friend
a report for work
a grocery list
a paper for school

Now place the items from your list in one of these two categories: **everyday/functional writing** or **extensive writing** and answer the questions that follow.

Everyday/functional writing	Extensive writing

1. Which type of writing follows set conventions?
2. Are the writing processes different? In what ways?

5.14 Product-oriented vs. extensive writing tasks

Writing takes on many forms in our lives, everything from jotting down phone messages to writing research papers, and the processes we use to write vary greatly depending on the purpose of the writing task. As you saw in Task 5.3, some of what we write is highly **instrumental**, writing for an immediate, **functional** need such as filling out a credit card application. Extensive writing, for example, a letter to the editor or an argumentative essay for a class, entails attention to genre, audience, and the academic language that goes with each of those. Extensive writing also requires more planning and revising than short functional writing products. Table 5.5 provides examples of both functional and extensive writing tasks that may be common in different areas of learners' lives. How does this compare to your own list in Task 5.3?

Table 5.5 Types of Writing Tasks

Functional Writing Tasks	Extensive Writing Tasks
Work-related: filling in forms to report defects of parts or accident reports writing résumés	Work-related: thank you letter or email after a job interview responding to email requests
Academic: completing registration forms filling in an online request for a book or an article at the library	Academic: lab journals essays research papers
Personal: addressing letters filling in a calendar	Personal: letters to the editor letters of complaint to a landlord

The first thing you may notice is that functional writing tasks have set conventions while extensive writing tasks entail attention to genre, audience, and academic language specific to that genre, as depicted in Figure 5.4.

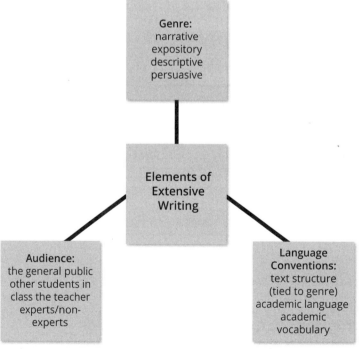

Figure 5.4 Elements of Extensive Writing

Students aspiring to attain a high-school equivalency, to retrain or get re-credentialed in their field, or pursue postsecondary training or education, need to work on these elements of extensive writing; they need to access a variety of sources and then cite them appropriately in their writing. Writing conventions themselves are socially constructed and the academic genres common in one society may not be present in another. Starting an essay with a thesis statement is not a universal rhetorical practice and acceptable topics in academic writing differ across cultures as well (Hinkel 2014).

In their survey study of over 270 teachers' practices for teaching writing to adult English language learners, Fernandez, Peyton, and Schaetzel (2017) found that there was limited instruction on writing genres other than narratives, little attention paid to audience (i.e., writing for a truly communicative purpose), or the academic language needed to express ideas clearly. Teachers in the study cited working on the types of functional writing tasks outlined above (e.g., résumés) but the following writing tasks were found to be the most prevalent, with 50 or more teachers responding that they often or sometimes include this as part of writing practice: grammar and punctuation exercises; class notes; short answers to essay questions, and biographical or personal writing. Johnson and Parrish (2010) found only five percent of adult educators assign research papers while nearly half of community college faculty in two-year programs assigned them in their classes. They, too, found that the most common text genre in both reading and writing instruction was narratives. It's a misconception that extensive writing tasks should be reserved for intermediate to advanced level learners and in this section, we will look at ways to lead all learners to writing for a variety of purposes.

Writing tasks that follow set conventions and for which the reader has specific expectations, for example, an online form for reporting an absence at school or work, may merit a more **product-oriented approach** to teaching. These types of functional tasks are not open to interpretation by the writer and often follow conventions that are specific to a particular task. Extensive writing tasks, on the other hand, can benefit from the stages of brainstorming, drafting, editing, and rewriting in a **process-oriented approach.**

5.15 Writing from the beginning: product-oriented tasks

As part of an emergent-literacy curriculum (see 5.4) or with learners who have print literacy in their L1 but are beginners in English, learners need practice in handwriting, spelling, basic grammar structures (tense, word order, subject-verb agreement), and punctuation, among other things. These skills can be integrated throughout instruction and in any type of lesson with beginning learners. This section contains an array of writing activities that can be characterized as form-focused and primarily product-oriented. Since many daily, product-oriented writing tasks are completed in an online environment, this is an ideal way to integrate practice with digital literacy skills as well (e.g., emailing a teacher about an absence, filling forms in online) (Harris 2015a; 2015b).

Vanishing Letters
Copying words, making lists, or labeling objects have great benefit for emergent writers, provided that practice is motivating and helps learners to strengthen their writing skills. **Vanishing letters** (Brod 1999) helps learners to build confidence in writing words on their own. Learners begin by copying a complete word, and then the teacher removes one letter at a time until the students write the word on their own. This example could be in a lesson on writing addresses (note the upper case S and A when the word is part of an address):

Street	Avenue
S _ r e e t	A _ e n u e
S _ r _ e t	A _ e _ u e
S _ _ _ e t	A _ _ _ u e
_ _ _ _ e t	_ _ _ _ u e
_ _ _ _ _ t	_ _ _ _ _ e
_ _ _ _ _ _	_ _ _ _ _ _

This technique works equally well with sentences or short paragraphs using vanishing words. This can be included as one of the activities in a whole-part-whole lesson (5.4 D) using words that are familiar to students.

Many of the everyday writing tasks that involve simple prose, for example, writing notes to school or leaving a message for a coworker, can be developed through **scaffolded writing** (Brod 1999; Gibbons 2015). With this technique, the teacher provides a sample text with key information left out. In this day and age, reporting a child's absence at school is normally done by phone or online, but a common reason to write a note is when a child needs to leave school early or when filling in permission slips for a school field trip. The tasks we assign should replicate real-world purposes for writing.

Dear _____,

_____ needs to leave school early today for _____. I will pick her up at _____.

Thank you.

Yours truly,

_____

Similar to scaffolded writing is the use of **sentence frames**, which provide a framework for developing short prose pieces. In the student-produced World Travel Book (see 5.10), the teacher provided students with sentence frames such as these:

I come from _____.

_____ is in _____.

In my country, people _____.

We eat _____.

The capital is _____.

The sentences generated through this task were then combined to develop simple paragraphs. Each piece of work was reviewed by the teacher or a volunteer and then the students typed the final drafts.

Dictation
Dictations have been used throughout the ages in language teaching. Provided that the content of sentences or passages that are used is meaningful and related to the content of instruction, dictation is an excellent way to help learners build confidence in their writing, and to check their ability to transfer what they understand orally to writing. Dictation is commonly done in pairs, making it an interactive task as well, as students check for understanding and ask for clarification. Here are just a few ways to make dictation meaningful (note that learners can write, type, or even compose a text message of what they hear):

- In a lesson on making appointments by phone, dictate name and phone numbers to a partner. To practice pronunciation of number pairs 13/30, 14/40, etc., dictate phone numbers, addresses, or simple equations that use those numbers. Have students practice on their own phones, or seated, back-to-back to rehearse using the numbers.
- Dictate short passages or class-generated texts that, once checked for accuracy, are used for reading or further writing practice (parallel writing, vanishing words).
- Dictate vocabulary words that have been covered in class for review and to practice spelling.

Teachers can also set up a **running dictation** where the text is placed in one part of the room and one learner must go from the text to a partner to recall as much of the text as they can at a time.

This task promotes additional skills related to peer-peer clarifications. Text content can draw on class discussions, vocabulary, or other content of use and interest at a given time.

Dictocomp/Dictogloss

An alternative to strict dictation is a guided writing technique called dictocomp or dictogloss. The teacher reads a short text, for example, a paragraph, story, or even a short article depending on the level of the learners. After reading the text aloud two or three times at normal speed, the teacher writes key words on the board and has the students write what they can recall from the text. The story and key words provide learners with content while giving them practice at writing in their own words.

Any of these form-focused activities can be used within any teaching approach or type of lesson, for example, as one of the practice activities in a contextualized language lesson (3.6).

5.16 Extensive writing

In addition to gaps between the *types* of writing tasks found in many adult education classes as compared to those required for careers and further education is the *amount* of writing students do in these two settings (Fernandez, Peyton, and Schaetzel 2017; Johnson and Parrish 2010). Fernandez, Peyton, and Schaetzel (2017) found that teachers of beginning to low-intermediate adult ELs had learners, on average, write no more than a paragraph a week. We start this section with an example of how we can build academic writing skills that attend to genre, audience, and academic language with learners at virtually any level, provided we give them the right supports.

In this sample for an intermediate-level class, we begin with pre-writing by generating ideas on the topic of caring for the elderly using an interview task and graphic organizer to record ideas. This approach allows us to first develop academic language through conversation (Egan and Parrish 2019; Zwiers and Crawford 2011), which can then serve as a bridge to more academic writing. Learners gather information from class members about different ways people care for the elderly. Then they use a paragraph frame, or academic writing scaffold, a technique that supports learners' development of academic discourse (Graff and Birkenstein 2014) to write a two-paragraph essay about the class's practices.

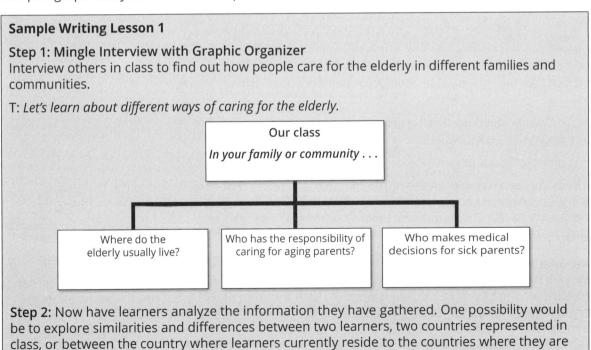

Sample Writing Lesson 1

Step 1: Mingle Interview with Graphic Organizer
Interview others in class to find out how people care for the elderly in different families and communities.

T: *Let's learn about different ways of caring for the elderly.*

Our class

In your family or community . . .

Where do the elderly usually live?

Who has the responsibility of caring for aging parents?

Who makes medical decisions for sick parents?

Step 2: Now have learners analyze the information they have gathered. One possibility would be to explore similarities and differences between two learners, two countries represented in class, or between the country where learners currently reside to the countries where they are from. Provide a new graphic organizer such as a Venn diagram for each question:

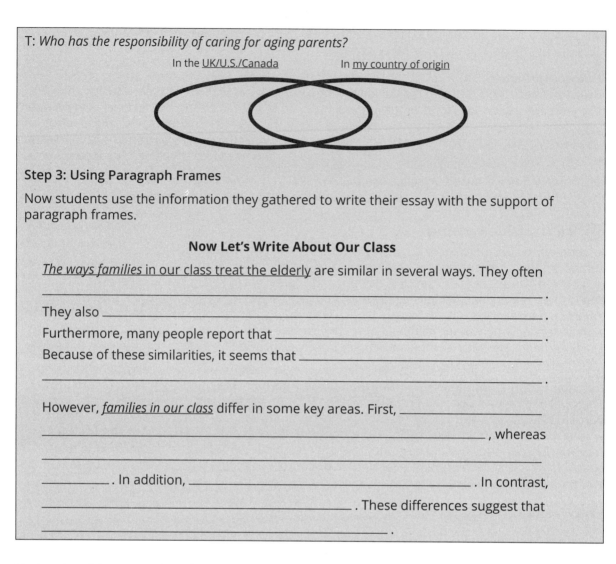

T: *Who has the responsibility of caring for aging parents?*

In the UK/U.S./Canada   In my country of origin

Step 3: Using Paragraph Frames

Now students use the information they gathered to write their essay with the support of paragraph frames.

Now Let's Write About Our Class

<u>*The ways families* in our class treat the elderly</u> are similar in several ways. They often

_____ .

They also _____ .

Furthermore, many people report that _____ .

Because of these similarities, it seems that _____

_____ .

However, *families in our class* differ in some key areas. First, _____

_____ , whereas

_____

_____ . In addition, _____ . In contrast,

_____ . These differences suggest that

_____ .

Notice that this approach to developing a short essay includes practice in valuable skills beyond writing:

- Communicate ideas clearly when speaking
- Categorize information
- Challenge assumptions

The paragraph frame provides academic language forms that correspond to the text genre: transition words to show similarities and contrasts, and simple present tense with adverbs of frequency to talk about routines. Learners can then explore a new topic for comparisons and use the class-generated sample for parallel writing, and then move on to more independent work.

Parallel writing

Writing from models, or **parallel writing,** is another way to scaffold academic writing for learners. Parallel writing begins by providing students with a written model focused on a particular text type or genre or specific writing conventions, for example, writing a paragraph with a topic sentence and supporting ideas. Learners begin with activities to draw their attention to text features as in this example:

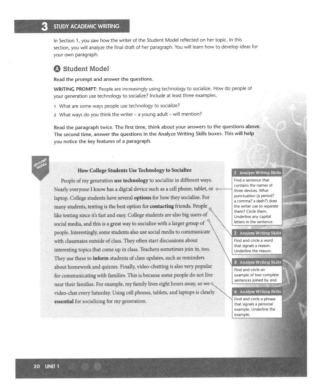

From Bohlke, Lockwood, and Hartman (2016) *Final Draft 1*

From there, learners outline this paragraph and eventually write their own following the model provided but with their own ideas and content. Activities to prepare them to write on their own could include conversations with a partner, brainstorming, and organizing their ideas with graphic organizers. After-writing activities could include sharing the essay with a partner, giving and getting feedback, and rewriting. Parallel writing is used at all levels of instruction; models simply become more complex and varied as learner level increases.

Extensive writing tasks generally benefit from a process-oriented approach, which entails pre-writing, planning, drafting and revising. Table 5.6 outlines stages common to a process-oriented approach.

Table 5.6 A Process-Oriented Approach to Writing

1 Identify the purpose for writing	Relay information to a friend in a letter Academic purposes (essays, research papers, scientific reports)
2 Identify the intended audience	An office worker reading a form A friend reading a letter An employer reading a report A class colleague interested in learning something new
3 Prepare for writing	Brainstorm key ideas alone or with a partner
4 Organize ideas	Organize ideas using **graphic organizers, word webs** Start with an interactive, oral task to generate content for the writing Make outlines
5 Teach the academic language needed	The academic language functions and forms needed to write in this genre

6 Write multiple drafts	Write ideas first, worry about mechanics later
	Write multiple drafts
	Share drafts with a peer
	Self/peer edit
7 Revising	Revise and write final draft

The next sample lesson demonstrates how a teacher can employ a process-oriented approach in a lesson on writing résumés with a group of low-intermediate level students in a work-readiness program.

Sample Writing Lesson 2

1. Pre-writing: T: *Did you work in your country? What work did you do? Were you paid or was your work unpaid? If you worked outside your home, how did you find that job? What did you need to send to the employer? What do you need to do here?* (Send in an application or write a résumé).

Class brainstorms information to be included (pairs first; and then one student invited to write information on board). All ideas are accepted and then learners can look for overlaps between what they brainstormed or what is expected in their countries and what is typically included in a résumé in their new country of residence.

Items to include on a résumé			
work experience	hobbies	age	family situation
education	sports	training	languages

Learners look at three sample résumés written by former students who have found jobs and identify the categories and the types of information included in each. Teacher elicits similarities and differences between what the class predicted and what they found on the samples (e.g., age and family status not included North America).

2. Organizing information: Creating word webs

With a partner, students write what they have done in each category and create a word web for each one: personal information, education, jobs, etc.

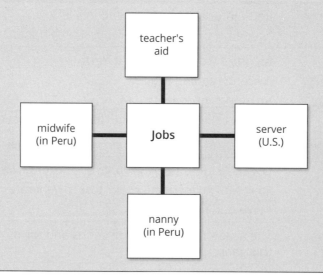

Next, learners transfer information from the word webs to a timeline to organize the information chronologically.

3. Writing first draft: Create first draft of résumé

4. Peer-reading: Classmate Revision Checklist

Classmate Revision Checklist

Writer's name: ＿＿＿＿＿＿＿＿＿   Checker's name: ＿＿＿＿＿＿＿＿＿

1. Are all categories included on the résumé? Do all apply?   YES   NO

   (If you circled *no*, note what is missing.)

2. Can you understand everything your classmate wrote?   YES   NO

   (If you circled *no*, underline unclear parts of the résumé. Ask your

   partner to revise the unclear part.)

3. Are the verbs in the correct tense?   YES   NO

   (If you circled *no*, circle the missed verbs and help the writer correct them.)

5. Revision: Revise draft using feedback from peers

There has been a long-standing tradition of using a process-oriented approach in academic ESL courses as it leads to a clearer and more accurate product. Adult learners with limited experience with academic writing need very clear guidance, scaffolds, and supports throughout this process (Weigle 2014). Even at advanced levels, there are many learners who appreciate the opportunity to see examples of what a particular type of writing should look like, for example, a lab report or literature review (Kim Koffolt—personal communication).

5.17 Graphic organizers as a scaffold to learning academic skills

Part of understanding genres includes recognizing the organization of a text, both as a reader and as a writer, which is why many of the sample lessons in this chapter include graphic organizers (timelines, Venn diagrams, cause-effect charts, flow charts). Including graphic organizers in reading and writing lessons gives valuable practice in organizing knowledge, seeing the text structure, and note-taking, skills shown to have a positive impact on learner performance in academic settings (Di Tommaso 2005). Using graphic organizers in reading lessons to analyze text has been shown to increase reading comprehension as well (Jiang and Grabe 2007). It takes time to acquire effective organization and note-taking skills, though, so explicit techniques should be introduced early and often (Parrish and Johnson 2010). Table 5.7 provides suggestions on the best match between some text types/genres and the type of graphic organizer best suited for working with that text type.[5] Consider all the graphic organizers included in Part I of this chapter (and throughout the book) and note the connections between the text types and graphic organizers that were chosen, e.g., the timeline for the story of Obama's life, the chart for the science of happiness reading.

---

[5] A search for any of these types of common graphic organizers will lead teachers to many websites with free and downloadable templates.

Table 5.7 Graphic Organizers and Reading/Writing Genres

Reading/Writing tasks/Genres	Possible Graphic Organizer
Short narrative; personal stories	time lines, tree diagram, linear string
Description	KWL charts, tree diagrams, main idea web, circle diagram
Write a résumé	word webs, time lines
Biographies	KWL; time lines
Process	linear string; flow chart
Division and classification	hierarchy diagram
Compare and contrast	Venn diagram, compare/contrast charts, T-charts comparison matrix
Cause effect	flow charts, cause/effect charts

5.18 Using dialogue journals with adult English learners

Developing fluency in writing is just as important as developing oral fluency, and **dialogue journals** are an ideal way of promoting written fluency. A dialogue journal is regular and ongoing written conversation between teachers and learners (or among learners) without the constraints of controlled, product-oriented tasks and it can be done with pen or paper, via email, or with a shared document depending on learners' digital literacy skills and access to technology. Learners read and write for a genuinely communicative purpose—the content is real; the teacher response is authentic. Teachers may get a glimpse of what a learner is facing at home or with family, as the following exchange between a teacher and learner illustrates (Isserlis 1996a: 46):

Oct. 2

. . . (my son) is better because He take medice. Thank you for you answer. I and my family are well. And we had a good weekend. Thank my dear teacher . . .

Oct. 23

. . . How old is (your son) now? Does he sometimes watch TV in English? I think he's lucky, because he is growing up hearing 2 languages-he'll be able to know Spanish and English. Do your other kids speak both languages, too?

Oct. 23

. . . (my son) have 2 ½ year old. When He Born he weingh 2 Pounds now he have 27 pounds. he Barn from only sixth month. Some times he watch cartoons But he liked played with her toys. He Can said some words in English. Yes my other Kids speak English and Spanish.

In later exchanges, the student shares problems she is having with high blood pressure. Janet and her student are communicating about topics that may not come out in the more "public" classroom setting. Isserlis (1996a), Peyton (1993), and others have highlighted many of the benefits of dialogue journals:

- A focus on communicating personal ideas, thoughts, and feelings can free learners from the fear of making mistakes.
- Learners are writing for an interested and attentive audience.
- Rapport and, hopefully, trust is built between/among learners and teachers.

- Learners can recognize the progress they are making as their entries become longer and more complex.
- Common learner issues emerge in a safe, private manner which can then shape /inform curriculum. (Note: if an issue is particular to one student e.g., a disclosure of abuse, a theft or other personal matter, it is important to ask that learner's permission to discuss the topic and to give the learner an option to disclose her/his issue to other students or not).

Reading and responding to dialogue journals is very time-consuming for the teacher and learners. There are a number of ways to make this valuable learning tool manageable for everyone.

- Provide designated class time for journal writing.
- Have well-prepared and trained volunteers respond to journals every other week as long as the volunteers have been in the classroom regularly and have built some trust with learners. The dialogue should not be with someone seen as a stranger to the learners.
- In large classes, have half the class hand in journals one week, and the other half the next.

Teachers need to realize that dialogue journals are not intended to be a form-focused endeavor, and the response should be first and foremost about the content of what learners have written. This is not a time to correct learner errors, but rather an opportunity to recognize areas for growth in learners' written language, which can then become the focus of later lessons. For those teachers who want to make corrections or give feedback about learner language, limit the corrections to one or two areas, for example, verb tenses or verb agreement. Another option is to let learners know that for one entry a week, you will respond to their grammar. Additionally, you may wish to compile common sorts of errors (without identifying the writers) and share several of them as part of a grammar mini-lesson within class time, as appropriate to focus of the class. As learners become more proficient, they may ask that the teacher make more corrections. When teachers get a glimpse of learners' lives and concerns, teaching may become more learner-centered, and dialogue journals are an ideal vehicle through which this can happen.

5.19 Technology and writing

Many of the technological tools available to adult education programs provide excellent vehicles for developing writing skills (see full discussion of uses of technology in Chapter 8) and they also provide an opportunity for learners to write for a broader audience (Harris 2015a). Here are just some of the many ways to embed meaningful use of technologies with writing skills development.

- In project-based learning, learners create a web page, a newsletter, or a class-generated blog as the final product.
- The *Change Agent* readings provide a place for reader comments. Do the same with student writings in a blog or wiki with a space for reader comments.
- Use shared documents and wikis to allow learners to collaborate on their writing, a skill valued in academic settings.
- Create simple forms yourself that replicate online forms in learners' lives, for example, online health forms, applications, product registrations, or ticket orders. Learners submit the form to the teacher to assess for clarity (Harris 2015b).
- Have learners create PowerPoint presentations, and if using a tool such as VoiceThread, they can solicit reader/viewer comments and contributions.
- Use online graphic organizers for pre-writing (or for reading tasks as well).
- Determine with students what word processing features you will use when giving feedback or having them do peer feedback on word-processed writing (comments, highlighting, underlining, boldface).

- Show students how to use grammar checkers, synonym checkers, or a free program like Ginger that provides alternate phrases. Adult education specialists at EdTech (2013) suggest these activities with a "rephraser" software:
  - Demonstrate with the class using a text projected for the class. Before using the rephraser, ask students if they can suggest alternatives; generate the new phrases and discuss the different forms and their functions; discuss which are appropriate in what context.
  - Ask students to come up to the computer and type some of their own phrases; have students form groups and see which group can come up with the most or best alternative phrases.
  - Go over student writing in class. (Be careful to keep the writing anonymous or ask the student's permission.) Have students download the software and show them how to use the software.
- Connect with other programs by establishing ePals to practice writing fluency.
- Email can be used for conducting peer reviews and providing feedback of written drafts.

5.20 Responding to learner writing

An initial response to writing normally focuses on the content of what has been written rather than the form. From there, a teacher needs to ask him or herself: What is the purpose of the writing task? In the case of emergent writers, getting words down on paper is a great achievement in and of itself, as with the following sample:

This learner came to class with basic literacy skills in his first language and emergent skills in English. The teacher, Janet, shares her ideas about the new hands-free driving law that outlaws the use of hand-held phones while driving and solicits the learner's opinion as well, but she does not correct any errors. The journal is a vehicle for learners to express opinions about current events as well as more personal reflections, as in the second entry. Janet focuses on form in writing through other types of activities in her class such as sentence frames, LEA, and parallel writing.

If a learner were writing a résumé, a cover letter, or an essay, the approach to feedback would be different given the audience for the writing. Many of the considerations in Chapter 3 (Table 3.3) apply here as well, particularly who the learner is and what the purpose of the task is. After a response on overall content, feedback to writing begins in the same way oral feedback is given: indicate where the errors are, but don't correct them for the student. The following are some guidelines for teachers to keep in mind:

• Always begin with a response to the content of what learners have written. Provide feedback on what is clear in their writing: *I enjoyed learning all of these details about your family members,* or *You supported your argument with evidence from the reading we did in class.*

• When responding to longer pieces of writing, develop rubrics or assessment checklists that include the categories of content, organization, discourse (e.g., overall organization, topic sentences, transitions), syntax, vocabulary, and mechanics (e.g., spelling, punctuation) (Brown and Lee 2015).

• Develop consistent conventions that your learners can understand: *sp* for spelling, *T* for tense, underlining for wrong word choice. There are many editing conventions, but it is often best to develop a set of editing marks with your students so you know they are understood.

• Provide opportunities for peer review and revision through conferences or group time.

• Develop a realistic sense of what a given learner is capable of producing and do not expect perfection or try to rewrite their work. Do remember what learners have done and chart their progress by photocopying completed journals, noticing errors that persist or diminish as part of ongoing planning and instruction.

Like so many teaching processes and routines, responding appropriately to learner errors takes practice. Teachers need to have a clear idea of what a learner is capable of, and then provide encouragement and feedback that is accessible to that learner. Patience should prevail . . . language isn't learned overnight!

Conclusion
Attaining literacy in a second language means far more than learning to decode and write words. Literacy involves activities that are conducted in rich social contexts between and among individuals. Attaining literacy in English broadens learners' opportunities; it allows them to attain certain jobs, help their children with schoolwork, and correspond with teachers and others in the community. English language educators have the task of determining their learners' literacy needs and selecting approaches and contexts for teaching reading and writing that are the most suitable for them.

Key Terms

On your own, or with a partner, provide an example or brief definition for each concept:

Checklist of Key Terms	
environmental print	
functional texts	
schema theory	
receptive skills	
digital literacy	
visual literacy	
top-down processing	
bottom-up processing	
pre-literate, non-literate, low-literate, low-educated	
language experience approach	
whole-part-whole approach	
phonics	
jigsaw reading	
text-dependent questions	
process-oriented approach	
product-oriented approach	
scaffolded writing	
graphic organizers	
dialogue journals	

Before doing these activities, revisit your answers to the questions at the beginning of the chapter.

1 Reading Skills Development

If you are already teaching and work with pre- or non-literate learners, conduct a whole-part-whole lesson beginning with a language experience (see LEA) with your students. Implement activities suggested in Section 5.5 and reflect on the benefits the approach has for your learners. Reflect on any difficulties learners experience and think of alternatives that you might try the next time you use this approach. Also notice any variations you implemented in order to meet your students' needs and strengths.

If you are working with learners with more developed literacy, choose an authentic text (a short reading, learner-written materials, an article) that relates to an upcoming unit you are teaching, but for which you haven't integrated reading practice before. Using this text, develop and implement a reading lesson including pre-reading, two reading activities that provide practice with reading strategies in Table 5.4, and a follow-up activity. After you teach the lesson, reflect on the successes learners had as well as any difficulties they experienced. What would you do differently the next time you teach a lesson like this?

If you are not teaching, collect one sample functional reading text and one longer informational text (a book review, an article). Then, analyze the reading strategies and skills needed to understand the texts you choose, for example, reading nutritional information requires understanding of numeracy and charts. Create two different activities that would give learners practice with reading these texts.

2 Helping Learners with Writing

If you are already teaching . . . reflect on and discuss (or write about) these questions:

What are your learners' writing needs?

How much of the writing you teach is functional and form-focused? How much of the time do you work with learners on more extensive writing tasks?

Choose one writing need and develop and implement a writing lesson that addresses it.

If you aren't teaching, look at integrated-skills ESL textbooks for three different levels of instruction.

1. What reading and writing practice is provided?

2. Is the focus on functional reading and writing or intensive reading and extensive writing?

3. What approach is used to teaching writing: product oriented, process oriented, or a combination of the two?

Cardiff, P., Newman, K. and Pearce, E. (N.D.) *Reflect for ESOL,* London: Action Aid. Available at *http://www.skillsforlifenetwork.com/?atk=964*. Developed for teaching or working with refugees, asylum seekers, or long-term immigrant groups in the UK. Using an empowering participatory process, it links language learning to the analysis of broader issues in learners' lives. Literacy and language development are based on rich visual materials related to learners' immediate experiences.

Grabe, W. (2009). *Reading in a Second Language: Moving from Theory to Practice*. New York, NY: Cambridge University Press. This book provides a thorough overview and analysis of important theories of reading and their implications for reading instruction.

Schaetzel, K., Kreeft Peyton, J. and Fernandez, R. (Eds). (2019) *Teaching Academic Writing to Adults Learning English.* Ann Arbor, MI: University of Michigan Press. This new volume contains chapters on teaching academic writing to adult English language learners from literacy-level to advanced.

Wrigley, H. and Guth, G. (1992) *Bringing Literacy to Life: Issues and Options in Adult ESL Literacy.* San Mateo, CA: Aguirre International. The authors provide information on methods and approaches, assessment, technology, teacher development as well as promising practices from literacy programs. Available at *http://www.cal.org/caela/esl_resources/BringingLiteracytoLife.pdf*

Sources for Literacy-Level Texts:

Bow Valley College. *ESL Literacy Readers*. Calgary, Canada: Bow Valley College *https://globalaccess.bowvalleycollege.ca/learners/readers.php*

abeEnglish *http://www.teachabcenglish.com/*

Sources for readings/reading lessons on current events:

NewsELA *https://newsela.com/*

ReadWorks *https://www.readworks.org/*

Commonlit *https://www.commonlit.org*

Story of Pandau (5.3): In the upper half of this cloth there are scenes of harvesting corn, pounding rice, and feeding animals. The third tier of images shows shamanistic ceremonies and the bottom tier shows traditional courting customs. The mother of the bride is furious when she learns from a messenger that her daughter has been seduced by her would-be husband and threatens the messenger with a stick.

Text for Sample Reading Lesson 2 (written by the author)

The Science of Happiness

In the past, psychological research focused primarily on disorders rather than on what characterizes "happy" people. More recently, researchers are exploring the connections between feelings of gratitude and levels of happiness, and many suggest that there are different kinds of happiness enhancers (Mangels 2008).

One of those happiness enhancers is called the gratitude journal, <u>which is</u> when people keep track of things they are grateful for in a diary. In one study, **it was found that** subjects who took time to consciously count their blessings in a gratitude journal on a weekly basis significantly increased their overall satisfaction with life over a period of six weeks, whereas a control group that did not keep journals had no such gain (Lyubomirsky, Tkach, and Sheldon 2004).

Another way to boost happiness is to perform acts of altruism or kindness, <u>for example</u>, playing music at a nursing home, helping a friend with childcare, doing yard work for an aging neighbor, or perhaps writing a letter to an aging relative. Lyubomirsky, Tkach, and Sheldon (2004) **found that**, as with the gratitude journal, doing five kind acts a week, especially when they were all completed in a single day, gave subjects in the study a measurable boost in satisfaction as compared to those in the control group.

Martin Seligman, considered the founder of this line of research, has experimented with similar techniques in controlled trials in large experiments conducted over the Internet. **He found that** the single most effective way to boost your feeling of joy is to make a "gratitude visit." A gratitude visit <u>means</u> writing a testimonial thanking a relative, teacher, mentor, friend—anyone to whom you owe a debt of gratitude—and then visiting that person to read him or her the letter of appreciation. The long-term effects of this practice were not as long-lasting as some of the others, though (Seligman, et al. 2005).

The last technique, which Seligman says is less powerful but more lasting than a gratitude visit is an exercise that he calls "three blessings." <u>For this technique</u>, an individual should write down three things that went well that day and why. **He found that** people who do that each day are less depressed three months later and continued to be six months later as well (Seligman, et al. 2005).

It's important to note that these studies have been conducted in Western, individualistic cultures where striving for self-satisfaction may be an acceptable practice. In more collectivist cultures, this focus on self-improvement may be at odds with beliefs about the good of the group as opposed to the individual. Also, definitions of happiness are culturally bound, so finding suitable measures for purposes of doing research can be problematic (Mangels 2008).

Lyubomirsky, S., Tkach, C., and Sheldon, K. M. (2004). Pursuing Sustained Happiness through Random Acts of Kindness and Counting One's Blessings: Tests of Two Six-Week Interventions. Unpublished raw data. doi:10.1037/1089-2680.9.2.111

Mangels, D. (2009). The Science of Happiness. *Berkeley Scientific Journal, 12*(2). Retrieved from *https://escholarship.org/uc/item/9c00g8js*

Seligman, M. E. P., Steen, T. A., Park, N., and Peterson, C. (2005). Positive Psychology Progress: Empirical Validation of Interventions. *American Psychologist, 60,* 410–421.

6 | Planning for Teaching and Learning

> **To consider before reading this chapter:**
> - What considerations should come into play when planning lessons?
> - What are some ways to build continuity from one lesson to the next?
> - How can the level and amount of teacher language affect learning?
> - How can we check learner understanding throughout lessons?

Part I: Lesson planning

6.1 Introduction

Planning for teaching and learning is a complex process that needs to take numerous variables into account. This chapter focuses on the decisions teachers make within their courses and from one lesson to the next: *What is the overarching purpose of the lesson? How does it connect to the broader curriculum? What are the objectives of the lesson and what final tasks will assess achievement of those objectives? How can I connect the lesson to learners' lives? What materials will I need? What do I need to review from previous lessons? What standards am I accountable to in my program?*

This chapter covers three important areas of planning for teaching and learning. First, we explore the processes teachers use in day-to-day lesson planning as well as the ways careful planning can help promote learner success in a lesson. Then we turn to the importance of planning for some of the key interactions that take place in all lessons, including introductions, directions to activities, transitions, questioning techniques, and comprehension checks. You will learn that those are not elements of a lesson to be left to chance, especially for those new to teaching English. Finally, we explore the importance of developing learner autonomy through the development of learning strategies so that students can continue to progress in their language development outside of the classroom.

Getting Started

Planning takes on many forms for different teachers: some carefully script their lessons, while others keep key questions in mind as they choose activities and materials, simply writing reminders for themselves. From my own experience, all teachers benefit from detailed lesson plans with objectives that are clearly articulated, a list of materials, descriptions of activities and interactions, assessments, and prepared questions to be used in introductions to a topic, directions, transitions, and comprehension checks. This is not to imply that the plan should dictate every twist and turn the lesson takes—a good teacher is one who takes the learners' lead. From my observations, however, it is clear that learners who feel that there is purpose and direction in a lesson are more likely to participate in class and contribute to discussions. Careful planning also builds teacher confidence, which in turn inspires confidence in the learners.

📋 **Task 6.1**

I asked several teachers to describe how they plan for their classes for adult English language learners. Some of the teachers responded in terms of long-range planning, and others talked about what they do day-to-day to plan each lesson. Read excerpts from their responses below and write examples of what these teachers consider related to each of the areas listed in the the chart below. Add some of your own ideas to the chart as well.

Lesson Planning Considerations	
1. Learner needs	
2. Outcomes/Objectives	
3. Standards	
4. Review	
5. Learner involvement	
6. Materials	
7. Tasks/Activities	
8. Assessment/Evaluation	

Colleen (Integrated-Skills ESL program)
I consider lesson objectives in terms of both language and content/skill standards, modalities involved, and how they might naturally intertwine, and how I'm going to assess whether or not the students have met those objectives. I think about how I will connect this lesson to the previous lesson, and to students' prior knowledge and overall unit and personal goals. I think about the order and complexity of activities and tasks. In this day and age, I also think about how I can scaffold/integrate digital literacy tasks into instruction. Finally, I figure out how I will help students notice their progress before they leave and how I will preview and connect our learning to the next lesson. And, if I remember, I try to find ways to imbue intrigue and humor to help keep a relaxed atmosphere, though that is often spontaneous.

George (Integrated Education and Training: Construction)
When working with students with occupational learning goals, I begin by hashing out what they will need to be able to do in the workplace. I then try to make a project or task that simulates a relevant workplace task. For example, for my construction class, I had students design, bid, and construct a model shed for a backyard based on the needs of a volunteer homeowner. Then I think of all the tasks and skills needed to complete the project and design lessons to lead up to the building of the shed, the project's outcome. I also try to incorporate academic skills that will serve the students' progress to other career and life goals through modules that are relevant to the needs of successful completion of the project, a well-built shed. So, these may include math lessons on measurement and area, readings on shed building and design, and presentation lessons for sales and marketing.

Nikki (Advanced ESL and College and Career Preparation)
When planning lessons, I base each unit on a theme. I am guided by three questions: "What academic vocabulary do my learners need to understand, discuss, and contribute to this theme?" "What structures do my learners need to understand and construct in order to discuss and contribute to this theme?" and "What reading skills do my learners need to enhance in order to be better close readers or in order to navigate the literature of this unit?" These guiding questions help me set content and language objectives and to start thinking about what my learners need to be able to do. Once I have set objectives, I plan ways to assess learner outcomes and activities that will get them there. I try to provide balanced activities that allow learners to meet objectives independently, in pairs, and in small groups.

Dan (Large Adult Education Center Literacy-Level Class)
Planning for me always starts with the thematic unit; the over-arching theme or line of inquiry of the coming weeks or months. Then I look at the individual parts that make up that theme and what I can address in the allotted time. These are the main content and skill goals for the students in my class. Then I get to the fun part of planning the techniques and materials I think are going to help us get towards those goals, hopefully in a sequential way that builds upon previous lessons and cycles back for review. As I'm doing that, I look to see which standards I think I am addressing and see if there are any more opportunities to adjust the lesson to include more standards work. This last part is newer to me so it takes some thinking, but it also keep things fresh trying to teach familiar topics in new ways.

Follow-up: These excerpts illustrate the range of considerations that go into planning lessons. While each of these teachers answered the question "What goes into planning the ESL classes you teach?" differently, there are some common themes and considerations in their responses, particularly in regard to determining learning objectives, identifying themes and major outcomes, and organizing the lesson in relation to learners' needs and previous learning.

In her work on course design, Kathleen Graves (2001) suggests that the process teachers use to plan for learning is best represented as a system of interconnected variables, which includes assessing needs, formulating goals and objectives, defining the context for learning, articulating beliefs, conceptualizing content, developing materials, and designing an assessment plan. While her work focuses on the larger process of designing whole courses, her emphasis on planning as a cycle, not only a set of steps to follow, is echoed in many of the teachers' thoughts on lesson planning above. In the discussion that follows, we examine these key areas of lesson planning:

- Identifying expected outcomes and clear learning objectives
- Determining learner strengths, needs, and expectations
- Connecting lessons to learners' lives and needs
- Aligning instruction to program standards as required
- Choosing materials that are relevant to the learners
- Balancing activities and content in a lesson
- Connecting one lesson to the next
- Gathering evidence of learning to assess learner achievement of objectives

We will see that all of these factors come together as a system for planning that can be flexible and responsive to learner backgrounds and needs.

6.2 Identifying learner needs

In the current landscape of adult education, many programs have adopted content standards that are focused on college and career readiness for adult learners (Chapter 10 includes an in-depth discussion of standards alignment). As discussed in Chapter 2, even intergenerational literacy and English language civics programs are placing more emphasis on work preparation than they did in the past. Even in a standards-driven environment, learners still need to have a voice in our planning and we always need to situate language acquisition in contexts that reflect learners' life circumstances and the purposes for which they are using English. Many learners come to classes to gain language skills to achieve personal goals, e.g., to communicate with grandchildren and/or go to the doctor by themselves, along with more academic and career-focused goals.

More often than not, a program has determined **learning outcomes** for each level (these may be based on state or national standards or benchmarks). If there is an assigned textbook, that, too, may shape the curriculum. In order to ensure instruction meets the needs of learners whose motivations and expectations vary greatly, a teacher needs to collaborate with learners to identify the goals for instruction within any program model.

There are a number of ways students can have a voice in shaping instruction and the teacher's job is to develop tools and techniques for eliciting learner input that are manageable for the learners. For students with developed literacy skills, brainstorming, writing down, and ranking their wants and needs are manageable tasks. Low-literacy learners can articulate and prioritize their wants and needs as well by using pictures and drawings that represent their ideas. At a family literacy program I visited, a teacher asked mothers to articulate parenting and language goals, and then had them create visuals using photographs and drawings, which were posted throughout the room. Another teacher had learners create collages of their goals and aspirations, which they presented to others in class.

Learners can complete can-do surveys based on the outcomes that have been determined in a particular curriculum or for a particular lesson. Imagine you are starting a unit on filling in job applications online. Create a simple pre-assessment with the major outcomes of the unit and a simple can-do rating scale.

	I can do this.	This is a little difficult for me. I can do it with some help from others.	This is very difficult for me. I need a lot of help from others.	No way, I can't do this. It's too difficult.
Find the company website.				
Link to the application.				
Fill in the application on a computer.				
List my experience.				
What else do you need to learn? Tell me here.				

Can-do descriptors adapted from CAELA Network (N.D.) *Assessing Learner Needs in the Adult ESL Classroom*

The results of a survey like this allow a teacher to prioritize instruction, focusing on those areas of most concern for a group as a whole. Many programs use individual learning plans and goal setting as part of the intake process, but these processes should not be one-time events that occur only at the beginning of a course. Learners should revisit and rearticulate their needs on an ongoing basis, which means that needs assessment becomes an integral part of day-to-day planning (more on ongoing assessment and self- assessments are covered in Chapter 9).

Lesson planning approaches

Avoiding the "fun" activities-driven approach: backward design

I have found that many teachers new to ESL put too much emphasis on activities before considering learner needs, final outcomes and standards, objectives, context, and connections to previous learning. I always remember the time when a student teacher in our Certificate Program came to my office for advice about her upcoming lesson in the practicum. Our conversation went something like this:

Betsy: So what theme or language area do you have in mind?

Chris: I really want to do a find-someone-who mingle about personal interests.

Betsy: Well, that might be an activity you could use at some point, but it all depends on the objectives you have for the lesson. What have you noticed the students need more work on as you've observed the class these past weeks?

Chris: Well, I know that a lot of them want to talk about jobs, but I really thought that activity you demonstrated on personal interests was fun.

What is guiding Chris's decisions about what to teach in the lesson? Like Chris, many teachers think of teaching as a series of activities when, in fact, the activities may be among the last things to consider in planning. As the conversation continued, I urged Chris to determine some kind of culminating outcome related to the theme of jobs, and then to identify the skills and language around that outcome that might be useful for these students. She ended up doing a lesson on reading job announcements, which led to mock interviews the next day. She included a personal and professional interests survey as one of her pre-reading activities.

Starting lesson planning by first determining what the desired results are for a lesson is called backward design (Wiggins and McTigue 2005). From there, teachers need to determine the evidence of learning they plan to gather (final activities, products), and only then do they choose or develop the lesson activities, tasks and materials, as depicted in Figure 6.1.

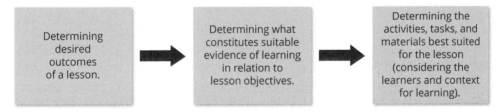

Figure 6.1 Using a Backward Design Approach to Lesson Planning

Jamie teaches pre-beginning ESL and English for childcare center jobs. See how she applies the backward design approach in her setting, a large community-based program that serves large numbers of refugees who have settled in Minneapolis.

> *I use backward design in the lesson planning process. The instructional objectives (or desired outcomes) frame the entire lesson. These instructional objectives are derived from content standards (CCRS, TIF, and Northstar[1]), as well as any career-specific standards. I then consider when and how assessment will occur during the lesson, and these assessments can be either formative or summative. The instructional objectives are then written in student-friendly language, so students will understand what they will be learning and why they will be learning it. All lessons have the same*

---

[1] These represent the College and Career Readiness Standards for Adult Education, the Transitions Integration Framework, and Northstar Digital Literacy Standards

> routines, so learners can focus on content instead of trying to figure out what they are supposed to do. I use the same learning task formats—but the content changes from week to week. Finally, I consider how I might scaffold up for my more advanced learners.

When we might apply "central" design
In this standards and outcomes-driven approach to backward design planning, where do approaches such as the Language Experience Approach, project-based learning, or a fully participatory approach as outlined in 2.10—where the outcomes emerge collaboratively with the learners and as a lesson progresses—fit in? This is where we may draw on a more **central design** (Richards 2013) approach, where a teacher begins with class materials and activities, then builds the lesson from there. In the case of LEA where a class generates its own text or in a lesson where a problem in learners' lives is the basis for instruction, central design may make more sense than backwards design. What is essential is that our planning be purposeful and in keeping with the needs of learners in our classes. Even with more participatory approaches, we can have a very clear road map for the direction of the lesson; the outcomes will be related to the final products created collaboratively by learners with the assistance of the teacher.

Additional considerations
Equally important in the planning process is ensuring that your lessons have a balance of interactions, language skills, and learning modes. McKay and Tom (2000) compare a balanced lesson to a balanced meal, where a lack of balance will make the lesson less than satisfactory for many of the learners. They suggest that teachers evaluate their choices of activities in a lesson in terms of groupings, skills, difficulty, and learning modes; there should be a variety of interactions and learning modes and a logical progression of difficulty as learners move to a culminating task in the lesson. Tarone and Parrish (1994) found that learners may exhibit variation in accuracy across different language tasks; learners may do extremely well on a discrete-point, fill-in-the blank activity, yet show minimal accuracy when using the language in an open-ended task; the communicative demands of a task may affect performance. These findings underscore the importance of providing an array of activity types to practice particular language points within each lesson.

Planning should also account for the level of critical thinking, overall challenge, and rigor that the tasks, topics, and teacher questions generate in a lesson. In evaluating a lesson, teachers can ask themselves the following questions:

- Do the activities challenge learners to create extended and meaningful responses, rather than one-word utterances?
- Does the lesson move learners beyond gathering factual information to analyzing and interpreting information?
- Have I included questions and tasks that elicit deep analysis of material, even with beginning-level learners?

The topics we choose also have an impact on learning. If you were enrolled in a language class, would you rather learn about celebrations and holidays or differences regarding deep cultural values and beliefs? In programs and curricula for newcomers, the topics themselves are often quite basic and represent tasks learners may have figured out on their own and/or with the support of family members (e.g., reading bus schedules). We can include topics that engage the intellect of learners; those can derive from interests they have expressed to you through needs assessment or informal conversations. Table 6.1 provides examples of the topics that could supplement what you might find in a curriculum with more of a life-skills orientation.

Table 6.1 Engaging Topics in a Life-Skills Curriculum

Topics Found in Many Adult ESL Curricula	Content That Could Be Added
Getting around the community ⟶	Local, national, or world geography; demographics (population, languages spoken, religions)
Talking about life experiences ⟶	History; current events; immigration trends
Foods and healthy eating ⟶	Causes of common diseases; mental health issues; access to medical services
Celebrations and holidays ⟶	Cultural traditions; sociology and anthropology
School ⟶	Educational systems and practices; accessing educational opportunities; benefits of first-language maintenance (using the L1 with kids at home)

(Adapted from Parrish 2015b)

Finally, we always need to consider the learner-centered principles outlined in Section 1.3. Those can and must be enacted in our lessons, even when external standards might be guiding our planning. Ignoring those principles can lead to a lack of motivation and agency on the part of learners.

6.4 Sitting down to plan

As was evident in the teacher accounts at the beginning of the chapter, lesson planning varies depending on the teaching context, program curriculum, and even the approach or philosophy to teaching. While program standards and outcomes are there to guide your planning, each class develops its own road map to meet its destination; lesson plans become the teacher's road map. If you are using a textbook, sometimes the themes and activities in the book determine the objectives for the day. In a class using the Language Experience Approach, the class-generated text becomes the focus of many of the teacher's decisions about what areas of language to practice. Some components of lesson planning logically precede others, for example, researching a grammar rule and patterns before designing an activity that practices that grammar point, or choosing the context or theme before collecting visuals and realia. Table 6.2 outlines the areas a teacher needs to consider in planning.

Table 6.2 Lesson Planning Components

1 What is the expected outcome for the lesson (or unit)?	Will students create a poster, write a report, make a presentation, or build something as in George's occupational class?
2 What standards does the lesson seek to address?	In a lesson where learners gather information from peers on a topic and then write a report, are they working towards a standard like this? *CCR Writing Anchor 1* *Write arguments to support claims in an analysis of substantive topics or texts, using valid reasoning and relevant and sufficient evidence.* Regardless of program standards, how can you layer the lesson with rigorous academic and career readiness skills needed in today's world (e.g., using graphic organizers in reading lessons to practice note-taking)?

3	What will the students accomplish in this lesson? The answers to this question become the **learning objectives** for the lesson.	Identifying and articulating clear learning **objectives** for the day helps to guide learning. These should reflect what *learners* will accomplish through the lesson, not on what the teacher does in the lesson, and they represent the necessary components needed to accomplish the broader lesson/unit goal or outcome. If the lesson outcome is to have a class debate on a topic, these may be some of the learning objectives: • Students will present opinions on a topic. • Students will present evidence from course readings to support claims. In a literacy-level class working on word families with vocabulary from a class-generated text, an objective may be: • Students will be able to sort words from a story in sets according to the initial consonant sounds regardless of spelling (e.g., fish/photo). In multilevel classes (which is the norm in adult ESL), be aware that you may need to have varying expectations of learners.
4	What specific **targeted language** do I want the students to produce? What are the language functions and language forms (grammar and vocabulary) they will need to be successful with the tasks I assign?	You need to identify the **language** students need in order to accomplish the real-world tasks that you assign. The **targeted language** is the linguistic focus for the day. If you want to end your lesson with small group discussions where learners take a position about a reading, is one objective for students to produce phrases for elaborating on others' ideas in a discussion? Are they learning phrases for interrupting others politely? If you are working on making claims with evidence, do you want them to use phrases such as, *According to the reading* . . .? In a lesson on writing résumés, you may want to focus on simple past tense.
5	If I am teaching grammar or an academic language function (e.g., making comparisons), what do I need to know about the form and meaning of the grammar?	If students are talking about life circumstances and creating a short autobiography, you may need to work on the present perfect tense: *Subject + have/has + past participle* (I have lived here for seven years). Do you know what a past participle is? Do you know when to use *for* or *since* with this structure? Do you know when we use this tense in English instead of the simple past (I moved here in 2012)? Even if you don't teach explicit grammar rules or use the grammar terms with students, you need to do your homework about the forms (see suggested grammar resources). In a lesson on making comparisons, what *language forms* do we use to show differences and what do we use to show similarities? What about phonological considerations? Consider the various pronunciations of the –ed endings or ways we place emphasis on certain words in a polite request.

6	If this is a reading, writing, listening or speaking lesson, what skills and strategies will learners practice?	In a reading lesson, students may need to read for the main idea and then for details. How will I get them to do a close reading for details and to make inferences about the text?
		In an LEA lesson, students may use the class-generated text to practice sequencing or recognizing sound-spelling correspondences.
		In listening to a short, authentic video, students may be asked to listen for details and practice note taking.
		Note: We should strive to have a balance of reading, writing, listening, and speaking throughout units, so keep that in mind when planning.
7	What contexts or themes could I use that are relevant to students, the objectives, and the targeted language?	Many times your program has identified learning outcomes for the level you are teaching. Contexts or themes you choose to meet these outcomes can vary depending on your students. If there is a unit on transportation, what forms of public transportation do they use? Perhaps they already know how to manage the systems in their community, so you can choose more challenging content such as exploring the benefits to the community of a new light-rail system. Use their life circumstances as the context for presenting and practicing language.
8	What materials have been provided and what are some authentic materials, visuals, realia, etc. that I could use related to the context?	Evaluate how well the materials that have been provided (the program curriculum or a textbook) meet the learning outcomes of the lesson. In a basic skills class for newcomers, you may add circulars or online ads for lessons on shopping. In a lesson on choosing a school for their children, local school websites could be used. Bring in authentic informational charts and graphs related to lesson themes to give learners practice managing a variety of text representations.
9	What are the digital literacy skills associated with the learning outcomes?	In a lesson on issuing a complaint to a landlord, learners will most likely do this with an online form; create a semi-authentic form that learners can fill in on their phones. In an advanced writing class, using shared documents to give learners practice with collaborative writing and with using word processing tools would match real-world digital literacy practices.
10	How does this lesson relate to previous lessons? What do students already know? What can I recycle?	Constantly review and recycle language and themes from one lesson to the next. We do not learn something after one try. Also consider logical sequencing, for example, a lesson on identifying personal skills should precede a lesson on writing résumés. Good textbooks usually do the sequencing for you, or can provide models to consider/adapt.
11	What activities best serve to move learners towards meeting the lesson objectives?	Choose and develop tasks and activities that naturally generate the targeted language that is the focus for the day. If a learning objective is "Learners will make suggestions using correct modals (you could, you should, you might)," create a situation where there is a genuine need to use this language, for example, having students give advice to one another on how to access resources in the community based on personal experience.
		Choose and create activities that allow learners to use the language they need to know in *their* lives.

12 How will I evaluate learning outcomes?	Always end the lesson (or a series of lessons) with an activity or task that allows learners to *demonstrate* their level of comfort and ability with learning objectives for the lesson. Observe and take careful note of areas that are most difficult for them so that you can review and recycle in later lessons. Ask learners to reflect on what they learned each day. In lessons with a concrete artifact (written piece, poster, small group presentations), use a rubric or checklist to assess learning.

📋 Task 6.2

Examine the following lessons from Chapter 3 in Section 3.3 using the questions below. Sample Lesson 1: *Talking about expenses*; Sample Lesson 2: *Sharing life stories/simple past tense*

1. What is the final outcome, culminating product or task that will provide evidence of learning?

2. What are the learning objectives and how are they articulated?

3. Is there a balance between whole group, small group, and individual work? Is the grouping appropriate for the task at hand? How would you describe the progressions of learning activities?

4. What language skills has the teacher integrated? Is there a balance of reading, writing, listening, and speaking?

5. Where is there attention to critical thinking or digital literacy?

6. Does the teacher promote a variety of learning modes (tactile, kinesthetic, visual)? Will this lesson appeal to a variety of learning preferences?

7. In what ways are the activities and materials connected to the learners' lives?

8. How successfully do you believe the activities might move learners towards meeting the objectives of the lesson and what tasks serve to assess that learning?

Follow-up: Compare your answers with others in your class. Are there any things that you would do differently in the lessons you evaluated? You can use this checklist to reflect on and evaluate your own lessons and those that you observe.

This section has examined the many considerations teachers need to take into account as they plan lessons from one day to the next. How does all of this relate to the lesson planning requirements of a school? What does the final lesson plan look like? Is there a set convention for lesson plans? Many districts provide teachers with templates for lesson plans. The problem with that is that no one template could possibly account for every type of lesson; that is why I have presented lesson planning as a process that brings multiple considerations together. Both Jamie and Colleen shared a general sequence to their lessons as follows:

Jamie: *To address these objectives, activities are planned in the following sequence: introduction, explanation and modeling, guided practice, independent practice, and extension. For my pre-beginning learners, this looks like the "I do, We do, You do" approach in which new concepts are scaffolded and there is gradual release of control to students.*

Colleen: *Additional considerations include how to make the lesson as student-centered as possible (including strategic groupings, individual or team tasks, and ratio of student to teacher* *talk time), as well how to scaffold academic language and tasks, including explicit instruction and gradual release of responsibility, controlled practice to more communicative practice.*

Many adult education programs apply the stages that Jamie referred to above: introduction, explanation and modeling, guided practice, independent practice, and extension. Colleen also refers to moving from more controlled to more communicative tasks in her planning process. See how the following example templates mirror those general stages; these lesson plan templates in Table 6.3 illustrate a range of lesson types and designs. Remember that there are samples in Chapters 3, 4, and 5.

Table 6.3 Sample Lesson Plan Templates

Reading lesson (see Chapter 5 for sample lesson plans) **Class description:** Setting: Time: Materials: Assumptions:	**Final lesson outcome:** **Standards addressed** (as appropriate): **Objectives:** Learners will: (These objectives will be related to reading strategies: anticipate content, read to confirm prediction, make inferences, make claims based on evidence in the text, etc. Depending on the pre- and post-activities, there may be listening, speaking, writing, or vocabulary objectives as well.)	**Lesson stages:** Pre-reading: Reading activities: Follow-up/post-reading:
Integrated and contextualized language lesson (see Chapter 3 for sample lesson plans) **Class description:** Setting: Time: Materials: Assumptions:	**Final lesson outcome:** **Standards addressed** (as appropriate): **Objectives:** Learners will: (These will be related to the competencies and functions presented and practiced in the lesson as well as linguistic competence: grammar, vocabulary, spelling, and pronunciation)	**Lesson stages:** Engage with language in a real-world context: Draw learners' attention to patterns and check learning: Engage in practice for meaningful purposes: • Focus on accuracy • Focus on fluency Application/extension: Assessment/evaluation:

LEA lesson / Whole-part-whole approach	Final lesson outcome:	Lesson stages:
(See Chapter 5 for lesson guidelines with these approaches)	**Standards addressed** (as appropriate):	Conduct experience and generate story or provide simple text:
Class description:	**Objectives:**	Engage learners with the story; relate to own lives:
Setting:	Learners will:	Provide multiple language activities that revolve around the text:
Time:	(These will start with completing the experience and the other objectives will relate to developing basic literacy: copying the text, identifying sounds/ letters, categorizing words starting with same sounds, etc.)	Engage with the theme of the text and connect to their own lives (application/ extension)
Materials:		
Assumptions:		

Find out what the expectations of your program are and design lessons that are in keeping with those expectations while at the same acknowledging that there is no "one size fits all" plan.

6.5 Building continuity from day to day

Teachers need to think beyond day-to-day planning in the choices and decisions they make about their lessons. Dan refers to planning at the unit level and then he looks at the individual parts that make up that theme. Andrea uses a whole-part-whole language experience approach in her class with emergent readers (see 5.4. D). See in Table 6.4 how planning in her context is done in one-week blocks.

Table 6.4 A One-Week Plan for a Literacy-Level Class

Each class period: three hours

Monday	Tuesday	Wednesday	Thursday	Friday
Preview vocabulary (pests, product names). Make predictions about experiences class will have at hardware store. Field trip to the hardware store to buy pest-control products.	Recount the experience at the hardware store. Use this to generate LEA story. Write story together. Copy story; give story a title.	Read aloud and silently. Sentence scramble (reorder words in sentences from LEA story). Sequence sentences from story.	Multiple tasks on sight words, word families. Cloze activity with text (leave out all verbs).	Co-construct dialogue for calling landlord. Role-play calling landlord to report issue in apartment.

At this level, learners take part in only one or two activities a day, so a teacher needs to think of balancing learning not only within a lesson, but also across lessons over an extended period of time. If we look at only one class session in the one-week plan above, there may not be a lot of variation of skills, modes of learning, or interactions. But if we look at the whole week, we see a very balanced plan that includes reading, writing, listening, and speaking as well as the language for making a complaint to a landlord.

Another way to build continuity in ESL classes is to establish **curricular routines**. When I asked Kristin about her lesson planning process, she started by talking about routines:

Kristin (literacy-level class for emergent readers)

My lesson planning process really starts with routines, for example, the writing out of dates, describing the weather, recounting their previous day's activities, or a letter of the day. I know that my learners spend less time struggling to understand directions when I reuse familiar routines and formats so each day's content has a routine tailored to it. I can focus on differentiating the content for the specific learners I'm serving that day.

Early in her career, my colleague Celeste shared with me that planning for 15 hours a week with the same group of intermediate-level learners was a daunting task. She decided to build some routines into her weekly plan: a listening lesson every Wednesday after the break, a reading lesson on Thursday, Fridays for the computer lab, all related to the overarching theme for the week. Here is an outline of the reading routine she used every Thursday:

1. At the beginning of class, each table was given one word used in the context of the reading and had to create a simple definition and picture for their word (Celeste chose words that build schema for the reading).

2. Each group sent a member from their table to the board to present their word.

3. Based on these key words, Celeste elicited predictions about the story and wrote them on the board. Learners then read to confirm those predictions.

4. Learners read for more detail with specific questions that were assigned as homework.

Celeste chose short readings that related to themes she was covering that week. I observed her class on two separate Thursdays and was struck by how quickly the groups engaged in these pre-reading activities. No time was lost in trying to explain the tasks and the learners took control of the entire process.

A final example for building continuity in lesson planning is to develop units or a series of lessons around a line of inquiry (Vinogradov 2016). The figure below shows how a series of lessons revolve around the question: *What are the benefits of early childhood education?* Notice the ways that digital literacy, reading strategies, writing, vocabulary, and grammar are woven together as learners work towards creating the culminating product: a poster on the benefits of preschool and the options available to them in the community.

Exploring Preschool in the U.S.: High-Beginning/Low-Intermediate

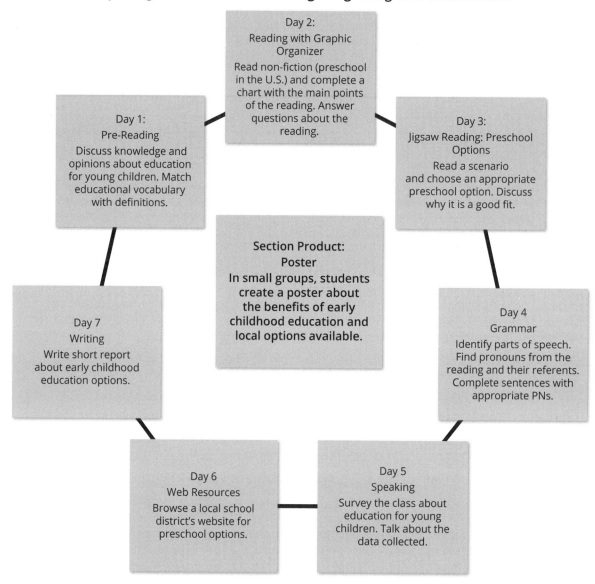

Day 2:
Reading with Graphic Organizer
Read non-fiction (preschool in the U.S.) and complete a chart with the main points of the reading. Answer questions about the reading.

Day 1:
Pre-Reading
Discuss knowledge and opinions about education for young children. Match educational vocabulary with definitions.

Day 3:
Jigsaw Reading: Preschool Options
Read a scenario and choose an appropriate preschool option. Discuss why it is a good fit.

Section Product:
Poster
In small groups, students create a poster about the benefits of early childhood education and local options available.

Day 7
Writing
Write short report about early childhood education options.

Day 4
Grammar
Identify parts of speech. Find pronouns from the reading and their referents. Complete sentences with appropriate PNs.

Day 6
Web Resources
Browse a local school district's website for preschool options.

Day 5
Speaking
Survey the class about education for young children. Talk about the data collected.

St. Paul Public Schools, R. M. Hubbs Center for Lifelong Learning

Conclusion

Planning lessons is a complex process that needs to take into account learner strengths, needs, and expectations. When using backward design, we start by identifying final outcomes and our assessments before mapping out the lesson activities or tasks and procedures. Teachers identify learning objectives that are achievable and related to what the *learners* will do in the lesson, not what the teacher will do. Those objectives should promote higher order thinking skills and challenge the learners to go beyond basic skills development. Using themes, projects, routines, lines of inquiry, and review all help to establish continuity and build learner confidence. Regardless of the approach you use to lesson planning, lessons need to be flexible and responsive to what happens on any given day, while at the same time guiding the learners and teachers on the best path possible to meeting the learning objectives. In the next section, we turn to the importance of planning for interactions that occur within every lesson so that teacher language, directions for activities, or checking questions enhance rather than get in the way of learning.

Part II: Teacher and learner interactions

6.6 Teacher language

The language that teachers use in class, or **teacher talk**, can have a tremendous impact on learner success with a lesson. This teacher talk falls into several categories:

> Directions for activities
> Direct instruction   Warm-up chats
> Transitions   Feedback   Questioning
> Comprehension checks

Teacher talk is appropriate in an ESL class provided that it is conveyed using language that is *accessible* to students. Which of these teacher instructions in French can you understand?

a.   Écoutez et répétez, s'il vous plait.

b.   Ouvrez vos livres à la page 76.

c.   J'aimerez que vous m'écoutiez et que vous répétiez les phrases suivantes après moi.

d.   Si vous voulez, vous pouvez ouvrir vos livres à la page 76.

I am guessing that many of you could ascertain the meaning of items a. (*Listen and repeat, please*) and b. (*Open your books to page 76*); they are direct and to the point, and within the reach of most learners, especially when combined with gestures. But what about c. (*I'd like you to listen and to repeat the following sentences after me.*) and d. (*If you would like, you can open your books to page 76.*)? Unless you've studied French, I imagine that many of the words were out of your reach. Items c. and d. include **extraneous teacher talk**, i.e., the majority of the words are not needed to convey the intended message. Not only that, but the language used is indirect and grammatically complex. It may seem that no teacher would use language like samples c. and d. with learners new to English, but as you read the examples below, you may be able to imagine yourself saying these things:

e.   Would you mind moving over there next to Alexis?

f.   Who can tell me what is happening in this picture?

g.   What kind of weekend did you have?

h.   The first thing we're going to do today is a paired reading.

In fact, many teachers new to teaching English fear that by simplifying their language too much, they will talk down to students, which is a valid concern. Minimizing teacher talk does not mean dummying down language to the point of using incomplete, unnatural utterances.

On the other hand, using indirect, polite language can make the directions ineffectual to the learner who hasn't acquired polite modals or indirect questions. *"What did you do this weekend?"* is much easier to understand than the question: *"What kind of weekend did you have?"* Giving a step-by-step account of each stage in your lesson (*The first thing . . . , Now I'll give you a handout . . .*) adds no value to the instruction. All of the items above represent the way we naturally interact with other highly proficient English speakers; in an ESL class, excessive words can clutter the air, making it difficult for the beginning-level learner to pull out what is truly important.

6.7 Maximizing learner involvement

Connecting instruction to learners' lives, using project-based and participatory approaches, and including ongoing classroom-based assessments (see Chapter 9) are all ways to maximize learner involvement (Finn Miller 2010). Learner involvement is also about the roles students take on during the lesson. With every decision you make about a lesson, you need to think about the roles and responsibilities learners take on so that they are doing most of the work and taking the lead. When teachers in our program reflect on their lessons, I ask them a question that I learned from Jack Richards at a TESOL Convention session on teacher reflection: *What did I do in this lesson that my learners could have done?* This question has become something of a mantra for me because far too often I see teachers doing all of the work for the learners.

📋 Task 6.3

Read each of these excerpts from adult ESL lesson plans and answer these questions:

What are the roles of the students and teacher in each one?

What does the teacher do that the students could be doing?

How can you change the scenario so that the students take on more of a teaching role?

Sample 1: Review of sequence words and imperatives (workplace English class)

> T gives each student an item from a kit for building a small bookshelf.

> T gives each step of the instructions: *First, place the top of the table face-down on a flat surface.* Learners come to the front of the room and complete their step when called out.

Sample 2: Correcting a listening activity after viewing an authentic how-to video online

> After completing a listening activity, T displays a graphic organizer that learners filled in while listening and elicits correct answers from the whole class, typing in responses she hears.

Sample 3: Practice of numeracy using grocery ads

> T calls out the names of two items in a newspaper circular. Students scan to find items and tell teacher which item is a better deal, taking into consideration the number of ounces, price per pound, etc.

Follow-up: The instructional choices the teachers made in these lessons are sound in terms of the content they have chosen and the activities they have prepared, but what is lacking is an awareness of learner responsibility and involvement in these segments. If these teachers asked themselves the question: *"What did I do in this lesson that my learners could have done?,"* they may have come up with some of the solutions you found in the task above. How could Sample 1 be constructed so that the learners are conveying the instructions for building the bookcase? How could learners give one another feedback after a listening task in Sample 2? As you plan your lessons, critically evaluate the roles and responsibilities you've given learners *before* you walk into class. The more learners take responsibility for activities, the better; the more you are talking and leading, the more they are only listening and following.

6.8 Giving directions

One of the most important (and most difficult) things for new teachers is learning how to give clear directions. If the students don't know what they are supposed to be doing, they won't get very far. My mottos have always been "Just do it!" and "Less is more."

"Just do it!" represents the need for teachers to demonstrate, or *do* an activity, rather than explain it. Once having demonstrated the activity with a student, have two students try to demonstrate one example before handing the activity off to the whole class.

"Less is more": the fewer words used, the better. Lengthy or multistep explanations are difficult for beginning-level learners to follow. Identify the steps to the activity, and demonstrate each step, one at a time, as it is needed to complete the task at hand.

📋 **Task 6.4**

Look at the sample activity.

Talking About Interests and Hobbies

1. How do you like to spend your time after work or on the weekend? Circle three things you like to do. Cross out three that you never do. Write three other things you like to do in your free time.

swim	visit family	listen to music
go to the library	garden	cook for friends and family
visit friends	sew	watch television
take walks	exercise	read

Three other things you like to do: _____

2. Now talk to the other students in class and find the person who has the most things in common with you. Ask that person the following questions:

   How often do you do that activity? What do you like about that activity?

   What are some things you did in your country that you can't do in the U.S.?

Now read two versions of directions for completing the activity. Which directions are more effective and why? Talk to your partner or write your answers in your journal.

Sample Directions for Activity: Talking About Interests and Hobbies

Version A

Teacher distributes handout to class.

Teacher: Now you are going to talk about things you like to do after work or on the weekend. I want you to circle three things you like to do, cross out three you don't like to do, and add three more of your own. After you finish, talk to people in class and find the person who has the most in common with you. Ask them the questions at the bottom of your handout.

Version B

Teacher: Mai, what do you like to do on the weekends?

Mai: I like to read.

Teacher: So do I. (T projects sample handout on white board and circles "read.") Do you ever sew?

Mai: No.

Teacher: Neither do I. (T crosses off "sew.")

(T distributes handout to class.) "Marco, what do you do on the weekend?"

Marco: Play soccer. (T uses questioning look.)

Teacher: Do you see soccer on the list? (points to overhead)

Class: No. (T asks Marco to write it in on the blank. T and class now read instructions together.)

Teacher: What do you circle?

Class: Things we do on the weekend.

Teacher: What do you cross out?

Class: Things we don't do.

Class completes Part 1 individually and then T gives instructions for Part 2 through a similar demonstration.

Follow-up: What is the key difference between the two versions? In Version A, the teacher describes the activity, but doesn't demonstrate what learners need to do. She doesn't check for understanding or have learners interact with her. While Version B might seem longer, there are no lengthy explanations. The teacher is having a meaningful conversation with the students as she demonstrates the activity. The teacher and students walk through a sample of the activity together; she asks checking questions that allow learners to demonstrate their understanding, and most importantly, she models what they need to do.

6.9 Checking learner understanding

A literacy instructor who was new to working with immigrant families shared the following incident with me:

> We organized a special after-school meeting with families in our program. I told my students that we would be meeting from 2:30 until 4:30 in the school cafeteria. I arrived at 2:20 to set things up and waited for the families to arrive. Two of the families came at 2:30, but the others arrived between 3:00 and 4:00. One family came right before we were finishing up the meeting. I was so surprised and quite disappointed. I asked the families why they came so late and they appeared confused, saying they came between 2:30 and 4:30 as instructed.

As someone who has worked with language learners for over 30 years, this story did not surprise me at all. For one thing, in many cultures, coming between 2:30 and 4:30 means arriving *any* time between 2:30 and 4:30. I also know that many people who have not had experience working with immigrants do not check for understanding when they give instructions, or if they do, they often ask, *Do you understand?* or *Is that clear?*, to which the students say yes or nod their heads. In this case, what the learners understood was quite different from what the teacher intended. Understanding can be about:

• Language: The learners misunderstand the words used by the teacher.

• Culture: The students' cultural concepts may be different, e.g., the use of *from_ to _* to denote a time frame.

- Background: The learners' understanding and interpretations of events are shaped by their own life experiences, which are different from the teacher's and from their classmates'. This means that everyone in the same room can have different interpretations of the same events.

Why do people say they understand when in fact they may not? There are a number of reasons, many of which are true for all of us:

- The learners believe they have understood.
- They want to show respect for the speaker; in some cultures, saying, "I don't understand" means, *You weren't clear so I couldn't understand you.*
- They may want to save face (as we all do).

Given these factors, teachers need to check for understanding in ways other than asking, "Do you understand?" Had the literacy teacher used **checking questions** like the following, there may not have been confusion about the start time of the meeting:

Teacher: The meeting is from 2:30 to 4:30. So, what time do you need be in the cafeteria? Class: 2:30. (If they reply that they can arrive between 2:30 and 4:30, you can clarify and check again. The checking question reveals the holes in comprehension without intimidating the students.)

Teacher: How long is the meeting? Class: Two hours.

This same approach can be used when teaching language points.

Grammar: You have been working on the present perfect (I *have lived* here for 12 years), which the students confuse with the simple past (I *lived* there for 12 years).

Teacher: I have lived here for 12 years. When I did I move here? Do I *still* live here?

Vocabulary: Teacher: I need to hire a babysitter for my kids. I want someone who is *prompt*. Does a prompt person come late or on time? My kids get off the bus at 3:00. What time does the babysitter need to be at my house?

Notice that these checking questions allow the learner to demonstrate their understanding. This kind of checking can be done in nonverbal ways as well, for example, *Yes/No* cards that are held up in response to a question. Asking students to complete simple tasks can serve to check understanding as well, for example, placing words on a continuum to show degrees:

Least to most frequent: *never, rarely, sometimes, often, always*

Strength of likes/dislikes: *hate, don't like, like a little, like a lot, really like, love*

📄 **Task 6.5**

The following phrases were used in a beginning level, intergenerational family literacy class. The italicized word in each example seemed to be new for many learners. With a partner or on your own, choose the question(s) that would best check a beginning learner's understanding of the word in italics, or write a checking question of your own. Number one has been done for you.

1. You'll need to bring a record of your child's *vaccinations*.

    a. <u>Who gives vaccinations?</u>

    b. Do you understand vaccinations?

    c. <u>What do vaccinations stop?</u>

In number 1, a. and c. allow the learner to demonstrate that they understand that a doctor or nurse gives vaccinations and that vaccinations stop diseases. Question b. could elicit a "yes" with no guarantee of actual understanding.

2. They encourage the schools to provide *nutritious* meals.

   a. What does nutritious mean?

   b. Give some examples of nutritious foods.

   c. Which of these foods are nutritious? *candy, an apple, whole grain bread, cheese, potato chips*

   d. _____

3. *Transitions* can be difficult for young children.

   a. When do transitions happen?

   b. What is a transition?

   c. Do you know what transition means?

   d. _____

Follow-up: There may be some variation in your responses, but what is important is that the questions you chose or wrote allow learners to *demonstrate* their understanding of a concept. The questions themselves need to be comprehensible to learners as well, and taking the time to plan and script these questions in advance benefits everyone.

6.10 Questions to promote critical thinking

In Chapter 3, we explored how using Bloom's Taxonomy of higher-order thinking can guide the development of classroom tasks to promote critical thinking in adult ESL classrooms. It can also guide the questioning techniques we use, posing questions that move beyond recall and up to analysis or application. Imagine you were to encounter a reading and accompanying questions like these in the curriculum you are using:

Where does Josephina work?
What are her hours?
How many brothers and sisters does she have?
How does she help her mother?

Read the story about Josephina's daily activities and answer the questions.
Josephina's New Job
Josephina has a new job. She now works at Family Mart. She works part time from 7:00 in the morning to noon. Now she can be with her two younger sisters and brother in the afternoon and then go to school to work on her English in the evening.
Josephina usually helps her sister with homework in the afternoon. Sometimes they go to the playground near their house. They often help their mother. They wash clothes and help clean the house. Josephina enjoys her new schedule.

(Adapted from Parrish 2015b)

Notice that all of the questions are display questions that require no analysis or interpretation of the text. Learners could scan the text to answer the questions without necessarily understanding much of what they have read. While we may start with questions like those, what happens if we ask learners questions like these?

- When does Josephina take her brother and sister to the playground? Do you think they go every day? How do you know?
- What do they do more often: help their mom or go to the playground? How do you know?
- How is Josephina's life different? How do we know?
- Why do you think she likes her new schedule?

Now learners need to look at the text closely to answer the questions. They need to interpret the meaning of *sometimes, usually,* and *often*, so they are getting practice with some basic academic language. They need to interpret that her new job reflects a positive change based on the word "enjoy" and analyze how time to work, help family, and continue to go to school could be affecting her satisfaction. This example demonstrates how the questions we ask lead to differing levels of thinking.

In many classrooms, we see a traditional teacher-led question-and-answer routine called Initiate-Response-Evaluate (I-R-E) (TEAL 2013). This routine may check for factual information but it does not always encourage higher-order thinking. In an I-R-E sequence, the teacher initiates a question that normally has one right answer. This is followed by teacher feedback and involves the teacher working with one student at a time. One improvement over this is to wait for a number of replies and ask the whole class to weigh in on which is correct. Let's see how we can create questions that prompt higher levels of thinking. In their book *Making Thinking Visible*, Ritchart, Church, and Morrison (2011) encourage questioning techniques that serve to reveal a learners' thinking process. They propose three ways of accomplishing this:

- Modeling an interest in ideas: By asking genuine questions of learners, those for which the teacher doesn't already know the answers, we encourage a climate of reciprocal learning.
- Constructing understanding: These are questions that serve to advance learners' understanding by connecting and extending ideas, or by making interpretations.
- Facilitating and clarifying thinking: The key question here is, "What makes you say that?" (34). The authors suggest that this question reflects a high level of genuine interest on the part of the teacher.

Ritchart, Church, and Morrison (2011: 31–36)

In addition to these teacher questioning techniques is the need to provide English language learners with the actual *language* frames they will need to make that thinking visible (Zwiers and Crawford 2011), for example, *It would seem to me; As I consider all the evidence . . .*

Prompting learner questions
It is not only the teacher who should be asking questions that really matter. Rothstein and Santana (2011) suggest a technique called the **Question Formulation Technique (QFT)** for turning questioning in the classroom over to students. They argue that learners haven't always been encouraged to ask the questions in school but that by doing so, they deepen their engagement and understanding of content. Learners need a process for generating questions that can be used for any number of purposes in the classroom: in response to a reading, to explore a new topic, in preparation for a project. QFT entails these steps:

- Generating questions: Generate as many as possible without judgment and without trying to answer them right away.
- Categorizing questions into closed- and open-ended questions: What are the pros and cons of each? What happens if we turn closed questions into open-ended questions?
- Prioritizing and using the questions: Teachers and learners together decide on how to use the questions. Which will best lead to creative thinking with the task at hand? How can the questions bring multiple perspectives together?

Consider how you could use QFT in a jigsaw reading lesson (see 5.8), in project-based learning, in a problem-solving task (see 4.9 G), or even for analysis of grammar point in a contextualized language lesson (see 3.3).

Some important reminders

Whether you are giving directions, organizing activities, eliciting language, asking checking questions, or giving feedback, here are some important reminders for working with those new to English.

- Use plenty of **wait time** during whole class instructional time. Tsui (2001) notes that this is a time when learners may feel particularly vulnerable as others are awaiting a reply. Early research on wait time (Rowe 1986) suggests that even increasing wait time to three to four seconds results in greater student output. My own observations (of myself and others) have shown me that most teachers are guilty of giving far too little wait time after asking students a question.

- Provide alternatives to teacher-whole group questioning. Oftentimes the most confident students are the ones who volunteer answers right away. Give learners some thinking time, time to record some ideas, and then opportunity to engage in partner practice before reporting to the whole group.

- Students may come from cultures where students do not question teachers (Chowdhury 2003). Let them know that requests for clarification, simplification, or repetition are welcomed and expected. Teach the phrases they'll need to ask for clarification, e.g., *Could you please repeat that?* Provide learners with language frames that represent other common interactions or routines in your classes.

- Frequently check for understanding. Do not assume that a nod or "Yes, I understand" means the student has understood.

6.11 Learning strategies development

Learning shouldn't stop when students walk out of the classroom.

While this statement might seem obvious, helping learners to recognize and use learning strategies to learn outside of class takes conscious effort on the part of both teachers and learners. What are language learning strategies?

📋 **Task 6.6**

Suppose you are in another country and you need to buy a fingernail clipper. You speak some of the local language, but you have no idea what the words are for fingernail clipper. How could you ask for this item without using the name for it? Talk to a partner or write your ideas below:

_____

_____

Follow-up: In order to make yourself understood, you probably used one of the following **compensation strategies:**

- Using mime or gesture
- Defining the word or explaining its function
- Using a synonym
- Getting help from someone who speaks the native language and your language

---

All of these represent ways of being resourceful and getting what you need in another language, rather than giving up and leaving the store. Compensation strategies are just one type of language learning strategy that can be taught within any type of ESL curriculum. Doing so empowers learners to progress and actively learn on their own. These strategies are any tools or tactics that learners employ to learn more effectively and more autonomously. Different strategies serve different purposes, but they can be used in any combination. Rebecca Oxford (1990) proposes two classes of strategies: direct strategies and indirect strategies as shown in Table 6.5.

Table 6.5 Direct and Indirect Learning Strategies

Direct Strategies	Indirect Strategies
Memory Strategies	**Organizational Strategies***
Those that help you to remember language, for example:	Those that help you plan for and organize learning, for example:
• Sorting words into logical categories • Using sounds and images to remember words	• Setting goals and objectives • Seeking opportunities for practice • Connecting new information with known information

Cognitive Strategies	Affective Strategies
Those that enhance understanding, for example: • Recognizing and using phrases • Repeating new language • Summarizing	Those that improve your emotional state for learning, for example: • Using relaxation techniques • Rewarding yourself • Keeping a language learning diary
Compensation Strategies	Social Strategies
Those that help you overcome limitations, for example: • Guessing through visual or other clues • Asking for help • Using mime or gesture	Those that promote learning cooperatively, for example: • Asking for clarification • Asking for correction • Interacting with proficient users of the language

*Oxford calls these metacognitive strategies. For a full description and discussion of Language Learning Strategies, see Rebecca Oxford (1990) *Language learning strategies: What every teacher should know*, Heinle and Heinle.

While much research is still underway to determine which strategies work best for given learners and under various conditions (Cohen and Griffiths 2015), good language learners employ strategies that make them more conscious about how they learn, that allow them to monitor the success of learning, and to manage their time, affect, and effort, leading to greater self-efficacy overall (Oxford 2016). Developing effective language learning strategies is a goal that merits attention in any English language class, regardless of the focus of instruction and regardless of learner level (Reimer 2008). That is what prompted the developers of the Transition Integration Framework (TIF) (ATLAS 2016) to include the category of **Learning Strategies** among the essential skills needed for transitioning to new opportunities at school or work and in the community. The framework includes broad skills related to learning strategies (LS), each with numerous subskills, for example:

LS Skill 2: SWBAT . . . Apply appropriate strategies to organize, retain, and review materials in order to aid in understanding and recall

Subskills:

a. Employ a variety of strategies for categorizing information (sorting words logically, alphabetizing, pros and cons)

b. Select and use graphic organizers appropriate for a task (T-chart for pros and cons, Venn diagram for compare/contrast)

c. Choose and apply preferred note-taking strategies based on personal preference or task (lists, outlines, word maps, highlighting, two-column notes)

d. Choose and use strategies for reviewing, evaluating, and summarizing information (oral retell, flashcards, outline, highlight main points)

LS Skill 3: SWBAT . . . Apply appropriate strategies to compensate for and fill in gaps in knowledge

Subskills:

a. Ask for repetition and clarification of unknown language and concepts

b.	Compensate for unknown language using paraphrase or circumlocution (using other words to describe or work around an unknown word)
c.	Use context and what you know to figure out or guess meaning of language
d.	Identify appropriate resources and/or means to fill in gaps in knowledge (ask a teacher, consult a dictionary, online search)

(ATLAS 2016)

Within the TIF, there are examples of how learners at various levels and in various contexts can practice each subskill, as depicted for LS Skill 2-Subskill b. in Figure 6.2.

Learning Strategies (LS) Continued...

Skill 2:
SWBAT... Apply appropriate strategies to organize, retain, and review materials in order to aid in understanding and recall

Sub Skills:
   a. Employ a variety of strategies for categorizing information (sorting words logically, alphabetizing, pros and cons)
   b. Select and use graphic organizers appropriate for a task (T-chart for pros and cons, Venn diagram for compare/contrast)
   c. Choose and apply preferred note-taking strategies based on personal preference or task (lists, outlines, word maps, highlighting, 2-column notes)
   d. Choose and use strategies for reviewing, evaluating, and summarizing information (oral retell, flashcards, outline, highlight main points)

LS Skill 2-Sub Skill b: Select and use graphic organizers appropriate for a task (T-chart for pros and cons, Venn diagram for compare/contrast)

	Complexity →		
Sample Activities	Read or listen to a short topical narrative* and put key events into a linear string.	Read a short text or listen to a brief online talk about a topic* and choose between 2-3 graphic organizer options that best represent the text (e.g., *description* – use word web, *narrative*- use timeline).	Read an article or listen to a podcast about a topic of interest.* Create a graphic organizer that best represents the organization of the information and use it to takes notes.
Technology Activities:	Read a topical narrative* and put key events into a linear string using an easy to use online graphic organizer such as *readwritethink* webbing tool.	Read a short text about a topic* and choose an online graphic organizer from a website such as *exploratree* to best represent the text (e.g., *description* – use word web, *narrative*- use timeline).	Read an article or listen to a podcast about a topic of interest.* Create an online graphic organizer that best represents the organization of the information and use it to takes notes.
Community	* Community topic	* Community topic	* Community topic
School	* School or educational topic	* School or educational topic	* School or educational topic
Work	*Workplace topic	*Workplace topic	*Workplace topic

Figure 6.2 Example of How to Teach LS Skill 2 Subskill b. of the Transitions Integration Framework (ATLAS 2016: 19) Reprinted with permission.

Making strategies explicit throughout instruction

In a listening lesson

In a class where the students do regular listening activities, both from the textbook and from authentic sources such as news reports, podcasts, and interviews, the teacher always begins with pre-listening activities. Each time she does that, she makes it explicit to her students that this strategy allows them to anticipate content and check their predictions as they listen. The teacher then shares how she uses that same strategy at home to practice listening to the news in German online:

> *Just as you need to improve your English, I am working on my German because my family and I are going to Germany this summer. Luckily, I can find news in German online each night. I don't know much German yet, but before I listen, I write down all the events I heard about that day, either in conversations with people, on the radio or in the newspaper in my language. Then when I listen in German, I try to hear some of those key words. I can always understand some names of countries and people, and some other words that sound like English. I want you to try doing that with the news in English every day.*

In a vocabulary lesson

In Section 4.9 C, we saw a categorizing task where students sort descriptive words for personality traits (e.g., reliable, emotional, manipulative) into these three categories:

Positive   Either Positive or Negative   Negative

By creating logical groupings of the vocabulary, the learners **engage** with the words by discussing them in groups; they analyze possible **connotations**; they **repeat** the words multiple times verbally; they **reason** as they justify their choices. The teacher now shares:

> *This is a good way to organize new words that you learn. It helps you to remember them better if you put them in groups like the ones we made on the board. Each week, keep a list of new words you learn and hear. At the end of the week, see what categories you may be able to create and justify your choices.*

Integrating learning strategies development into your lessons is one more way that learning and teaching can promote successes and accomplishment for your students. Just as with teacher-student interactions, the teaching of learning strategies should not be left to chance or taught haphazardly. Strategies should be presented, practiced, and made explicit throughout instruction as an integral part of your lessons. In fact, research indicates that more positive results are shown if strategy training is taught in connection with specific content (O'Malley and Chamot 1990).

As noted in Section 3.3, a systematic approach to vocabulary acquisition (Dutro and Kinsella 2010) includes writing and pronouncing a new word a few times; breaking down long words into syllables and identifying the word stress; explanations in student-friendly language; visual representations; and structured oral and written tasks. Susan Finn Miller's *vocabulary workouts* provide these supports and if used systematically in class, can be used for independent practice and review.

Vocabulary Workout

New Word or Phrase	Explanation	Examples
approach /ap-**PROACH**/ (verb)	To do something in a specific way or manner	Students often have a specific way or **approach** to studying new vocabulary. Students also usually have a certain **approach** for solving a math problem.
approach /ap-**PROACH**/ (noun)	A way of doing something or a way of solving problem	Teachers use different approaches when teaching. For example, some teachers **approach** their teaching by using technology in their class. Other teachers don't use technology in their approach.

Conversation Practice:

Q: What is a healthy approach to dieting?

A: A healthy _____ to dieting includes eating a lot of _____ (noun) and only a little _____ (noun).

Writing Practice: When taking a test, reading the questions first can be a(n) _____ (adjective) _____.

My Sentence:

Jessica Jones (personal communication) provides language frames learners need to talk to their classmates about their word attack skills. In doing so, she promotes skills for learning new words independently.

What does _____ mean?

I think _____ means _____

For example, _____

My dictionary says _____ means _____.

Can you show me the meaning of the word or sentence?

I'll try to draw it.

Here's a good picture on my phone.

Maybe I can act it out.

I don't think I can show this.

Conclusion

In this chapter, the discussion of planning for teaching and learning has included far more than writing a lesson plan before walking into an English language class. Teachers need to prepare for classroom interactions and integrate learning strategies instruction into lessons. They need to find ways to build continuity from one lesson to the next. While many of these teaching routines become second nature for experienced ESL teachers, those new to the profession need to be mindful of the importance of all of these elements to assure that learners have an optimal learning experience.

Key Terms

On your own, or with a partner, provide an example or brief definition for each concept:

Checklist of Key Terms	
course goals/outcomes	
objectives	
targeted language	
curricular routines	
display questions	
teacher talk/extraneous teacher talk	
checking questions	
Question Formulation Technique (QFT)	
wait time	
language learning strategies	

Before doing these activities, revisit your answers to the questions at the beginning of the chapter.

1 Lesson Planning

If you are already teaching, use the lesson-planning guidelines in Table 6.2 as you plan an upcoming lesson. Afterwards, reflect on the ways that using these guidelines helped your planning. What areas had you overlooked before? In what ways did using the guidelines affect the outcomes for learners in that lesson?

If you are not teaching, talk to an ESL teacher about the class she or he teaches and write a class description based on the information she or he gives you. Choose a unit from the textbook that the class is currently using and prepare a lesson plan using the lesson-planning guidelines in Table 6.2. If possible, ask the teacher for feedback about your plan.

2 Giving Instructions

If you are already teaching, audio or video record a portion of your lesson when you are giving instructions to your students. Transcribe your instructions and answer these questions:

a. Do I demonstrate or describe the activity?

b. What modeling do I provide? Do I break the activity down into logical steps and give learners only the information they need to complete each step?

c. How do I check for learner understanding? Do I have students try the activity before the whole class undertakes it?

How did you do? Are you satisfied with your instructions, or did you discover some areas where you might improve? Rewrite the instructions to reflect any changes you would like to make the next time you use this activity.

If you are not teaching, choose an activity in an ESL textbook and script the instructions you would give for the activity. Think of how you would demonstrate the activity as well as the techniques you would use to check that learners understand what they need to do. Practice giving the instructions to a classmate, friend, or family member and ask for feedback about your instructions using the questions above.

3 Checking Understanding and Questioning Techniques

If you are already teaching, identify key vocabulary and grammatical or functional language in an upcoming lesson and prepare checking questions to use with your learners. Remember that good checking questions allow learners to <u>demonstrate</u> their understanding. Avoid: *Do you know . . .? Do you understand . . .? What does ___ mean?* After the lesson, reflect on how successful you were at checking learner understanding. Is there anything you would do differently if you were teaching this lesson again?

If you are not teaching, choose a unit in a textbook and do the same exercise. Practice your checking questions with a partner in class.

Grammar References for Teachers

Azar, B. (2017). *Chartbook, 5th Edition*. White Plains, NY: Prentice Hall. The Chartbook draws on the classic Azar grammar series with concise explanations, timelines, and examples of grammar points, particularly the tense/aspect system of English.

Swan, M. (2017) *Practical English Usage, 4th Edition*. Oxford: Oxford University Press. This grammar reference answers questions that teachers and learners ask about English grammar and vocabulary with clear explanations and examples.

Thornbury, S. (2017) *About Language, 2nd edition.* Cambridge: Cambridge University Press. This book asks: "What is it that a teacher needs to know about English in order to teach it effectively?" It develops teachers' language awareness through a wide range of tasks, which involve them in analyzing English to discover its underlying systems.

Lesson Planning

Michaud, C. and Reed, M. (2010) *Goal-Driven Lesson Planning for Teaching English to Speakers of Other Languages.* Ann Arbor, MI: University of Michigan Press. This text shows teachers how to take any piece from English language materials—an assigned text, a newspaper article, an ESL activity from a website, etc.—and use it to teach students something about language.

Wiggins, G. and McTigue, J. (2005) *Understanding by Design, Expanded 2nd Edition*. Association for Supervision and Curriculum Development. For those particularly interested in backward design, this text guides educators in the design of curriculum, assessment, and instruction with templates and tools for planning.

Learning Strategies

Nation, P. (2014). *What Do You Need to Know to Learn a Foreign Language?* School of Linguistics and Applied Language Studies. Victoria University of Wellington, New Zealand. *https://www.victoria. ac.nz/lals/about/staff/publications/paul-nation/foreign-language_1125.pdf*. This free, online text is designed for learners of foreign languages. It gives teachers ideas on how to highlight strategies with their learners.

Oxford, R. (2016) *Teaching and Researching Language Learning Strategies: Self-Regulation in Context, 2nd Edition.* New York, NY: Routledge. This text provides discussion of self-regulation and agency. It shows applications of learning strategies in all language skill areas and in grammar and vocabulary.

7 | Managing Learning in Adult English Language Classes

To consider before reading this chapter:

- What are the characteristics of a multilevel class?
- How can teachers differentiate instruction to meet a wide range of needs, backgrounds, and levels in an adult English language classroom?
- What would an optimal learning environment for adult English learners look like?

Part I: Creating optimal learning environments

7.1 Introduction

Multiple elements of a lesson, which are often less tangible than the written plan, textbook, or materials the teacher has prepared, contribute to the relative success of that particular lesson. Identifying those factors and accounting for them in the planning stages can have a tremendous impact on learning. In the first part of this chapter, we examine the impact factors such as multilevel classes, the classroom environment, variable attendance, or pairing/grouping of students can have on learning, with a focus on turning challenges into opportunities for learning. In the second part of the chapter, we turn to suggestions for working with learners with particular needs, for example, students with learning disabilities, physical disabilities, or those who have experienced trauma. Let's start by looking at Valentina's class.

Getting Started

 Task 7.1

Read the description of Valentina's class and answer the questions with a partner or in your journal:

Valentina teaches a low-intermediate/intermediate class of 35 adults enrolled from a variety of countries, including Liberia, Vietnam, Mexico, Ecuador, China, the Ukraine, and Bosnia. She works at a community-based program that offers only three levels. Some learners have advanced degrees from their country and others have limited or interrupted prior formal schooling. Their backgrounds with technology and digital literacy skills range broadly from an engineer who has worked with sophisticated computer programs to someone who has hardly used a computer. Her program has an open-enrollment policy, which means that students are joining the class weekly. Many of the students have jobs and attend class sporadically so attendance varies from 12 to 35 students. Some students seem mostly interested in long grammar explanations and written activities; others seem eager to engage in discussions. The classroom is used by other programs at her school, so she hasn't been able to make use of the space as she'd like. She can't keep posters, resources, or learning supports on the walls. She knows her students would benefit from more interaction with one another, but she's not sure how to organize pair and group activities in her small space. Valentina has always been very forthcoming in helping her students with personal issues (calls to landlords, rides to appointments), but lately this has made her feel uncomfortable because a few students seem to be placing too many demands on her personal time or aren't making the effort she feels they could to resolve issues on their own.

1. Identify issues that could have an impact on learning and teaching.

2. What could Valentina do to turn some of these challenges around? Think in terms of learner roles and responsibilities, course content, tasks, teaching and learning strategies, and the classroom environment.

Issues/Challenges	Opportunities

Follow-up: Valentina is working with a multilevel class, managing varying experiences and expectations, and managing open enrollment. These are among the topics we will look at in the chapter. As you read, look for possible solutions to the challenges you identified above.

7.2 Working with multilevel classes

Teachers like Valentina may feel ill-prepared for accommodating the multiple levels, expectations, and needs of the learners in class. These variables affect learners' feelings about classes as well. In studies on learner attrition and attendance, learners have noted mixed literacy skills, minimal peer support, and irrelevant materials as reasons for leaving programs (Brod 1990). Learners can feel that course content is at odds with their perceptions of what they should be learning, for example, academic readiness instead of a lesson on cooking without any focus on skills related to numeracy or measurement (Schalge and Soga 2008).

The fact is, multilevel classes are a reality of just about every ESL program and should not be seen as a deterrent to learning. Many would argue that multilevel classes allow for richer interaction among students, promoting multiple perspectives, peer teaching, and multifaceted learning. The question is: What are some effective ways to make multilevel classes rich and productive learning environments for all students? This discussion needs to begin with an understanding of what multilevel actually means. Is it only a question of language proficiency?

📄 **Task 7.2**

Take a few minutes to brainstorm as many characteristics of a multilevel class as you can.

What are the characteristics of a multilevel class?
variation in proficiency levels   *different school experiences*

Follow-up: The simplest view of multilevel classes is that some learners are very proficient and participate all the time, and others are non-communicative, leading the teacher to think they lack skills in English. In reality, it can be difficult to gauge learner ability across language skills; "Sometimes . . . we assume that the silent student doesn't understand when in fact [his] listening skills may be quite strong. Similarly, confident speech may mask very limited literacy skills"

(Bell 2012: 88). Reticence to participate should not be attributed to willingness to learn or to levels of competence; the outward behaviors students exhibit in class have as much to do with experiential and affective factors as they do with language proficiency (Carter and Henrichsen 2015). Bell (2004), Isserlis (2009), and Tomlinson (2014) propose a multitude of factors that contribute to an individual's learning profile. Central to Tomlinson's work in differentiation is to avoid viewing any of these differences as deficits. Table 7.1 presents four broad categories of variables that can affect learning along with some of the factors teachers need to consider when planning for instruction.

Table 7.1 What Does Multilevel Mean?

1 Experiences with Education	Factors to Consider
Prior formal and/or informal education	• Number of years of schooling (formal or informal) • Experience learning other languages • Comfort with sitting in a classroom
Expectations about learning/ teaching	• Content, e.g., work readiness, citizenship • Language focus, e.g., grammar, reading, writing, listening, speaking • Approaches to teaching; group/pair work • Willingness, comfort, and ability to speak up in class • Views of teacher as expert • Student-teacher roles; differing norms of student-teacher interactions, inside and outside of class
Literacy skills	• First and second language literacy • Preliterate, nonliterate, or low-literate (Table 5.1) • Ease with digital literacy
2 Cultural Background	**Factors to Consider**
Classroom behaviors and expectations	• View of teacher as expert • Differing norms regarding pair/group work • Differing norms of student-teacher interactions, inside and outside of class • Roles related to gender and age
Tensions among groups in the class	• Political unrest between students' countries of origin • Tension between different clans from the same culture • Status within country of origin
First/primary language	• Similarities or differences with English or other first languages in class, e.g., Spanish has far more in common with English than does Chinese
3 Individual Factors	**Factors to Consider**
Identity and investment	• Degree of sense of belonging in the new country, community, and in the class

Obstacles to learning **Another box for *presence,*** ***ability to attend to learning***	• (Dis)abilites • Health and mental health • Un/employment status • Experiences of trauma, violence or abuse • Worries, concerns, stressors beyond classroom
Motivation	• Reasons for learning English: personal, professional or academic • Voluntary learning vs. compulsory learning • Vision learners have for themselves; self-concept as learners
Personality/ways of being in the world	• Introverted vs. extroverted • Analytical vs. intuitive • Degree of flexibility with trying new ways of learning
Age	• Effects on attention span, eye sight, hearing • Physical stamina: ability to sit, stand, move about

Preferred approach to learning	• Preference for:
	  - saying and doing things
	  - writing everything down
	  - observing demonstrations
	  - individual vs. group work

4 Situational Factors	**Factors to Consider**
Situation in the new country	• Length of time in the country • Workload, family demands • Part-time or full-time student • Socioeconomic condition • Housing conditions and food security • Racism, xenophobia • Discrimination based on sexual orientation
Access to English outside of class	• Time and effort devoted and available to learning English outside of class • Amount of input in English from online sources, television, radio, family, friends, or coworkers • Opportunities for meaningful interaction in English outside of class • Facility with and availability of technologies for learning (e.g., high-speed Internet for accessing learning tools or videos)

Given the tremendous number of variables at play in all adult education classes, creating lessons that account for so many diverse needs may seem impossible. The fact is, we can never meet everyone's needs all of the time; what we can do is be aware of these variables and differentiate instruction accordingly. According to Tomlinson and Imbeau (2010), differentiation represents a view that classrooms should be places that maximize each learner's capabilities. What do educators of adult ELs need to take into consideration as they create this optimal learning environment?

7.3 Establishing goals in multilevel classes

There is a direct connection between adult learner persistence and learners' perception that their goals are being met (Comings 2007; Comings, Parrella, and Soricone 1999). In a study on adult ESL learner absenteeism (Schalge and Soga 2008), adult ESL learners expressed frustration about the mismatch between their goals and teacher expectations of them. While teachers in this study attributed absenteeism to issues such as transportation and childcare, the learner participants reported a mismatch between their goals and instructional decisions regarding content and pacing (too slow) in the class. Learners were not able to identify any clear assessments of their learning and reported feeling bored in the class when the teacher covered topics such as organizing one's home or cooking rather than teaching academic skills they felt they needed. They also desired more direct instruction from their teacher. Learner expectations may be in direct conflict with the teacher's view of herself as a facilitator of learning.

Even when learners are gaining self-confidence in English and feeling less marginalized in their communities, they still express frustration with unmet personal and professional goals (Cooke 2006). It is through a careful assessment of learner needs and an open conversation about learner goals that mismatches like these may be addressed. One way to bridge the gap between learners' diverse needs is to identify and negotiate shared goals, which results in more realistic expectations for the whole group (Balliro 1997).

Group goal-setting tasks

A. Four corners

Four corners is a technique used widely in language classrooms for a variety of purposes, one of which can be group goal setting and needs assessment. The teacher posts signs that represent learning content, outcomes, or even processes for learning in the four corners of the room. These can be proposed by the teacher or they can be brainstormed by the learners themselves. Learners move to the corner of the room that represents their greatest need or interest. Learners could repeat the process for their second choice. Once in their groups, learners can share why they chose that corner. Possible categories for group goal setting could be:

Learning preferences: Starting with a prompt such as "When learning new information . . ." or "When learning a new skill . . .", the four corner signs are: *I learn best when talking. I learn best by doing activities with others. I learn best by listening and taking notes. I learn best working alone.*

Language skills: Greatest need/or strengths in listening, speaking, reading, writing

Digital literacy skills: Use email to communicate. Find information online. Apply for jobs online. Pay bills online.

Learning outcomes: In a unit on job explorations: Describe my work history. Describe my skills. Search for jobs online. Apply for jobs online.

Primary focus (topics or content) of learning: Environmental issues. Technological advances. Educational systems. History.

In literacy-level classes where learners have minimal print literacy, pictures of situations and themes can be used instead of words; learners can work collaboratively to choose those that are the most important to them, then tally the group results (Shank and Terrill 1997).

B. Polling
Electronic polling can be used as a digital alternative to four corners. If the teacher projects the results to an online poll, the learners see in real time what is important to the group as a whole. Polls can be implemented using any number of free tools (e.g., PollEveryhere, Socrative, Google Forms) to create a short needs assessment at the start of a term, unit of instruction, or lesson. Learners use their phones or devices to enter choices. If not all learners have a device in class, teams can be assigned and one learner enters responses that reflect the group's consensus. Polling can also be done by a show of hands, post-it notes, or other non-digital means.

C. Can-do statements
Learning outcomes expressed as "can-do" statements can make goal setting accessible for learners at any proficiency level. To establish content goals in a literacy-level class, a teacher can post these statements across the front of the classroom.

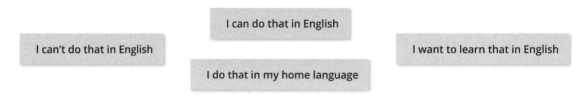

Including the category, "**I do that in my home language**" acknowledges that many activities in learners' lives are conducted in their first language. Call out the following literacy practices and have learners stand next to the appropriate can-do statement:

- Read to a child
- Read emails from school
- Help a child with homework
- Read the mail
- Read email from friends or family
- Write email to friends and family
- Write letters to friends or family
- Read a newspaper, print or online

Alternatively, first have students brainstorm literacy practices in their lives and use those for the basis of this task. This task allows learners to see that there are varying needs and abilities in class. It can be used at the beginning a unit of instruction and repeated at the end of a unit, adding the question, "What can you say/do/write/read now?"

D. Generating and prioritizing group needs
Working in teams, learners generate lists of the language/skills/knowledge they need to develop in various areas of their lives, for example, at home, for education, at work, or in the community.

Each team creates a poster for one assigned area (home, work, school, community) to share with the group and to post in the classroom. Students circulate to each poster and put a check mark next to common needs in order to start prioritizing group needs. Needs can be added to the posters and revisited to identify progress, and priorities can be reorganized each month (or more often).

E. Defining group expectations about learning/establishing ground rules
Balliro (1997) highlights the importance of students taking responsibility for their own learning in the multilevel class. Establishing class ground rules promotes an inclusive classroom environment

where learners express their expectations from the start of a class. At the lower-proficiency levels, learners can take part in a discussion using sentence starters like these:

A good teacher _____.   A good student _____.

We (the students) will _____.   The teacher will _____.

The responses become the ground rules for the class, which are written and displayed in the classroom. In a more advanced level class, learners can explore their expectations regarding forms of address, interaction styles, ways of giving and receiving feedback, or ways of operating in group tasks, which could result in ground rules like these:

- Respect all class colleagues, even when you do not agree with their point of view.
- Listen carefully; do not interrupt.
- Keep an open mind.
- Be open to being challenged.

(The Teaching Center 2009)

Learners in Ivana Ferguson's class create posters and during a gallery walk, the other learners indicate agreement by adding check marks to suggestions proposed by classmates as in Figure 7.1.

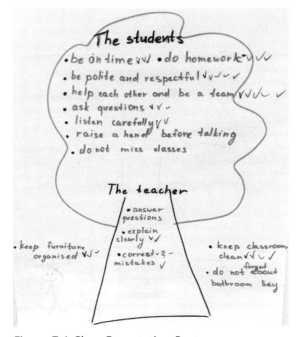

Figure 7.1 Class Expectation Poster

Making these expectations public allows learners to recognize the variation in expectations of the group.

The techniques in this section give all learners a voice in the needs assessment process, and they build cohesion and cooperation among the group members from the very start of the class. These tasks make public the varying needs that exist within the group, which may help to minimize frustration around unmet needs or perceptions that the teacher is not aware of individual needs. This also provides teachers with insights about learners' needs and expectations as they plan for differentiation in adult English language classrooms.

7.4 Differentiation in English language classes

Differentiation consists of tailoring instruction to account for and address varying learner profiles, interests, and readiness. Keeping overall learning outcomes in mind, the content, process, and products of a lesson or unit are adjusted so that all learners can make gains in their language development that are in keeping with their abilities and needs (Tomlinson and Imbeau 2010). Considering overall desired learning outcomes of a lesson or unit, we modify instruction as follows:

What we need to modify . . .	Based on learner . . .
Content: What do learners need to know and understand? This can include content knowledge such as economics or numeracy, as well as the language learners need to be successful in a lesson/unit.	**Readiness:** How well prepared are learners for the content, skills, and language demands of classroom tasks?
Process: What approach allows learners to make sense of the content?	**Interest:** What content, knowledge, and skills will be of most interest to learners and, by extension, motivate them?
Product: How do learners demonstrate what they have learned?	**Affect:** How might learner attitudes, emotions, or feelings affect learning?
	Learning profile: How do learners approach learning? How might learning preferences or cultural expectations about teaching and learning roles vary among learners?

(Tomlinson and Imbeau 2010: 15–17)

Let's use the high-intermediate decision-making task presented in Chapter 4 to consider how these elements of differentiation come together. In a class exploring entrepreneurship in their community, learners consider a variety of options for starting a small business.

Learning Outcome:

Present the pros and cons of starting a particular small business in your community based on evidence.

Task: Look at these three types of businesses and discuss which you have the skills and expertise to develop.

Restaurant

Food truck

Small market

Start with online research in teams.

- Create groups based on which type of small business interests you most.
- Choose a targeted neighborhood.
- Research the number of similar businesses in the area.
- Research spaces available for rent or lease, or the cost of purchasing a food truck.

Discuss the pros and cons of starting their type of business for the targeted area based on the information gathered. Present findings to the class either at the board, with a PowerPoint presentation or a poster.

In order to determine the ways in which the teacher needs to differentiate instruction, we start by examining the content, process, and product for this task. What language, skills, and knowledge do learners need in order to be successful with this task? How will learners go about meeting the outcomes? What will the teacher assess (the process, product, or both)? By doing this analysis of the task demands, as shown in Figure 7.2, the teacher can determine the kinds of adjustments she may need to provide so that all learners can contribute meaningfully to the task.

Decision-Making Task: Starting a Small Business		
Content	**Process**	**Product**
Concepts: entrepreneurship, small business	• Determine personal skills/interests	• A poster or PowerPoint to present findings
Language functions:	• Create like-interest groups	• In-class presentations done as a gallery walk or whole-group presentations depending on class size
• Ask for and give opinions	• Conduct a web search	
• Make suggestions	• Discuss pros/cons of options	
• Describe options	• Present findings to others	
• State preferences	• Listen to presentations and ask questions of classmates	
Language forms:		
• Modals of possibility (we can/could) and advisability (we should)		
• "*Wh*- question" forms (e.g., How many...?)		
Vocabulary: renting vs. leasing, competition, availability, benefits, drawbacks		
Critical thinking skills:		
• Evaluate the reliability of a web page		
• Analyze options		
• Identify and evaluate pros/cons of each option		

Figure 7.2 An Analysis of Task Demands

Tomlinson and Imbeau (2010) provide a framework for differentiation that aligns the instructional components to be considered (content, process, product) and learner variables (readiness, interest, and learning profile). Figure 7.3 illustrates how to apply that process to the decision-making classroom task and shows the differentiation the teacher could make based on learner variables. Note that these examples illustrate the types of differentiation one could make; these would be based on the needs of a given group of learners.

	Learner Readiness	Learner Interest	Learning Profile
Content	• Direct learners to a variety of web sources that have level-appropriate language. • Pre-teach the vocabulary and work on pronunciation (word stress). • Provide language frames for the language functions, e.g., stating preferences: *I'd rather ___ because I know a lot about . . .* *If you ask me . . .; I think the best option is . . .*	• Choose professions that you know are of interest to the learners (i.e., not necessarily those presented in the task). • Start by having students generate a list of possible small businesses. • Elicit prior experiences with small businesses in students' countries of origin. • Start with readings about immigrants who have started their own businesses.	• Provide links to videos as well as readings to appeal to varying strengths and learning preferences. • Provide differentiated questions, some that gather basic factual information and some that require more analysis based on learners' reading or listening comprehension levels.
Process	• Have class generate a list of questions to use while doing web searches. • Model a web search as a class. • Use a jigsaw approach to lighten the load, learners choosing what questions to address (see 5.9). • Encourage translanguaging, using the L1 as a resource, when exploring sources and in discussions; for note-taking (see 7.5 J).	• Discussion of pros and cons of starting your own business. • Learner-created groups based on interest.	• Provide time for independent work and reflection. • Provide options for developing products: shared electronic files; marker and paper; photos taken with phones. • Provide graphic organizers to organize ideas: T-chart for pros/cons discussions; mind map for organizing sections of the final product.
Product	• Allow for varying outcomes (e.g., poster or PowerPoint with extensive script vs. a video or podcast for those with stronger oral skills). • Use an assessment rubric that allows for information presented in words (written or oral) or images.	• Draw on student interests in developing final product, for example, someone more interested in numbers and data works on numerical displays. • Have students generate questions to use during gallery walk.	• Allow for varying formats for the final product (e.g., poster, PowerPoint, video, skit, podcast, a short manual, FAQs, tip sheets). • Encourage learners to use images, video or sound clips in the presentations.

Figure 7.3 Model of Differentiation for Classroom Tasks

7.5 Additional practices for working with multilevel classes

As we have seen, teaching multilevel classes does not mean preparing multiple lesson plans each day; rather, it's a question of providing multiple options within the same lesson or unit. What follows are some practical suggestions for adapting lessons, including ways to vary tasks and learner roles, multiple options for activities, and using self-access materials, all in keeping with the ideas of differentiation outlined above.

A. Allow for learner choice and use open-ended tasks

Classroom activities that have one set outcome can be frustrating for learners who are unable, for whatever reason, to complete the task in the allotted time frame. One way to avoid this is to provide learners with a choice of items to complete within a given time frame, allowing for variation from one student to the next. The following example illustrates this strategy, which can be used when learners are practicing any language function or workplace competency. Assume that the instructor has already presented the language needed for making requests and asking permission at the workplace. The following scenarios are cut up and passed out to students, with extra copies left on a table in the room. Students mingle and make polite requests or ask permission of others in class; students can choose to grant or refuse the request. When a student is finished with one scenario, he or she chooses another one on the table and continues the task. This activity gives all learners a chance to practice at their own pace. Students are also given the choice of scenarios allowing them to choose those for which they feel most prepared. Whether students complete one or eight scenarios, they can feel the accomplishment of completing the piece(s) of the activity they select. In order to motivate learners to take on a greater challenge, suggest that they complete at least one more item than they did during the previous class.

Sample Scenario Strips:

You are in the lunchroom and want to look at someone's newspaper.

You forgot your wallet at home and need to borrow money for a soft drink.

You don't feel well and want to leave work early.

You need time off for a doctor's appointment.

You want a coworker to help you understand an employee announcement.

B. Assign different tasks to different ability level students

Creating a variety of task types with the same outcome for one lesson can be an obstacle for part-time teachers who have limited paid preparation time, so consider developing materials like those below cooperatively with other teachers. A file of multilevel tasks can be created and shared by all the teachers at your site. Varying task complexity and providing a simpler version of task for lower-proficiency level learners have been shown to promote increased output of targeted language features (Kim 2009).

In a vocabulary lesson on jobs, different groups are given one of the following tasks:

Option A: Prepare a set of visuals on cue cards like these:

Have learners sort the jobs according to whether they are typically done indoors/outdoors/either; typically held by men/women in your country; require special training/no special training.

Option B: Prepare a set of cue cards with names of professions written on them and do the same as Option A. Sort words into these categories as well: jobs people in the group have done; jobs they'd like to try.

Option C: Small group discussion with these questions (name of profession written along the side of page):

What jobs do people do outdoors/indoors?

Which are typically held by men/women in your culture? What about in this country?

Which of the jobs would you be interested in and why?

What experiences have you had in your daily life with any of these workers or occupations?

Option D: Learners identify the jobs they do at home and in their community and then consider the skills associated with each one. See how many of these are transferable skills for jobs outside of the home.

Tasks I Do at Home and in My Community	Skills Required
Helping my kids with homework	Reading, math, organizing, planning
Managing my household	Reading labels, advertisements, Looking up deals online, Making to-do lists, planning, organizing, Making decisions
Sharing childcare with neighbors	Making arrangements by phone and email, Planning activities for kids

All four options allow learners to practice vocabulary associated with jobs in ways that are accessible to them. In Option A, learners with limited literacy skills can rely on the visual representations of the jobs. The categories for sorting the words do not require extensive analysis and completing the task does not require extension use of language. However, successful completion of the task demonstrates that the learners understand something more than the definition of the job title. Option B requires that learners can read the names of the jobs and sorting the words into categories requires more discussion and critical thinking than in Option A. Option C allows more advanced learners to discuss the jobs in more depth, bringing personal experiences and interpretations to the discussion by sharing, communicating, and presenting across groups. Option D represents what might work well with a group of learners who haven't worked outside of the home and who may not see themselves in the jobs presented in the curriculum. This approach acknowledges and expands on skills developed through jobs at home. Consider how these same modifications could be used with other content (e.g., housing, transportation, educational options).

C. Multilevel listening tasks

Any time you use a listening passage in a lesson, there are a variety of ways you can have learners work with the same passage. One routine I have often used in my English language classes is to play the daily news headlines to expose learners to authentic language. News broadcasts are delivered very quickly, as are most truly authentic listening passages, so the challenge is to prepare tasks that are accessible to varying ability levels. The alternative tasks below serve to illustrate the types of activities you could do with *any* passage, one from an assigned textbook, an interview, or an online video clip.

Using the morning news headlines (video or audio):

Option A: Give a visual cutout card of the country and have the students hold up their card if their country is mentioned. If there is a large map in the room, students can stand by the map and point to countries they hear mentioned. This could be done on a local or national scale as well.

Option B: Hand out pictures of things mentioned in the news. Students hold up their picture as the item or person is mentioned (you often find corresponding photos in the online or print newspaper for the same day).

Option C: Give a list of countries (or cities and states), key words, or names that are covered in the news. Students check off the words as they hear them.

Option D: Elicit from learners the stories they have heard in the news that week. Invite a learner to write those on the board and have the other students write that list in their notebooks. As they listen, they check off those stories that were mentioned.

Option E: List news topics on a handout and have students circle the topics that are covered in the news as they listen.

weather	crime	sports
national	international	local
government	people	business

One recording can be used to accomplish all of these activities, with different learners taking part in different activities. The tasks require minimal preparation and the places and names would likely appear in later broadcasts, allowing the teacher to recycle the tasks in later lessons.

Teachers can vary the degree of difficulty of listening and reading activities in textbooks by assigning only half of the items to some students, who then share their answers with students who completed the other items. Different pre-reading/listening and post-reading/listening activities can be assigned depending on ability level. When I taught a listening lesson based on a video clip about a controversial language teaching method used in China, I provided two options for follow-up, the first for the learners who had very high oral proficiency and had expressed their desire to have more discussions in class. The second option was designed for learners at the low-intermediate level, who sometimes struggled with tasks that were too open-ended.

Option A:

Learners worked through a set of discussion questions about language learning and teaching preferences, followed by a ranking activity whereby students rated the degree of importance of different elements, e.g., pair/group activity; use of visual aids. They prepared a list of what they agreed they wanted in a language class, which they presented to the whole class.

Option B:

What are the best ways to learn a language? Write words or draw pictures for each of these things:

The classroom	The teacher	The students	The activities

The categories provided in Option B made the task more concrete than an open-ended discussion; those who had limited literacy skills could use pictures or symbols, while others in the group simply transcribed their contributions. The final outcome was to create a poster representing the ideal language class. This alternative to a discussion activity proved very successful for the low-intermediate level learners. Providing two options allowed for multiple outcomes (each group chose the language to include and the ways to present information), and the options appealed to a much greater array of learning preferences.

D. Jigsaw activities

The jigsaw activities explored in Chapters 4 and 5 are ideal for multilevel classes as they allow for differentiation of the texts and the tasks assigned. Jigsaw involves assigning different readings or listening passages or different tasks to different groups of learners. (readworks.org is an excellent source for informational texts on current issues, as it provides multiple levels of the texts on the same topic; elllo.org provides the same option for short listening passages on a variety of topics).

E. Assign varying roles

One of the core principles of cooperative learning is that each member of a group needs to have a clear role and purpose in order for the cooperative learning task to be successful. In a multilevel class, more advanced students can quickly dominate, leaving little room for participation by less advanced or quieter students. Here are some possible roles that can be assigned to students with particular strengths:

- Students with stronger literacy skills can be scribes during group activities, particularly for those tasks that have an outcome to report to the whole class. They can be given sentence starters such as: *If I understand, you said _____. Is that correct?* Such sentence starters can help learners understand their roles in the group and the expectations/responsibilities of their role.
- Learners who are hesitant to speak can be timekeepers and be given cue cards with sentences like these: *We have 10 more minutes. We need to finish in 5 minutes.*
- Students who tend to dominate discussions could act as facilitators with some set ground rules; their job is to make sure everyone participates a set number of times. This allows the more verbal and perhaps more advanced students to participate while making them aware of the

need for others to have a chance to speak. They could be given language frames like these: _____, we haven't heard from you yet. _____, did you want to add anything?

These roles are interchangeable, i.e., everyone can be the timekeeper or facilitator. The idea is that each person knows what his or her role and purpose is as a group member, in addition to the responsibility of completing the activity itself.

F. Use different versions of the same dialogue or text: scripted; semi-scripted; discourse chains
Many textbooks have dialogues designed to present or provide opportunities to practice language; teachers and learners can also create dialogues collaboratively. The following variations demonstrate what you could do with one dialogue on calling a landlord about an issue in an apartment for learners with varying ability levels. Some learners may feel safest simply practicing a written dialogue, while others are ready to move on to something far more challenging. Learners with limited literacy will have difficulty reading a dialogue, but may be ready to practice based on visual cues.

Version A: Scripted Dialogue (First brainstorm a list of problems and create a word/phrase bank: I have bedbugs. The trash wasn't collected. The heat isn't working.)

> **Tenant:** I have a problem in my apartment.
>
> **Landlord:** What's the problem?
>
> **Tenant:** (Choose from problems brainstormed)
>
> **Landlord:** How long have you had this problem?
>
> **Tenant:** It started _____ ago.
>
> **Landlord:** What unit are you in?
>
> **Tenant:** I'm in _____.
>
> **Landlord:** Please fill in the repair request online to set up an appointment.

Version B: Semi-Scripted Dialogue

> **Tenant:** I have _____ in my apartment.
>
> **Landlord:** What's _____?
>
> **Tenant:** (Choose from problems brainstormed.)
>
> **Landlord:** How long _____ this problem?
>
> **Tenant:** It started _____ ago.
>
> **Landlord:** What _____ are you?
>
> **Tenant:** I'm in _____.
>
> **Landlord:** Please _____ the repair request online to set up _____.

Version C (for students with limited literacy skills):

Show a picture of the problem (leaking sink; water on the floor)

Students create their dialogue based on those visual cues.

Version D: Discourse Chain

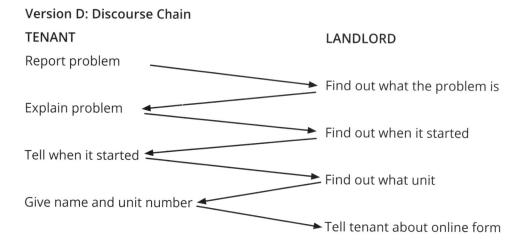

TENANT	LANDLORD
Report problem	
	Find out what the problem is
Explain problem	
	Find out when it started
Tell when it started	
	Find out what unit
Give name and unit number	
	Tell tenant about online form

G. Use role plays with very complex to minimal roles; use picture prompts with no words

Role plays can be used successfully with learners at all levels provided that the students understand directions and role descriptions. In a multilevel class, there may be students for whom written role descriptions are too complex and incomprehensible. An alternative to role plays with prescribed roles is to provide a picture of a scene and allow learners to choose who they want to be and what they want to say (Ladousse 1987). A scene on video with the sound off can also be used, played through one time and then freeze-framed for reference by the students as they prepare their role play. Upon showing the scene, let each group work together to choose their parts and prepare and practice their role play. Find pictures, take photographs, or record scenes of:

- A visit to the doctor
- A tenant showing a problem to a landlord
- A student meeting with an advisor
- Coworkers discussing a problem at work
- An accident scene
- A parent-teacher conference

H. Language Experience Approach

The Language Experience Approach (for full discussion, see 5.4 A) is generally viewed as an approach for working with emergent readers and writers, but it can be used very effectively in a multilevel class as well, even with high-level reader/writers. As the teacher elicits stories orally from the group, the advanced learners can make suggestions, corrections and/or spell words for the class, sharing the teacher's role. Another option is to pair mixed-ability students to create texts, using these steps:

- Start with a shared event, an important event in their lives in the last (week, month, year), something they've done before class, or provide a written or visual prompt to elicit a story related to the themes in your curriculum. These texts can begin at the sentence level with beginners.
- Students practice telling the story silently to themselves; ask students to think through the beginning, middle, ending, as well as key points in the story. A simple graphic organizer could be provided for those students who want to take notes. When ready, students tell the story to their partner.
- Pair more literate learners to transcribe stories of a partner with more limited literacy skills.
- To practice keyboarding skills, one student can tell a story as the other types the story.

- Those with limited literacy skills can draw pictures or verbally recount stories. These verbal accounts could be audio recorded and used for other class activities such as generating and answering questions, developing dictations, word lists, or practice with basic typing skills.

Any of these student-generated texts are then used by the whole class for other practice activities.

I. Self-access materials and computer labs

Self-access options can range from thematic classroom stations with activities that can be completed individually or in small groups, to self-access centers, use of phone apps for additional practice, and computer labs. Providing such additional learning options can increase self-directed learning beyond the course curriculum (Nash and Kallenbach 2009). The choices a program makes depend on its size and resources. In this section, the focus is on classroom self-access materials (computer software and distance learning materials are discussed in more detail in Chapter 8).

In preparing self-access materials, clear instructions and answer keys are crucial in order for the work to be done autonomously. Activities and tasks should be ones that are familiar to learners so that they can get started without teacher assistance. Some of Valentina's students (discussed at the beginning of the chapter) expressed a desire to have more grammar practice. By providing grammar activities in self-access centers, she could meet their needs while continuing to work on other areas of language with the class. Some students may desire additional practice with listening or reading. Bell (2004) suggests that learners keep a log or portfolio of independent work they have completed. The following list of sample options are easy to develop and can be used over and over by different groups of learners:

Table 7.2 Classroom Self-Access Options

- Prepare sets of vocabulary words that have been covered in class and have learners sort words into logical categories; create a story using the words.
- Have learners create and/or learn to access digital flashcards on their phone using a free program such as Studystack *https://www.studystack.com/* or Quizlet *https://quizlet.com/*.
- Create sentence strips using language taught in class, class-generated stories, or functional dialogues that students need to put in a logical order. Provide all possible orders in the answer key.
- Provide book/stories and recordings (commercially produced, or ones you've recorded). Short stories or high-interest articles that can be completed in one or two class periods are ideal. Have a color-coded leveling system so learners can choose texts that are appropriate for their level (Bell 2004).
- Have students record stories using their phones to share with family or others in class.
- Provide grammar review activities with answer keys (from published materials or at websites such as Anglo-link *https://anglo-link.com/* or English with Jennifer *http://englishwithjennifer.com/*.
- Develop listening lessons using listening passages from commercial ESL textbooks, news broadcasts, podcasts, elllo.org, or YouTube. Provide students with preview questions, comprehension questions to answer while listening, and follow-up questions that can be answered in a journal.
- Create an in-class reading corner with graded readers, high-interest articles, and short stories. Have students keep a reading log (stories read, record of main ideas/summary, and reactions).
- If doing project-based learning, have a permanent station where learners can complete portions of the project the class is currently working on.

In situations where the ESL teacher shares the classroom with other programs, these self-access materials can be stored in small crates and brought in and out of classrooms.

J. Encourage translanguaging

Translanguaging describes a learner's use of their entire linguistic repertoire across all languages they know (Velasco and García 2014), which for many adult learners may be two, three or more. When students, families, and teachers draw on translanguaging, they are applying "flexible language practices that contradict monolingual language policies and ideologies . . ." (p. 264). In other words, translanguaging views the learner's other language(s) as a resource with equal value to the additional language being learned, not as something that is a deterrent to learning a new language. García (2013) views translanguaging as a democratic endeavor that promotes social justice by giving equal voice to all learners, both inside and outside of classrooms. Consider the benefits of translanguaging in the scenarios below:

- A pair of students question one another in their first language as they work on a paired reading task using texts written in English.
- Learners in a class doing project-based learning on issues of dire concern to them (reporting sexual harassment at work, enrolling a child in a bilingual program, what to do when approached by an immigration officer) conduct research using complex texts in their L1. The final products (posters for a gallery walk) are in English (Van Dyke-Kao and Yanuaria 2017).
- Learners first talk among themselves in their L1 when the teacher poses a question to the whole group.

In these scenarios, translanguaging allows learners to affirm their understandings of content that they may have read or listened to in English. It allows them to access a broader range of sources and information they need in order to complete a complex task (creating a poster on a critical issue).

Van Dyke-Kao and Yanuaria (2017) report enhanced outcomes in their adult education program when making translanguaging strategies explicit to adult ELs. Learners in their program are encouraged to:

- Use home language for note-taking while listening to/reading in target language
- Repeat and review content in home language while studying
- Talk to peers in their home language when discussing assignments
- Brainstorm for assignments in the home language
- Draft writing assignments in the home language
- Think in home language while speaking or listening in the target language
- Compare languages to develop metalinguistic awareness (How are linguistic features similar or different?)

(Van Dyke-Kao and Yanuaria 2017)

Translanguaging also involves knowing *about* and making explicit the differing features of the target language and the L1, for example, word order differences: red shoes, zapatos rojos; verb choice: I am 13 years old, Yo tengo 13 años (I have 13 years). These translanguaging practices counter a tendency found in some educational circles of dichotomizing academic English and the home language, often situating home language practices as less valued (Rosa and Nelson 2017).

K. Leverage classroom volunteers

Many programs have volunteers or college students completing service learning in adult ESL classrooms and having assistants like this in the class is an asset in a multilevel classroom. Volunteers with more training in working with ELs can provide mini-lessons to specific groups of learners. They can circulate and monitor group work, assist with responding to student work, or conduct assessments. They can take charge of stations set up around the room or lead discussion groups. It is important that volunteers be instructed on effective group facilitation so that they do not dominate groups.

7.6 The classroom environment

Getting started: Take a few minutes to visualize what you would want to see when you walk into a language classroom. What do you see on the walls, what objects are in the room, how are the seats arranged? All of these features have an impact on learning, particularly for learners new to English and/or to adult learning contexts. Everything from wall charts with the alphabet, common phrases, and vocabulary to student-produced work displayed on the walls can enhance learning. Unfortunately, sharing classroom space in large institutions can make covering the walls with visual aids impractical. Many of the items below could be moved in and out of a classroom if necessary.

- Create bulletin boards with language experience stories, student writings, drawings, photographs; in sites with shared classrooms, display these in school entrances or hallways.
- Display projects completed by previous classes and the current class.
- Display helpful phrases around the room that represent class interactions and routines: *What does _____ mean? Can you repeat that, please?*
- Display helpful phrases for sustaining group discussions, e.g., discussion starters, opinion phrases, clarification phrases.
- Label objects around the room: chalkboard, door, window, table, chair, and any other visual aids, especially in literacy-level classes.

It is important that classes be as inviting and comfortable as possible. Create seating arrangements before students arrive, or ask students who arrive early to class to help you. Make sure the seating arrangement is appropriate for the mode of instruction you will be using. It may be that a horseshoe with seats facing the front is best for a teacher-led presentation. Perhaps the class starts with small groups checking homework together, which would require seats arranged in clusters. The classroom arrangement should be part of your planning process and not left to chance.

7.7 Managing large classes

The participatory and learner-centered practices described in this book include extensive learner interaction and input, which some teachers find daunting with a class of 30 to 40 students (not to mention classes of 50 to 200, common in many settings around the world). Some teachers shy away from communicative activities all together because they are concerned that it will be too chaotic or unmanageable. Pairing students and using cooperative learning, however, are among the ways you can assure that learners get ample opportunities to practice language and receive feedback and support from peers. A class based primarily on teacher presentation or lectures would mean almost no practice time for students.

Another common concern for teachers with large classes is difficulty keeping up with individual student progress as well as lack of time to correct student work or respond to dialogue journals in meaningful ways. All of this points to the need to promote learner autonomy so that students do not rely solely on the teacher for guidance throughout the lessons, and to build peer feedback and support into instruction.

- Create activities with built-in peer feedback and/or correction. For written tasks, provide Student A with half of the answers to a particular set of questions and Student B the other half. Ideally, make copies on different colors to make the distinction between the two versions of the activity more obvious. After completing their items, learners read their responses and receive feedback from their peers. For speaking practice, use information-gap activities, which allow for immediate feedback from peers. Provide answer keys for homework (a shared online document on the class web page, projected at the start of class, or on handouts that you collect for later use) that pairs or small groups can work through together. Some weeks, have peers read and respond to dialogue journals, once you've modeled ways of responding—perhaps giving them small opportunities to respond to short writing from classmates before responding to journal entries.

- Give answer keys to selected students around the room and have them become the experts who provide feedback to others in class. This role can be assigned to students at any level.

- Model and thoroughly check for understanding of activities *before* students begin to work in pairs or groups; otherwise you will find yourself with multiple groups or pairs in need of help once the class has started an activity.

- Make yourself available to the pairs or groups in class; monitor progress, take notes for individual students or small groups that can be distributed or emailed to students after an activity. There may not be time to give everyone feedback at the end of the class.

- Learners may be more reluctant to speak up in front of a large group of peers. When practicing language points, provide ample models and then let students practice in pairs before calling on individuals. This gives them time to "rehearse" their responses.

- Use **think-pair-share-square** or **stand and talk** (VanDerWerf 2017) as a class routine. For "think-pair-share-square," pose a question and let students think about it; then pair up and talk about it to a partner. Finally, have students share answers with another pair of students before reporting to the whole class. With "stand and talk," learners think about their answer to a question and then stand to talk to someone not at their table. Both of these techniques can be used anytime in class: when brainstorming vocabulary, answering pre-reading or pre-listening questions, working on math problems in a numeracy class, or practicing a particular language point. It allows all students the opportunity to participate and use language, even if they do not volunteer to speak in front of the whole class.

- Establish class routines for starting and stopping activities—switching lights on and off, ringing a bell or chimes, raise of a hand from the teacher—or decide as a class what that signal will be. Avoid shouting over the students to get their attention.

- Establishing rapport in a large class takes time. Teachers can create **base groups** or **cohorts** who spend time together each class period to check homework, answer questions, or complete particular activities. Designating base groups of learners who enter the program at the same time can provide learners with a support system and sense of community (Nash and Kallenbach 2009). In classes that include a significant amount of discussion and debate, or where project-based learning is common, try creating groups who stay together over a set time period (three to four weeks).

- Students in large classes complete their work at different times, so it is important to promote learner autonomy. Provide reading corners with books, newspapers or magazines, self-access materials, or ongoing dialogue journal assignments or links to online materials that learners can access on their phones. Have multiple options ready or extension activities focused on the same materials.

- Assign student mentors to new students to help them feel that they are a part of the class.

The suggestions above are useful for any class, large or small, but serve to enhance student interaction in those situations where the teacher cannot be accessible to all of the students all of the time.

7.8 Open enrollment

Many ESL programs have an **open-enrollment** policy, which means that learners are allowed to enter a program at any time throughout the duration of a course rather than only at the beginning of a term, or at regularly determined intervals. There are many legitimate reasons for using open enrollment:

- Immigrants and refugees arrive in communities throughout the year and need to be able to enter a program right away.
- Adult learners' life circumstances can change dramatically, requiring that they step in and out of programs.
- It is thought that due to high attrition rates, classes would be far too small by the end of a term if managed enrollment were used. Keeping classes full may fulfill state or national funding requirements.
- Programs seek to support as many learners as possible with limited funding (Chisman and Crandall 2007) and open enrollment allows for greater flexibility for working adults.

The result for teachers in some programs is that students come in and out of classes on a daily, or even hourly basis. This presents the teacher and the class with a number of challenges (Comings 2007; Condelli and Zaidi 2003; Scogins, Thompson, and Reabe 2008):

- Goal-setting with individuals when there are no volunteers or intake personnel available
- Keeping track of learner progress
- Knowing for whom and how many learners to plan for each day
- Building a sense of community and cohesiveness
- Making sure new learners don't feel left out when entering a group
- Helping learners catch up to the rest of the class
- Providing lessons that build upon one another
- Limiting gains on program assessments and accountability measures

While the challenges are great, there are a number of things that teachers can do to improve learner involvement in an open-enrollment program:

- Use peers as tutors. Learners at a higher proficiency level benefit from teaching others. As with volunteer teachers, instruct them on how to give a brief orientation to incoming students and assign them to the new arrivals.
- Invite existing learners to welcome in new arrivals; develop routines in classrooms where students gain confidence to welcome visitors, new students, and others coming into the classroom and to explain classroom processes and routines.
- Take full advantage of volunteers. Instruct them on how to give a brief orientation to incoming students and assign them to the new arrivals.
- Develop a simple introductory task that learners can complete if they arrive in the middle of a class: a simple goal-setting task (*In this class I want to . . .*); a simple survey of needs and interests; a set of visuals depicting needs and interests that they can choose from.
- In large classes, understand that you can't and shouldn't interrupt the lesson each time new students arrive. Greet them and have them introduce themselves to the class, and assure them that you will talk to them during the next break.
- Provide independent learning tools that review missed material or give learners further practice through self-access materials (see 7.4 I).

These practices can help to minimize disruptions caused by open enrollment.

7.9 Managed enrollment

While there are a number of strategies and techniques that a teacher can employ for making open enrollment classes more manageable, many programs are implementing a policy of **managed enrollment**. In using managed enrollment, a program determines a set time period during which learners can enroll in classes, most often at the beginning of each term. There are programs that allow enrollment only one day or evening per week, which is an improvement over those that have students entering every day, or even throughout a given class period. The program described below permits students to enroll at the beginning of short terms (8-9 weeks), ensuring that those students who are on waiting lists will not need to wait an indeterminate amount of time to enter classes.

When MiraCosta College's non-credit ESL program had an open-enrollment policy, there were as many as 300 students on a waiting list each term. Their records showed that only 25% of students attended regularly for a complete semester, which is representative of many programs. Changes in grant requirements for federal funds used learner gains on standardized tests as the basis for funding rather than student attendance (Ramirez 2001). All of these factors led MiraCosta to pilot a managed-enrollment program, which proved to have tremendous success.

MiraCosta changed to five nine-week sessions per year, with enrollment allowed only during the first two weeks of class. Those not admitted are placed on a waiting list for the next session. Students who miss more than three to five classes are dropped and put on the waiting list for the next session. These changes to programming led to the following outcomes:

- A rise in retention from less than half to over 80%
- Promotion to the next level at the end of each session rose from 3% to 25%–30%.
- All students on waiting lists were admitted to the following session.

Another study found that there was a positive impact on learner gains when adult education programs offered high-intensity, managed enrollment classes (Chisman and Crandall 2007). When learners were given the option between enrolling in low-intensity/open enrollment classes (those that meet three to six hours per week) or high-intensity/managed enrollment classes (those that meet as many as 25 hours a week), a higher percentage of students chose the latter. Of course, such high-intensity instruction may not be feasible for some working adults, and high-intensity courses are also much costlier to run. With a move to more career contextualized Integrated Education and Training programs in adult ESL, these high-intensity/managed enrollment courses are becoming more and more prevalent (Nash and Hewett 2017).

7.10 Pairing/grouping students

📋 **Task 7.3**

Most of us are likely to have had experience working in pairs or groups at work, in classes, or at conferences with varying degrees of satisfaction and success. Think of a pair or group activity you recently took part in and reflect on what made the activity successful (or not successful) for you. What was engaging and what was unhelpful? Think about the assignment of group members, roles of members, the purpose of the task, and anything else that had an impact on the success (or lack of success) of the activity and write your answers in your journal or talk to a partner in class.

Pair/group activity: _____	
Assignment of group members	
Roles of members	
Purpose of the task	
Other factors?	

There are many factors to consider when creating pairs and groups in a lesson, and the advice I give new teachers is not to leave it to chance. Ability level may seem like the most obvious factor, but there are others as well, including gender, family relationships, learner expectations, and the purpose of the pair/group activity.

Ability level: There are benefits to both like-ability and cross-ability pairs and groups, but a teacher needs to make choices about activities and learner roles to make the most of these different groupings. In the case of beginning-level learners, it can be intimidating to work with someone who is far more advanced in their language proficiency. I have observed beginning level students participating more openly and productively with students at a similar level as they complete a task at a comfortable pace and level of complexity. Sometimes learners with more advanced proficiency levels appear to be more challenged if working with others at an advanced level as well.

There are, however, some advantages to cross-ability groupings. For one thing, mixed-ability groups mirror more authentically what learners will encounter outside of class in work meetings or interactions in the community. More proficient students can provide beginning-level students with valuable language input. Helping others and acting as a peer tutor has value as well, but it is important that the learners perceive that there is a benefit to taking on this leadership role. Remind students that one of the best ways to learn is to teach others. Here are just a few examples of roles and activities for cross-ability groups:

- In paired activities where one student is the information holder and one is the information receiver (e.g., in an information-gap task), give lower-proficiency-level learners the role of information holder. This approach has been shown to promote greater output from the lower-proficiency level learners than when placed in the role of information receiver (Dao and McDonough 2017).
- Have more literate students transcribe stories of emergent reader/writers or let them be the note-takers in mixed-ability group tasks.
- To practice listening and following instructions, have more advanced students give verbal instructions to beginning-level students, who arrange pictures, fill in an information grid, etc. The input from a peer is likely to be comprehensible to the beginner.
- In jigsaw activities, give the higher-level learners more demanding questions to answer.
- When using a computer and projector to review particular content, invite computer-savvy students to the keyboard to click forward/backward as the class participates in answering/responding to onscreen cues, quizzes, and prompts.

Gender: In a class I recently observed, when one of the women was assigned a male partner for a pair activity, she turned her chair so as not to face him. While she completed the task as assigned, I had to ask myself how she felt, and wondered whether the teacher had given any thought to the groupings she chose. In fact, she had not; she simply asked students to work with the person sitting next to them. In this particular instance, it was clear that the learner would have been much more comfortable with a female partner. Learners from many cultures may be more comfortable with same-gender partners, at least until they get to know their classmates well, in some instances, but possibly not at all in others.

Family relationship: In a class I observed over a ten-week period, a married couple came to class together, sat together, and moved into groups together. Once in their groups, the husband dominated, interrupting his wife whenever she tried to participate. In conversations with her before and after class, it was clear to me that she was actually more advanced than her husband. The teachers I was observing were uncomfortable separating them—they thought it could be disrespectful and also very conspicuous if they asked the husband to move to another group. The teachers hadn't thought to employ less obvious ways to separate them, for example, having learners number off one, two, three and having all the ones together, the twos together, and the threes together (other grouping strategies are below). Once they tried this, the couple worked separately with no complaints at all.

Learner expectation: If it is clear that learners are unaccustomed to doing pair and group work, it is the teacher's job to explain the benefits of student-student interactions in class. As adults, students appreciate knowing why their teachers are using particular techniques and are often open to trying new things if they know what the benefits to them are. Relating what you do in the classroom to what the learners need to do in the real world is one way to present pair and group work. If you ask the students to observe how and when they need to use English outside of the classroom, it will quickly become apparent that interactions outside of the classroom are not between them and a teacher figure. It is also important to reassure learners that you are listening and monitoring their English during pair and group activities. Take notes as you listen and give learners feedback, either individually or as a whole group wrap-up. Consider asking learners for feedback after completing particular activities or at the end of each class (see exit ticket ideas in 9.5 e.), and/or asking them to rate their own participation and engagement on a scale of one to ten.

Purpose of task: Teachers who embrace learner-centered, communicatively-based approaches to teaching often assume that pair and group work is always better than individual or whole group work. When a teacher asks pairs of learners to complete a matching or a fill-in-the blank activity, there is often silence in the classroom. Why is that? The purpose of the activity does not lend itself to pair work; it is easier, and, from the learners' standpoint, more efficient to complete the activity on their own. If you want learners to communicate with one another, it is essential to provide tasks that promote a genuine reason to communicate with a partner (e.g., interviews, jigsaw). In planning pair and group work, ask yourself: *Would this activity best be done alone or with a partner?* There are times when copying sentences, filling in sentences, and writing stories are useful, and best done individually. Consider too, as suggested above, authentic ways in which adults do and don't work together in contexts beyond classrooms.

Strategies for creating pairs and groups

From the discussion above, it is clear that it is often necessary to plan grouping arrangements in order for learners to engage fully with an activity. There are times, however, when pairs and groups can be created randomly. In fact, in classes where multiple pair or group activities are done each day, it will be important to vary the groupings. Creating groups can become a communicative activity of its own by having students gather together based on certain criteria, perhaps reviewing vocabulary or language from a recent lesson:

1. Type of work they want to pursue

2. Type of job they held in their country

3. Month they were born

4. Number of people in their immediate family

Think of two more possibilities:

_____

_____

Learners need to communicate with one another in order to form groups. Groupings can also relate to the content of the lesson. In a reading lesson exploring the topic of personality and birth-order theory, the teacher can start by having learners create groups according to their birth order, including an "only child" group. Once those groups are established, the teacher then proceeds with the lesson. It is important not to overuse this technique; regrouping many times in a lesson with different criteria would be confusing.

As an alternative to numbering students off (as suggested above), the teacher can review vocabulary the class has worked on recently (e.g., the names of seasons, academic subjects, job titles) by assigning a word to each student and having students form like-word groups:

> Teacher (walking around the room): *Spring, summer, fall, winter, spring, summer, fall, winter,* around the room until all students have a season. (The teacher can start the sequence and have the students continue it around the room.)

> Teacher: *The spring group will work over here* (pointing to one part of the room), *the summer group here,* and so on.

Students benefit from repetition of words and phrases that they are learning. In lieu of partner or group tasks, line activities, concentric circles, or four corners (see 7.3) can be used to maximize practice, while maintaining interest through interactions with several class members.

Line activities: One line of students stands in the same spot for the activity; a second line of students faces the first. For a warm-up activity, pairs can respond to set prompts: *What do you do on the weekend? Tell me about your job.* After a few minutes, one row moves down one student so that a new pair is formed. This technique can be used for pre-reading or pre-listening questions as well, allowing the students to hear and consider multiple perspectives on a topic. Zwiers and Crawford (2011) recommend providing language prompts for elaborating and building on others' ideas each time students move to a new partner *(I just heard from _____ that . . .; Had you considered . . .?)* so that each exchange becomes richer and more in-depth.

Concentric circles: Similar to line activities, form two concentric circles with equal numbers of students (if there is an odd number of students, the teacher can join one circle). The students interact with the person facing them, then the outer circle rotates one student to form new partners.

7.11 Establishing appropriate boundaries

ESL teachers are often students' only liaison to mainstream communities and they may rely on teachers for assistance in areas that go beyond learning English. I think many ESL teachers appreciate the advocacy roles that they take on, and are willing to provide far more than language support for students. But when does it go too far? When does a teacher's involvement become either excessive or inappropriate? Many teachers and program staff have questions and concerns about the following issues:

1. Invitations:
    -   Entire class to teacher's home for party during or outside of class time
    -   Entire class to park/restaurant or other neutral location for party during or outside of class time
    -   Invitation from student to go for coffee or dinner at student's home
2. Gifts
3. Hiring of students
4. Transportation of students (appointments, shopping, job interviews)

5. Advocacy:
   - Making non-emergency phone calls for housing/medical/police
   - Teaching students to drive
   - Writing letters for students (other than for verification of attendance, job references, etc.)
   - Helping students find jobs

What follows are a list of questions teachers can ask themselves to determine the appropriateness or potential for misunderstanding, legal repercussions, or problems of a given situation. There are so many variables that are unique to any situation, so a "yes" answer to these questions does not necessarily mean that your interactions are inappropriate. Answering "yes" to many of the questions, however, should signal the potential for problems.

Table 7.3 Establishing Boundaries: Questions to Consider

1 Have I considered safety and liability issues—for staff and for students?	You need to consider what the liability issue would be if you had a car accident with your student during class time. You also need to consider program/agency regulations and rules regarding employees' liability.
2 Will this activity put the ability of the student to participate in class and meet their goals at risk?	If the situation doesn't go well, the student may feel uncomfortable about returning to class.
3 Is there any sense of obligation for either the student or the teacher?	A student may feel they need to return a favor to a teacher, which may affect their participation in the program.
4 Is this activity something that you would consider doing with any or all of the students in the class (i.e., non-exclusive)?	Anything you do that appears to give only some students preferential treatment (hiring them to do work, driving them to appointments) could make others feel excluded.
5 Would I be able to read about this in the paper?	If there's the risk that your interaction with a student could appear the slightest bit inappropriate, you probably shouldn't take part in it.
6 Have I made appropriate referrals, as needed?	Students often come to us for legal advice, concerns about landlords, etc. If you are not an expert, your assistance may do more damage than good. Refer the student to the appropriate assistance agency.
7 Have I been transparent with students about the limitations of my role?	The norms between teachers and students in ESL classes are often less formal than what learners have encountered in their countries. This is a time to be direct and transparent about your role and responsibilities to them as a teacher.

📄 Task 7.4

Let's look at a scenario a teacher may encounter. Read the situation and ask yourself the questions in Table 7.3. Should Barbara have accepted her student's offer? Why or why not?

Barbara has an ESL student who was an auto mechanic in his country. He has started repairing cars at his home and has offered to do a minor repair for Barbara. Thinking it would be helpful to give him the business, she decides to have him do the work. A couple of weeks later, she realizes the problem hasn't been solved, and in fact is a bit worse. She takes her car into the garage she normally uses and has the repairs completed. The student didn't do any damage to her car, and she was in no danger driving it, but she feels funny about telling him the problem wasn't corrected.

Follow-up: The key questions in this situation revolve around liability and jeopardizing the student's ability to continue in the program. What if Barbara had an accident after the repair was made? Even if the student's work had absolutely no influence on the accident, how might it appear to the student? Does the student have a license to do the kind of work he did? Could he get in legal trouble? Are there contexts in which giving work to a student might also have bearing on the perceived power differential between teachers and learners?

Conclusion

In this section, we have looked at the impact different learner and classroom variables have on learning. Given that any class is comprised of individuals with varying backgrounds and needs, all adult ESL classes can be characterized as multilevel. ESL teachers have no choice but to accommodate an array of learner strengths and needs in every class they teach. Teachers need to make careful decisions about group assignments, learner roles, the classroom environment, appropriate boundaries, and more. The overarching goal should be to provide a context for learning that is as welcoming and as accessible as possible to a wide range of learners.

Part II: Serving learners with particular needs

7.12 Learners with learning disabilities

One of the most difficult assessments to make in working with English language learners, children or adults, is whether or not a student has a **learning disability (LD)**. This term refers to any number of disorders affecting one's ability to acquire language, mathematical or reasoning skills. While not learning disabilities, behavioral and social interaction issues may accompany some learning disabilities. These disabilities may stay with individuals throughout their lives (National Joint Commission on Learning Disabilities 2016).

Many of the classic signs of learning disabilities that experts look for in native English-speaking learners do not necessarily signal a learning disability in English language learners. ELs and learners with an LD may exhibit challenges in following directions, phonological awareness, understanding sound-symbol correspondences, recognizing sight words, or retelling a story in sequence. Both groups may have poor memory, problems with concentration, and get frustrated easily (Klingner 2015). The difference with ELs is that these behaviors will normally change over time and the underlying reasons for the behaviors are different; the behaviors could be attributed to lack of experience with formal education, lack of literacy in the first language, or limited exposure to English outside of the classroom (Schwarz 2009). Traumatic events (emotional and physical) can also contribute to challenges faced by both groups; those with learning disabilities, however, are "hardwired"—their brains function in ways that make learning difficult and require educators to find alternative and multiple ways of helping these learners learn.

Of course, there are adult ELs with learning disabilities; the question is *How to know if there is a problem?* Many of the LD characteristics are present with beginning-level ELs (Hamayan, et al. 2013; Simons Loustalet 1999), and all learners may exhibit some of these problems. However, if a learner has many of these problems on an ongoing basis, there could be cause to consider ways of addressing these difficulties over time (with or without a diagnosis of a learning disability). The following are some persistent signs of a learning disability with adult ELs (Simons Loustalet 1999)

Difficulties with:

- decoding, rate, and fluency when reading
- handwriting and spelling
- organizing thoughts in writing and speaking
- processing information and following instructions
- attention and concentration
- distinguishing between similar sounding words in listening and speaking
- visual processing, such as reversing letters or tracking lines on a page

Few of us are experts in the field of learning disabilities, so ESL professionals need to learn how and where to access appropriate referrals within the school system and the community at large, and assist learners to make the contacts they need. Learners have the right to a formal diagnosis if it is merited. A diagnosis of a learning disability gives a learner access to certain **accommodations** that remove any barriers to completing a task in school or in the workplace, for example, allowing additional time for test taking or text-to-speech tools for learners who have difficulty decoding print (Byrnes 2000).

Formal diagnoses of adult second language learners can be difficult to obtain. Tests used in the public schools have been designed for the K–12 audience, and most have been normed with native English speakers. A valid assessment needs to be conducted in the home language;

however, test administrators may not be familiar with the adult learner's language or culture (Schwarz 2009). Many assessments ask learners to report learning disabilities, which can be highly problematic with immigrant or refugee learners. The term "learning disabilities" may not exist in their language and the concept may be highly stigmatized in their culture (U.S. Committee for Refugees and Immigrants 2007). With or without a formal diagnosis, educators can gain knowledge about the following with the aid of an interpreter if needed:

- the learner's background and history
- the learner's prior academic experiences (formal vs. informal; literacy levels in L1)
- whether problems acquiring or using the home language were present
- whether the issue of concern has persisted over time
- patterns of significant strengths and weaknesses
- characteristics of the home language vs. the target language (PANDA N.D.; Schwarz 2009)

7.13 Universal Design for Learning

Universal Design for Learning (UDL)[1] is a framework for designing inclusive and effective curriculum, assessments, and materials (CAST 2018). When applied in the adult ESL classroom, learners are given multiple options for expressing themselves, for engaging with materials and with one another, and information is presented in multiple ways. The goal is to eliminate any unintended barriers to learning that may be found in curricula. A variety of means and methods would be used to present information to learners along with necessary scaffolds. Learners have a variety of options for demonstrating their understanding, which may include assistive technologies; learners are encouraged to provide responses that are oral, written, or visual (CAST 2018). This framework is compatible with the learner-oriented approaches for teaching English to adult learners outlined in Chapter 2, particularly project-based learning, participatory learning, and cooperative learning (TEAL 2010) and in keeping with the model for differentiation outlined in Section 7.4, where the content, process, and products are adjusted according to learners' profiles and readiness.

Horton and Hall (2005) and PANDA (N.D.) recommend many techniques, strategies, and accommodations for working with adults with learning disabilities that are in keeping with UDL. Many of these techniques are intended to provide additional structure and predictability to instruction.

Table 7.4 Supporting Adult ELs with Learning Disabilities/Recognized Challenges

Classroom Strategies

- Determine learners' strengths and build on those strengths.
- Structure lessons and activities; provide information in clear, sequenced steps.
- Provide and articulate timeframes for completing activities.
- Provide checklists of tasks completed.
- Reinforce learning using visual and other sensory aids; have learners handle materials; use color-coding when possible/appropriate.
- Use demonstration more than explanation.
- Give frequent positive feedback and help learners recognize success.
- Use memory aids such as mnemonics or graphic organizers.
- Teach ideas concretely; make directions specific, concrete, and understandable.

---

[1] For a complete overview and UDL guidelines, visit *http://udlguidelines.cast.org/*

Accommodations: while accommodations is generally a term used to seek extra time or other supports for formal testing or alternative ways of functioning in a workplace, the term is used here to remind teachers of ways of assisting learners in ongoing ways within ESL classroom settings and beyond.

- Allow extra time on tasks.
- Provide access to materials in a combined audio and print format; use text-to-speech or speech-to-text technologies.
- Provide well-trained tutors to read material aloud or assign a peer coach.
- Have shorter work periods and frequent breaks; allow adequate time for transitions.
- Allow alternative methods to demonstrate learning (e.g., oral instead of written response; underlining a correct answer instead of writing it out).

(For an extensive list of accommodations, see *Accommodating Adults with Disabilities in Adult Education, 2nd edition* (2005). University of Kansas Center for Research on Learning *http://das.kucrl. org/projects/accommodating-adults-with-disabilities-in-adult-education-programs* and the PANDA Minnesota Adult Basic Education Disability Specialists website *http://mn.abedisabilities.org/*)

The area of learning disabilities and adult ESL merits far more attention than can be provided in this section. Online resources providing comprehensive information, resources, and further links are provided in the resources list at the end of this chapter.

7.14 Learners with physical disabilities

A number of years ago, I walked into the first evening of an adult ESL class that was to be taught by student teachers in the certificate program I coordinate. I always teach the first class while the student teachers observe, and on this evening, we were expecting a group of 12 high-beginning Russian students. I had prepared a lesson on making introductions, talking about jobs held before coming to the U.S., personal interests, and wants and needs for the English class they were starting. I included practice with basic *wh-* questions for interviewing one another about their personal histories, wants, and needs. I relied heavily on visual aids to depict professions; I planned to use the flip chart and PowerPoint for model sentences and prompts for practice. As the class was about to begin, two young blind men from Poland joined the group.

These two students had heard about the class from a community agency and took a 50-minute bus ride to get there. I had to make some major adjustments to my lesson plan, many of which I believe enhanced learner participation by all of the students as the sighted students described pictures and activities, and read instructions to the blind students. The learners expressed enthusiasm about the opportunity to return every Tuesday and Thursday evening in the dead of winter. My concern was whether or not the student teachers in the program had been given adequate tools and strategies for dealing with the new makeup of the class. Much of what they had read and learned about in the months before the practicum relied on using visual representations (pictures, written models, labels around the rooms) and written texts and activities.

My story illustrates the unpredictability of every teaching situation and the need for teachers to be resourceful and flexible. For teachers in a large district, the first step is to inquire about and locate appropriate resources available through their school or community. Does their school disabilities service provide tutoring support? Are special materials and adaptive tools available, for example, large print readers or text-to-speech tools? To my delight, the four student teachers in our program immediately started brainstorming adjustments they would need to make in upcoming lessons. They proved to be extremely resourceful teachers and highly sensitive to their students' strengths and needs. Here are just two examples of how they incorporated a variety of instructional means and learning modes into lessons that followed that term.

> In a lesson on getting around the neighborhood, asking for and giving directions, and names of common services (restaurant, bank, grocery store, etc.) one teacher prepared a tactile information-gap using specially designed maps. Masking tape marked the roads, a coffee bean represented the coffee shop, a penny represented the bank, and a piece of fabric presented the laundromat. Students worked in pairs and, each one with a different map, gave directions to their partner on how to get around their assigned neighborhood.

> In a lesson on clothing and colors in the assigned textbook, the color swatches and pictures in the book were going to be of little help in making the language meaningful to the blind students, so the teacher added the dimension of fabric types and texture to the lesson. For one of the practice activities, learners stood in a circle and were given an article of clothing. The teacher put on music and had the students pass the articles to the left until the music stopped, at which point the learners described what they had in their hands in terms of fabric type and texture. This continued until everyone had chance to describe several items. The activity elicited words such as these: corduroy, wool, fur, soft, rough, furry, bumpy, smooth.

If you have learners with physical disabilities or limitations, you need to plan lessons following the Universal Design for Learning (UDL) principles outlined above and, when possible, consult with deaf and blind resource workers. Also consider the following:

- *Are there multiple representations of materials used and are multiple modes of learning encouraged (visual, oral/aural, kinesthetic, tactile)? Do classroom aids enhance learning (visual aids, audio/video recordings)?* The teachers I worked with used an incorporated hands-on, physical activity that helped to make language practice equally effective for both blind and sighted students. A learner with hearing problems would benefit from visual reinforcement, both pictorial representations and words written on the board. In the example above, using varied and interesting textures made the lesson much more relevant to blind students, i.e., that is how they would probably describe a piece of clothing. Older students with impaired vision struggle with small visuals or small print, so it is important to use large, vivid photographs, drawings, and print. Also, make sure lighting is adequate in the room. For learners with hearing problems, providing closed captioning may be helpful when using videos or transcripts from the teacher's book when doing in-class listening tasks.
- *Are there multiple means of expression and flexible options for demonstrating learning provided in the lesson?* In one lesson, some learners could voice record answers to a task on their phone and email a sound file to the teacher while others complete written responses. For a class project, some learners can write a paper while others create a video or give an oral presentation.
- *Do you provide multiple means of engagement? Do the instructional techniques accommodate all the learners?* The teacher who uses mingles and multiple groupings in most lessons needs to think of ways to accommodate a learner with mobility problems, making the lesson equally rich for all learners. The tactile information gap accommodated the needs of the blind students.

Not all students will necessarily indicate that they have a disability, so it is up to the teacher to be observant and to ask the questions above, regardless of whether or not you are aware of students with physical disabilities or limitations. Build the habit of checking in with students who you know do have particular needs. As noted in the section on learning disabilities above, an in-depth exploration of working with learners with physical disabilities is beyond the scope of this text. Additional resources are provided at the end of this chapter.

7.15 Victims of torture or abuse

A potential obstacle to learning is past experiences with torture, or past or present experiences of domestic abuse or other forms of trauma. The Canadian Center for Victims of Tortures (CCVT, 2018: website) states: "Torture is a cruel epidemic that touches every part of the world. In the past five years, Amnesty International has documented its use in 141 countries." The consequences of torture are long-lasting, and students in your classes may be living with the effects for years, if not a lifetime. Those effects include an inability to concentrate, feelings of disorientation, disrupted sleep patterns, post-traumatic stress, depression, or side effects of prescribed medication.

As ESL professionals, our primary responsibility is to provide language instruction. Trying to counsel learners in any way will cause more harm than good, so referring learners to appropriate counseling services is key. However, there are means of making students who have experienced torture or trauma more comfortable while they are in our classrooms. The CCVT offers these suggestions for teachers working with victims of torture:

For learners who exhibit difficulties with concentration:

- Keep lessons short and provide frequent breaks.
- Give brief instructions followed by demonstrations.
- Include physical activity when feasible for the students; hands-on tasks are easier to complete than those that require sitting passively listening.

To minimize the possibility of activating painful memories:

- Avoid discussions that deal with politics and religion in a controversial way, i.e., the merits of one leader or form of government over others.
- Avoid using pictures and situations that are violent in nature, for example those involving robberies, imprisonment, fires, and arrests. Photos depicting doctors and doctors' offices can be troubling because of the involvement physicians may have had in the torture they experienced.
- Discuss the content of presentations with guest speakers before they come into your class.
- Avoid unconscious racist behaviors; be aware of your own assumptions and biases; similarly, don't assume that everyone shares your views. (See Awareness of Implicit Biases at the Yale Center for Teaching and Learning *https://ctl.yale.edu/ImplicitBiasAwareness.*)
- Be aware of teaching practices that involve too much stimuli. Survivors have increased sensitivity to external stimuli and too much frantic movement, for example TPR activities, could be a reminder of violent experiences.
- Avoid loud sudden noises. If calling the group to attention, find ways that are minimally invasive to hearing or sight (e.g., a small bell, a raised hand).

Finally, the CCVT recommends that doors, blinds, and curtains be kept open as much as possible and, if the weather permits, at least one window. Assure learners that if they need a break at any time during the lesson, they are free to step outside for a few moments. Have the learners organize the room the way they would like it to look.

Immigrants who are experiencing the trauma of abusive relationships within a new culture, living with the effects of surviving political persecution, or witnessing violence in their homelands, may be hesitant to seek help, nor even know where to go or whom they can trust. Cultural norms and support systems may be very different from what they knew in their own country. A social worker working with undocumented migrant workers shared with me the fear of deportation many victims face. Even documented immigrants and citizens are often wary of government involvement in their lives. Again, locating local counseling services that specialize in the area of trauma and abuse is the first step to take. Janet Isserlis (2000; 2009) makes the following recommendations for working with students who are or have been victims of trauma or abuse:

- Build connections with community resources. As educators, we can ease potentially tense relationships between students and service providers. Find out what happens when one calls an emergency hotline so that learners will know exactly what to expect when they call: What questions will be asked and is language assistance available? What assurances of confidentiality are there? Consider providing instruction in the language they'll need to make these calls (CCVT,

2018: website). Victims of violence hotlines are available to men and women; avoid framing issues of violence against women, per se, especially if so doing might call unwanted attention to any one learner's situation. The overarching rationale is to make learning safer for *all* students in the group.

- Provide safe avenues through which concerns about violence can surface, for example, conversation circles, readings, or dialogue journals.
- Allow learners to share as much or as little information about themselves as they want, particularly when they are just beginning to study together. Let learners know that while they are invited to share information about their lives, they are not obliged to do so (Isserlis 1996b). Avoid asking directly about childhood experiences. Frame questions so that learners can reply with "I'd rather not say." (Isserlis 2009: 46).[2]
- Allow learners to determine their own level of participation in classroom activities.
- Accommodate for learners who may need to absent themselves from class for long periods of time; for example, offer distance learning as an option, and make sure they know they are welcome to return at any time.
- Validate learners' strengths. This is crucial for adults who have received negative messages about themselves or their learning abilities.
- Encourage translanguaging to build community and foster contributions to class.

Informed by trauma-informed theory (Mollica 2006) and approaches in multimodal expressive therapies (Murray, et al. 2010), the New England Literacy Resource Center initiated the Managing Stress to Improve Learning project. In this project, teachers introduced a variety of stress management and self-regulation strategies as part of the daily routine of the classroom, such as stretching and breathing exercises, guided meditations, and daily check-ins. The project also includes the integration of expressive arts activities as part of the learning process and one of those is the Altered Shoes project, inspired by the movement to transform everyday options into pieces of art.

> "We thought an altered shoe project would allow students to reflect on their life journeys —where they have walked, where they are walking now, where they want to walk—by using imagery, color, and collage. The project allowed for a range of entry points and engagement —from sensory engagement to written reflections." (New English Literacy Resource Center N.D.)

(Photo and learner account from the SunPost)

Colleen Crossley works with learners who have experienced extreme trauma before coming to the U.S. as refugees. The Altered Shoes project provided an outlet for self-expression while also teaching about metaphors, symbolism, sequencing, and idioms. Students read the Langston Hughes poem, "Mother to Son," and listened to the song "Walk a Mile in My Shoes." The photo of one learner's altered shoes and the significance of the project for that learner are portrayed below.

> This learner's shoe design was inspired by a Langston Hughes poem, "Mother to Son." She used popsicle sticks to create a stairway, and placed crystals above the stairs to represent a line in the poem: "Life for me ain't been no crystal stair." Two clothespins on the tongue of the shoes represent the learner and her brother. "Life has never been good to me. Every time it starts good, it will go right back. That's the meaning of my shoes: my life has been building from the day I was born. My life is crystals that I never get to reach at the end," she said.

---

[2] Teachers can use the classic Jazz Chant (Graham 2000), Personal Questions and, "I'd rather not say," to reinforce responses to personal questions.

Conclusion

Not all ESL teachers are experts in working with students who have particular needs, so they must be aware of their own limitations in regard to helping students who may have learning disabilities, physical or developmental disabilities, mental health issues, or post-traumatic stress disorders. ESL professionals need to learn how and where to access appropriate referrals within the school system and the community at large, and assist learners to make the contacts they need. Teachers need to be active listeners and observers at all times and challenge themselves to create lessons that are inclusive and responsive to all students.

On your own, or with a partner, provide an example or brief definition for each concept:

Checklist of Key Terms	
differentiation	
discourse chain	
think-pair-share-square	
open enrollment	
managed enrollment	
line activities	
concentric circles	
learning disability	
Universal Design for Learning (UDL)	
accommodations	

Before doing these activities, revisit your answers to the questions at the beginning of the chapter.

1 Adapting Activities for Multilevel Classes

If you are already teaching, choose a lesson you recently taught, but that was difficult for some learners to complete (perhaps those whose literacy skills are less developed than others', quiet students, students unaccustomed to working in groups). Consider the **content, process** and **product** of the lesson. Then think about the learners in that lesson with regard to **learner readiness, interests,** and **learning profiles.** Develop two variations for activities in that lesson that would differentiate instruction and make the lesson more accessible for learners who struggled in the lesson.

If you are not teaching, select a lesson from an ESL textbook. What problems would learners with minimal literacy skills have completing this lesson? Choose one activity and develop an alternative task that meets the same language objectives, yet is more accessible to learners with limited literacy.

Choose a listening or reading passage in an ESL textbook and create multiple options (e.g., assigning different roles, creating different comprehension questions, designing different follow-up activities) for working with the passage.

2 Learning from Others

One of the best ways to develop a repertoire for managing ESL classes is to talk to other teachers about what has worked best for them. If you are already teaching, make notes of something you've tried with success for the areas listed in the chart below. Then, ask at least two other teachers at your school for suggestions of ways they have responded to these areas with success. If you are not teaching, visit a school and interview teachers and/or observe classes and gather ideas that you may be able to use in the future: This is a good opportunity to join one of the LINCS online communities of practice *https://community.lincs.ed.gov/*.

Ways of Managing Adult ESL Classes	
Adapting an activity for multilevels in class	
Handling open enrollment	
Working with learners with disabilities	
Managing large classes	
Setting up the classroom	
Managing pair and group work	

Differentiation and Multilevel Activities

Bell, J. (2004). *Teaching Multilevel Classes in ESL, 2nd edition.* Toronto, Ontario: Pippon Publishing and Dominie Press. This is an excellent text on the challenges and suggested practices for managing multilevel adult ESL classes.

Hess, N. (2001). *Teaching Large Multilevel Classes.* Cambridge: Cambridge University Press. This text is rich with ideas for managing large, multilevel classes, including ideas for motivating students and establishing class routines.

Tomlinson, C. and Imbeau, M. (2010). *Leading and Managing a Differentiated Classroom.* Association for Supervision and Curriculum Development. While focused on K-12 education, this text provides a model for differentiation that is appropriate for any level or setting.

Working with Learners with Particular Needs

Bridges to Practice/Success for Adults with Learning Disabilities is a series of guidebooks to help educators and counselors recognize, screen for, and address diagnosed learning disabilities. While not developed for ESL professionals, anyone concerned about learning disabilities and adult learners will find this site very helpful. The series is online through Literacy and Learning Disabilities Special Collection at *http://ldlink.coe.utk.edu/home.htm*.

The U.S. Committee for Refugees and Immigrants (USCRI), Assisting Refugees with Disabilities Program: Resource Guide for Serving Refugees with Disabilities guide includes information about resources for serving adults and children with disabilities, assistive technology, benefits for refugees with disabilities and more. Available at *https://refugees.org/wp-content/uploads/2015/12/Serving-Refugees-with-Disabilities.pdf*.

Taymans, J. (2010). *Learning to Achieve: A Professional's Guide to Educating Adults with Learning Disabilities,* Washington, D.C.: National Institute for Literacy. May be downloaded in PDF or HTML at *http://lincs.ed.gov*.

8 | Selecting Instructional Materials and Resources

To consider before reading this chapter:

- How do you decide what materials to use in your classes?
- What digital learning and technologies do you integrate into your instruction?
- How can you supplement a textbook or curriculum that has been assigned to a class you teach to better meet the needs of learners?

Part I: Evaluate, select, and supplement textbooks and materials

8.1 Introduction

Among the many decisions teachers need to make is the selection of appropriate instructional materials. With myriad textbooks, online curricula, learning apps, online learning tools, computer software, videos, and classroom aids available, how can an ESL teacher make the right decisions? In the first part of this chapter, we consider criteria for evaluating and selecting textbooks or published materials and curricula. We then look at ways to supplement and adapt materials in order to meet the needs of a particular group of students. We also consider the importance of taking learning outside of the classroom through activities such as field trips, scavenger hunts, interviews, or surveys. While earlier chapters have addressed distance learning and digital literacy skills, the second part of this chapter takes a much closer look at digital learning and technology integration in adult ESL curriculum and instruction.

Adult ESL programs take a variety of approaches when it comes to selecting and adopting materials. The assumption that all students will purchase and have a textbook in hand, as is common in many instructional settings, is not necessarily the case in adult education. In some instances, a program purchases class sets of textbooks for classroom use only, and these sets are used with different classes from one term to the next. The books are not given to the students to keep but may be available for purchase at the school bookstore for those who want their own copies. Some programs have developed their own curricula that teachers are either required or encouraged to use. In some cases, a program maps out a curriculum that draws on available online materials or published textbooks, or **open educational resources (OERs)** where teachers can find teacher-made materials around a variety of core themes.

Getting Started

 Task 8.1

What do you look for in class materials (textbooks, online curricula, supplementary materials)? Brainstorm all of the considerations you make and then identify the five criteria that are the most important to you. For those of you already teaching, draw on experiences from your program. Those of you new to teaching can draw on the skills and knowledge you have gained through your training and this text.

Considerations in Selecting Textbooks and Course Materials

Five most important criteria:

1. _____
2. _____
3. _____
4. _____
5. _____

I asked several practicing teachers what they look for when choosing course materials. Here are the responses from two veteran ESL teachers. Do you see any similarities between their responses and your own? Read what Renada and Lyle have to say and identify factors that you and your classmates or colleagues had not considered, and then add them to the box in Task 8.1. You will revisit and use this list at the end of this chapter in the application tasks.

Renada

With the new state and federal requirements that ESL courses are standards aligned, one of the first things I look for when selecting Adult ESL course materials is whether the materials are aligned. Beyond that, I also look for materials that have been designed with adults in mind, meaning that the content is relevant and respectful of the language needs that are most pressing for adult learners. I would also look to see whether the materials offer an opportunity for students to develop critical thinking skills. Finally, a newer consideration would be whether there is an online component to the materials. It is becoming more and more important to have materials that can be accessed electronically, both inside the classroom and independently by the student on their own time.

When it comes to published materials, Renada adds considerations such as the usefulness of the teacher's manual and whether or not there are masters that can be photocopied for some activities.

Lyle

The material and exercises need to be relevant and engaging, but not overwhelming or intimidating. I look for materials which learners could comfortably use independently as well.

There are a variety of relevant, timely topics addressed in fairly concise units which are more broadly appealing and considered generally important to ELL adults. I also look for a balanced approach to both functional skills and academic development. Texts or curricula should integrate all the communication skills and offer a wide variety of ideas and support related to teaching and learning these skills. A very important part of this is the critical thinking component. I look for material which fosters further development of higher order thinking skills.

I look for material that is multicultural in nature—that takes into account the lifestyles, approaches, perspectives, and experiences of people living in other cultures as well as of those who are adjusting to life in the United States. I think it's crucial to use sound educational materials to not only facilitate the development of literacy skills (including digital), but also to assist in the successful transition into a new culture and society. I also like materials that have a problem-solving component in order to help learners feel/become more empowered in their lives.

Follow-up: Every program is unique and learner variables, program expectations, fiscal restraints, and technological resources, among other things, will have an enormous impact on the decisions that are made about the selection of appropriate curricula, textbooks, software, and other materials. This chapter focuses on the following decisions that classroom teachers need to make:

- When given different books to choose from, how will I know which is best for students?
- How can I adapt and supplement the text or curriculum I'm using?
- What other resources can I draw on, both inside and outside of the classroom?
- What technologies will enhance learning?

We begin with a process for selecting and evaluating textbooks.

8.2 Types of textbooks

In a discussion of textbooks, it is important to make distinctions among the types of materials available to teachers. There are many different types of textbooks to choose from, and while not each one fits cleanly into a category, there are some key categories worth noting.

a. **Core series** consist of a sequence of books for beginning through high-intermediate or advanced-level learners. All skill areas are integrated and grammar points, functions of language and vocabulary are normally presented in each unit. Ideally, these texts have intentional integration of critical thinking skills as well as the 21st-century skills such as team work, collaboration, and problem-solving. Most core series written with an adult ESL audience in mind have correlations to current standards or assessments.[1] Core series normally consist of a multimedia package, including an accompanying website with web-based activities, audio/video, pre- and post-assessments, and teacher texts with suggestions for lesson planning and implementation.

Like core series, **integrated-skills texts** provide practice in all skills areas, but are not part of a multiple-level, multi-media series. They function as stand-alone resources to which teachers may add other elements.

b. **Grammar texts** come in many forms. There are core grammar series, ranging from beginning to advanced, that include grammar presentations and practice, both written and oral. They may be accompanied by audio/video support and websites for learners and teachers. **Reference grammars** are those texts that list the rules of form and usage of grammar structures. They do not contain activities for learners and would not normally be used as the textbook for an ESL class. Many teachers keep a reference grammar in the classroom for learners to check or clarify a grammar point, or for the teacher's own reference as questions arise.

---

[1] In the U.S., College and Career Readiness Standards, English Language Proficiency Standards, CASAS, BEST; in Canada, the Canadian Language Benchmarks; Skills for Life in the UK; the Australian Core Skills Framework).

c. **Skill-specific texts** provide learners with a focus on the development of a particular skill area (reading, writing, listening, speaking, or vocabulary). A good text will provide learners with practice in all skill areas; however, the emphasis is on development of strategies to become, for example, a more effective reader (e.g., predict, read for gist, find meaning of new words in context), writer (e.g., pre-write, organize ideas), listener (listen for specific information), or speaker (e.g., ask for clarification, speak with intelligible pronunciation).

d. **Literacy texts** are intended for learners with limited literacy skills. The texts often include passages written by ESL learners, and include practice in both top-down skills such as predicting, reading for gist, as well as bottom-up skills such as copying, filling in letters, and recognizing sound/spelling correspondences.

e. There are **content-based texts** for particular subject areas (citizenship) and career-focused texts for learners preparing for specific jobs and industries (nursing, retail, culinary arts). Texts for those seeking a high school equivalency focus on subject areas such as math, language arts, or social studies.

f. Also worth considering in this section are the multitude of **teacher resource books** that provide teaching suggestions and activities for skill areas, grammar, functions, competencies, and vocabulary. These books can provide teachers with a wealth of information for supplementing and adapting core texts.

8.3 Evaluating and selecting textbooks

No textbook can provide everything needed in a class; it is just one of many resources from which programs develop their curriculum. The process of choosing materials starts by asking these questions:

- Will I use an assigned text and follow it throughout the class? How will I supplement it with other activities as well as authentic materials?
- Will I follow a curriculum developed by my program or state?
- Will I create all of the materials myself?
- Will I work with colleagues to create units that we can share?

Unless you have unlimited time on your hands and you are also an expert materials writer, the last two options are often not realistic or even desirable. Writers and publishers spend a lot of time and energy assessing the needs of programs and are constantly producing new materials (some better than others) from which teachers can choose. For those teaching 20 or more hours a week with little or no paid preparation time, having a textbook as a backbone to a curriculum can have many advantages. There are also a few potential pitfalls of which teachers, particularly those new to the profession, need to be aware. Table 8.1 outlines both the benefits of using a textbook as well as some cautionary notes that need to be considered.

Table 8.1 Benefits and Drawbacks of Using Textbooks

Benefits of Using a Textbook	Potential Drawbacks of Using a Textbook
• It assures a measure of structure, consistency, and logical progression in a class. Textbook writers have taken a considerable amount of time and effort to produce material that is logically sequenced and is as comprehensive as possible.	• Not all of the content corresponds to the needs of learners and it may require a substantial amount of supplementing and adaptation. • It may not allow for the degree of learner input desired by both the class and teacher.

- It minimizes preparation time for teachers with heavy teaching loads and little time to prepare.
- It allows learners to review the material and preview other lessons.
- It meets a learner need/expectation of having something concrete to work from and take home for further study.
- It provides those new to teaching with guidance in course and activity design as well as grammar and other aspects of English.
- It may provide multiple resources: online activities for self-study, audio/video, pre- and post-assessments.

- Inexperienced teachers may rely too heavily on a textbook, following it in lockstep sequence regardless of learner strengths, wants, and needs.
- Textbooks can be costly for small community-based programs that have limited funding; learners may not have the means to purchase books themselves.

In weighing in on the benefits and drawbacks to using assigned textbooks, the most promising practice is to select a text that corresponds as closely as possible to the needs of the learners, the program, and the teacher, and supplement it with activities from teacher resource books, digital learning tools, authentic materials, or learner-generated texts as needed. Selecting the text that has the best fit for learners becomes essential, which means that selection committees and teachers need to take the selection process seriously, taking into consideration a number of variables.

Central to both Renada and Lyle's considerations for materials selection is a focus on the fit between the materials and the learner, which is in keeping with the principles of learner-centered teaching introduced in Chapter 1 (1.3). Remember that learner-centered teaching doesn't suggest that the teacher no longer has a role in the classroom. In fact, a truly learner-centered class takes considerable teacher direction and one of the ways that a teacher directs learning is through the choice of suitable materials. In assessing the extent to which a text would be responsive to learners, a teacher needs to consider the questions in Table 8.2.

Table 8.2 Textbooks and Principles of Learner-Centered Teaching

Learner-Centered Principles	Questions to Consider When Selecting Texts
All learners bring to class rich knowledge and experiences that must be validated.	Does the text include activities that activate learners' prior knowledge about the context or theme of the unit? Are there warm-up and previewing tasks?
The content of instruction is relevant to the students' needs and interests and draws on their experiences and knowledge.	Are the contexts and themes in the chapter relevant to learners' lives? Who are the people represented in the text? In what ways are they represented? Are they depicted in roles to which learners could relate and that are respectful to adult learners?
Learners have active roles in the classroom and control the direction of activities.	Are there interactive tasks? Do the activities allow learners to take direction of activities, or is everything written with a teacher-led mode of learning in mind?
Classroom interactions and tasks are authentic, representing how language is used in the real world.	Does the language produced through the activities in the text represent authentic use of language?

Learners acquire strategies that help them learn inside and outside of the classroom without the help of a teacher.	Are learners presented with and given practice with learning strategies that they can use outside of class (e.g., predicting, guessing)?
Classroom tasks challenge learners and promote higher-order thinking skills.	Do tasks require learners to employ higher-order thinking skills—to analyze, evaluate, or synthesize information? Do questions move beyond display questions, those which ask only for factual information?

Byrd and Schuemann (2014) suggest that the fit between the text and the program as well as the fit between the text and teacher need to be considered as well. Does the text adequately address the core program outcomes? Does the text correspond to standardized tests and standards that are used to assess students? Are there means of assessing learning within the text? Are the supporting materials going to help me in my day-to-day planning? If it is a career-focused text, does it represent the latest trends and career pathways in your area? Ronna Magy shared that not only did she use government employment data in choosing topics for her textbook on choosing a career pathway (Magy 2017), she interviewed employers in those fields to determine the job and language demands of those careers (Magy—personal communication). All of these considerations can come together to create a checklist for evaluating textbooks. The textbook evaluation checklist below incorporates questions about the learner, the program, and the teacher.

Table 8.3 A Textbook Evaluation Checklist

1 Disagree 2 Agree 3 Strongly agree			
1 The textbook and the learner	1 2 3		Strengths and weaknesses
a. Learner knowledge and experiences are validated and activated through schema building activities.			
b. Contexts for presentation and practice relate to learners' life circumstances.			
c. People in the book are depicted in non-stereotypical roles, and roles to which learners can relate.			
d. The material challenges students and promotes higher-order thinking skills.			
e. Language practice represents real-life use of language. Examples of realia (application forms, etc.) are authentic. Online practice presents authentic applications of digital skills.			
f. The text provides learners with a wide variety of activities and modalities for learning as well as communication using appropriate technologies.			

2 The textbook and the curriculum	1 2 3	Strengths and weaknesses
a. The text adequately responds to the outcomes of the program.		
b. The book contains assessment tools that can be used to measure progress in our program.	1 2 3	
c. The language and content corresponds to the core standards and assessments used by the program/state.		
3 The textbook and the teacher	1 2 3	Strengths and weaknesses
a. The approach used in the text corresponds to my beliefs about teaching and learning and represents current knowledge and research about teaching and learning.		
b. The supplements, resources, and teacher aids are adequate. The teacher's edition provides helpful suggestions and guidelines, especially for new teachers.		

8.4 Selecting and evaluating online curricula

In reviewing online curricula, many of the questions in the textbook evaluation checklist can guide you, but there will be some additional considerations to make. What is the source and who developed the materials? Is it an open educational resource (OER) and is it connected to a reputable organization? If not, the resource is more likely to disappear in time. If it is from a commercial site, there may be hidden costs or restrictions placed on teachers or learners. Have the materials been vetted by educational experts (for example, curriculum and materials added to the LINCS website have been reviewed by experts)? Does the online curriculum provide a comprehensive scope and sequence with clear learning outcomes?

8.5 Choosing literacy-level materials

Many literacy-level programs use learner-generated texts through the Language Experience Approach or the whole-part-whole approach discussed in Section 5.4. Emergent readers need materials with limited print on the page, clear visuals, and relatable topics, which is why learner-generated texts are ideal. If using textbooks or online curricula for literacy-level learners, the teacher needs to add some key questions to the textbook evaluation checklist:

Does the material build on learners' knowledge of spoken language and build literacy from there?

Does the material provide practice in basic literacy development (copying letters and words, phonemic awareness, spelling) while at the same time presenting and practicing other areas of language? Is the vocabulary supported with clear, unambiguous visual support?

Is the material age-appropriate? (Some programs choose phonics materials that have been developed for children.)

📋 **Task 8.2**

Look at this excerpt from a unit in a phonics-based series for emergent readers, *What's Next?*, and consider the questions on the previous page.

Lesson	Topic	Phonics	Sight Words
1: Introducing Samsam and Adam	Introductions	short *a* *d, m, n, s, f* *sh, th*	are, her, his, is, she, the, they, this, what name

From Conklin (2011) What's Next? Book 1 New Readers Press

The teacher's guide provides suggestions for previewing the text; learners start by talking about what they see in the pictures. They work through a series of tasks to practice the targeted sounds and sight words, for example, listen and write missing letters (_____ am; _____ ad; th _____) or listen and circle the word they hear (Sam/sat/sad). Comprehension questions are supported with visuals and require only a *Yes/No* response:

Reading Comprehension: Circle *Yes* or *No*.

1. Samsam is a man.   Yes   No

2. Adam is a man.   Yes   No

Follow-up: The characters and theme of this literacy-level textbook could be highly relatable for adult newcomers. There is extensive literacy skills practice based on the story. Previewing activities would meet the need of starting with oral language and building from there. The drawings are clear and could be supplemented with online images projected on the screen in the classroom (a larger map of the U.S., a picture of the school learners attend).

There are a number of other series for emergent readers, for example, *Easy English Readers* from *abc English*, with visual supports and topics that are relatable to adult learners. Materials with clear photographs have been shown to be more accessible and less ambiguous for those learners with limited prior formal schooling (Bruski 2012).[2]

Do you want fish?

No, thank you.

Do you want bread?

Yes, please.

(From abc English Easy English Readers: www.teachabcenglish.com)

8.6 Adapting and supplementing textbooks

Even after careful selection of a textbook, a teacher often needs to adapt and supplement with material that is more relevant or accessible to learners, to challenge them, to provide additional practice, or to appeal to a greater range of learning styles. It is important to maintain the overall theme, sequence, and flow of a curriculum when making modifications. Here are just a few recommendations:

1. *Adapting units and activities to meet broader needs:*

    a. Evaluate a chapter ahead of time in terms of relevance to learners' lives and interests, and prepare visuals and realia that will make the material more meaningful to students.

    b. Evaluate the lesson ahead of time in terms of difficulty. Could the vocabulary, grammar, or functional language be more challenging? If so, brainstorm other words, forms or phrases around the same theme that you want to present and practice. Are there many words that you anticipate will be particularly difficult in this lesson? If so, be prepared to demonstrate those words through multiple means, both visual and aural/oral.

    c. Some texts may favor a particular learning style. Think of ways to enhance the lesson to appeal to many learning style preferences. For learners who have difficulty understanding written or verbal explanations of verb tenses, use simple timelines to illustrate the meaning of the grammar (Azar 2017). Incorporate tactile and kinesthetic learning by using manipulatives—realia, flashcards, or pictures.

    d. Before working with a dialogue or story in the book, co-construct a similar dialogue or story with the class. This allows for learner input and assures that the language used is within the learners' reach. Learner-generated texts will have a stronger connection to the learners' lives. The students can compare their text to the one in the book, providing them with more than one way to express themselves and communicate with others.

---

[2] An online series from Bow Valley College, *ESL Literacy Readers* (*https://globalaccess.bowvalleycollege.ca/tools/esl-literacy-readers*), aims to authentically represent events and issues that a typical newcomer may experience, for example, using public transportation, enrolling a child at school, or looking for a job. Clear photos and simple language make these highly accessible and they are accompanied by audio and a teacher's guide.

2. *Activities and materials for supplementing a textbook:*

a. Incorporate a video clip or short authentic reading text related to the theme of the unit. In a grammar lesson on the simple future and making predictions, show the morning weather forecast. Give learners a simple listening task to complete:

Monday	Tuesday	Wednesday	Thursday
High _____	High _____	High _____	High _____
Low _____	Low _____	Low _____	Low _____

In reporting their findings, students use the simple future tense: The high will be 70° on Tuesday. This allows learners to see how the grammar is used in real-world contexts. The same can be done by sending the learners to a weather app on their phones.

b. Supplement activities in the book with easy-to-prepare information gaps or grid activities like the following example. In working on the simple present and routines, have learners copy a grid like this from the board:

Name	When you get up	On weekends	In the evening

Learners mingle and gather information about their classmates by asking and then report their findings:

What do you usually do when you get up?

What do you do on weekends?

c. Add data collection and analysis with a one-question interview.

This technique (see 4.9 E for a detailed description and example with academic language frames and a graph-creation step) adds practice with academic language, critical thinking, graphic literacy, teamwork, and effective communication, and can be used with any topic and at any proficiency level. Many textbooks include a series of questions to practice with a partner, but you can use those for a one-question interview instead. You can use this task to build on a theme in a unit, as in this example:

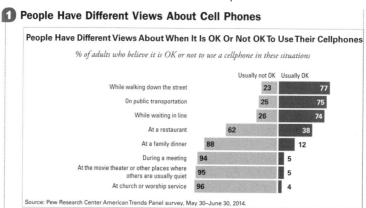

Ventures Student Book 2, 3rd edition (Bitterlin, et al. 2018)

Use interview strips like these:

---

1. How often do you use a cell phone when walking down the street?

| Very often | Often | Not very often | Never |

---

2. How often do you use a cell phone during a family dinner?

| Very often | Often | Not very often | Never |

---

3. How often do you use a cell phone while waiting in line?

| Very often | Often | Not very often | Never |

---

d. Select additional practice activities from any of the multitude of teacher resource books available, for example *Grammar Practice Activities* (Ur 2009) (see resource list at the end of the chapter). Most of these books contain a listing of activities by topic, grammar point or language function, making them easy to cross-reference with more theme-based textbooks or curricula. Any of the interactive speaking activities outlined in Section 4.9 can be used to supplement a textbook or curriculum as well.

e. Teachers can add news clips, scenes from television programs, short how-to videos or public service announcements to supplement their lessons. Video viewing should be anything but a passive endeavor for the learners. A video is simply another form of text (like a listening or reading passage) that needs to be accessed through pre-viewing/pre-listening, viewing and listening activities, and follow-up activities.

Videos have an advantage over audio in that learners can look for visual clues, facial expressions, gestures and body language to aid in their understanding. Video provides learners with more vivid representations of language use in a variety of contexts, e.g., in countries around the world, or in various work settings. Learners can view a segment with the sound off and then identify nonverbals and discuss how the people in the scene are feeling. They can predict what people are talking about or watch a scene and co-construct a dialogue that corresponds to the scene. The teacher can stop a scene and have the class predict what will happen next.

Another way to use video is to record learners as they role-play interactions, give presentations, or enact a skit. This can provide learners with immediate and powerful feedback on their performance, and keeping a collection of videos throughout a term can demonstrate for learners the progress they have made.

8.7 Making use of teacher editions

Whenever I conduct workshops or teach classes on textbook selection with teachers new to ESL, I get the same reaction to beginning-level and literacy-level ESL textbooks: *How could I possibly spend more than five minutes on this activity? How could this unit take up an entire class period?* Good beginning-level ESL texts are those that make use of large, clear visuals, minimal clutter, and simple instructions. For those new to teaching, it is understandable that they may have difficulty knowing how to fully exploit a page like the one below.

📋 Task 8.3

How would you exploit this page with a group of beginning-level English learners? Take a few minutes to brainstorm ideas with a partner or write ideas if you are on your own.

From *Ventures Basic, 3rd edition* (Bitterlin, et al. 2018)

Follow-up: What makes a text complete for the teacher is a clear, comprehensive teacher's edition that provides guidelines on materials, previewing tasks, activities implementation, and extension. Now look at the suggestions for this lesson from the teacher's edition of *Ventures Basic, 3rd Edition*. It includes ideas for warm-up, practice, and extension. It includes teaching tips for working with literacy-level learners. Those who are more experienced will not necessarily follow these recommendations to the letter, but for the new teacher, this teacher support is invaluable. Compare these recommendations to the ideas you brainstormed above.

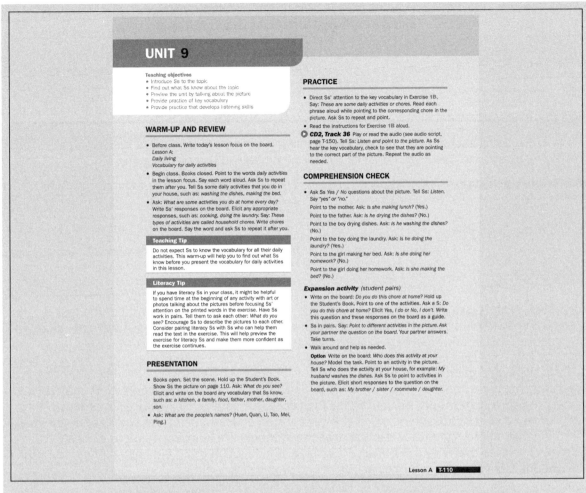

From *Ventures Basic, 3rd Edition Teacher's Edition* (Bitterlin, et al. 2018)

8.8 Taking learning outside of the classroom

Given the limited amount of time learners actually spend in ESL classes, it is crucial that teachers provide opportunities to take learning beyond the four walls of the classroom. We know that a feature of effective ESL teaching and learning is authenticity of content and tasks. We do the best we can in classrooms to replicate authentic use of language; we use authentic materials for listening and reading practice; realia connects new concepts to the outside world. But taking learning outside of the classroom expands learners' opportunities to engage in meaningful and authentic exchanges with others in their community. The question is what should students be asked to do? Are whole-group field trips, which require extra funds and transportation, practical or even possible? Are there tasks other than field trips that can provide an extension to learning?

 Task 8.4

Before we go on, brainstorm activities learners could do outside of the classroom. You can include ideas for class field trips, but also think of individual tasks that learners can complete in the community, on the job, or at home. Of course, we can promote extensive online independent learning, which will be included in the next section of this chapter.

Taking Learning Outside of the Classroom

Follow-up: Activities that take learning outside of the classroom may fall into one of the following categories. See if your answers in Task 8.4 fit any of these categories.

a.   Field trips: group or independent

b.   Scavenger hunts

c.   Surveys/interviews

d.   Community events and resources

Regardless of the tasks you choose to assign, the key to successful completion of the task is preparation done beforehand in class. Let's look at examples of tasks for each category along with suggestions for preparing learners in class before they go out on their own.

A. Field trips (group and independent)

Programs that have transportation (a van, bus, easy access to public transportation) may take students to libraries, schools, museums, performances, or community services in order to complement and enhance their curricula. An integrated education and training class might visit a company that employs individuals in the area the students are learning about (e.g., health care, auto mechanic) so that they can observe firsthand what a job in that field entails; they could speak to someone from human resources about hiring practices.

Preparing for a field trip is much like conducting pre-listening or pre-reading activities; you need to activate the learners' prior knowledge and expectations about what they are going to experience when they get someplace. The teacher also needs to preview vocabulary and pre-teach key questions they may need to ask once they get there. Finally, students need to go on the field trip with a specific task to complete, in pairs or individually.

For those programs with limited funding and no access to transportation, **independent field trips** with a purpose can be assigned. Rather than taking the entire class somewhere, students explore a location in their neighborhood (See 8.2. for how to do the same with web searches). Everyone can visit the bank near their home to gather information about opening an account. Afterwards, the class can compare which bank has the lowest fees. The class can conduct research on the most cost-effective shopping options: a local co-op, a large supermarket, or a farmer's market. Which offers the freshest food and best prices? Which has foods the learners prefer to buy? Learners create questions of interest to them, conduct their research, and bring the information back to class for analysis. Learners can choose destinations in their community based on their personal needs and interests. After any field trip, learners can conduct paired interviews to gather information about their community (Parrish and Pecoraro 2002).

Paired Interview to Debrief Field Trips

1 What did you see? Did you talk to anyone there? Who?	
2 What was one new thing you saw or did?	
3 What did you bring home from your trip? Examples: library book, food, cloth, information, schedule	
4 How did the field trip help you?	
5 Was speaking English easy or difficult? Why? Did you have any trouble saying what you wanted to say in English? When did this happen?	

B. Scavenger hunts

Scavenger hunts can be conducted for a variety of purposes. Learners can gather information from stores and services in their neighborhoods, their children's school, from work, or from the Internet. At the beginning level, learners can complete a scavenger hunt through observation, as in Sample 1. The information they bring back to class can be used to personalize lessons on places in the community or giving directions.

Sample 1:

Find stores and services in your neighborhood. Write the names of the places you find.

For buying groceries	For washing clothing	For buying gasoline
_____	_____	*Pump and Go*
_____	_____	_____
For buying clothing	For buying medicine	For opening a bank account
The Clothes Horse	_____	_____
_____	_____	_____

Higher-level learners might read manuals and talk to others to find the information they need, as illustrated in Sample 2. This example is designed for learners who are already working and can be used in conjunction with a unit on safety and work.

Sample 2:

Look for the following information at your job. You may look at signs or manuals at your job, or you can talk to your coworkers.

---

1 Do you know how to report an accident? Find out how to report an accident.

2 Where can you find first aid at your workstation?

3 What hazardous materials are at your workplace?

4 What safety precautions do you need to follow?

5 How many breaks can you take?

6 What should you do if you feel sick at work?

Write three more things you want to find at your workplace:

_____

_____

_____

C. Surveys/interview

As with field trips, surveys and interviews should be conducted for a concrete and meaningful purpose. It is up to the learners (with the help of the teacher) to develop questions that are appropriate and connected to the curriculum. Here are just a few examples of the types of tasks adult English learners might complete:

- Interview someone who has a job in an area of interest to you. What training did they need for this job? How did they find their job?
- Interview someone whose first language is not English and who speaks English at work. What helps them communicate with others on the job?
- Interview someone who has become a citizen. How did they prepare for the test? What suggestions can they give you to practice for the citizenship test?
- Interview a teacher or other parent at your child's school. What are some suggested homework routines (when and where should children study)? What are some good resources for homework (teacher phone lines, websites)?

D. Community events and resources

For those students living in large urban areas, there may be free or low-cost concerts or other performances, community education classes, health services, or legal services from which they can benefit. The learner may be more inclined to take advantage of them if the teacher uses materials about these resources in class. One teacher shared student outcomes that resulted from a lesson she conducted with her class on community education: one class member enrolled in a basic computer class, another took advantage of an exercise class, and another ended up *teaching* a class about her language and culture (Celeste Mazur—personal communication).

E. Project-based learning

Project-based learning (PBL), described in detail in section 2.10, can inform learners about resources, both material and human, available to them in their communities around issues of concern to them. Learners can explore issues such as these:

- Immigration reform with visits from local human rights groups
- Exploring first language maintenance and its benefits (interviews the other immigrants, English language education experts)

Civic participation and community action sourcebook (Nash 2001) includes reports on several other projects initiated by ESL classes, including projects on AIDS awareness, domestic violence, bringing transportation to a rural community, and peace and tolerance.

Conclusion

Textbook and materials selection depends on learner variables, program and teacher needs, as well as available resources, and making sound decisions can make all the difference for everyone involved. Adapting and supplementing the materials we choose can bridge the gaps that exist between a textbook and learner needs. This can be achieved by adding visuals, realia, and authentic materials, by adjusting activities to promote more interaction, and by addressing the needs of learners in today's digital-rich world—the focus of the next part of this chapter.

Part II: Digital learning and technology integration

8.9 The place of digital learning in today's world

In the first edition of this book, most of this chapter focused on selecting print materials with a section on computer assisted language learning (CALL). How things have changed in 15 years! In this day and age, in which digital literacy is as commonplace as print literacy, digital learning needs to be embedded in all that we do and at all levels of adult English language instruction. Just as with print literacy, competence with digital literacy has an impact on an adult's employability, health, and civic engagement (Batalova and Fix 2015). Digital literacy tasks have been included in sample lessons throughout the book, but in this section, we dig deeper into the overall goals of digital learning, ways of assessing learners' digital skills, and guidelines for choosing what tasks and tools to use. We also consider how technologies can promote more independent learning, allowing learners to persist in their education even if they can't come to a brick-and-mortar school every week.

Many times, adult educators make erroneous assumptions about learners' digital skills. In fact, even those without access to computers may be very savvy when it comes to communication apps and navigation tools on their phones. Just as teachers' skills will vary, so will learners'. "ELLs and their teachers are part of a continuum of digital literacy experience and skills. Education, age, income, access to technology, social networks, and family members' use of digital technologies are some of the many factors that influence the digital literacy of ELLs." (Harris 2015a: 2). Even so, learner access to reliable broadband needed for some learning tools and the ability to use devices to access information and solve problems can vary greatly (Rosen and Vanek 2017). The good news is that Tyton Partners (2016) estimate that "55%–75% of the 4.1 million adult education students in programs today have smartphones" (p. 17). That said, not all learners have affordable access to the Internet. Later in this section we will see how we can leverage that mobile technology inside and outside of the classroom.

Getting Started

📋 Task 8.5

With a partner or in your journal, brainstorm all of the things you have to do in your personal and professional life that are digital. If you are currently teaching, which of these tasks and tools do you work on with English learners?

Digital practices in your personal and professional life	Tasks and tools you include (or could include) in your curriculum with English learners
Use a navigation app on my phone	

I asked leaders in digital learning to share with me what they believe teachers should know about digital literacy and technology integration in adult ESL instruction.

As you read their responses, take notes about the following:

1. What was affirmed for you?

2. What surprised you?

3. What was clarified for you?

4. What questions do you have about this topic?

Since one of our teaching principles is to teach English in authentic contexts, we need to include digital contexts throughout our English language instruction. For example, communicating with children's teachers is done through email or some other digital messaging system. In workplace and educational settings, collaboration is very often done online in shared documents like Google docs. That means that we need to teach the language skills in those contexts. I often say to teachers, think about what you have to do in your life that is digital. Your students need to do those same things and you need to help them have the English language and literacy skills to do those things.

Kathy Harris, Director of the Learner Web in the Department of Applied Linguistics at Portland State University

There are three primary uses for technology in classrooms: 1) to develop learners' digital skills through direct instruction, practice, and application, 2) to meet the teacher's instructional goals (such as assessment, differentiating instruction to learners' unique needs, or soliciting learner input), or 3) to transform instruction in ways that would not be possible without the use of technology. For example, video chat tools can bring guests from anywhere in the world to speak in your classroom, virtual reality hardware could allow learners to go on field trips to distant locations, from coral reefs to the pyramids of Giza, or mobile devices could be leveraged by learners to create and share videos advocating for adult education funding. Technology in the hands of a skilled teacher can expand learners' horizons. But we must be careful not to rush to use a technology just because it is new and exciting. All technology use in classrooms should be purposeful. Teachers need to think carefully about the goals they have for themselves and for learners and which technology will best help them achieve those goals.

Susan Wetenkamp-Brandt, Educational Technology Manager, Minnesota Literacy Council

Classroom technology integration and digital literacy should be thought of as two sides of the same coin. Done well, technology integration can both support digital literacy and transform learning in classroom, enriching it with real world tasks mirrored in our technologically-rich society. Selection of technologies should be driven by the digital literacy learning needs and skills of learners; these strengths and challenges need to be balanced with both the level and quality of support available in the classroom and the difficulty or newness of the content being taught.

Jen Vanek; Director of the IDEAL Consortium, EdTech Center, World Education

Technology integration, using digital hardware or software, in an adult ESL class should begin with instructional goals or objectives, not with a search for the latest "cool tool." The broad question teachers and program or school administrators should ask is, "What are we trying to accomplish, what do we want adults to be able to learn and do, and are there digital tools that will help us to do that better?" Learning about technology should be part of a language-learning goal. For example, if there is a writing goal, that may be the time to teach how to use a word processing tool, in the context of the language-learning goal. A simple way to think about this is to incorporate a technology objective, where relevant, as part of each language-learning lesson plan.

David Rosen, Moderator, LINCS Community of Practice, Integrating Technology Group

These colleagues have identified a variety of themes, which will be addressed in this section:

- The components of digital competence in today's world
- Integration of digital skills in all lessons and at all levels
- Aligning learning with overall learning objectives
- Innovative and meaningful applications and using technologies for learning

Let's start with the components of digital competence for adult learners.

8.10 Components of digital competence

Digital learning encompasses a whole array of skills, as depicted in Figure 8.1.

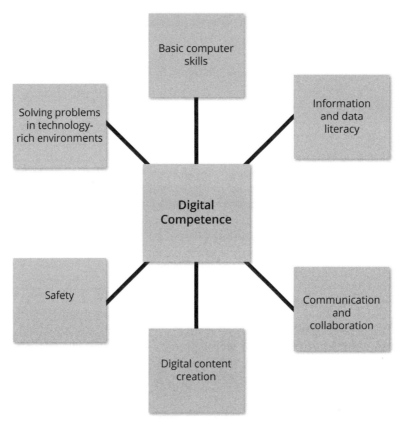

Figure 8.1 Components of Digital Competence (Categories from DigComp 2.0: The Digital Competence Framework for Citizens and Northstar Digital Literacy Standards (N.D.)

Considering what you brainstormed in Task 8.5, along with the recommendations from the four technology leaders at the beginning of this section, can you find examples that correspond to the categories above? Any time teachers work on basic word processing, saving documents, or creating attachments, they are working on basic computer skills. Developing a PowerPoint presentation as a culminating product in project-based learning represents digital content creation. Table 8.4 provides examples of each of the six components of digital competence:

Table 8.4 Components and Examples of Digital Competence

Components of Digital Competence	Current Examples (These May Change!)
Basic computer/digital device skills: using the tools to access information	Turn devices on and off. Use a mouse, touch pad, keyboard, and touchscreen as input devices. Find, open, close, save, and create files. Locate, open, and close programs and applications. Recognize email and web addresses. Create and send emails; add and read attachments. Locate and open a browser, use search box, and open and close tabs. Enter information into online forms; use the tab key to navigate.
Information and data literacy: evaluating and managing information	Evaluating the accuracy and reliability of information. Making use of hyperlinks to follow desired/required path of information. Differentiating between relevant and non-relevant information.
Communication and collaboration: interacting using digital tools	Using apps for communication. Using email to communicate with teachers. Using shared documents to work on a project at school of work. Collaborating with others using virtual meeting spaces (e.g., Skype or Zoom).
Digital content creation and the tools needed: word processing, Excel, PowerPoint	Making a presentation for a class or conference. Composing a research paper. Collecting and analyzing data for a project.
Safety: protecting data, personal security	Recognizing phishing and other scams. Creating strong passwords.
Solving problems in technology-rich environments	Defining a problem to solve or decision to make. Formulating questions. Accessing information to solve a problem or answer a question.

Examples drawn from Harris 2015a; 2015b; Vuorikari, et al. 2016; *DigComp 2.0: The Digital Competence Framework for Citizens; Northstar Digital Literacy Standards (N.D.)*

8.11 Building language and digital skills at the same time

As language teachers, we can support language acquisition while at the same time addressing these essential digital competencies. We first need to identify the digital tools and tasks that will advance student learning and that mirror authentic use as in Kathy's example of emailing a child's teacher, the expected means of communication with most teachers nowadays. As both David and Susan noted, the decisions we make about what technologies to use or digital literacy skills to address should be driven by the objectives of the lesson and the needs of the learners. Finally, digital skills need to be integrated at all levels of instruction:

New teachers need to know that they should not wait until learners have mastered print literacy to begin introducing digital skills. Because print literacy and digital literacy are so closely intertwined, learners need to develop both skill sets simultaneously. No matter what level of print literacy the learners have achieved, there are digital literacy activities and applications they can engage with.

Susan Wetenkamp-Brandt

Each time you teach a unit, you should ask yourself these questions (Harris 2015b):

- What real-world tasks related to the lesson themes are typically undertaken in a digital environment?
- What activities could be added or adapted to this lesson or unit so that learners can work on them digitally?

Harris (2015b) provides clear examples of digital skills used in contexts that are often addressed in core ESL texts and curricula, along with the English language acquisition focus of each (Table 8.5). This kind of analysis assures that a teacher is considering the language and digital learning objectives at the same time, rather than trying to use the "latest cool tool" as David cautions us against.

Table 8.5 Integrated Digital Tasks and Language Focus

Topic or Theme	Digital Task	English Language Acquisition Focus
Children's education	• Email the teacher • Use online field trip permission and volunteer applications • Find information on school website	• Communicate informally through writing • Convey personal information • Scan for information
Employment	• Email cover letter and résumé as attachments • Use online job application forms • Search for a job online	• Communicate formally through writing • Convey personal information • Read carefully for information
Consumer information	• Use technical support by chat or email • Complete online forms for product registration or warranty • Compare products using consumer reviews	• Communicate informally through writing • Read technical questions for understanding • Read for understanding, synthesize
Community	• Locate addresses on map and navigation help • Find ESL classes available or volunteer opportunities	• Read maps for information • Scan for information
Transportation	• Find local public transportation system and routes • Find bus/train arrival times • Complete an online credit application for car purchase	• Read maps for information • Scan for information • Convey personal information

(From Harris 2015b)

In addition to determining the digital skills needed in today's world, we need to determine learners' digital literacy skills. A valuable tool for assessing learners' (and teachers') digital skills is the Northstar Digital Literacy Assessment *https://www.digitalliteracyassessment.org/*. The assessment and standards cover basic computer skills, common operating systems, email, social media, and information literacy. After each assessment, a report highlights the information mastered and the areas in need of improvement. This allows the instructor to customize instruction for learners, and the learners know what areas they need to work on as well. When ESL teachers take the assessment, it reveals their own strengths and gaps.

Teachers can also create targeted in-class needs assessments like this information-grid task (Harris 2015b). Learners mingle and tally results; the teacher can learn what the primary needs of the class are and gear instruction accordingly.

I can . . .	Yes	No
take pictures with my phone.	III	IIII
take videos on my phone.		
send text messages.		
send pictures with a text message.		
use my phone to find translations of words.		

We also need to determine learners' access to devices (computers, smartphones, tablets) in the classroom, home, and community.

- What devices do they have?
- What is their access to Internet/data?
- What are they already using technology for?
- How much upfront technology training/orientation do they need to use the technology? To navigate the course?

(*Ascher Webber and Wrigley 2018*)

8.12 Digital learning tasks for the language classroom

What follows are sample activities that combine language objectives with one or more of the areas of digital competence outlined in Table 8.4. Any digital task may involve a certain amount of trial and error for learners and teachers alike, so it is important to pair learners more comfortable with the digital skills being practiced with learners who may be less so (Harris 2015b). It is also important to note that recommendations on digital learning may never stay up to date. As Kathy Harris shares:

> Things that adults need to be able to do in the digital world are changing and will continue to change. This is true for us as teachers and for students. That means that we all need to get comfortable experimenting in digital spaces that are unfamiliar. That might mean a website that looks different than the last time you were there, an app that you use in class that has gone away, or a new thing that is being done digitally. While this may sound challenging, it is actually quite liberating to know that we don't have to be the one who has all the answers with digital literacy!

Therefore, the samples that follow should be viewed as illustrations of the *types* of tools and tasks you might choose. Those included here can be used at any level based on the content you are teaching and the needs of learners. As you read these examples, consider these questions and take notes:

- Does the task advance learning in a meaningful way?
- Does the task represent authentic, real-world digital practices?
- What does the example inspire you to try in your own setting?

Constructing texts

An authentic use of technology is to construct written texts using a word processing tool. During LEA (5.4) lessons, learners can type[3] the class-generated text, leading to these combined language and digital learning objectives:

Language objective: Learners will be able to copy a class-generated text

Basic computer skills: Learners will be able type the story using a word processing tool.

Similarly, during paired dictations, learners can type what they their partner says instead of writing with pen and paper, thereby providing practice with typing using a word processing tool. At the most basic literacy levels, learners can create labels and cover sheets with their name, themes, and dates for their class binders.

Filling in forms

In all aspects of life and work, we fill in online forms:

- Ordering merchandise online
- Providing medical information

What else? Find examples in Table 8.5 and add ideas of your own. Make a list with a partner or on your own.

Teachers can create simple forms using any number of online form makers, creating something that mirrors the language learners have practiced in a unit and is as authentic-looking as possible (Harris 2015b). If you're unsure about how to create forms, you can search YouTube for an instructional video for whatever form maker you plan to use. Adding practice with online forms helps learners with a number language and digital literacy skills, including:

- Conveying personal information
- Spelling names, places, and basic personal information
- Reading for specific information
- Keyboarding; navigating a web page

What else?

Using online quizzes to assess learning

In the lesson on job vocabulary in Section 3.4, we can add an in-class quiz using any number of freely accessible online quiz makers.

---

[3] Learners can practice typing/keyboarding using one of many online apps. Teachers can link to one of these on the class learning management system (LMS) or a class web page.

What is his job?

Skip

4

0
Answers

▲ electrician

◆ carpenter

● farmer

■ florist

(Developed by author using Kahoot)

These online quizzes provide teachers with immediate feedback on achievement of the language objectives while also letting learners practice the basic skills of entering URLs and passwords online; they can point and click on the correct answer. Learners are also exposed to tools they can access to create digital flashcards or their own quizzes for independent practice.

Web searches

Adult basic education learners report that the Internet gives them access to information through print and videos that they wouldn't have had access to in the past (Rosen and Vanek 2017). Most websites and online materials, though, have been designed for an audience with advanced English skills. As with any form of authentic text, a teacher needs to create activities that facilitate the learners' abilities to make educated guesses about where to find information and to read selectively to find what they need on the site.

In a lesson on the climate and weather, learners can go to a website to gather information about the weather where they live now, or the weather conditions in their own country. The teachers can provide URLs for sites to visit, or learners can enter their city and weather into the search engine. These sites often use minimal print and vivid visual presentations with maps and weather symbols, making them ideal for those learners who have limited literacy. Learners work towards these language objectives: spell their city name, read selectively for high and low temperatures and weather conditions, and compare weather in their current city and home city, as well as these basic computer skills: browse for cities and weather using a search engine and navigate a web page.

We can also use information gap activities when doing web search tasks. The example below includes practice with selective reading, followed by an information-gap activity where pairs of students share the information they gathered from their local Department of Motor Vehicles (DMV) website on getting a driver's license (this task can be modified using the state or national website on how to get a driver's license). This example is based on a typical DMV site in the U.S. Same-group students (A or B) may work collaboratively to gather the information they need and then they are paired (A-B) to exchange their information. This approach lightens the web search load and builds in communicative practice at the same time.

Student A	Student B
You are at the Department of Motor Vehicles website. You need to find the following information for yourself and your classmates.	**You are at the Department of Motor Vehicles website. You need to find the following information for yourself and your classmates.**
1. The website gives nine steps to follow to get an original driver's license. What are the first five steps?	1. The website gives nine steps to follow to get an original driver's license. What are the last four steps?
2. Click on <u>DMV office</u>. Find the office closest to your home.	2. Click on <u>DMV office</u>. Find the office closest to your home.
3. Click on <u>make an appointment</u>. What number do you call to make an appointment?	3. When are DMV offices closed?
4. Click on <u>social security number</u>. What can you use to show your SNN?	4. Click on birth date and legal presence. Give three examples of documents you can use as proof of birth date and legal presence.
5. Click on <u>vision exam</u>. How good does your vision need to be? What happens if you don't pass the vision test?	5. What is a passing score? How many times can you take the test?
Now ask your partner what they found at the website and record that information. Share what you learned as well.	Now ask your partner what they found at the website and record that information. Share what you learned as well.

We need to consider authorship, content, and currency, as well as design and navigation when evaluating websites for use with ESL students. Some key questions to consider are what Kathy Schrock calls the five Ws:

Who	• Who wrote the pages and are they an expert?
	• Is a biography of the author included?
	• How can I find out more about the author?
What	• What does the author say is the purpose of the site?
	• What else might the author have in mind for the site?
	• What makes the site easy to use?
	• What information is included and does this information differ from other sites?
When	• When was the site created?
	• When was the site last updated?
Where	• Where does the information come from?
	• Where can I look to find out more about the sponsor of the site?
Why	• Why is this information useful for my purpose?
	• Why should I use the information?
	• Why is this page better than another?

Kathy Schrock ©2001-2016

We also need to make sure the site is free of bias and stereotypes. Learners can use these same questions for evaluating the legitimacy of websites.

Cooperative learning tasks: jigsaw and paired reading

In the sample reading lesson in Chapter 5 on the science of happiness (5.8), learners read and completed one section of a graphic organizer in the jigsaw reading lesson. What happens if that stage is completed using a shared cloud-based document? Pairs or small groups can first work together to fill in their section of the grid. As the sections of the grid are populated, the class reads what has been written (as opposed to the mingle and share in the original plan, which practices oral/aural skills). Not only do learners read for specific information—define one happiness booster and result from research; use reporting language in constructing a summary of the article—they also practice digital communication and collaboration when using a collaborative word processing tool to share information and construct an overview of an article.

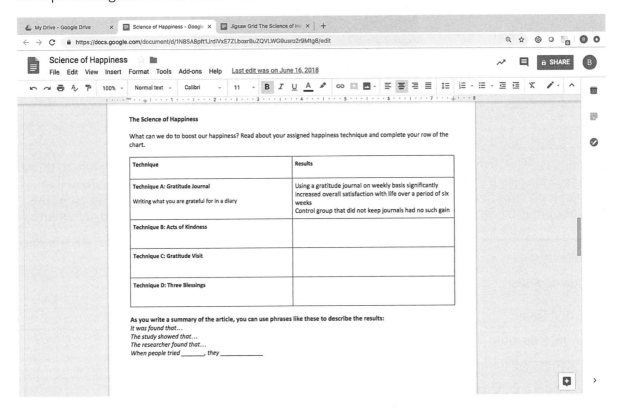

There are a number of reading resources that allow different learners to explore the same topic through different readings (ReadWorks and NewsELA are two free sources). *The Change Agent* (see 5.10) is an excellent source for content written by and for adult learners, each issue including several articles on a theme. This makes the magazine ideal for jigsaw tasks or for paired reading (5.8 and 5.9). Peterson (2018) shares how learners can work collaboratively to respond to writing prompts in a shared document using different color fonts to highlight the various perspectives; learners could then look for commonalities and differences and write a synthesis of class views on a topic. Learners can choose a partner to respond to using the commenting feature.

Learner-generated content

Nell Eckersley (2017) suggests that teachers and learners alike are better at consuming information with technology, for example, watching YouTube videos or gathering information online, than creating information using technology: "We are generally pretty strong in our consuming of information via technology, but for many creating and curating are not skills that are practiced. If teachers are creating with technology, they often think that they have to be the creators and the students are the consumers. But one of the most powerful aspects of the technology today is that students can be creators too" (Eckersley 2017).

Garden video project

Mary Zamacona's learners at the Open Door Learning Center of the Minnesota Literacy Council worked on a garden movie project.

Learners worked in the school's community garden and groups of learners created a two to three minute video giving a tour of the school garden and instructions for how to cook one food item. Developing a storyboard (Figure 8.2) was but one of the many activities conducted as part of this 16-week project. Learners also entered data about the garden's progress in a shared document.

Simple Storyboard

Title of Video:

Group Name:	Group Members:
1. Introduction Welcome to the garden	
2. Show and name the vegetables in English. Does it grow in your country?	
3. Explain how to cook vegetable one.	
4. Closing: Say why the garden is important for the school. Thank you	

Figure 8.2 Story Board for Developing Video

Creating connections

A common practice in English classes is to have students teach others about their countries of origin. In the past, that normally took the form of a poster, but today we can take others to the street where we lived or the place where we shopped, using web-based virtual maps with 360°

street views (Shiring 2017). Students can create digital stories using any number of freely available web-based, collaborative tools that allow for use of audio, video, slides, and narration as well as movie-maker applications. Digital storytelling entails any combination of text, videos or photos, audio narration, or music (Stanley and Dillingham 2017). In a reading lesson on photo archives and memories, Jessica Jones (personal communication) has students choose a picture on their phones, then stand and mingle to share the photo/memory before moving on to the creation of a more formal presentation. Learners load at least three photos to their personal cloud-based drive and create a slideshow to present to the class. Learners can take and share pictures on any theme related to the curriculum (Gaer 2011), whether it is pictures of a favorite place or, in a lesson on our environmental footprint, photos of "green" practices in the community.

Problem-solving

PIACC (2009) proposes three dimensions to problem-solving in technology-rich environments. Figure 8.3 illustrates this process with examples English learners may encounter.

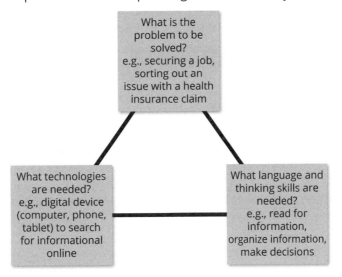

Figure 8.3 Dimensions of Problem-Solving

We start with a scenario adapted from Northstar Digital Literacy to model the problem-solving process with learners. In this example, learners work on reading information presented visually (a chart), writing in a spreadsheet, searching for information online, and they also engage in discussion skills as they compare the various criteria for the jobs presented to Alejandra's needs.

> The Hernandez family lives in St. Paul, MN. They spent a lot of time at the hospital this year. Alejandra had a baby, her son Miguel broke his arm, and her husband Antonio was very sick and in the hospital two times. Now they have high medical bills to pay.
>
> Antonio makes a good salary, but not enough to pay the medical bills. Alejandra stays home taking care of the baby while Miguel is at school. Antonio works nights. They have a strict budget, but they still need a little extra money to pay the bills.

Alejandra has decided to look for a part-time job and has these criteria:

- Work when Miguel is at school (8:30-3:30)
- Temporary
- Part-time
- At least $10.00 an hour

Learners are asked to consider which job sites to search; sample sites are provided and the teacher and learners complete a spreadsheet like this:

	A	B	C	D	E
1	**Job Title**	**Description**	**Location**	**Pay**	**Days**
2	Part-time nanny	Childcare; twin boys; nine months old	Burnsville	$13/hour	Weekdays: M-F
3	Nanny for three children	Meet kids at school; walk to home	St. Paul	$12/hour	Weds/Thurs evenings
4	Part-time for one infant	Childcare for three months; one baby	St. Paul	$11/hour	Mon and Weds 9:00–3:00

(Based on Northstar Digital Literacy Information Literacy Assessment)

Learners then make a decision as to which job is most suitable for Alejandra based on her criteria. Next, learners consider criteria for their own job search, visit the job sites, create their own spreadsheet, and determine which job is most suitable for them.

📋 **Task 8.6**

Consider other topics/themes that would that work well for a problem-solving task. What technologies would be most suitable and what language and thinking skills would the task require?

Digital communication tools
Email, text messages, chat rooms, discussion forums, blogs, and social media are tools that can promote interaction at a distance between teachers and learners, among learners, and with individuals all over the world. In writing classes, shared documents or email are vehicles for sharing drafts and receiving feedback outside of class time. Some of these tools are particularly important for learners preparing for entrance into post-secondary academic programs where faculty expect a high level of computer and Internet literacy and knowledge (Johnson and Parrish 2010) and they promote independent learning, the focus of the next section.

8.13 Using technologies for independent learning

In a large survey of adult education teachers and administrators, practice for students outside of class, opportunity for self-paced learning, and personalization of learning were cited as the greatest benefits of technology in adult education (Newman, Rosbash, and Sarkisian 2015). Workers need access to flexible learning opportunities and open educational resources so that they can continue on a path to acquiring more language and skills (OECD 2016). Teachers can extend learning through cloud-based shared documents, discussions through social media groups, blogs or wikis, emails, and more using learners' mobile devices (Vanek, et al. 2016).

Integrated mobile learning
Chapter 2 includes a description of **distance learning** options, one of which was MOBILE UP! (see 2.20). Like MOBILE UP!, Cell-Ed pilot projects include very short learning modules with an audio lesson, a follow-up text from the "coach" to reinforce learning, and an interactive quiz to

assess and apply learning. Learners can study any time, during break times at work, on the bus, or at home. Learners in the pilot expressed appreciation for texts from coaches and for the ability to learn at different times and in different ways. As students became more comfortable using the program, they shared it with peers around the country, who then joined the Cell-Ed pilot program. A great advantage to this program is that no data plan or Internet access is required (Ascher Webber and Gaer 2016).

The processes used in the Cell-Ed project could be used with any adult English learners. Teachers can send out questions for review, pre-writing, or homework that learners respond to by text. Teachers can have conversations with learners, add extensions to readings, or ask students to search for additional information (Ascher Webber and Gaer 2016). Gaer (2011) provides examples of the types of message we might send to learners that represent authentic reasons for this mode of communication (i.e., reminders, inquiries):

- We missed you in class today. Will you be coming tomorrow?
- Please bring _____ to class tomorrow.

Learning management systems and class web pages

Anyone who has taken an online course has used a learning management system (LMS), which hosts the materials, online discussion forums, assignments, and tools for independent learning. There are free LMSs for teachers such as Schoology or Emodo that ESL teachers can use to support independent learning for students in their classes. Alternatively, teachers can create a web page to provide learners access to additional materials for independent learning. Alison Shank's page for her intermediate, integrated skills English language class provides learners with supports for monthly units as well as links to self-access materials that learners can use on their own outside of class.

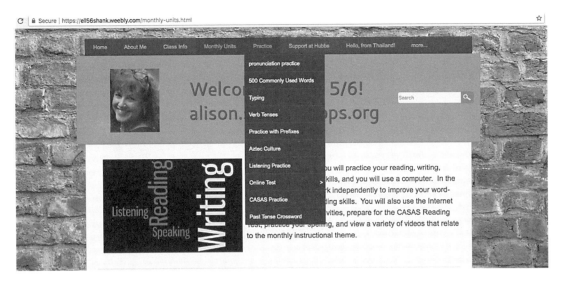

8.14 Learning software and apps

The selection and evaluation of software and learning apps for digital learning and language practice must be taken as seriously as any other choice made by ESL teachers. Learning software and apps are changing and emerging every day and these guidelines can assist new teachers in making the best choices possible for their learners (Gaer 1998, Healey and Johnson 2002).

- Does the language and content of the software or app reinforce or complement my curriculum?
- Does it meet the goals of the learners?

- Is it easy for students and teachers to learn and use?
- Is the language and content familiar and relevant to students?
- Will it work on any device (phone, tablet, or computer)?
- Does it require students to use their own data or can they operate it on the school's Wi-Fi?
- For classroom use, does the software allow for pair activities in cases where I have few computers or digital devices?

Other challenges arise in the selection and implementation of software in English language curricula. In programs with open enrollment, software needs to be simple enough to use so that learners can be trained to use it quickly as they enter the program. Assigning veteran students as trainers is one way to overcome this obstacle (Gaer 1998). Yet another consideration is the cost of software, which can be prohibitive for small community-based programs. Most large programs have someone on staff who can handle questions about costs and licensing agreements. Whether we recommend or assign software or an online curriculum, we need to make sure that any links to sites or videos are accessible to all levels of technology users. Downloading a video may use up an inordinate amount of a learner's data plan allowance and there are still many learners who may have limited access to computers and reliable broadband (Rosen and Vanek 2017), so we need to be selective about what we assign and make sure learners can view and use materials.

Conclusion
The technology leaders cited in this chapter have made a compelling case for the integration of technology in ESL instruction from the very beginning levels of instruction. Teachers recognize the need to integrate digital learning for authentic purposes. Doing so allows adult learners to acquire the digital skills needed in today's world as well as to access to an abundance of information from every corner of the globe. The ESL teacher's job is to create purposeful and achievable activities, to choose tasks and tools that align with instructional and learner goals, and to support learners in developing digital literacy in ways that are at their pace and within their means.

Key Terms

On your own, or with a partner, provide an example or brief definition for each concept:

Checklist of Key Terms	
core series	
integrated-skills texts	
literacy-level texts	
independent field trips	
problem-solving in digital-rich environments	
mobile learning	
learning management systems	

Before doing these activities, revisit your answers to the questions at the beginning of the chapter.

1 Textbook and materials evaluation

Look at the list of criteria for choosing materials that you generated in Task 8.1 and consider what you would add now after reading the chapter. **If you are already teaching**, evaluate texts that you could use for at least two of the groups you currently teach. Evaluate one core text for each level, as well as one skill-specific text (reading, writing, listening, speaking or grammar) for each level: four texts in all. You may practice using the textbook evaluation checklist in Section 8.3 as well. **For those of you who are not yet teaching**, evaluating a textbook has some limitations. You do not have a learner audience as a frame of reference for your evaluation. Therefore, create a description of a class based on an observation you have completed. Evaluate two core texts and one skill-specific text (reading, writing, listening, speaking, or grammar).

2 Adapting textbooks and materials

If you are already teaching, choose a unit in a book or curriculum (online or developed by your program) that you recently used that did not respond adequately to your learners' needs. **If you aren't teaching,** choose a unit from an ESL textbook or online curriculum and identify ways in which you think it could be enhanced using ideas from sections **8.1.6 Adapting and supplementing textbooks** and **8.1.8 Taking learning outside of the classroom,** or any of the ideas for digital learning integration in Part II of the chapter.

3 Developing a problem-solving, web-based activity

If you are teaching, consider an issue of concern to your learners that can be explored through digital tools and resources (see Figure 8.3. for the problem-solving components in a technology-rich environment). Develop a problem-solving task like the one in Section 8.2. Remember to consider the problem to be solved, the technology needed (also find websites you could send learners to), and the language and thinking skills the task requires. As you choose websites for exploration, consider the five Ws in Section **8.12** when selecting sites.

ESL textbooks

You can visit publishers' websites for extensive listings of adult ESL materials, including core series, literacy-level texts, integrated skills texts, grammar books, videos, software, and more.

Teacher Professional Books for Ideas to Supplement Textbooks or Curricula

Any of the *New Ways in Teaching* series from Teachers of English to Speakers of Other Languages (TESOL) *http://www.tesol.org*

Maley, A. (2017) *50 Creative Activities*. Cambridge: Cambridge University Press.

Ur, P. (2016) *100 Teaching Tips.* Cambridge: Cambridge University Press.

Ur, P. (2009) *Grammar Practice Activities*. Cambridge: Cambridge University Press.

Digital Learning and Technology Integration

Clandfield. L. and Hadfield, J. (2017) *Interaction Online: Creative Activities for Blended Learning*. Cambridge: Cambridge University Press.

Goldstein, B. and Driver, P. (2014) *Language Learning with Digital Video.* Cambridge: Cambridge University Press. The book contains a variety of generic, easy-to-use, practical activities as well as a number of ready-made worksheets for specific video clips. Activities require minimal preparation and are suitable for a range of ages and levels, and for both the experienced and less experienced teacher.

Harris, K. (2015) *Integrating Digital Literacy into English Language Instruction: Issue Brief* and online professional development module. LINCS ESL Pro Project. Washington D.C.: U.S. Department of Education, Office of Career, Technical and Adult Education *https://lincs.ed.gov/programs/eslpro*.

Jenkins, R. (2015) *Integrating Digital Literacy into English Language Instruction: Companion Learning Resource*. Washington, D.C.: U.S. Department of Education, Office of Career, Technical and Adult Education *https://lincs.ed.gov/programs/eslpro*.

Vanek, J., Simpson, D., Johnston, J. and Petty, L. (2016) *IDEAL Distance Education and Blended Learning Handbook, 5th edition.* Boston, M.A.: World Education.

Walker, A., and White, G. (2013) *Technology Enhanced Language Learning: Connecting Theory and Practice*. Oxford, UK: Oxford University Press.

SOME USEFUL WEBSITES (SEE THE RESOURCE PAGE AT CAMBRIDGE UNIVERSITY PRESS FOR THIS BOOK FOR ADDITIONAL RESOURCES)

EdTech of World Education As noted at their web page, "educational technologies advance at rapid speeds." EdTech experts help to identify, design, implement, evaluate, and promote best practices in leveraging technology to accelerate learning. There are articles, teaching tips, and links to webinars on digital learning and technology integration. *https://edtech.worlded.org/*

The Northstar Digital Literacy Assessment *(http://www. digitalliteracyassessment.org)* assesses digital skills through online, self-guided modules.

The ESL Literacy Network *(https://esl-literacy.com)* is for professionals who work with English learning adults with little formal education and limited literacy. Created at Bow Valley College in Calgary, Canada, users may find the online ESL literacy readers *(https://esl-literacy.com/readers)* particularly useful. The readers include sound, clear images, and simple language.

9 | Assessing Learning and Teaching

Part I: Formal and informal assessment processes

9.1 Introduction

Assessment occurs every day in ESL programs. Adult English learners may take standardized tests for placement and advancement; they complete entrance interviews and educational plans at intake. Assessment occurs as teachers observe students and provide feedback, and as learners provide feedback to one another. Teachers conduct in-class assessments to measure performance and achievement in relation to student goals and course outcomes; learners assess their progress as well. Assessment plays an important role in program evaluation and accountability. Finally, teachers undergo assessment; a supervisor may formally evaluate them; teachers may also engage in self or peer assessment for professional development purposes. All of these processes are complex and require careful planning and implementation.

Getting Started

 Task 9.1

Take a few minutes to think about these questions and write down a few notes:

- How have you been assessed as a language learner? If you haven't studied another language, think of any type of assessment you have experienced as a learner.
- Now think of *one* of those assessments. What was the purpose of the assessment?
- How did you feel taking the assessment?
- Do you think that it was an accurate measure of your skills?

I reflected on these questions for Mandarin classes I audited several years ago. In one class, I had daily Chinese character quizzes (we had to memorize 10 a day); we had unit tests and one final oral interview. As someone who was used to getting good grades in school, I was disheartened when quizzes were returned to me with a low grade. However, when I attended events with people from China, I was gratified to find that I could make a little small talk in Mandarin. I didn't feel as though assessment techniques used in class measured the gains in my communicative competence. The teacher in this class used **formal assessments**, some **formative** (representing my ongoing development during the course) and some **summative** (a measure of my achievement at the end of unit or course). No doubt, learners in our classes have the same need to see their progress and we need to find assessments that accurately reflect gains they are making in their language development.

A different view of assessment

In another class, the teacher took a very different approach to assessment. On the first day of the term, we each created a flash card with an activity we learned about in Mandarin 1, using a character we could remember. I was thrilled because I remembered how to write *watch movies*.

Then, we walked around the room asking others whether they liked our chosen activity. What was the purpose of this assessment? This first-day activity was both **diagnostic** (showing the teacher how comfortable we were asking and answering questions about personal activities) and **formative** (getting feedback that contributed to our learning). This was an example of a **classroom-based assessment**, using a regular classroom activity (a mingle) to assess learning.

Up until now, this book has focused on what teachers and learners do in the classroom. As we turn to the topics of assessment, accountability, and standards in this chapter and in chapter 10, it is time to consider how everything ESL teachers do fits into the bigger picture, as described by administrators from Australia and the U.S.:

> *Teachers come with enthusiasm for creating engaging lessons, but have to quickly understand a very complex system. Funding for different programs is usually linked to strict compliance related to curriculum delivery, assessment frameworks, and reporting of learner progress, which can often seem incompatible with good teaching practice. It is possible for administrators and teachers to work together to ensure that program delivery meets learner needs as well as compliance requirements.*

Margaret Corrigan
Manager, Carringbush Adult Education, Melbourne

> *Teachers want to teach, but there are greater goals than theirs. Teachers come to programs with good training and good intentions, but may not know what drives the system. Teachers need to know what data to collect for accountability purposes, and as they gain more time and experience in the program, more about broader national philosophical initiatives that drive policy. And finally, they need to know how to reconcile learner goals with program goals that don't appear, at first glance, compatible.*

Diane Pecoraro
Long-time ABE/ESL Minnesota State Specialist

This chapter focuses on assessment processes that are used day-to-day in classrooms and for these broader accountability purposes. Chapter 10 turns to the issue of standards and how those relate to accountability systems at the state or federal level.

9.2 Assessment dilemmas

As Margaret and Diane point out, the perception of many ESL teachers is that their primary job is to teach. While this is absolutely true, programs are accountable to funders in terms of gains in learner performance, and teachers need to have the tools to gather information that can provide evidence of learner progress and achievement of goals.

Task 9.2

Read the following assessment dilemmas. Identify the issues involved in each one and list the teachers' concerns in the box below:

Assessment dilemmas

a. *I have always used a participatory approach, developing a curriculum from my learners' expressed needs. My program uses assessments that focus on many skills that we don't necessarily work on in my class. I find that my students aren't promoted to the next level as quickly as before, but I don't want to teach to a test that doesn't represent what I do. Also, I'm feeling pressure from my supervisor to adjust my approach to teaching.*

b. *My learners are highly motivated and work very hard at improving their English. We use a standardized test to place learners, and a different version of that test at the end of each class level, but I don't know how to show them that they are making progress during the class. I teach level-1 students, many who have limited formal education from their countries. They have a lot of difficulty with test-taking. Because of this, I don't know if the test really captures all that they've learned. I'm thinking I should do more on testing strategies in my class, but we have so little time together.*

c. *I find assessment to be the most difficult part of my job. We need to write a report on every student at the end of the term, but I always feel like I don't have enough meaningful data about my students' progress. I know this is important because our coordinator uses our assessments in reporting progress under our federal grant. I need to find ways to conduct meaningful and reliable assessments in class.*

Assessment Issue	Teacher Concerns
Standardized tests	*Learners don't have experience with testing. Don't know if I should work on test-taking skills in class.*

The concerns of these teachers are echoed throughout the adult ESL community. What teachers really want to know is: *Are students learning and are my classroom practices helping them learn?* Many teachers question the need to spend significant amounts of class time on assessment. Many new teachers (and experienced ones, for that matter) do not feel that they have the expertise to design tasks and tools that measure progress, nor do they appreciate the need to assess learning on a continual basis. MaryAnn Cunningham Florez, manager of an adult education program in Virginia that serves around 6,000 learners each year, shares the connections she sees between assessment, accountability, and standards. She highlights the multiple ways teachers can gather information about learner progress and then use that information or data to plan instruction and measure achievement in relation to learner needs, and in relation to program accountability standards.

As a teacher, you use data from different sources to create instruction that is relevant, engaging and productive for learners. You draw feedback from the students about their needs and goals; you look at intake assessments to see what they are bringing to the table; you become a social scientist of sorts, constantly observing, recording, and analyzing what students are doing; you tap into the theories and approaches and strategies you have gained from your professional training and experiences about what is best practice. Standards and accountability are another source of information to help you in this process: what should students at this level be able to do and what are your students achieving or not achieving?

Programs need to employ a variety of processes that, in combination, provide all of the different stakeholders (learners and their families, teachers, programs, and funders) with the information they need. As we will see, teachers and programs should use assessments that reflect the integrative nature of language and literacy, as opposed to viewing language as a discrete set of skills to be measured (Wrigley 2008). This can be a challenge with standardized tests alone, which is why we need to assess learners in multiple ways and on a continuous basis.

9.3 Clarifying terms

The topic of assessment can be daunting due to the many assessment terms and concepts. In this section, I pose some common questions, and follow them with brief explanations. There are a number of resources available for those interested in a more in-depth study of test construction and assessment overall (see resource section).

A. What is the difference between testing, assessment, and evaluation?

Testing typically refers to those times when we measure "a person's ability or knowledge in a given domain, with an emphasis on the concept of *method* and *measuring*" (Brown and Lee 2015: 489). **Assessment** is a broader term that encompasses day-to-day observations as well as a variety of alternative assessment tools that will be explored later. **Evaluation** entails an in-depth study of assessment results to determine the effectiveness of programs.

B. What do I need to know about practicality, reliability, and validity in assessing students in my classes?

Practicality refers to the feasibility of implementing a particular assessment or test. Conducting one-one-one interviews of learners at the end of class may be practical if you have 15 students, but not if you have 40. Is the tool you are using reliable? **Reliability** means that the assessment tool would result in consistent outcomes if administered more than one time or if rated by more than one assessor. What is the **validity** of the test results? Does the tool assess what it is intended to assess? A basic literacy assessment conducted in English may not adequately measure what a learner actually knows about literacy practices overall. Are results related to what a learner knows about English (vocabulary or structures) or to experiences with reading or writing overall (e.g., perhaps is nonliterate in the L1)? The learner may also be unfamiliar with the cultural references in the task (Wrigley 2008). Does the test correspond to what was taught and what learners can reasonably be expected to know and does it assess the targeted skills? In one of my Mandarin classes, the teacher had us answer listening comprehension questions by writing out answers in Mandarin characters, but another had short multiple-choice items written in English. This second teacher's assessment was a more valid measure of our *listening* skills since we didn't have to read and process questions, and then write in Mandarin at the same time. This worked because all the learners in the class shared the same first language, English. This is something an ESL instructor could consider doing if all the learners share the same first language.

C. How are placement, diagnostic, achievement, and proficiency testing different?

Look at Table 9.1 for a summary of these types of tests.

Table 9.1 Test Types and Purposes

Placement testing	Where should a learner be placed in a program? Placement testing is conducted for the purpose of identifying the level most suitable for a learner. While some programs use a standardized test for this purpose, the placement testing may also include interviews, surveys, or an in-house placement test that adequately differentiates learner levels.
Diagnostic testing	What do learners already know and what do they need to learn in relation to course outcomes? A diagnostic test reveals a learner's competence in relation to the outcomes of a particular class. In a class that focuses on speaking and pronunciation, the diagnostic test assesses oral skills; in a career-focused class, the test assesses strengths and weaknesses for that particular work setting. Teachers employ a variety of tasks for the purpose of diagnosing learner needs, including interactive tasks, role plays, writing samples, and observation by the teacher.
Achievement testing	What have learners gained through a unit or course? In many programs, standardized pre- and post-tests are given to ascertain achievement, for example, CASAS (CASAS stands for Comprehensive Adult Student Assessment System and is commonly used in adult education programs in the U.S.). This can be appropriate in cases where the program outcomes are strongly tied to what the standardized test measures. Alternative assessments are commonly used to determine achievement.
Proficiency testing	What is the learner's overall competence? A proficiency test is not designed for a specific course or set of outcomes. It may be used to determine someone's readiness for academic work, for example, the TOEFL (Test of English as a Foreign Language) or IELTS (International English Language Testing System), which are given to thousands of students throughout the world hoping to enter universities in English speaking countries or English-medium universities around the world. IELTS is also used as part of the immigration processes in Canada, the UK, and Australia.

9.4 Standardized tests

It is important to understand what standardized test can do and what they cannot do. Standardized tests are typically used to differentiate among learners at different levels in order to determine the most appropriate level for them within a program, or to determine whether or not they have made progress in relation to a norm or criterion. Standardized tests can be **norm-referenced**, which means that scores reflect a comparison to a group (or norm), or the test taker's performance in comparison to other test-takers. A norm-reference test may be used to determine cut scores for the distribution of scholarships in a college setting. Alternatively, standardized tests can be **criterion-referenced**, which means that scores reflect a comparison to a set of outcomes (or criterion), for example, a citizenship test (Kunnan and Grabowski 2014). Standardized tests are administered and scored using procedures that are uniform and consistent (Bailey and Curtis 2015). As a result, test scores can give a broad and consistent view of learner progress within and across levels, programs, and states. These test scores may be only part of the picture, though, as these state-level administrators share:

> Local adult basic education (ABE) programs and states are now expected to report more outcomes for their students. Federal accountability measures move beyond just traditional educational gains via assessment to now include diploma attainment, employment, wages, and postsecondary enrollment for participants after they exit classes.

Brad Hasskamp (Adult Secondary Credential and Education Policy Specialist)
Astrid Liden (ABE Professional Development Specialist)
Minnesota Department of Education

Now let's consider what standardized tests cannot do. When used for placement, they cannot tell us what individual learners want and need as they enter programs. Because of a lack of test-taking experience, a learner's score may not reflect his or her real strengths and prior knowledge. When used to measure level change, unless the test mirrors program outcomes, it cannot provide us with learner progress and achievement in relation to unique learner or program goals. Nor can it depict learner achievement of more elusive skills, for example, increased use of learning strategies, or reading daily to a child. That is why standardized tests must be only one of many assessment tools used in adult ESL.

📋 **Task 9.3**

Most any program you work in will use standardized tests for placement, achievement, or for reporting outcomes to state agencies. Find out what standardized assessments are used in your program, state, province or region and for what purposes (placement or achievement). Conduct a web search and talk to program administrators in your area. Common standardized tests used in adult ESL are included here, but you may also need to add your own.

Assessment	What is the focus and how it is used?
BEST Literacy	
BEST Plus 2.0 **Basic English Skills Test**	
CASAS **The Comprehensive Adult Student Assessment System**	
IELTS Life Skills	
TABE	
TABE CLAS-E	
ESOL Skills for Life	
Add others:	

In reviewing a variety of tests, it becomes evident that different standardized tests emphasize different skill areas. Some are more appropriate for literacy or beginning-level learners, for example, the BEST (Basic English Skills Test) is often used with new immigrants with very limited English. It can even be used with pre-literate students, and those with little or no spoken English, through tasks that require only pointing to a picture. As a classroom teacher, chances are you will not be the one selecting or administering the test; however, it is beneficial to have a general understanding of what learner test scores represent. Also, in cases where standardized tests are used throughout the program to measure learning gains, there are some things that can be done that do not require "teaching to the test."

- Carefully examine the content of tests used and check to see when and where test items correspond to course outcomes and learner goals.
- When you cover a particular skill or competency that you know is assessed on the test used by your program, tell students that this is something they may encounter on the test.
- Periodically use activity types that mirror formats used on the standardized tests, for example, multiple-choice activities in reading and listening lessons to get learners used to that format (not as a test item per se).

In a literacy class that has been working on giving directions and understanding prepositions of direction, one of the practice activities includes the same format learners encounter on the standardized test used in the program. In the same class, the teacher does a group matching activity with images and words students will encounter on the test. She shared with me that the assessment is decontextualized and the questions are very random as compared to what learners encounter in her highly contextualized lessons. This matching gives learners practice with sounding out the words and working with decontextualized images/drawings, which can be difficult for literacy-level learners to interpret (Bruski 2012).

Learners in Kristin Klas's Literacy-Level Class Preparing for the Standardized Test

Many textbooks include activities that mirror the multiple-choice with bubbles format found on most standardized tests.

Assessments will, ideally, assess the sorts of higher-order thinking skills presented in Section 3.6, and reading test items should assess the kinds of higher-order reading strategies discussed in Section 5.7, especially at the intermediate to advanced levels.

📋 **Task 9.4**

Take a look at the sample test item (text followed by two sample questions) from the CASAS Reading Goals Series Level D, which corresponds to advanced ESL. Decide which of these higher-order reading strategies are assessed and how:

- Evaluating an argument and identifying specific claims in a text
- Analyzing the evidence a writer provides to support a claim

- Analyzing conflicting views on the same topic
- Synthesizing information

Anything else?

Is the College-to-Job Path the Best Route to Higher Employment Rates?

PRO
By Luke Dubois

How can job openings and unemployment statistics occur simultaneously? Why are the unemployed not able to land these available positions? The answer lies in a skills gap resulting from an education system that does not train enough people to meet employers' needs. What is the best way to minimize this gap? By far, the most advantageous solution is to create a path from our educational institutions to companies in need of workers. Such partnerships anticipate the number of skilled workers a company will need and create educational curricula that fulfill this demand. One example is a well-known European car manufacturer that is operating in the United States and forming a partnership with a community college. The company provided input on the tools to train students in using the machinery at their manufacturing plant and contributed to the content of the coursework. This mutual arrangement gives the company skilled workers and provides the college with increased job placement rates to attract new students. Hence, the college-to-job path benefits the country as a whole by increasing the number of educated members of society, a win-win situation for all indeed.

CON
By Nadine Ng

College is not an automatic fit for everyone. In fact, in recent years the number of college students who actually complete their degree has been only slightly above the fifty percent range. The remedial classes that many students end up enrolling in can prolong the time needed to complete degree requirements, making college seem too time-consuming to finish. In addition, in an attempt to develop well-rounded graduates, colleges often make it a mission to expose students to a wide curriculum, which results in a lengthier path leading to lower student graduation rates. In contrast, vocational training programs that do not burden students with additional college requirements are the most logical route to successful job training and placement. To avoid setting up students for failure, we must ensure they are qualified to complete training programs successfully by requiring entrance exam scores. Students who complete vocational programs receive a certificate of completion showing they are ready to work in many industries. Society should focus on expanding the number of graduates from these programs, as their job placement results appear more promising.

16. Nadine Ng's argument supports the claim that a college education is not for everyone by explaining that _____.

   A. many students who start college never graduate

   B. a college education limits students' career choices

   C. a majority of students transfer to vocational courses

   D. colleges put too much emphasis on remedial classes

17. What would be the *best* alternative title for this article?

   A. Why Is College Ultimately the Best Route to Career Success?

   B. How Much Education Do Effective Workers Really Require?

   C. Is College or Vocational Training the Ultimate Answer?

   D. Are European Companies Transforming the Labor Market?

From CASAS Reading Goals Series Samples (2018)

Teachers can create reading tasks that assess these higher-order reading strategies and that mirror this format.

Standardized test results provide only a partial view of learner ability and achievement. There are alternative means of capturing learner progress and achievement that engage learners in ways that more closely mirror instruction, many of which are more meaningful to teachers and students alike. These **formative** assessments that do not entail a formal paper-pencil test or standardized test fall under the umbrella of **alternative assessment.** A variety of alternative assessment techniques are described in the next section, including observation, performance assessment, learner self-assessment, and dialogue journals, among others.

9.5 Alternative assessment

Alternative assessment aligns with many of the principles of learner-centered teaching:

- It is program-based and reflects the content/context of the course in which it is used.
- It mirrors the approach to teaching used in the classroom, meaning it is likely to be more comfortable for learners.
- It allows learners to demonstrate accomplishments in ways that reflect natural use of language.
- It captures ongoing, continuous progress.
- Many alternative assessment techniques (performance assessment, dialogue journals, group projects) involve interaction among learners or between teacher and learner in communicative ways.

Alternative assessments can be used for both **formative** and **summative** purposes. **Formative assessments** are those that provide learners and teachers with immediate feedback and are said to focus on assessment for learning. They can even direct a teacher to make adjustments at the moment. **Summative assessments** are those that measure learner gains in relation to a set of learning objectives at the end of an instructional unit of study. Before reading about alternative assessment techniques, complete the following task.

📋 Task 9.5

Imagine you are teaching the lesson on expenses outlined in Chapter 3 (see 3.3). The learners work with an authentic informational text (a pie chart of expenses) to explore average expenses of people in the U.S. to their own expenses. The objectives for this lesson are the following:

Functional:
- Compare and contrast expenses among residents of the U.S.
- Compare and contrast their own spending habits to those presented in a graph

A. Observation

Careful **observation** of learning is a way to capture learning in the moment and allows teachers to make adjustments to teaching so that learners can find the best means of learning. It also allows us to notice those times when a learner makes gains and then backslides, a normal part of learning, and hopefully to notice what approaches to teaching and learning promote the most success for learners. Teachers observe learning every day, but are they always assessing learning in the process? A teacher may report that the class did very well on an activity, but is not able to report specifically *what* went well, *who* was engaged and successful in the lesson, and who wasn't.

When a teacher has a clear idea of what she or he is observing *for* in the classroom, **observation** can be a valid formative assessment tool. This starts with articulating clear objectives in a lesson and observing for evidence that learners are moving towards meeting those objectives, then noting what happens in class in relation to those objectives either during or after the lesson. Is it only language that should be assessed? Assessing a learner's ability to use and interpret graphics, think critically, or employ learning strategies are equally important. The sample observation tool in Figure 9.1 consists of a simple teacher-made grid with the day's objectives and space for recording progress. This example corresponds to my lesson on expenses in 3.3.

Lesson Objectives	Evidence of Progress
Students will be able to compare and contrast expenses among residents of the U.S. and compare and contrast their own spending habits to those presented in a graph.	*All but two students contributed to the discussion at the beginning, saying things like "People spend a lot more on housing than on food." During the mingle, comparing U.S. expenses to their own, all of the students interviewed at least three others.*
Grammatical: • Make comparisons using "spend *more* on _____ *than* _____;" "*as much on _____ as _____*" • Use qualifiers to show degree of differences (considerably, somewhat, a little).	*I elicited the grammar from them with success after we analyzed the pie chart together, so that showed who already had knowledge of the structures. I heard Alex struggle with the structure during the mingle (he said "spend more better on housing." I wonder if he thinks "better" is a marker for comparisons? It was hard to elicit "considerably" and "somewhat," but when we did a continuum on the board, they placed those in order from least to most.*

Vocabulary: categorize types of expenses	The only category that they had a hard time with was "charitable contributions." Great when José started giving personal examples (I give clothes to my church). His example seemed to make it easier for everyone.
Speaking/pronunciation: use proper word stress on vocabulary (exPENSes; contriBUtion)	They had a really hard time hearing the stress. When we started using both clapping and humming along with the bubbles, everyone started adding words to the right columns. I'll have to remember to use that multimodal approach with this group. When the word was a cognate with Spanish, they tended to say the words with syllable final stress (contributiON).
Critical thinking: • Compare U.S. Labor and Statistics chart to their own expenses • Categorize expenses	The final activity of interviewing and then creating their own graph for the group pushed everyone to both contribute and create a lot of original language and thought.

Figure 9.1 Sample Observation Tool

An alternative to writing notes is to record these reflections on your phone or computer immediately after a class. Zoshak (2016) calls these immediate recorded reflections "tiny talks" and suggests that using them as a tool for reflection between novice teachers leads to highly constructive analysis of practice. While it may be unrealistic to maintain records like these on a daily basis, print or recorded, doing so even weekly or biweekly allows a teacher to analyze in more detail the learning that is going on in class. The same can be achieved on a more immediate, smaller scale. Teachers can add post-its or notes in the margins of handouts and lesson plans on learner success and teaching effectiveness. This daily documentation and reflection can feed into the planning of subsequent lessons. A practical benefit of observation and ongoing assessment is that the job of writing progress reports at the end of the term is far easier and far more meaningful as a teacher draws on data collected during the term.

B. Performance assessment

Performance assessment involves learners demonstrating their ability to perform a real-life task, for example, calling in sick to work or requesting a meeting with a child's teacher by email. Central to performance assessment is the development of a **rubric** for evaluating learner outcomes on the task. What criteria should I use for evaluating performance? What language forms, functions, and vocabulary are needed to perform the task successfully? What extra-linguistic features of language (tone, nonverbals) should learners make use of to be intelligible if it is a speaking task? The sample in Figure 9.2 illustrates what a rubric to assess *writing an email to a child's teacher to request a meeting* could include.

Assessment Rubric

Task: writing an email to request a meeting with a child's teacher

1 needs improvement

2 adequately conveys information

3 very clearly conveys information; few errors in grammar or spelling

	1	2	3	Comments
Uses appropriate opening				
Makes request appropriately				
Gives reason for meeting				
Gives times when available to meet				
Uses appropriate closing				

Figure 9.2 Performance Assessment Rubric

In order for performance assessment to be a meaningful measure of learner competence, the task learners perform needs to be as authentic as possible and reflect the language and skills that were taught. Ask yourself these questions about the performance task:

• Does it measure what has been taught?

• Does it mirror real-world problems?

• Can students demonstrate their knowledge and skills?

(CAELA Network 2007: III-B-47)

When possible, use authentic materials such as real forms, work documents, or appropriate online tools (have learners email you a mock response to a child's teacher). In workplace programs, observe and assess learners performing tasks on the job. Conducting frequent performance assessments may not be practical in a large class. As an alternative, learners can observe peers doing the performance task and complete a rubric like the one above. When done as a class routine, peer assessments provide learners with valuable feedback on their progress.

Rubrics can be used for all kinds of learning tasks and outcomes. Teachers in Minnesota created an #IamABE curriculum, with this goal:

> We realized that one of the main issues we were facing is that many community members outside our classrooms did not understand how legislation was affecting our students. We also didn't have outlets for our students to share their ideas, needs, and complex identities that weren't overshadowed by our own political leanings. So, we set out to create that space.

The curriculum includes lessons on First Amendment rights, voicing one's political opinions on social media, and provides a foundation for elevating student voices through social media. The lessons are aligned to state content standards and the teachers developed assessment rubrics to measure progress. Figure 9.3 shows how a rubric can be used to assess participation on group tasks and critical thinking, along with writing outcomes.

Name: _____	1 Emerging	2 Developing	3 Satisfactory	4 Exemplary
Student participated in large group recall and categorization of stereotypes (Learning Strategies 2).	S did not participate, or quietly observed.	S contributed by speaking in their L1 to a classmate who translated and/or their contributions were off topic.	S contributed at least once to the whole group discussion in L2 and their contributions were on topic.	S contributed multiple times to the discussion and encouraged others to participate.
Student participated in small group sort of stereotypes (Critical Thinking 1).	S did not participate, or quietly observed.	S contributed by speaking in their L1 to a classmate who translated and/or their contributions were off topic.	S contributed at least once to the whole group discussion in L2 and their contributions were on topic.	S contributed multiple times to the discussion and encouraged others to participate.
Student can articulate (*yes or no*) if statement or picture reflects a stereotype and give reason (Critical Thinking 2 and 4).	S did not respond when asked.	S responded in L1 and/or their response indicated they did not understand the question.	S responded in L2 and their response reflected understanding.	S responded in L2 and was able to give a simple explanation as to why.
Student can produce clear and coherent *I am* statements to refute stereotypes (Writing Anchor 4).	S cannot produce a response.	S produced a response but response did not refute a stereotype, or response in L1 to another classmate who translated.	S produced a response in the L2 to refute a stereotype, but it requires some clarification.	S produced a response in the L2 that is clearly refuting a stereotype discussed in class.

Figure 9.3 Assessing Project Outcomes with a Rubric (Klas and Kreil 2017 #IamABECurriculum)

C. Checklists
Checklists are less complex than rubrics and can be used to track ongoing achievement of lesson, unit, or course objectives. The sample in Figure 9.4 is for a literacy-level program where emergent readers are acquiring foundational reading skills.

Sample Foundations Checklist

Date:	Oct. 18-22
Purpose of Assessment:	Assessment for learning
General Learning Outcome:	Interpret formatted text
Specific Learning Outcome:	Interpret lists, charts and tables
Task:	Naming and ordering letters

Conditions:
- task is familiar
- task is modeled/prompted by instructor

	Participates in choral rote reciting of alphabet	Contributes orally to naming various letters	Spells name aloud	Using a model and working in pairs, puts alphabet flashcards in order	Uses finger for tracking on a model while class recites alphabet
Nyabile	✓	✓		✓	✓
Farida	✓		✓	✓	✓
Adam	✓	✓	✓		

Figure 9.4 Checklist of Foundational Reading Skills (Bow Valley College (2011) **Learning for Life: An ESL Literacy Curriculum Framework***)*

The sample in Figure 9.5 is for assessing a persuasive essay with high-intermediate to advanced learners. A checklist like this can be used by leaners for self-assessment or for peer feedback as they work on drafts of their writing.

Persuasive Essay		Comments
Make my position clear	Yes/No	
Provide background in the introduction	Yes/No	
Have three arguments to support my position	Yes/No	
Support my arguments with evidence	Yes/No	
Use appropriate citations	Yes/No	
Summarize key points in conclusion	Yes/No	

Figure 9.5 Assessment Checklist for a Persuasive Essay

Notice that the items in the checklist correspond to the features of that particular writing genre. A checklist for assessing a paragraph describing a process would include: ordering steps correctly, using appropriate transitions, (*First, the next thing, finally*), using imperatives, including a reminder or warning (e.g., *It's important to remember...*).

D. Quiz-quiz-trade

Quiz-quiz-trade is a cooperative learning technique developed by Kagan and Kagan (2009) that can be used to assess learning of any content covered in class. The teacher prepares question/answer cards (ideally as many questions as there are learners, but there can be duplicates). Students mingle and pair up. They do not show their card to their partner.

Student A asks Student B the question and coaches the partner as needed using the answer provided on the card.

Student B asks Student A the question and coaches the partner as needed.

Students switch question cards and then move on to a new partner.

This technique is especially useful for reviewing material from a lesson or unit. The question cards in Sample 1 could be used after the reading lesson on the science of happiness in Section 5.8, assessing learners' content knowledge from the reading.

Sample 1: Assessing content learning

Question 1:	Answer:
According to the research on happiness boosters, what was the effect of using a gratitude journal on a weekly basis?	Those who took time to consciously count their blessings in a gratitude journal on weekly basis significantly increased their overall satisfaction with life over a period of six weeks, whereas a control group that did not keep journals had no such gain.

Question 2:	Answer:
Give two limitations of this kind of research.	Studies have been conducted in Western, individualistic cultures where striving for self-satisfaction may be an acceptable practice. In more collectivist cultures, this focus on self-improvement may be at odds with beliefs about the good of the group as opposed to the individual.
	Definitions of happiness are culturally-bound, so finding suitable measures for purposes of doing research can be problematic.

The question cards in Sample 2 are for a class that has been working on the language of academic conversations.

Sample 2: Assessing linguistic knowledge

Question 1:	Possible answers:
What can you say to bring someone into a discussion?	• We haven't heard from you yet.
	• _____, what do you think about this?
	• I'd like to know what _____ thinks about this.

Question 2:	Possible answers:
What are three ways to disagree politely with someone in a discussion?	• But don't you think that . . .?
	• I see what you mean, but . . .
	• But isn't it really a question of . . .?
	• I take your point, but . . .
	• Yes, but on the other hand . . .
	• But all the evidence suggests that . . .

E. Exit tickets/exit questions

There are any number of ways to use exit tickets or exit questions, for example, when I had to answer my Mandarin teacher's question using the language of the day before exiting the room. This formative assessment tells the teacher if learners need additional practice or further instruction. It also gives learners a chance to organize their ideas and engage in metacognition (thinking about their thinking and learning). Possible formats for exit tickets are:

- **3-2-1**

  After a reading: three things you discovered, two things that interest you, one question you still have. At the end of a lesson or unit: three things you learned; two ways you'll use this information outside of class; one thing that still confuses you.

  This can be done with post-it notes, index cards, or through online polling.

- **Mini-quizzes**

  Two to three questions related to the learning objectives of the day.

- **Reflection on learning**

  What did you learn today that you hadn't considered before? What did you learn today that was most useful?

F. Dialogue journals: oral and written

Dialogue journals provide a vivid record of learner progress as well as an ongoing sense of growth for the learner, making them an ideal vehicle for ongoing assessment. Audio-recorded oral journals can be used in much the same way written journals are used through an ongoing spoken dialogue between a teacher and learner. When I used oral dialogue journals in an advanced speaking/pronunciation class, I responded first to the content of what the learners told me, then provided language feedback for those areas where word choice or pronunciation affected intelligibility. At the end of term, the learners had the satisfaction of hearing themselves at the beginning and end of the class. This form of assessment may have limited practicality in very large class, but could become more so with the help of volunteers.

G. Video/audio recordings at intervals

It is difficult for teachers and learners to perceive progress in oral proficiency because most of the products we keep tend to be written ones. While we may have a sense that a learner is more fluent, creating records of that progress is easy to do through occasionally audio or video recording learners' enacting a role play, a short conversation, telling a story, or giving presentations. After recording at regular intervals, review a compilation video with learners so that they can recognize their development and growth.

H. Portfolio assessment

A portfolio is a collection of learner work (selected by the students) that is representative of accomplishments made in a class or during a term of study. It may include writing samples, written exercises, projects, video recorded presentations, audio recorded stories, digital stories, drawings, readings and accompanying activities completed, learning logs, or even letters from teachers or employers. Planning for the portfolio can become an activity by having learners brainstorm and discuss what they would like to include. This is also a time for the teacher to clarify the purposes and benefits of creating a portfolio. Canada has recently implemented Portfolio-Based Language Assessment (PBLA) in lieu of standardized testing to assure consistency and standards of quality of ESL programming for adult immigrant learners across the country (Centre for Canadian Language Benchmarks 2017).

I. Work samples/group projects

Evaluating group projects can provide insights into learners' ability to distribute tasks, work on a team, and present information clearly, either through a final written product or presentation. As with performance assessment, a teacher can create a rubric for assessing the final project, which can be completed by the teacher, the learners, and the audience who sees the final product.

J. KWL charts: What do I know? What do I want to learn? What did I learn?

This strategy is used for multiple purposes: to activity prior knowledge on a topic, to set learning goals, and to assess learning. At the start of a unit, learners work in small groups and brainstorm everything they know and everything they want to learn about the topic. Their responses are compiled to create a group chart on the board, projected on a screen, or as a wall chart. At the end of the unit, learners go back to the chart and assess what they learned and compare those outcomes to their learning goals.

What Do I Know?	What Do I Want to Learn?	What Did I Learn?

Figure 9.6 KWL Chart

9.6 Learner self-assessment

Learner self-assessment should be an integral part of an ESL class. The benefits are numerous:

- It allows students to reevaluate the goals they have set for themselves, to recognize their progress in relation to those goals, and to identify new goals revealed as they progress.
- It heightens their awareness of the goals and outcomes of the program and allows them to identify their strengths and needs in relation to those outcomes.
- It helps them identify how they learn best; reflect on what they can do as learners (not just what the teacher does as a teacher).
- Develops a skill common in many workplaces, but that is new for many immigrants.
- Gives learners a voice in their education and in shaping the curriculum; they can see themselves as one of the many stakeholders.

Self-assessment needs to be a daily routine that can start with something as simple as asking learners to reflect on that day's lesson (or any of the exit ticket ideas above):

What is one thing you learned that was new for you and particularly helpful?

How will what you learned help you in your daily life, at home, work, or in the community?

During review the following day, ask learners if they used anything from the previous lesson outside of class. Did they notice any of the new words they learned on signs, on the news, at work, or anywhere in their community?

At the end of a unit, learners can reflect on what they learned as well as how they learned best. The teacher can develop a simple task like this one for my lesson on expenses in 3.3:

Think about your learning.

1. The most useful thing I learned in this unit (or this week) was _____.

2. I still want to learn _____.

3. I learned best by working:

    _____ with the teacher and class _____ alone _____ with a partner.

4. The most useful activities were:

_____ looking at the pie chart and talking about everyone's expenses.

Figure 9.7 Lesson Self-Assessment

In order to highlight learner achievement in relation to the specific language outcomes in a lesson or unit, students complete a **learning log** or checklist with can-do statements (can be the same used as a needs assessment). Think back to the lesson on job titles and responsibilities in 3.3, which addressed these learning objectives:

Vocabulary:
- Match job titles to visuals
- Match jobs to job responsibilities
- Say job titles with correct word stress
- Categorize types of jobs (e.g., indoor/outdoor; work alone or with others)

Grammar:
- Students will be able to use simple present tense to talk about jobs (e.g., a butcher cuts meat)

Learners can complete a learning log like the one in Figure 9.5.

I can name all the jobs presented in the lesson.
Yes___ No ___ Some ___ Write what you remember:

I can pronounce the names of jobs clearly.
Yes___ No ___ Some ___ Which ones need some more work:

I can describe what people do for their jobs.
Yes___ No ___ Some ___ Give one example:

I can say which jobs are outdoors or indoors.
Yes___ No ___ Some ___ Give one example of each:

These were easiest for me today (√ what was easy):
Listening _____
Speaking _____
Reading _____
Writing _____

These were more difficult for me today (√ what was difficult):
Listening _____
Speaking _____
Reading _____
Writing _____

Figure 9.8 Sample Learner Log

9.7 Using assessment results for accountability purposes

The assessment techniques and tools outlined above provide fairly immediate results to those stakeholders in the classroom, i.e., learners and teachers. But what about those stakeholders who are outside of the classroom? In a discussion of **accountability**, it is crucial that classroom teachers hear from stakeholders that are outside of their classrooms. I asked several state adult ESL specialists and program coordinators what they see as the signs of a successful program. I also asked which **performance indicators** are the most important to them. Their responses give classroom teachers insight into the kind of data they need to gather about learner progress.

📋 **Task 9.6**

First, reflect on this question:

In your opinion, what are indicators of a successful program?

Now look at this list of the most common themes that emerged from administrators. How does this compare to your own list?

Successful programs are those that . . .
- Meet the goals the students have established for themselves.
- Build personal connections with the teachers and among learners.
- Prepare learners for the demands of the 21st century.

Important indicators of success are . . .
- Gains on standardized assessments
- Attainment of learners' personal goals
- Job attainment; job improvement
- Entrance into job training and further education
- Attainment of high school equivalency
- Increased learner earnings
- Learner retention
- Learner persistence
- Learners as partners in their children's education
- Independent learning (online, learning circles, etc.)
- Increased community involvement
- Cultural adjustment

> *A strong program will find that balance between meaningful classroom work, navigation to self-efficacy, and customer service.*
>
> Adrienne Fontenot, Director of Adult Learning and Educational Programs

Follow-up: All of those I spoke to identified learner involvement and attainment of personal goals as signs of success. While measures on standardized tests are still important, it is clear that other means of assessment need to be used to capture gains such as employment, cultural adjustment, or attainment of personal goals. You have already learned about numerous means of assessing learning and teaching, all of which can be used to gather data that provides all stakeholders with evidence of learner achievement and suitability of programming.

Look at five examples of learner outcomes that need to be assessed and reported. What do you think would be the most suitable assessment technique (e.g., performance assessment, dialogue journals) for measuring achievement of each outcome?

You need to . . .	What assessment tool could you use?
Capture gains in writing using evidence from sources to support claims.	
Determine how learners are working on their language skills outside of class.	
Find out how learners are involved in the community outside of school and/or work.	
Know whether learners have achieved employment goals.	
Capture improved intelligibility in pronunciation over time.	
Find out if learners are doing independent reading or reading to their children more frequently.	

The best assessment tools are those that are compatible with the content of instruction, or the outcomes being assessed, as well as the approach to learning and teaching used in your class. This means that you need to use multiple means of gathering data to capture the breadth of learning that occurs in a class. Table 9.2 reviews assessment tools and techniques and describes how they can be used for accountability purposes. See if any of your ideas from Task 9.7 are included in the table.

Table 9.2 Tools for Gathering Data for Reporting Progress

Portfolios	Make learners aware of program standards and accountability expectations. Have them collect work for their portfolio that corresponds to the standards and accountability requirements of your program. This includes in-class work as well as achievement of employment and other personal or educational goals. Portfolios can take the form of a binder or learners could develop an online portfolio (folders or a simple web page).
Performance assessments	Conduct performance assessments that align with program outcomes and standards and keep rubrics as a record of learner achievement. This technique is useful for assessing outcomes of competencies such as reporting an accident at work or calling in sick. Rubrics for assessing writing can be used and kept as well.

Recorded samples	Audio/video record performance assessments or speech samples periodically to capture progress over time. If you are looking for improvement in intelligibility of pronunciation, recorded speech samples are crucial.
Learner writing samples / Journal entries collected over time	As with recorded samples, writing samples gathered over time are a powerful means of capturing development in writing ability.
Projects	Collect projects and identify the standards covered through the development of the project. Document outcomes using checklists or rubrics that delineate the standards.
KWL charts What do I know? What do I want to learn? What did I learn?	Save KWL charts as a record of learning goals and achievement of those goals.
Reading logs	Record titles of books read, brief summaries and feelings about the book, both for personal reading and books read to children.
Learner folders / Print or digital	Keep a folder for each student with all test scores, learner goals, and any information gathered using the techniques above.

Checklists of learner achievement of program outcomes are commonplace in adult ESL programs. Sometimes they are developed by the program and used program wide, and other times the teacher and learners develop checklists themselves. These can be particularly helpful for tracking progress of non-linguistic goals such as improved employment, community involvement, or educational attainment. The sample learner checklist (Figure 9.9) includes a number of these types of goals.

How am I doing with my English skills?

Since I started this class...

1	I read more in English.	Yes/No
2	I attend more events in my community.	Yes/No
3	I communicate more with teachers.	Yes/No
4	I applied for a new job.	Yes/No
5	I got a promotion at work.	Yes/No
6	I got a new job.	Yes/No
7	I talk more to my co-workers.	Yes/No
8	I find information online more easily.	Yes/No

I also _____.

Three goals I still have:

1 _____

2 _____

3 _____

Figure 9.9 Sample Learner Checklist

In an Integrated Education and Training program (see 2.19 D), these assessment checklists are ideal for measuring achievement of content and language outcomes. For example, in a class in English for Retails Jobs, checklist items might include:

I can describe product features.	1 strongly disagree	2 disagree	3 somewhat agree	4 agree	5 strongly agree
I can handle customer complaints.	1 strongly disagree	2 disagree	3 somewhat agree	4 agree	5 strongly agree

Any of the tools recommended for initial needs assessment (see 6.2 and 7.3) or for diagnostic purposes can be revisited at the end of a unit of instruction or course and results can become a part of a learner's record or portfolio.

Conclusion

Far too often teachers fail to make use of the information and data they gather through the assessment processes outlined in this section. Sharing the results of standardized tests and alternative assessments with learners allows them to see the benefits of testing and assessment. In programs that allow time for teacher collaboration, sharing results with colleagues provides a means of building cohesion among classes in the program, as well as a means of identifying common strengths and weaknesses of instructional practices.

- Inform students of their successes on tests and alternative assessments as well as the areas in which they need improvement.
- Show them the link between their results and subsequent instruction. For example, the outcomes of a performance assessment on returning items to the store indicate that the class needs more work on this competency. Show them those results and the ways the new lesson will help them to improve in this area.
- Collect and use the results of learner self-assessment. Show them the link between those assessments and subsequent instruction so that they see the ways in which they have an impact on instruction.
- Compare the outcomes of assessment with other teachers in the program. Also share the assessment tools themselves so that the processes used throughout the program become more consistent.

In this section, I have explored the place of standardized tests and alternative assessment tools commonly used in adult ESL programs. A fair assessment reflects what students have learned and is conducted in ways that are familiar to students. Developing valid means of capturing learner performance and achievement is paramount, not only for the benefit of teachers, program administrators, and funders, but most importantly, for learners. Seeing progress motivates students; observing and recording learner outcomes has a positive impact on teaching. Equally important is intentional reflection on our practice as part of an assessment loop, as depicted in Figure 9.10.

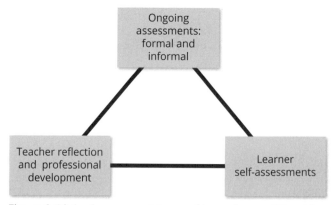

Figure 9.10 An Assessment Loop of Learning and Teaching

Part II: Assessing teaching effectiveness and continuous teacher development

9.8 Introduction

One of the primary goals of assessment is to determine the extent to which instructional practices meet the needs of learners. Observant teachers modify content, activities, and techniques as they observe for and reflect on learner outcomes in their lessons. Teachers also need to be deliberate about their growth and professional development; teacher change takes intentional and purposeful reflection. In this section, we explore processes for teacher reflection and personal development, including peer- and self-observation, learning logs, journals, communities of practice, and mentoring.

📋 Task 9.8

Discuss these questions with a partner or write answers in your journal if you are on your own:

- How do you assess the effectiveness of the work you do (as a teacher or as a professional in another setting)?
- How do you continue to grow in your professional life?
- How do you collaborate with others to work on issues you face in your class or at your job?

9.9 Self-directed professional learning and development

In the past, it was common practice for schools to hold required workshops and trainings that may have had little connection to what teachers needed or wanted to work on in their practice. More recently, teachers are given choice in their professional development plans (Crandall and Finn Miller 2014).

A. Leveraging social media and online sources

With time constraints and limited resources for professional development (PD), there are many things teachers can do to promote professional learning on their own. Jayme Adelson Goldstein, a professional development specialist, highlights a number of ways that we can leverage both social media as well as the myriad online resources out there for teachers.

> *Self-directed professional development is a 21st-century solution to the constraints (funding, scheduling, content) that often limit access to PD. Internet tools and social media make it relatively easy to engage in self-directed professional development. I always recommend starting with a few self-survey questions—Where do I need support with instruction? What do I want to know about x? Where can I find tools and resources to address my learners' needs? This way you can customize and focus on your needs and learners' needs—allowing you to choose the what, how, and when to learn. A quick perusal of online lists of best English language teaching practices and/or resources can help you determine which avenue(s) to explore. Set up email notifications whenever content on your selected topics is posted to the web. And "following" guiding lights in our field (researchers, authors, organizations) on social media can give you a "backstage pass" to someone closely associated with the topic you're exploring.*
>
> **Jayme Adelson-Goldstein, National Professional Development Specialist, Lighthearted Learning**

We can apply the same guidelines for evaluating the reliability of online teacher resources as we would for any website (see Section 8.12). A great place to start is to visit the websites for professional organizations for our field (see listings in the chapter resources).

B. Collaborative/cooperative development
Peer observation

As Jayme highlights, there are many ways that we can go solo in our professional development pursuits, but as she notes, one of the most valuable resources for teacher development is communication with other teachers. Research indicates that professional development should promote collaboration among teachers, draw on research to inform practice, and be extended over time, as opposed to the one-shot workshop (Burt,

> *Of course, professional learning is exponentially more valuable in collaboration with a colleague, and connecting through social media and virtual meeting spaces (like Skype and Zoom) makes it possible to find PD accomplices anywhere in the world.*
>
> Jayme Adelson-Goldstein

Peyton, and Schaetzel 2008; Guskey 2000; Smith 2010). Heavy teaching schedules, busy lives, and little preparation time are all obstacles to collaborative development among teachers, but finding a colleague for peer observations is well worth the effort. Recognizing the strength of this process, some administrators give release time once a term (or more in a few cases) to conduct peer observations. If this is not an option, find a peer with a different work schedule than yours and arrange to visit one another periodically, or video record a lesson and post it to a shared drive for peer observation. That way you could work with that "accomplice" anywhere in the world.

Just as with any form of observation, having a clear task and focus can make the experience richer. The task can be a set of questions that your peer wants you to respond to, questions you have about your own teaching, or an observation task that delves into a specific area of learning and teaching. The task below was designed for student teachers to use while observing peers during their practicum, but would work equally well for teachers observing one another in their own classrooms.

Sample Observation Task: Giving Learners Voice in a Lesson

As you observe, look for evidence that the teacher is accounting for these principles of learner-centered teaching.

Some principles of learner-centered teaching	Note evidence of this principle in practice
Learners' first language and culture are viewed as a resource for learning.	*I noticed a lot of peer support with the L1 when the learners worked in groups. That seemed to really clarify the task expectations for Greta and Vang.*
The content of instruction is relevant to the learners' needs and interests and draws on their experiences and knowledge.	
Learners make choices about content and classroom activities.	
Classroom interactions and tasks are authentic, representing how language is used in the real world.	

Possible questions for follow-up conversation with your colleague:

1. Share the information you gathered through the observation. First, find out how your colleague feels about the lesson. Did the instructional decisions account for these principles? What did both of you notice?

2. What learner roles and interactions did you observe? Where do you think the teacher was most responsive to learners' backgrounds, interests, and needs? Where might your colleague like to focus more attention on the learners? Brainstorm ways in which the lesson might be modified to give students more voice.

Lesson Study

Another collaborative process is called **Lesson Study**, described by professional development specialist Susan Finn Miller as follows:

> *Teachers in Professional Learning Circles can engage in the iterative Lesson Study process, which involves a group of teachers in designing a lesson together and then observing one instructor teaching that lesson. Those who are observing the lesson focus their attention on the learners in the class rather than on the teacher. The observers are interested in determining how well learners are achieving the goals of the lesson. In the follow-up PLC meeting, the teachers talk about their observations and make changes to the lesson to enhance its effectiveness—after which another instructor teaches the lesson.*
>
> *Research has shown that these job-embedded and collaborative forms of professional learning have a positive impact on teachers' practices as well as learner outcomes.*
>
> Susan Finn Miller, LINCS Moderator, Adult English Language Acquisition

Teacher collaboration with Lesson Study has been shown to improve teachers' self-efficacy, which has been associated with improvements in learning outcomes (Ciampa and Gallagher 2016; Chong and Kong 2012). In the Lesson Study process, colleagues can track learners' comfort and success with different teaching strategies and activities and a record like the one below can be kept. This example is from a beginning-level class for newcomers working on language for requesting information over the phone.

Activities/Techniques	Learner Comfort/Involvement
Role play	I noticed you might need to give them more time to practice language they need for the role play.
Making calls on cell phones from class	Seemed to enjoy this—lots of laughter. All but two pairs finished making their calls. Maybe we can try having them finish from home next time.
Selective listening	So many of the students wanted to write down everything from the recorded messages. Let's talk about ways to help them see the value of listening only for the info they need. This will help them a lot outside of class.

Figure 9.11 Assessing Effectiveness of Teaching Strategies During Lesson Study

Notice how the colleague teacher identifies aspects of the lesson that need adjusting; she's not just observing learner outcomes, but also teaching effectiveness. The next teacher who teaches the same lesson can now implement those adjustments and the colleague observers can track the impact those adjustments have on learning.

9.10 Journals and learning logs

I never kept a journal until I was asked to do so as a requirement in my teaching practicum in 1982. Journaling allowed me to process what had happened each day, to pose questions for myself or to ask my mentor. Looking back over my entries allowed me to see development in my thought processes about teaching and learning. Journaling does not need to be a solo endeavor. Teachers can work cooperatively with a peer or mentor using dialogue journals. Pairs or groups of teachers commonly create online forums for this purpose. An alternative to keeping a journal is to maintain a learning log in which the teacher records observations, reflections, insights, or questions about the teaching and learning that occur in a lesson.

I wonder what would happen if I tried . . .

The language experience activity worked well today—need to use that more often.

I was uncomfortable with Souling's questions about my colleague. I need to think of ways to handle situations like that.

Capturing these thoughts and reflections immediately after teaching is important, otherwise they tend to vanish from our memory.

Communities of Practice/learning and study circles

Another way to interact with colleagues is through the formation of **Communities of Practice** (CoPs), which are small groups of teachers devoting time to support one another through active listening and exploration of common issues and concerns they are having in their teaching. CoPs exist in any profession and represent any group with common goals seeking to develop personally and professionally (Wenger 1998). CoPs can be face-to-face or virtual, with

Teachers learn most when they have the chance to engage with one another about their work in professional learning circles.

Susan Finn Miller

teachers coming together from across a state, a region, or even from different countries. As part of the LINCS ESL Pro initiative (2015-2016) sponsored by the Office of Career and Technical Adult Education, a number of states formed CoPs based on their needs and interests and chose to work through online modules in one of these three areas:

• *Meeting the Language Needs of Today's Adult ELL*
• *Integrating Digital Literacy into English Language Instruction*
• *Preparing English Learners for Work and Career Pathways*

These online modules were developed with CoPs and professional learning circles/communities in mind and include reflection and application tasks for teachers and administrators. The LINCS ESL Pro suite of materials also includes issue briefs and digital magazines on each theme that are ideal for **study circles**, which is when teachers come together to deepen their understanding of a topic through readings, attendance together at conferences or webinars, discussion, and reflections. Many of the professional organizations listed at the end of this chapter also host CoPs and study circles, and they

Sometimes having someone else map out a PD path can be comforting. In that case, consider using the autonomous online courses at LINCS. And don't forget that members of professional organizations such as COABE and TESOL can take advantage of their recorded online sessions as part of their membership.

Jayme Adelson-Goldstein

offer webinars along with other professional development opportunities.

Action research

All of the processes above can lead to deeper exploration of your teaching through **action research**, which involves teachers identifying problems or issues in their teaching, gathering data or information about what is happening, researching the topic, and taking action in their classes. This kind of exploration, which is situated in the teachers' classrooms, is a powerful tool for ongoing personal development. Nunan and Bailey (2009) propose the following steps for conducting action research:

- **Identify an issue**: What is something that you are struggling with as a teacher? Is there an approach or strategy that you want to experiment with in your class? Any of the teacher development ideas outlined above, as well as the outcomes of the ongoing assessment tools described in Section I of this chapter, can provide possible topics for action research.
- **Gather information about the issue**: There are many ways to gather information about any area of teaching: read, conduct online research, talk to other teachers, observe others.
- **Use that information to design changes in classroom procedure**: Design activities, implement specific strategies that apply what you have learned through your research.
- **Implement this procedure**: Now try the procedure out in your classroom over a period of time.
- **Observe changes this implementation brought about in the classroom**: Observation takes planning; use observation grids/checklists, journals, video/audio recording, learning logs, and self-assessment to capture the changes that occurred as a result of the action research.
- **Reflect on the outcomes and implications of the process**: Keep a log or journal and share your findings with colleagues.

Action research can be as simple or complex as a teacher wants it to be. It is a common tool in teacher education programs, allowing teachers to apply the principles they are learning about to their classes. For those of you already teaching, it can be a way for you to apply principles you are learning about right now.

I engaged in a mentoring project with ESL teachers in the community with the aim of helping novice and experienced teachers implement learner-centered teaching practices through action research. The project sought to heighten teacher awareness of the impact their practices have on learner involvement and learning outcomes. The mentoring process began with observations and personal assessments to identify areas for exploration. In the second stage, the teachers conducted action research around the identified growth areas. I also provided targeted mentoring sessions on those targeted areas. The third stage consisted of follow-up observations and discussions of the effects changes in teaching practices had on learner involvement.

All of the processes the teachers and I engaged in could be utilized between peers, with a mentor and new teacher, or even individually as a means of observing and reflecting on one's own practice. All of the teachers began the cycle by completing this task:

The mentoring pre-activity
Provide examples of what learners and you are doing in your classroom that correspond to each of these characteristics of a learner-centered classroom (See Chapter 1 Section 1.3). In what areas are you most responsive to your learners' needs? What are some areas that would benefit from further research and experimentation in your classroom? We will use the outcomes of this initial assignment to determine the areas for focus during the first observation. From there, you will develop targeted observation tasks for me to complete as I observe the learners in your class, and for you to complete after your lesson.

Celeste was particularly concerned that quieter students in her class were not participating enough and that, provided the opportunity to do so, they would. She incorporated two concrete teaching techniques that she was very familiar with, but had not become routines in her teaching: think-pair-share and teaching the language of turn-taking more explicitly (e.g., *It's your turn. Do you have something to add? What do you think?*), and consistently asking learners to use that language. Her curriculum included a unit on job routines, including a focus on simple present tense and adverbs of frequency. In previous lessons, she used the learners' textbook but she was never satisfied that the material was relatable to students. See how she implemented the strategies above in a lesson on job routines to make her lesson more participatory and learner-centered:

- Learners moved to tables based on their type of job (here or in their country): retail; housekeeping; food service; education; office. This grouping strategy promoted a fair amount of communication among students as they determined which table was the best fit for them. This also worked in some higher-order thinking: categorization.
- Next, she used think-pair-share: *Think of activities you do on the job and work together to create a list of at least five items. Each member needs to add at least one example.* (She directed them to the turn-taking phases on the wall that they could use to elicit information from one another).
- Groups shared ideas as Celeste wrote activities on the board. Now Celeste asked what a good day or bad day on the job would be like, first modeling for herself:

  On a good day, I plan carefully.

  On a bad day, I speak too quickly.

Groups worked together again to create good day/bad day lists using a simple T-chart. As an observer, I recorded which learners contributed at my table and how frequently. The result was that two of the typically quiet students were among the most involved in the activities. Celeste and I continued the process over several weeks, each time focusing on a different aspect of learning and teaching. Celeste revisited the pre-activity at the end of the cycle, and the following is a sample of how the process affected her teaching:

- ***The learners control direction of the activities****. With the group-work language, students are politely, appropriately communicating with one another, encouraging participation of quieter students, developing English confidence, and learning great skills for outside of the classroom. Looking back at group work just a couple months ago and now, there is a great improvement.*

TESOL International Association recently released "The Six Principles for Exemplary Teaching of English Learners™" (TESOL 2018). These principles are:

Principle 1. Know Your Learners
Principle 2. Create Conditions for Language Learning
Principle 3. Design High-Quality Lessons for Language Development
Principle 4. Adapt Lesson Delivery as Needed
Principle 5. Monitor and Assess Student Language Development
Principle 6. Engage and Collaborate Within a Community of Practice

These principles are in keeping with those we have explored in this text and the resources provided by TESOL will give you inspiration for any of the teacher development suggestions outlined in this section of the chapter. All of these processes take intentional effort on the part of teachers. Taking time to truly reflect on what we do is energizing and allows us to collaborate with colleagues in new and meaningful ways.

9.11 Learners assessing instruction

The processes of assessment discussed throughout this chapter provide us with rich data about the effectiveness of learning and teaching, but there is one more important piece to the assessment puzzle: What do learners feel about instruction? How do students evaluate the effectiveness of our teaching? Research in K-12 education indicates that tracking progress can lead to greater learner achievement (Marzano 2009). As with all forms of assessment, teachers need to gather ongoing and meaningful input from their learners, but sometimes this can be difficult for both linguistic and cultural reasons:

Language obstacles: Learners may not have enough language to talk about instruction. Use bilingual aids or interpreters, or develop strategies by which learners can show or demonstrate their feelings through visuals.

Cultural obstacles: Understand that in many cultures, students would never be asked to evaluate their teachers. Develop means of evaluation that allow learners to provide meaningful feedback in non-threatening ways. Assure them that feedback does not affect their standing in the program. Use group consensus activities, which give a group opinion rather than a personal opinion.

Students may have an easier time talking about activities and content as opposed to the teacher and teaching. The following evaluation activity can be conducted on a regular basis (weekly, monthly) as well as at the end of a term as a final evaluation. List typical activities you use in class: role plays, interviews, debates, discussions, reading short articles, writing exercises, digital learning tasks, grammar exercises, listening activities. Also list content you have covered (healthy living, the environment, local elections). Have students complete sentences like these:

I liked doing _____

I didn't like _____

I liked learning about _____

I didn't like learning about _____

Next week/term I want to _____

To elicit group feedback, have small groups of students answer these two questions:

What have you learned (this week, month, in this class)?

What helped you learn best?

Invite a group representative to write their answers on the board, compile the lists, and ask the class to identify the five most common responses to the two questions. The outcomes of this activity provide the teacher with feedback about which activities had the most impact and which instructional strategies were the most beneficial for this particular group. In cases where the learners will continue on in the program, the teacher needs to inform them that these results will help shape the instruction in the next class, whether with the same teacher or with another teacher. Any of the exit ticket/exit question tasks in section 9.5 e. can also provide you with feedback on your teaching effectiveness. Your program may have a formal evaluation process, often conducted online. For this reason, frequent teacher-made online polls or online forms can be used to acquaint students with this process as well as to give you ongoing feedback.

Conclusion

Many forms of assessment have been examined in this chapter, including standardized tests and alternative assessment, as well as teacher assessment and ongoing professional development. Assessment results are also used to inform funders about program effectiveness and learner successes. All of these processes take careful consideration and planning. The information gathered allows teachers and program administrators, as well as students to monitor and adjust the strategies they employ to make learning and teaching as productive as possible.

On your own, or with a partner, provide an example or brief definition for each concept:

Checklist of Key Terms	
proficiency test	
placement test	
diagnostic test	
achievement test	
practicality	
reliability	
validity	
standardized tests	
alternative assessment	
formative assessment	
summative assessment	
performance assessment	
rubrics and checklists	
learner logs	
Communities of Practice (CoPs) and Professional Learning Circles/Communities (PLCs)	
action research	

Before doing these activities, revisit your answers to the questions at the beginning of the chapter.

1 Program intake

Every program uses different processes at intake to place students in the most suitable class. **If you are already teaching,** find out what processes your program uses. What placement test do they use (a standardized test or their own)? What other processes do they use at intake? Reflect on the following:

What do the test scores and any other intake procedures tell you about learners in your classes?

Describe two things you do once students are with you to have a more complete picture of their level and needs.

If you're not teaching yet, visit a site and ask the intake coordinator, an administrator, or a teacher what process they use for placement. If possible, look at copies of their intake forms and placement tests. Reflect on the following:

What would the test scores and intake process tell you about students?

Describe two more things you would do at the beginning of a course to have a more complete picture of their level and needs.

2 Developing performance assessments

If you are already teaching, choose an upcoming unit for which you have not developed an assessment tool before. Describe the task you will ask learners to perform (e.g., a role play, a real-life written task) and develop a rubric that you could use to assess learner performance with this task. **If you are not teaching,** choose a unit from an ESL textbook and do the same thing.

3 Learner self-assessment

Look at three ESL textbooks or online curricula and find out if they include any kind of learner-assessment at the end of the units, in the support materials (sometimes these are in the online tools), or periodically throughout the book. Choose one unit and develop a learner log and a reflective task that would allow learners to identify what they accomplished.

4 Continuous professional development plan

Identify an issue that you want to work on in your teaching. How would you like to learn more about that topic? Consider the ideas provided in Part II of the chapter. What resources will you draw on, with whom would you like to collaborate, and how will you assess the effectiveness of any changes you are making in your teaching? Here are some steps you may consider:

- Gather information about the issue (visit professional websites, read, talk to other teachers, observe others).
- Use that information to develop a procedure (technique, activity) that is new for you.
- Implement this procedure.
- Observe changes this implementation brought about in the classroom, particularly, what impact does that change have on student learning?
- Reflect on the outcomes and implications of the process with a colleague.

Assessment

Bailey, K. and Curtis, A. (2015) *Learning About Language Assessment, 2nd edition.* Boston, MA: Cengage. This text outlines the principles of second language assessment through three sections, beginning with authentic dilemmas from practicing teachers, followed by principles of assessment, and ending with inquiry-based activities.

Brown, J.D. (2005) *Testing in Language Programs.* New York, NY: McGraw Hill. This book provides teachers with tools for developing good tests, analyzing and interpreting test results, and improving tests so that they are fair and accurate measures of learner achievement.

Teacher Reflection and Self-Assessment

American Institutes for Research (2015) The *Adult Education Teacher Competencies.* Designed to identify the knowledge and skills needed by adult education teachers to improve student learning and performance. *https://lincs.ed.gov/professional-development/resource-collections/profile-833*

Danielson, C. (2009) *Talk About Teaching! Leading Professional Conversations.* Thousand Oaks, CA: Corwin Press.

O'Leary, M. (2014) *Classroom Observation: A Guide to the Effective Observation of Teaching and Learning.* New York, NY: Routledge.

ONLINE RESOURCES

LINCS *(https://lincs.ed.gov/)*

Through the LINCS Community of Practice, self-paced online courses, and searchable resources, adult education practitioners can collaborate and share ideas to improve educational outcomes.

Professional Organizations (these organizations also have local affiliates):

Teachers of English to Speakers of Other Languages (TESOL) *(http://www.tesol.org/)*

Coalition on Adult Basic Education (COABE) *(https://www.coabe.org/)*

National Association for Teaching English and Community Languages to Adults *(http://www. natecla.org.uk/)*

TESOL Canada *(https://tesolcanada.org/)*

Literacy Education and Second Language Learning for Adults (LESLLA) *(https://www.leslla.org/)*

The International Association of Teachers of English as a Foreign Language (IATEFL)

ProLiteracy *(https://proliteracy.org/)*

National College Transitions Network (NCTN) *(https://www.collegetransition.org/)/www.tesol.org.au/)*

10 | Standards and Accountability

To consider before reading this chapter:

- What standards drive practice and policy in adult English language programming in your context?
- How can teachers reconcile learner goals with program standards that don't appear compatible?

10.1 Introduction

Much, if not all, of what ESL teachers do each day could not happen without resources and funding from state and federal agencies. What are funders' expectations? Are they radically different from those of learners, classroom teachers, and program administrators? What **standards** do state and national funders hold programs to and how do they measure that those standards have been met? What do ESL teachers need to know about those standards, and how can they align instruction to meet them in ways that are consistent with learner goals and their own practice? Answers to these questions are the basis for this chapter. While accountability and standards may seem daunting, being accountable for what you do in an English language classroom is one of the responsibilities of the job; accountability and standards provide one means of capturing the achievement of students as well as the effectiveness of instruction.

10.2 What are standards?

Standards are a broad set of desired outcomes for learners from which programs develop their curricula. **Content standards** represent what students are expected *to know* and be able to do as a result of instruction, and **performance indicators or descriptors** show what learners need to do to *demonstrate* their proficiency within the content standards. Content standards are normally broad statements and the performance descriptors or indicators represent what can be expected at any given level of instruction as with this example from the English Language Proficiency Standards for Adult Education (US Department of Education 2016b: 21).

ELP Standard 1	Level 1	Level 2	Level 3	Level 4	Level 5
An ELL can ... construct meaning from oral presentations and literary and informational text through level-appropriate listening, reading, and viewing.	By the end of English language proficiency level 1, an ELL can ... use a very limited set of strategies to: • identify a few key words and phrases in oral communications and simple spoken and written texts.	By the end of English language proficiency level 2, an ELL can ... use an emerging set of strategies to: • identify the main topic in oral presentations and simple spoken and written texts. • retell a few key details.	By the end of English language proficiency level 3, an ELL can ... use a developing set of strategies to: • determine a central idea or theme in oral presentations and spoken and written texts. • retell key details. • answer questions about key details. • explain how the theme is developed by specific details in texts. • summarize part of a text.	By the end of English language proficiency level 4, an ELL can ... use an increasing range of strategies to: • determine a central idea or theme in oral presentations and spoken and written texts. • analyze the development of the themes/ ideas. • cite specific details and evidence from texts to support the analysis. • summarize a text.	By the end of English language proficiency level 5, an ELL can ... use a wide range of strategies to: • determine central ideas or themes in oral presentations and spoken and written texts. • analyze the development of the themes/ ideas. • cite specific details and evidence from texts to support the analysis.

As already noted throughout this book, standards have moved from being largely life-skills and competency-based to now placing greater emphasis on college and career readiness. This is particularly evident in the U.S. with the Workforce Innovation and Opportunity Act (2014) that emphasizes the need to prepare all adults for employment in high-demand industries and jobs that can lead to economic self-sufficiency. This legislation requires states to adopt rigorous content standards that prepare adults for the demands of post-secondary education and work. This move to standards leading to employability is a global trend. In fact, Gibb (2015) suggests that worldwide, standards today are quantifying learning in ways that are often counter to what we know about socially-constructed literacy practices, or practices that are truly learner-oriented. She cautions us that larger world-economic forces have had significant influence over standards in adult education, as opposed to in the early years when adult education was a "humanistic community-based practice" (p. 55).

> *Standards are about preparing students for the demands of college, careers, and civic engagement in a complex, global, information-rich, and technology-based society, allowing students to engage successfully with others in each of those contexts.*
>
> Dave Coleman, Los Angeles Unified School District

10.3 Standards frameworks and reporting

In Chapter 9 (9.7) we considered how assessment results can be used for program-level accountability purposes. In this chapter, we focus on national-level policies and standards that guide curriculum development within the context of adult ESL in English-dominant countries such as Australia, Canada, the UK, and the U.S.[1] Common to all of these countries is that English language instruction for immigrants and refugees is the responsibility of the government through funding and oversight of program delivery (Murray 2005). Educational policies are ever changing, so what's true today may not be in five years. At present, the standards, outcomes, or benchmarks in Table 10.1 are used for guiding curriculum development and in some instances, for defining measures of learner gains.

Table 10.1 Standards and Curriculum Frameworks Used in Adult ESL

Country[2]	Standards, Outcomes, or Benchmarks	Program Funding and Oversight
Australia	**Certificates I-IV in Spoken and Written English** (CSWE) constitute a national curriculum framework of spoken and written English language, literacy and numeracy for the federally run Adult Migrant English Program (AMEP). *http://www.ameprc.mq.edu.au/resources/cswe_2008*	National Adult Migrant English Program (AMEP); programs apply for competitive grants. The Australian Core Skills Framework is used to describe an individual's performance in the five core skills of learning, reading, writing, oral communication, and numeracy. *https://www.education.gov.au/australian-core-skills-framework*

---

[1] New Zealand was not included as there is no curricular framework specifically for adult English language learners.

[2] Europe's Common European Framework of Reference (Council of Europe 2001) provides descriptions that apply to competence in all languages across all levels. While used extensively in language programming, it is used less so in programs developed specifically for immigrant and refugee learners in these English-dominant countries.

The UK	Programs offer *ESOL Skills for Life* qualifications that draw from the **Adult ESOL Core Curriculum**, a framework for English language learning which defines the skills, knowledge, and understanding that ESOL learners need to demonstrate and it guides curriculum and instruction for ESOL teachers in a variety of settings. *https://cdn.cityandguilds.com/ productdocuments/skills_for_work_ and_life/english_mathematics_and_ict_ skills/4692/centre_documents/adult_ esol_core_curriculum_v1.pdf*	National Controlling Migration Fund; the controlling migration prospectus explains how local authorities can access the fund and makes clear that proposals for funding should demonstrate how they will benefit the resident community (Foster and Bolton 2018).
Canada	**Canadian Language Benchmarks** represent national standards in English and French for describing and measuring second language proficiency of adult immigrants and prospective immigrants for living and working in Canada. The benchmarks consist of a set of descriptive statements of language ability and communicative competencies on a leveled continuum. This framework is used for planning curricula for language instruction in a variety of contexts. *http://www.language.ca/home/*	Immigration, Refugees and Citizenship Canada (IRCC) funds Language Instruction for Newcomers to Canada (LINCS) and Occupation-specific Language Training (OSLT). Accountability now based on a Portfolio-Based Language Assessment (PBLA) based on the Canadian Language Benchmarks.
The U.S.	Under the Workforce Innovation and Opportunity Act (WIOA), states must adopt rigorous content standards. Many states have adopted the **College and Career Readiness Standards** (CCRS) for Adult Education. The **English Language Proficiency Standards (ELPS) for Adult Education** articulate the language needed to meet rigorous content standards; some states develop their own ESOL frameworks that integrate these national standards frameworks. CCRS: *https://sites.ed.gov/ octae/2013/04/22/college-and-career-readiness-ccr-standards-for-adult-education/*	States receive funding from the federal government, and disperse funds to individual programs through competitive grants. Funding may be earmarked for specific types of programming, for example, career pathways. States gather learner data from programs and report levels of performance with the U.S. Department of Education's **National Reporting System** (NRS), an accountability system used to measure the effectiveness of federally funded adult education programs. Data on three primary measures include indicators of employment, credential attainment, and measureable skill gains (i.e.,

ELPS:

https://lincs.ed.gov/publications/pdf/elp-standards-adult-ed.pdf

educational functioning level gain or receipt of a secondary school diploma). NRS authorizes which assessments (e.g., CASAS, TABE CLAS-E, BEST) can be used. The NRS educational functioning levels are based on the English Language Proficiency Standards for Adult Education.

It would seem that the move to college and career readiness standards in adult education makes sense in today's economic landscape. According to a 2011 study, those without a high school diploma are nearly twice as likely to be unemployed compared to those with even some college (e.g., a short certificate, some technical training) (Foster, Strawn, and Duke-Benfield 2011). Educational attainment affects the well-being of adult immigrants and refugees and their families and an adult education system that focuses on basic survival skills alone falls short of preparing adults to meet their full economic potential. Learners need adequate levels of English and academic readiness skills to pursue those career qualifications. Do these standards and associated assessments represent what learners know and need to be able to do in their lives and social contexts? Are all learners seeking employment, and should that be the primary focus of adult ESL instruction?

10.4 Placing standards in context

National standards, outcomes, or benchmarks are used as a means of building consistency across programs and authorized assessments are normally tied to those standards. In the U.S., while many applaud WIOA for better aligning federally-funded job training and adult education programs with the skills sought by businesses, the Migration Policy Institute's National Center on Immigrant Integration Policy (2015) raises concerns about whether this legislation could prevent states from using funds to serve immigrants and refugees, particularly those with limited prior formal schooling or limited literacy, who may not need or want workforce training. Educators in the UK expressed similar concerns, namely that national funding has favored programs serving higher-proficiency level learners or career-focused programs over programs that support literacy development for newcomers (Casey 2016).

In the U.S., both the English Literacy and Civics (EL Civics) and Family and Intergenerational Literacy programs funded under WIOA include workplace systems in their description, but those programs also aim to integrate English literacy and civics education to help immigrants and other English learners master English and navigate governmental, educational, and community systems (e.g., banking and health care). The optional indicators for reporting outcomes for English language civics and family literacy programs in the U.S. point to the sorts of outcomes to consider in *any* adult ESL program to assure that we are meeting a wide range of learner needs:

- Involvement in children's literacy related activities:
  - Reading to children
  - Visiting a library
  - Purchasing books or magazines for children
- Achieving citizenship
- Voter registration

- Involvement in community activities:
  - Attending or organizing meetings of neighborhood, community, or political organizations
  - Volunteering to work for such organizations
  - Contributing to the support of such organizations
  - Volunteering to work on community improvement activities

(National Reporting System 2017:57)

The Adult ESOL Core Curriculum and Canadian Language Benchmarks both include community involvement and strategies for independent learning among the desired outcomes. Among the theoretical underpinnings of the Australian Core Skills Framework are these:

- View core skills as complex social practices embedded in context, and influenced by purpose, audience, and contextualized expectations and conventions.
- Recognize that core skills are best learned within a context that the adult learner perceives to be relevant and important.
- View texts as serving particular functions in a social context and different texts have predictable language structures depending on their function.

Commonwealth of Australia (2012:3) *Australian Core Skills Framework*

As educators of adult English learners, we need to balance government mandates with learners' needs, goals, and backgrounds. Generally speaking, standards in the four contexts outlined above don't prescribe the content or topics of instruction.

📋 **Task 10.1**

Look at these sample standards and performance indicators for beginning to high-beginning English language learners. In what ways do these examples focus on college or career readiness? In what ways do they address broader language and literacy needs? How could they be addressed using learner-generated texts or content? Are some more prescriptive than others?

Standards Framework	Sample Standard	Performance Indicators
U.S. English Language Proficiency (ELP) Standards for Adult Education; ten anchor standards and for each one, five sets of leveled descriptors.	ELP 2: Participate in level-appropriate oral and written exchanges of information, ideas, and analyses, in various social and academic contexts, responding to peer, audience, or reader comments and questions.	By the end of English language proficiency level 1, an ELL can . . . • actively listen to others. • participate in short conversations and written exchanges about familiar topics and in familiar contexts. • present simple information. • respond to simple *Yes/No* questions and some *wh-* questions.
UK ESOL Core Curriculum (3 levels)	Speaking Level 1 Be able to obtain information from simple verbal communication	The learner will be able to: 1.1 Follow the gist of simple verbal communication. 1.2 Obtain necessary detail from simple verbal communication for a given task. 1.3 Follow single step verbal instructions correctly for a given task.

Canadian Language Benchmarks	Speaking Level 1: Interacting with Others	
For each level, provides a profile of ability; organized by the four skills (listening, speaking, reading, writing); four levels for each skill.	• Use and respond to basic courtesy formulas and greetings. [Interlocutors are familiar and supportive.]	• Responds appropriately to common greetings, introductions, and leave-takings. • Uses appropriate basic courtesy formulas. Indicates communication problems verbally or non-verbally.
Australian Core Benchmarks (five levels); organized around five core skills (listening, speaking, reading, writing); and numeracy across three domains: • Personal and community • Workplace and employment • Education and training	Oral communication level 1: 1.07 Gives or elicits basic information in a short, simple spoken context.	• Understands and responds appropriately in highly familiar oral contexts where exchanges are short and explicit. • Asks simple questions and makes statements with reasonable effectiveness where this involves short utterances and highly familiar content. • Responds to a request for clarification or repetition and makes statements with reasonable effectiveness where this involves short utterances and highly familiar content.

In this world of standards-based instruction, we need to keep the learner at the center of instruction. A standard related to interpreting information presented in diverse formats can be applied to texts that learners use in their own lives and that they bring to class, whether that be a diagram for putting together a table or the online grading portal used at their child's school. The standard below (English Language Proficiency Standard 2) could be addressed through a debate on an issue of local concern or through a problem-solving task related to a neighborhood or work issue. What are some other ways this standard could be addressed at the advanced level?

Standard	Level 5 (Advanced) Descriptors
ELP Standard 2 An ELL can participate in level appropriate oral and written exchanges of information, ideas, and analyses, in various social and academic contexts, responding to peer, audience, or reader comments and questions	By the end of English language proficiency level 5, an ELL can . . . • participate in conversations, extended discussions, and written exchanges about a range of substantive topics, texts, and issues. • build on the ideas of others. • express his or her own ideas clearly and persuasively. • refer to specific and relevant evidence from texts or research to support his or her ideas. • ask and answer questions that probe reasoning and claims. • summarize the key points and evidence discussed.

10.5 Standards in the classroom

In Chapter 1, I make the case for preparing all learners for the demands of the 21st century. In my context of adult ESL in the U.S., the introduction of the College and Career Readiness Standards for Adult Education prompted some key instructional shifts in the landscape of adult education, namely, that we are giving learners more practice with: (1) complex texts and the academic language in those texts; (2) reading, writing, listening, and speaking grounded in evidence from a text; and (3) building learner content knowledge through the use of content-rich, non-fiction texts (U.S. Department of Education 2013). I don't see these shifts as uniquely college or career focused; they represent ways that anyone can engage more deeply in their communities by accessing information presented in multiple formats.

Let's now see how we can align standards to diverse learner backgrounds and needs using any variety of teaching approaches, including task-based or project-based learning. To demonstrate how standards can play out in the language classroom, consider the Leisure Time Activities task in Section 2.9 task-based learning. Learners read and interpret information about leisure time activities among adults in the U.S. presented in a pie chart.

Task: Read this chart and answer these questions with your partner:

1. How much time could people spend interacting with others?
2. How much of the time can be spent outdoors?
3. How healthy are these practices? Why?

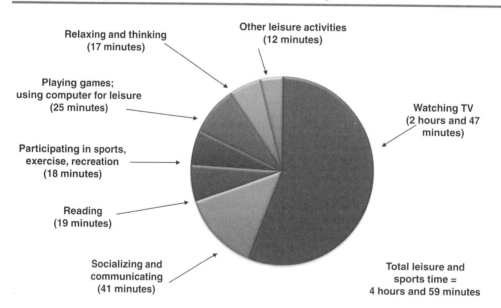

Leisure time on an average day

Relaxing and thinking (17 minutes)

Other leisure activities (12 minutes)

Playing games; using computer for leisure (25 minutes)

Watching TV (2 hours and 47 minutes)

Participating in sports, exercise, recreation (18 minutes)

Reading (19 minutes)

Socializing and communicating (41 minutes)

Total leisure and sports time = 4 hours and 59 minutes

NOTE: Data include all persons age 15 and over. Data include all days of the week and are annual averages for 2015.

From *Bureau of Labor Statistics, American Time Use Survey*

In order to work with this informational text, learners take part in a series of activities:

Step 1: Build background knowledge and pre-teach concepts (leisure vs. work/chores).

- Present visuals with photos
- Picture sort/categorizing

Step 2: Answer the questions about activities and health issues related to leisure activities using evidence from the chart to support their claims.

Step 3: Work with the language forms and functions needed to successfully complete the task:

- Pronunciation of vocabulary; word stress matching (words to stress patterns)
- Speculating using language like this:
  - I think people could . . .
  - People can do _____ alone or with others.

- Co-construct language for comparing and contrasting:
  - People spend (a little, much, considerably) more time _____ than _____.

Step 4: As a final task and outcome, conduct class research on own groups' leisure time activities and create their own pie chart. Compare their practices to those depicted in the pie chart.

📋 **Task 10.2**

In what ways are each of these English Language Proficiency Standards addressed with this lesson? Review the lesson and take notes here:

English Language Proficiency Standards addressed with this lesson	Justification for choosing that standard
ELP 1: Construct meaning from oral presentations and literary and informational text through level-appropriate listening, reading, and viewing.	
ELP 3: Speak and write about level-appropriate complex literary and informational texts and topics.	
ELP 4: Construct level-appropriate **oral** or written claims and support them with reasoning and evidence.	
ELP 10: Demonstrate command of the conventions of standard English to communicate in level-appropriate speech and writing.	

Now compare your notes to my analysis below of this lesson. The highly integrated, task-based approach and the use of an authentic informational text makes meeting a variety of standards quite natural. Notice that the task requires a high level of analysis and it prompts practice with a variety of language functions and forms. At the same time, the topic could be of interest to any learner, whether someone with specific career goals or one who is acquiring English to feel more confident in an English-dominant country.

English Language Proficiency Standards addressed with this lesson	Justification for choosing that standard
ELP 1: Construct meaning from oral presentations and literary and **informational text** through level-appropriate listening, reading, and viewing.	• Task-based on an informational text in graphic form (pie chart) • Requires learners to read closely and repeatedly and to extrapolate meaning beyond surface level understanding • Learners classify information from the pie chart; interpret information presented visually; draw conclusions about what is and is not healthy.
ELP 3: Speak and write about level-appropriate complex literary and informational texts and topics.	• Learners converse about a complex text (an informational graphic) and topic (healthy leisure time). • Learners formulate opinions based on information presented in the pie chart.
ELP 4: Construct level-appropriate **oral** or written claims and support them with reasoning and evidence.	• The final question requires learners to make a claim: "How healthy are these practices, and why?" in an oral exchange with a partner. • Learners need to cite evidence from the text to support their claim.
ELP 10: Demonstrate command of the conventions of standard English to communicate in level-appropriate speech and writing.	• Comparatives and superlatives • Simple present tense • Modals of possibility and probability (can/could) • Gerunds • "*Wh-* question" forms (e.g., How much time . . .?)

Now let's return to the teacher who used project-based learning, where learners developed a mosaic for the school, described very briefly in Chapter 2. The culminating project in Colleen Crossley's class was the creation of an "all are welcome here" mosaic. This project was part of an ongoing unit on the theme of civil rights where learners explored the critical issue of discrimination many immigrants may face in their communities. Learners read about the civil rights movement in the U.S., Jim Crow laws, and discrimination. They took part in a variety of discussion activities and writing tasks. The mosaic project addressed the language of following instructions, asking clarifying questions, and explaining a process to others.

Colleen's program uses the College and Career Readiness Standards for Adult Education and she shared the alignment between the overall unit on civil rights and those standards.

CCRS Addressed	Descriptors and Sample Tasks for Her Level
Reading Anchor 1: Read closely to determine what the text says explicitly and to make logical inferences from it; cite specific textual evidence when writing or speaking to support conclusions drawn from text.	**Level B:** Ask and answer such questions as who, what, where, when, why, and how to demonstrate understanding of key details in a text. Viewed and discussed art as a way to bring about social change; read about civil rights topics and heroes. Five Ws reading task.
Reading Anchor 2: Determine central ideas or themes of a text and analyze their development; summarize the key supporting details and ideas.	**Level B:** Determine the main idea of a text; recount key details and explain how they support the main idea. Used graphic organizers while reading texts to identify topic sentences and supporting details.
Writing Anchor 2: Write informative/explanatory texts to examine and convey complex ideas and information clearly and accurately through the effective selection, organization, and analysis of content.	**Level B:** Write informative/explanatory texts in which they name a topic, supply some facts about the topic, and provide some sense of closure. Wrote related paragraphs with topic sentences and supporting details Used graphic organizers and paragraph frames to support writing Grading rubric addressed: topic sentence, supporting detail
Speaking and Listening Anchor 4: Present information, findings, and supporting evidence such that listeners can follow the line of reasoning and the organization, development, and style are appropriate to task, purpose, and audience.	**Level B:** Report on a topic or text, tell a story, or recount an experience with appropriate facts and relevant, descriptive details, speaking clearly at an understandable pace. Shared the steps of, and participated in, making mosaics, first, with another class of beginning ELLs and then with senior partners at a senior center.

Standards should guide curricula; they should not dictate everything that happens in the classroom. The teacher's job is to guide learners to articulate their goals, and then look for overlaps between those goals and program or state/national outcomes and standards by which learners will be assessed. Teachers also select materials that respond to both learner needs and program standards.

Choosing standards-based textbooks

One way for programs to align instruction to standards is by adopting a **standards-based textbook series.** Publishers may provide alignments in the scope and sequence of the book or through online correspondence charts to, for example, College and Career Readiness Standards or the Canadian Language Benchmarks. Here's an example aligning a unit from a published text to the College and Career Readiness Standards used in the U.S.:

Unit 4 Health

Lesson F [Life Skills]	Reading Anchors 1, 2, 4, 7, 10 1) read closely to determine what the text says explicitly and to make logical inferences from it; cite specific textual evidence when writing or speaking to support conclusions drawn from the text. 2) determine central ideas or themes of a text and analyze their development; summarize the key supporting details and ideas. 4) interpret words and phrases as they are used in a text, including determining technical, connotative, and figurative meanings, and analyze how specific word choices shape meaning or tone. 7) integrate and evaluate content presented in diverse media and formats, including visually and quantitatively, as well as in words. 10) read and comprehend complex literary and informational texts independently and proficiently.

(From *Ventures Level 4 CCRS and ELP Standards Correlation Chart, 2nd Edition,* Cambridge University Press Website).

In this example from a career-contextualized text, *Road to Work* (Magy 2017), the college and career ready topics and skills that relate to standards are outlined:

Unit, Title, Pages	Theme	Career Clusters and Occupations	Language Functions	College and Career Readiness Skills	Informational Text	Critical Thinking, Problem Solving, and Paraphrasing
Unit 1 **Park Here!** Pages 14–19	• Moving up a career ladder	Transportation: transportation operations • Parking lot attendant • Automotive service technician and mechanic	• Discuss setting educational and career goals • Talk about getting a better job • Talk about moving up a career ladder	• Read closely • Respond to text-dependent questions • Cite evidence • Build vocabulary • Retell a story • Write about working as a parking lot attendant • Internet Research: career ladders	• Read about moving up a career ladder • Read an automotive service technician job description	• Paraphrasing

(From Road to Work, Magy 2017: 4*)*

In the U.S., many publishers provide correlations to standards of states with extremely large ELL populations, for example, California, Florida, Texas, and New York. While these correlations to standards are very useful, an important question to ask continually is: *Does the text align with learner goals as well as the program standards?* One can assure a measure of alignment between learner and program goals by providing ample opportunities for learners to reflect on what they've learned in a lesson and, more importantly, articulate how what they have learned can help them in their lives (see 9.6 for ideas on learner self-assessment).

10.6 Emergent learner needs and standards: two cases in point

Many programs, even those using a core series for instruction, utilize practices that allow the curriculum to emerge from learners' lives and needs, for example, project-based learning (2.11) or participatory problem posing (2.10). How do teachers reconcile the issues and concerns that emerge through these approaches with the standards and accountability systems that may be in place in their programs? The following cases illustrate how a teacher can align learner needs with different standards or outcomes.

In a visit to a low-intermediate adult ESL class, learners shared a number of challenges they had encountered over the previous few weeks. The teacher was concerned that the issues raised did not fit the program curriculum. As I analyzed the learner challenges, I was able to identify specific language needs that are common to many sets of standards. As you read the learner challenges, see if you can identify the language skills Diana and Chae need to develop in English.

Learner challenge 1

Chae tried to call school to report his daughter's illness. He couldn't navigate the voicemail system so he gave up. Not surprisingly, his daughter's teacher called him at mid-morning to find out where his daughter was. This student was highly motivated to learn the skills of calling the school and using voicemail systems. Now that the class is more focused on college and career readiness, the teacher isn't sure how working on navigating voicemail systems and leaving messages fits into her curriculum.

Learner challenge 2

Diana found that she had unknowingly purchased a very expensive service contract for the used car she recently purchased at a local car dealership. When she realized it, she had tremendous difficulty canceling the policy. She couldn't understand all of the options on the voicemail system when she called the dealership. When she finally got through to someone, she had difficulty describing the problem so she finally gave up and kept the contract.

I identified the following language needs. Diana and Chae need to . . .

- explain that there is a problem so that the others can understand.
- verify information during interactions like the one at the car dealership.
- be able to understand voicemail systems that offer multiple options.
- understand how and when to leave a voice message.
- read contracts; conventions of service contracts.
- learn how to recognize offers and refuse offers.

Now let's see how some of these learners' needs align with various standards we explored in Table 10.2. This time I included the College and Career Readiness Standards that are used widely in the U.S.

Table 10.2 Aligning Learners' Expressed Needs to Standards

Learners need to ...	English Language Proficiency Standards for Adult Education	College and Career Readiness Standards	UK Adult ESOL Core Curriculum	Canadian Language Benchmarks
• describe a problem so that the others (e.g., sales people, employers) understand.	ELP 2 Level 3 • Participate in conversations, discussions, and written exchanges about familiar topics, texts, and issues • Restate some of the key ideas expressed	Speaking and Listening Anchor 4 Level B: • Report on a topic or text, tell a story, or recount an experience with appropriate facts and relevant, descriptive details, speaking clearly at an understandable pace.	Speaking Level 2 2.3 express clearly statements of fact and short accounts and descriptions.	Speaking CLB 5 Level 2 IV. Sharing Information • Provides necessary information • Asks relevant questions • Repeats information and ideas to confirm understanding

• verify information during interactions such as the one at the car dealership.	ELP 2 Level 3 • ask and answer relevant questions • restate some of the key ideas expressed ask questions to gain information or clarify understanding	Speaking and Listening Anchor 1 Level B • ask questions to check understanding of information presented, stay on topic, and link their comments to the remarks of others	Speaking Level 2 2.4 ask questions to clarify understanding	CLB Listening 5 II. Comprehending Instructions • seeks clarification and confirmation if required
• understand voicemail systems that offer multiple options. • understand how and when to leave a message.	ELP 1 Level 3 • determine a central idea or theme in oral presentations and spoken and written texts • retell key details and answer questions about key details		Listening Level 2 2.4 listen to and follow short, straightforward explanations and instructions	CLB Listening 5 II. Comprehending Instructions • understand simple to moderately complex directions and instructions for generally familiar and relevant procedures • responds with actions to directions and instructions

In addition to these listening and speaking standards, this class could benefit from working on reading standards that may help them to access complex texts such as service contracts. The needs expressed by Chae, Diana, and others in their class are real and immediate. These learner challenges can now provide rich contexts for instruction that are relevant to the learners, while at the same time helping the students meet standards like the ones above.

The two cases in this section illustrate how learner input provides the content and context for instruction that is compatible with a variety of standards, and in many cases multiple standards. Here is a checklist of important reminders:

- Provide ongoing opportunities for learners to articulate their goals.
- Find out what standards your program uses for accountability purposes and to guide the curriculum, and look for places where learner goals align with them.
- Use textbooks or online curricula that correspond as closely as possible to outcomes and standards that address both learner and program needs and expectations.
- Use learner strengths, needs, wants, and dilemmas as the starting point of instruction.
- Develop assessment tools that capture learning in these areas.

Using standards is just one of your lesson-planning tools. Remember how Dan addresses standards in his lesson-planning process for his literacy level class (6.1):

*Planning for me always starts with the thematic unit; the over-arching theme or line of inquiry of the coming weeks or months. Then I look at the individual parts that make up that theme and what I can address in the allotted time. These are the main content and skill goals for the students in my class. Then I get to the fun part of planning the techniques and materials I think are going to help us get towards those goals, hopefully in a sequential way that builds upon previous lessons and cycles back for review. **As I'm doing that, I look to see which standards I think I am addressing** and see if there are **any more opportunities to adjust the lesson to include more standards work.** This last part is newer to me so it takes some thinking, but it also keeps things fresh trying to teach familiar topics in new ways.*

Standards need not be a noose around teachers' and learners' necks; use standards to guide, shape, and help you in the process of developing lessons that are, first and foremost, responsive to learners. Use standards to assure that you are holding learners to the highest expectations possible.

10.7 Standards and assessments

Standardized tests are used by programs as one measure of learning outcomes and they are often used to report level gains to funders. As a teacher, it is important to find out how program assessments are tied to standards. As an example, the CASAS assessment system is informed by both the College and Career Readiness Standards and the English Language Proficiency Standards for Adult Education. Test items assess foundational literacy, language and vocabulary (with a focus on the academic word list[3]), and literal comprehension of both informational and literary texts, as well as higher order reading strategies such as making inferences or determining an author's point of view (CASAS 2016).

It may be quite evident how we would assess literal understanding of a text, as reflected in this CCR Reading Standard Anchor 1 Level A performance descriptor: *Ask and answer questions about key details in a text.* However, it may be less evident how to assess outcomes on a standard such as this:

CCR Reading Anchor 7: Integrate and evaluate content presented in diverse media and formats, including visually and quantitatively, as well as in words.

Level A Performance Indicator: Use the illustrations and details in a text to describe its key ideas (e.g., maps, charts, photographs, political cartoons, etc.).

How does this CASAS level A test item assess both CCRS Reading Anchor 1 Level A and CCRS Reading Anchor 7 Level A performance descriptor?

---

[3] The Academic Word List contains words which appear with high frequency in English language academic texts (Coxhead 2000).

2. The pool opens on Sunday at _____.

    A.   5 AM

    B.   8 AM

    C.   10 AM

    D.   5 PM

(CASAS Level A Reading Goals Test Series sample test items, 2018)

At the beginning proficiency level, this item assesses the learners' ability to interpret information presented in a chart with visuals and text; in this case, signage they may encounter in their community. They can use the graphics to determine which line presents pool hours. By Level D for CCRS Reading Anchor 7, learners are assessed on their ability to: *integrate quantitative or technical information expressed in words in a text with a version of that information expressed visually (e.g., in a flowchart, diagram, model, graph, or table).* How does this sample item from the CASAS Reading Goals Test Level D series assess both CCRS Reading Anchor Standard 1 Level C (*Refer to details and examples in a text when explaining what the text says explicitly and when drawing inferences from the text*) and the CCRS Reading Anchor Standard 7 Level D performance indicator?

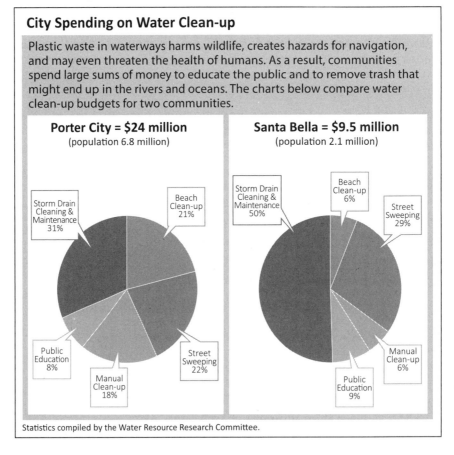

Test item:

According to the two charts, Porter City and Santa Bella spend the largest percentage of their water cleanup budgets on _____.

A.   Street Sweeping

B.   Beach Clean-Up

C. Manual Clean-Up

D. Storm Drain Maintenance

(CASAS Level D Reading Goals Test Series sample test items, 2018)

10.8 High-leverage instructional practices to meet rigorous content standards

What is common to many of the standards explored in this chapter is that they lead learners to collaborate with others effectively, think critically in community, work, and school contexts, and employ strategies for understanding oral and written text presented in a variety of formats, including digitally. They represent the kinds of 21st-century skills needed for access to information and full participation in communities in today's world. Teachers can help learners meet these skills through the routine implementation of high-leverage instructional practices across disciplines (a course focused on literacy development or a career-focused course) and levels.

There are various definitions of "high-leverage" practices. Research on helping English language learners access rigorous content standards (Ewert 2014; Neri, et al. 2016) consider **high-leverage practices** to be those that scaffold learning, address the academic language demands of a lesson, promote collaborations among learners, prompt higher-order thinking, and provide language needed to make that thinking visible. We have explored many such practices throughout this book. Table 10.3 highlights some of those practices along with 21st-century skills that are likely to dovetail with many of the standards that programs are currently using.

Table 10.3 High-Leverage Practices and 21st-Century Skills Addressed

Activity Type	21st-Century Skills Addressed
Jigsaw activities and paired reading	• Read closely • Present results to others • Interview others; present information to others • Synthesize information from multiple sources • Employ effective communication strategies
One-question interviews and data analysis	• Collect, organize, represent, and interpret data • Use and interpret tally marks • Represent data visually • Interpret graphs • Transfer information (data to graphs) • Summarize and synthesize information • Conduct "research" • Practice numeracy skills
Graphic organizers as while-reading or while-listening activities	• Recognize text organization and text genre • Organize and categorizing information • Practice note-taking

Information grid tasks / Interviews	• Note-taking using a grid
	• Communicate effectively using:
	  – clarification strategies
	  – follow-up questions for elaboration

Providing academic language frames or paragraph frames	• Using an academic register with sentence frames (two thirds of the class) • Transferring information (graphs to paragraph)
Short authentic video clips in listening lessons	• Practice with mini "lectures;" authentic, non-scripted language • Listen selectively • Practice note-taking
Analysis of real-world information (graphs, tables, charts)	• Cite evidence to support claims • Interpret information presented in diverse formats

When teachers use high-leverage instructional practices like these, they afford learners the opportunity to collaborate with others, employ a wide variety of critical thinking skills, and develop the language needed to express their ideas clearly.

Conclusion

I began this book with an examination of the unique strengths adult learners bring to English language classrooms as well as challenges they may face, and I have ended with a look at the larger picture of adult English language standards and accountability systems. These topics, along with everything in between, should be seen as interconnected with the learner at the center; each element in adult English language education systems should inform the others.

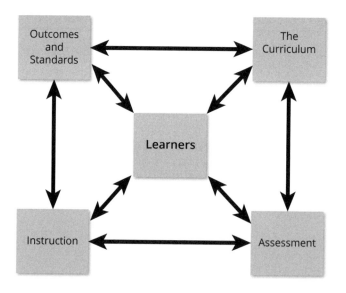

Our primary responsibilities as English language teachers are to the learners in our programs. Standards and accountability systems should be viewed as one means of providing and maintaining quality instruction. They should be connected to the lives and needs of learners, while at the time satisfying the needs of other stakeholders. I have argued, along with many other professionals in the field, that the most suitable approaches for working with adult English language learners within this system are those that are truly learner-centered. It is my hope that the principles and practices in this text will get you started on the road to teaching in a variety of settings, with diverse groups of learners, and in keeping with your own beliefs and strengths as a teacher.

On your own, or with a partner, provide an example or brief definition for each concept:

Checklist of Key Terms	
accountability	
content standards	
performance indicators or descriptors	
standards-based textbook series	
high-leverage practices	

Before doing these activities, revisit your answers to the questions at the beginning of the chapter.

1 Standards in your setting

If you are already teaching, answer as many of these questions as you can. Then do research on answers to those you were not sure about, or to add to your current understanding:

a.   What are the accountability requirements of my program and/or state/region?

b.   What standards guide my program?

c.   To whom is my program accountable and for what purposes?

d.   How can I align program standards with learner goals?

If you are not teaching, answer questions a., b., and c. by searching online for the Adult Education office in your area or by interviewing an adult English language teacher or program coordinator. For question d., describe two things you would do in an ESL class to align learner goals and program standards.

2 Aligning instruction to your program standards/outcomes

If you are already teaching, identify and describe three standards or outcomes for which learners need to be assessed in your program. Describe what you believe would be the best way to address those standards in your context and with your curriculum. Consider a lesson you recently taught and see if you can identify which standards are addressed.

If you are not teaching, ask a teacher in your area to share three outcomes or standards from a class she or he teaches or find a list of the standards for your state online and choose three for this activity. Describe what you believe would be the best way to address those standards in your context and with your curriculum.

3 Aligning learner goals to standards

If you are already teaching, identify three standards or outcomes that you believe overlap with learner goals you have elicited. Describe two ways you would connect the program standard to your learners' goals. **If you are not teaching**, find a list of the standards for your state or region (ask an ESL teacher or do an online search) and look for places where the *Learner Challenges* in Section 10.5 overlap with those standards.

Post-task

Looking back . . .

Go back to the statements you reflected on at the beginning of this book. With a partner or on your own, complete these statements again with your current beliefs about teaching and learning in adult ESL contexts. Afterward, discuss the ways in which your views have evolved or changed through the process of reading and working through the activities in this book, and by collaborating with others to develop your knowledge and skills for meeting the needs of adult English language learners.

Complete these statements with your current beliefs about teaching and learning in adult English language learning contexts.

1. Strengths and challenges adult learners may bring to the classroom are . . .

2. Some common purposes for learning English are . . .

3. Learning a second language involves . . .

4. If I walked into an adult English language classroom, I'd like to see . . .

5. Learners' roles and responsibilities in class are . . .

6. My responsibilities as a teacher are . . .

A selection of standards not already listed in this chapter:

Partnership for 21st-Century Skills (P21): Framework for 21st-Century Learning. Tucson, AZ: 2009. Available online *http://21stcenturyskillsbook. com/resources/*

The Northstar Digital Literacy Assessment provides comprehensive lists of digital literacy standards that can be included in curricula. *http://www. digitalliteracyassessment.org* assesses digital skills through online, self-guided modules.

Transitions Integration Framework (TIF), ATLAS (2013; Revised version 2016) The TIF defines the academic, career, and employability skills essential for adult learners to successfully transition to postsecondary education, career training, the workplace, and to enrich community involvement. *http://atlasabe.org/professional/transitions*

The Cambridge Framework for Life Competencies Life competencies grouped into eight areas: Creativity, Critical Thinking and Problem-Solving, Digital Literacy, Learning to Learn, Communication, Collaboration, Emotional Development and Social Responsibilities. We have then developed Can Do Statements to describe what learners should be able to do for each competency at each stage of the learning journey, including higher education and work. *http://www.cambridge.org/elt/blog/wp-content/uploads/2018/04/Life-Competencies-Digital-final.pdf*

Standards for Adult Education ESL Programs TESOL (2002) define quality components from a national perspective. Using program indicators in eight distinct areas, the standards can be used to review an existing program or as a guide in setting up a new ESOL program. While this predates the move to college and career readiness standards, the indicators are still highly relevant and could be used in programs in any part of the world.

OTHER USEFUL WEBSITES

National Reporting System website: This site provides adult education teachers, administrators and others interested in the adult education program reference material and training related to the guidelines of the National Reporting System in the U.S. Available at: *https://www.nrsweb.org/*

Centre for Canadian Language Benchmarks: The Centre for Canadian Language Benchmarks supports the national standards in English and French for describing, measuring and recognizing second language proficiency of adult immigrants and prospective immigrants for living and working in Canada. *http://www.language.ca/home/*

Glossary

academic language – language needed for work and school that includes, for example, discipline-specific vocabulary, language structures, and rhetorical conventions typical for a content area.

accommodations – allowances made for students with learning disabilities or physical handicaps that allow them equal access to all aspects of programs.

accountability – being answerable to program administrators and funders for instruction and learner outcomes.

acculturation – understanding of the beliefs, emotions, and behaviors of the dominant culture, without letting go of the first culture.

achievement test – measures what learners have gained through a lesson, unit, or course.

acquisition vs. learning – acquisition refers to natural, unconscious processes that children go through as they acquire their first language; learning refers to consciously learning the rules and patterns of the language.

action research – a process of teachers identifying problems or issues in their teaching, gathering data or information about what is happening, researching the topic, and taking action in their classes.

affective filter – Krashen's term for emotional barriers to learning, for example, high stress or embarrassment.

agency – the ability of individuals to take control of their learning in pursuit of their personal goals and aspirations.

alternative assessment – refers to tools to assess learning that are typically classroom based and ongoing, and reflect the outcomes of a particular course. Examples include performance assessment, observation, self-assessment, or portfolio assessment.

assimilation – is the complete absorption of the second culture practices, beliefs and norms.

backwards design – starting lesson planning by first determining what the desired results or goals are for a lesson, and building the lesson to achieve those goals.

balanced literacy approach – an approach to literacy development that draws on the principles of Whole Language teaching as well as more form-focused activities.

BICS – Basic Interpersonal Communication Skills.

behaviorism – refers to a theory that human beings learn new behaviors through a stimulus and response cycle.

BEST (Basic English Skills Test) – intended for new immigrants with very limited English. Includes listening, speaking, reading and writing.

blended learning – a combination of face-to-face and distance learning.

bottom-up processing – involves attempts to decode and understand a language word-for-word.

Bridge program – a program that prepares students to enter a particular academic degree or credentialing program.

CALL – Computer Assisted Language Learning is any means of enhancing instruction through the use of computer-based activities including software, the Internet, email, or basic word processing.

CALP – cognitive academic language proficiency.

career-contextualized ESL – programs that integrate English language skills development with general workplace, or transferable job skills such as effective communication with supervisors and co-workers or problem-solving at work.

CASAS (The Comprehensive Adult Student Assessment System) – an assessment system that includes an array of standardized tests for placement and achievement for reading, writing, listening and life skills.

central design – lesson planning that begins with class materials and activities, then builds the lesson from there.

chain drills – a teacher or learner asks a question, another answers and asks the next question in a chain fashion, until all learners have practiced the language.

checking questions – used so that learners *demonstrate* their understanding of new concepts (content, vocabulary, grammar, functions or competencies).

collaborative dialogue – interactions that help learners to co-construct language through collaborative activities.

communicability – the ability to meet communicative demands.

communicative competence – the ability to use language in a variety settings (at work, at a store, at home) with varying degrees of formality (with a friend vs. with a boss).

communicative language teaching – an approach to teaching that focuses on developing fluency and communicative competence through extensive interaction and use of authentic materials.

competencies – real-life tasks learners need to complete at home, in their communities or workplace, for example, calling in sick to work or completing a permission slip for a child's teacher.

competency-based education – an approach to education whereby language competencies become the basis for instruction. Language functions, grammar, vocabulary and skills are taught to assist learners in achieving the competencies.

comprehensible input – Krashen's term for language input that is understandable to learners. Language is made comprehensible through gestures, visual support, repetition or prior knowledge.

concurrent enrollment – enrollment in job-specific content classes along with supports or ESL classes that integrate the field-specific content.

content standards – refers to what students are expected *to know* and be able to do as a result of instruction.

content words – those words that are stressed within a sentence; those that carry the most meaning, for example, nouns, verbs, or adjectives.

content-based teaching – curricula which have a content area as the focus of instruction, for example, citizenship, math, social studies, or global studies. Content-based instruction is often used in pre-academic programs.

contextualized language lessons – focus on a particular language competency, function, grammar or set of vocabulary used in real-world contexts.

Cooperative Language Learning (CCL) – centers around group tasks where each member is held accountable for his or her learning, and where outcomes to activities are dependent on a genuine exchange of information among participants.

core series – consist of a sequence of books for beginning through high-intermediate or advanced-level learners that integrate instruction in all skill areas as well as grammar, functions, and competencies.

criterion referenced test – a test for which the scores reflect a comparison to a set of outcomes (or criterion).

critical period – the stage when one is best able to acquire a second language, thought to be from around three to just before puberty.

cultural competence – understanding cultural norms and practices.

curricular routines – daily or weekly classroom routines that make instruction consistent and predictable for learners.

diagnostic test – a test or assessment tool that determines what learners do and do not know in relation to the course objectives.

dialogue journals – learner journals that include an ongoing reader (usually the teacher) response.

differentiation – tailoring instruction to account for and address varying learner profiles, interests, and readiness.

digital literacy – using current technologies (which are ever-evolving) to evaluate, organize, communicate, solve problems and create information in our technology-rich world.

discourse chains – a controlled practice activity whereby learners are provided with the steps in a conversation (greet, request information, provide information) to complete with a partner.

discrimination task – a listening task used in pronunciation instruction whereby learners demonstrate their ability to discriminate between different sounds or different stress or intonation patterns.

display questions – questions for which one already knows the answer.

distance learning – instruction where there is a separation of place and/or time between the learner(s) and the instructor conducted through one or more media, for example video or on-line learning.

dominant culture – the majority and long-established culture of a society.

echoing – a teacher repeating verbatim what learners say in class, either correctly or incorrectly.

English Language Civics (ELC) – programs that promote active citizenship and participation in all aspects of the community including voting and civic involvement, involvement in neighborhood programs, and active participation in children's schooling.

emergent curriculum – a curriculum that develops around learners' expressed wants and needs.

English Language Acquisition programs (ELA) – programs that serve a broad population of learners without specific vocational or academic outcomes. All four skills and all areas of language are integrated into the curriculum.

environmental print – print that is found in the community or workplace such as street signs, billboards, warning signs, or store names.

extraneous teacher talk – less helpful teachers talk where the majority of the words are not needed to convey the intended message.

extrinsic motivation – motivation that derives from factors imposed on the learner by an outside force (e.g., requirement for a job, citizenship exam).

family/intergenerational literacy – these programs promote connections between homes and schools by promoting literacy among adults and their children so that children reach their highest academic potential.

financial literacy – the ability of learners to navigate financial systems; learn about issues such as online phishing and identify theft; acquire skills for meeting their financial needs and goals.

fluency – the ease with which one is able to communicate in a second language, even without accuracy in the language.

function words – the words that are typically unstressed within a sentence.

functional texts – reading texts that are used for an everyday, functional purpose, such as menus, phone books, or labels.

functions of language – represent the ways we use language forms and phrases in social interactions, for example, greetings and introductions, making invitations, making polite requests, or complaints and apologies.

funds of knowledge – knowledge all learners bring to class based on culturally and historically accumulated knowledge and skills that enable an individual or household to function within a given culture.

graphic literacy – the ability to use and understand pictorial symbols to convey meaning.

graphic organizers – any means to visually organize information, for example Venn diagrams, word webs, or charts.

i + 1 – is Krashen's term for input that is just beyond a learner's current level. This kind of input challenges, yet is accessible to learners.

identity – the ways that learners perceive themselves within their social networks.

independent field trips – are field trips that are completed by individual students outside of class time.

inductive approach – when language is presented in context first and learners deduce or figure out the rules with the teacher's guidance.

information-gap activity – refers to an activity that requires a genuine exchange of information in order for learners to complete the task.

Integrated Education and Training (IET) – programs where the occupational instructor and adult education instructor co-teach in the same classroom or coordinate instruction through

integrated-skills texts – provide practice in all four skills areas and typically integrate grammar, language functions, and competencies.

intelligibility – pronunciation that is understandable by the listener and does not interfere with communication.

Interactionism – a view that second language acquisition requires interaction between speakers. Language is made comprehensible through modifications or comprehension checks by both the speaker and listener.

intergenerational tension – struggles that emerge among generations in immigrant families as a result of conflicting values, beliefs, and norms between the first culture and the new culture.

interpersonal dialogue – dialogue for the purpose of communicating with others for personal reasons, for example, making small talk with a co-worker, talking to a friend about a concern at home.

intrinsic motivation – motivation that stems from a desire within the individual for personal growth.

investment – the degree to which a learner sees that his or her contributions are valued in a given social context.

high-leverage practices – those that: scaffold learning; address the academic language demands of a lesson; promote collaborations among learners; prompt higher-order thinking; and provide language needed to make that thinking visible.

higher-order thinking skills – a model for sequencing learning objectives that move beyond simple recall to include understanding, applying, analyzing, evaluating, and creating.

jigsaw reading (or listening) – refers to a reading or listening activity that involves different groups of learners reading or listening to different texts related to one theme, and then grouping with others in class to exchange the information they learned about in their text.

KWL chart – is a means of activating background knowledge, setting learning goals, and reflecting on learning. The chart contains three sections: What do I know? What do I want to learn? What did I learn?

L1 – an individual's first language.

Language Experience Approach (LEA) – an approach that starts with a class recounting a shared experience, which is transcribed by the teacher. The class-generated text becomes the basis for literacy instruction.

language learning strategies – tools learners employ to help them learn more effectively, remember or organize information, or compensate for lacks in their language.

language skills – the four language modes: listening, speaking, reading, and writing.

learner-centered – instruction that puts the learners' backgrounds, expectations, strengths, wants, and needs at the center of curricular choices and classroom practices.

learning disability – refers to any of a group of disorders manifested by significant difficulties in the acquisition and use of listening, speaking, reading, writing, reasoning, or mathematical abilities, presumed to be due to central nervous system dysfunction.

learning strategies – any tools or tactics that learners employ to learn more effectively and more autonomously.

learning styles/learning preference – a person's preference for understanding and processing information.

lesson study – a professional development process where several teachers collaboratively plan, teach, observe, revise and share the results of the same lesson taught with different learners.

linguistic competence – refers to the ability to use and understand language forms, including grammar, spelling, and pronunciation.

literacy-level texts – are intended for emergent readers who may have extremely limited literacy skills in their first language.

managed enrollment – refers to a practice of admitting students only at particular times in a program, be it once a week or once every six weeks. It is an alternative to "open enrollment," whereby learners enter programs on an ongoing basis.

meaningful practice – involves activities in which learners talk about information that is truthful and relevant to their lives.

mechanical practice – helps learners reinforce forms without necessarily creating meaningful utterances.

minimal pair – pairs of words that have only one phonemic difference, for example, bat and vat (/b/ and /v/).

minority cultures – groups that arrived in a country more recently than the dominant culture and make up a minority of the population.

monitor – Krashen's term for learned language acts as a monitor that edits and corrects language.

multiple intelligences – Howard Gardner's term for at least seven *intelligences* that learners draw on to process and understand the world: verbal/linguistic, musical, logical/mathematical, spatial/visual, bodily/kinesthetic, intrapersonal, and natural/environmental.

National Reporting System (NRS) – an accountability system used to measure the effectiveness of federally-funded adult education programs.

Natural Approach – an approach to teaching that starts with providing abundant comprehensible input to learners, much in the way children acquire their first language.

nonliterate – refers to students who speak a language which has a written form, but who don't read or write that language themselves.

norm-referenced test – a test for which the scores reflect a comparison to a group.

objectives – what learners will be able to do at the completion of a lesson. Objectives should be observable and/or measurable.

open educational resources (OERs) – online resources where teachers can find teacher-made materials around a variety of core themes, oftentimes vetted for quality by an educational body.

open enrollment – refers to allowing learners to enter programs at any time during a course or term.

outcomes – the desired results of instruction.

paired reading – working with two texts on the same topic. Pairs of learners read one of two assigned texts and then work with another pair of learners to combine the key concepts from their texts.

parallel writing – a guided writing activity that starts with a text that learners follow as model for their own writing.

Participatory Approach – drawn from Freire's work, a teaching that derives from learners' lives and personal issues within their social context so that they can take action to improve their lives.

performance assessment – an assessment tool whereby learners perform language tasks to demonstrate their competency with language. The assessor uses a rubric with specific criteria in order to determine learner achievement.

performance indicators – various means of providing evidence that learners are meeting program standards or outcomes, e.g., gains on test scores, achievement of personal goals, employment.

performance standards – represent what learners need to do *to demonstrate* their proficiency within content standards.

persistence – when learners continue learning through multiple means (classes, self-directed learning, distance learning) until meeting their educational goals.

phonics – is a view that literacy development is a linear process whereby learners first acquire sound-letter correspondences, with which they create words and then sentences.

placement test – is used to determine the most suitable level for a learner within a program.

practicality – the extent to which an assessment tool is practical to administer.

pre-academic ESL – programs that prepare ESL learners to enter academic settings.

pre-listening – activities that serve to activate learner prior knowledge about a theme before listening to a passage and completing listening activities.

pre-literate – refers to students who speak a language that does not have a written form, or has a form that is rare or has developed very recently (e.g., Hmong).

pre-writing – activities that prepare a learner to write, for example, brainstorming and organizing ideas.

problem posing – a process in participatory education whereby learners identify problems that are affecting their lives. These issues and concerns become the basis of further activities.

process-oriented approach – a multi-step approach to writing that includes pre-writing, ongoing feedback, and multiple drafts.

productive skills – speaking and writing skills.

product-oriented writing – focuses on the finished product rather than the process of writing.

proficiency test – measures a learner's overall competence.

Question Formulation Technique (QFT) – process for generating learner questions that can be used for any number of purposes in the classroom.

realia – real objects brought into class for demonstration or practice.

receptive skills – listening and reading skills.

reformulation – responding to learner errors by naturally restating learner language.

register – the level of formality as well as the academic language conventions that are suitable for a particular situation.

reliability – refers to tests that provide consistent results.

retention – the numbers of learners staying in a program and moving from one level to the next.

rubric – a scoring tool that attempts to communicate expectations of quality around a task. They aim to delineate consistent criteria for assessment and grading.

scaffolded writing – a writing tasks whereby learners complete a sample text with key information left out.

scaffolding – instructional techniques that help move students progressively toward stronger understanding and greater independence in the learning process.

scanning – reading a text only for specific information.

SCANS (Secretary's Commission on Achieving Necessary Skills) – refers to the soft skills needed to perform adequately in the workplace, for example, asking for help, working in teams, managing resources.

schema theory – suggests that prior knowledge shapes our expectations and understanding of what we hear; the closer our schema is to the content of what we hear or read, the easier it will be for us to understand.

semi-literate – refers to students who have some formal education or are able to read and write but only at an elementary level.

semi-scripted dialogue – dialogues that have some of the words provided and in which learners must fill in the missing portions to complete the dialogue with a partner.

sentence stress – refers to the words that are stressed within a sentence.

silent period – Krashen's terms for the initial period of language acquisition when a learner understands some language but is not able to produce it.

skimming – reading for the main idea or gist of a text.

Sociocultural Perspective – a view that learning is not an individual process but a social one. Grounded in the work of Lev Vygotsky, the belief is that understanding of language is co-constructed through collaborative activities, or **collaborative dialogue.**

sound/letter correspondences – the correlation between written symbols (letters) and the sounds they represent in a language.

stand and talk – a class routine where learners think about their answer to a question and then stand to talk to someone not at their table or in their group.

standardized tests – tests that are administered and scored using procedures that are uniform and consistent; typically used to differentiate among learners at different levels for placement purposes.

standards-based textbooks – those texts that are aligned to a particular set of (or sets) of standards, either state or national.

target language – has two meanings: 1) the second language learners are working to acquire; 2) the language focus of a particular lesson, for example, returning something to a store or the simple present tense.

Task-Based Learning (TBL) – an approach where instruction is based on real-world tasks that learners need to complete in the target language (an information-gap activity or development of a project) rather than on a set of language features that need to be taught.

text-dependent questions – those questions that require the learner to go back to the text and read carefully to find the information.

think-pair-share – a classroom routine whereby learners think of an answer or brainstorm ideas, then talk about it with a partner before sharing with the whole class.

top-down processing – involves making educated guesses about content based on prior knowledge and visual clues (facial expressions, context, etc.).

Total Physical Response (TPR) – a teaching method whereby learners respond physically to teacher commands and eventually commands from other learners.

transactional dialogue – dialogue that serves to transmit factual information.

transition programs – programs offered in adult education that are the most advanced and aim to develop academic skills.

translanguaging – the process whereby multilingual speakers utilize their languages as part of an integrated communication system. The L1 is seen as an asset and is leveraged to assist in the language learning process.

validity – refers to tests or assessment tools that test what they are intended to test.

visual literacy – represents the ability to process and represent knowledge through images.

Vocational English as a Second Language (VESL) – refers to courses that provide instruction in English needed for a particular vocation, for example, nursing or carpentry.

virtual field trips – are "field trips" that are completed through online searches, typically around a particular theme with particular tasks to complete.

wait time – the time provided for a learner to think of and respond to teacher questions.

Whole Language – is an overall philosophy to learning, which views language as something that should be taught in its entirety—not broken up into small pieces to be decoded.

whole-part-whole approach – an approach to emergent literacy development that begins with a whole text that learners understand and then moves on to phonics instruction.

word stress – refers to the syllable that is stressed within a multi-syllable word.

word web – a visual presentation of how words or concepts are interconnected, with a key word in the center and related words branching out from there.

workplace ESL – ESL programs offered at the workplace.

work-readiness programs – ESL programs that prepare learners for a variety of work settings.

Zone of Proximal Development (ZDP) – the distance between a learner's current developmental state and potential state the learner can reach provided they have the appropriate supports, or scaffolds, from a more expert listener.

References

Adelson-Goldstein, J. (2016). *Preparing English Learners for Work and Career Pathways: Companion Learning Recourse.* LINCS ESL Pro Project. Washington, D.C.: U.S. Department of Education, Office of Career, Technical and Adult Education *https://lincs.ed.gov/programs/eslpro*.

Adult Basic Education Teaching and Learning Advancement System (ATLAS). (2016). *Transitions Integration Framework*. Retrieved from *http://atlasabe.org/resources/aces/learning-strategies*.

Akomolafe, S. (2013). The invisible minority: Revisiting the debate on foreign accented speakers and upward mobility in the workplace, *Journal of Cultural Diversity 20*(1), 7–14.

Alan, B., & Stoller, F. (2005). Maximizing the benefits of project work in foreign language classrooms. *English Teaching Forum, 43*(4), 10–21.

An, D. & Carr, M. (2017). Learning styles theory fails to explain learning and achievement: Recommendations for alternative approaches. *Personality and Individual Differences, 116*(1) 410–416.

Anderson, L. W. & Krathwohl, D. R. (2001). *A Taxonomy for Learning, Teaching and Assessing: A Revision of Bloom's Taxonomy of Educational Objectives: Complete Edition.* New York, NY: Longman.

Anderson, N. (2014). Developing engaged second language readers. In M. Celce-Murcia, D. Brinton, D. & M. Snow (Eds.) *Teaching English as a Second or Foreign Language, 4th edition* (pp. 170–188). Boston: National Geographic Cengage Learning.

Ascher Webber, A. and Gaer, S. (2016). Learning on the go with mobile devices. Webinar offered Jan. May 6, 2016. EdTech Center. Boston MA: World Education. Retrieved from *https://edtech.worlded.org/resources/learning-on-the-go-with-mobile-devices/*.

Ascher Webber, A. and Wrigley, H. (2018). Innovative digital learning models for ELL immigrant adults, Webinar offered Jan. 209, 2018. EdTech Center. Boston MA: World Education. Retrieved from *https://edtech.worlded.org/resources/webinar-innovative-digital-learning-models-ell-immigrant-adults/*.

Auerbach, E. (1997). *Making Meaning, Making Change: A Participatory Curriculum Development for Adult ESL Literacy.* Washington, D.C. and McHenry, IL: Delta Systems and Center for Applied Linguistics.

Auerbach, E. (1995). "From deficit to strength: Changing perspectives on family literacy." In Immigrant Learners and their Families. G. Weinstein-Shr and E. Quinterro (Eds.) McHenry, IL: Center for Applied Linguistics and Delta Systems, Inc.

Auerbach, E. (1986). Competency-Based ESL: One Step Forward or Two Steps Back? *TESOL Quarterly, 20*(3), 411–429.

Azar, B. (2017). *Understanding and Using Grammar Chartbook, 5th edition.* White Plains, NY: Prentice Hall.

Bailey, K. & Curtis, A. (2015). *Learning about Language Assessment, 2nd edition*. Boston, MA: Heinle Cengage.

Balliro, L. (1997). Multiple levels, multiple responsibilities. *Focus on Basics* Volume 1, Issue *http://www.gse.harvard.edu/~ncsall/fob/1997/balliro.htm*.

Barnett, R. (2007). *A Will to Learn: Being a Student in an Age of Uncertainty.* Buckingham, England: SRHE and Open University Press.

Barry, M. & Egan, A. (2018). An adult learner's learning style should inform but not limit educational choices. *International Review of Education* 64(1), 31–42.

Batalova, J. & Fix, M. (2015). *Through an Immigrant Lens: PIAAC Assessment of the Competencies of Adults in the United States.* Washington, D.C.: Migration Policy Institute.

Bell, J. (2012). Teaching mixed level classes. In A. Burns & J. C. Richards (Eds.). *The Cambridge Guide to Pedagogy and Practice in Second Language Teaching* (pp. 86–94). New York, NY: Cambridge University Press.

Bell, J. (2004). *Teaching Multilevel Classes in ESL, 2nd edition.* Toronto, Ontario: Pippin Publishing and Dominie Press.

Belzer, A. & Pickard, A. (2015). From heroic victims to competent comrades. *Views of Adult Literacy Learners in the Research Literature Volume: 65*(3), 250–266.

Bernaus, M., Masgoret, A., Gardner, R. & Reyes, E. (2004). Motivation and attitudes towards learning languages in multicultural classrooms. *The International Journal of Multilingualism, 1*(2), 75–89.

Berry, J.W. (1997). Immigration, acculturation, and adaptation. *Applied Psychology, 46*(1), 5–34.

Bigelow, M., & Vinogradov, P. (2011). Teaching adult second language learners who are emergent readers. *Annual Review of Applied Linguistics, 31*, 120–136. doi:10.1017/S0267190511000109.

Bitterlin, G., Johnson, D., Price, D., Ramirez, S. & Savage. L. (2018). *Ventures series, 3rd edition.*

Bohlke, D., Lockwood, R. & Hartman, P. (2016). *Final Draft 1.* Cambridge: Cambridge University Press.

Bow Valley College (2011). *Learning for Life: An ESL Literacy Curriculum Framework.* Calgary AB: Bow Valley College. Retrieved from *https://globalaccess.bowvalleycollege.ca/sites/default/files/Curriculum_Framework.pdf.*

Brinton, D., Snow, M., and Wesche, M. (2003). *Content-Based Second Language Instruction, Michigan Classics Edition.* Ann Arbor, MI: University of Michigan Press.

Brod, S. (1990). Recruiting and retaining language minority students in adult literacy programs. *ERIC Digest.* Washington, D.C.: National Clearinghouse for ESL Literacy Education. (ED 321 621).

Brod, S. (1999). *What Non-Readers or Beginning Readers Need to Know: Performance-Based ESL Adult Literacy.* Denver, CO: Spring Institute for International Studies.

Brown, D. and Lee, N. (2015). *Teaching by Principles, 4th edition.* White Plains, NY: Pearson Education.

Bruski, D. (2012). Graphic device interpretation by low-literate adult ELLs: do they get the picture? *Minnesota and Wisconsin Teachers of English to Speakers of Other Languages.* Retrieved from the University of Minnesota Digital Conservancy, *http://hdl.handle.net/11299/162757.*

Bunch, G. C., & Kibler, A. K. (2015). Integrating language, literacy, and academic development: Alternatives to traditional English as a second language and remedial English for language minority students in community colleges. *Community College Journal of Research & Practice, 39*(1), 20–33. doi:10.1080/10668926.2012.755483.

Bureau of Labor Statistics (2017). *News Release Consumer Expenditures 2016.* U.S. Department of Labor. Retrieved from *https://www.bls.gov/news.release/pdf/cesan.pdf.*

Burt, M., Peyton, J. K., & Schaetzel, K. (2008). *Working with Adult English Language Learners with Limited Literacy: Research, Practice, and Professional Development.* Washington, D.C.: Center for Applied Linguistics. Retrieved from *http://www.cal.org/adultesl/resources/briefs/working-with-adult-english-language-learners-with-limited-literacy.php.*

Byrd, P. & Schuemann, C. (2014). English as a second or foreign language textbooks: How to choose them- how to use. In *Teaching English as a Second or Foreign Language*. M. Celce-Murcia (Ed.) Boston, MA: Cengage.

Byrnes, M. (2000). Accommodations for students with disabilities: removing barriers to learning. *NASSP Bulletin, 84*(613), 21–27.

CAELA Network (2007). Assessing learner needs in the adult ESL classroom. *The CAELA Guide for Adult ESL Trainers.* Washington, D.C.: Center for Applied Linguistics. Retrieved from *http://www.cal.org/caela/scb/III_A_AssessingLearnerNeeds.pdf.*

Cambridge University Press (2017). *Ventures Level 4 CCRS and ELP Standards Correlation Chart, 2nd Edition.* New York, NY: Cambridge University Press. Retrieved from *https://www.cambridge.org/files/3315/0661/2519/Ventures4_ELP_CCRS_Correlations_2017Aug.pdf.*

Canadian Centre for Victims of Torture. (2018). Torture and second language acquisition. CVCT Web page: *http://www.icomm.ca/ccvt/intro.html.*

Carter, S. J. & Henrichsen, L. E. (2015). Addressing reticence: The challenge of engaging reluctant adult ESL students. *Journal of Adult Education, 44*(2), 15–20.

CASAS (2016) *CASAS Reading Standards: The Relationship to the College and Career Readiness Standards for Adult Education and the NRS Educational Functioning Levels for ABE/ASE.* San Diego, CA: CASAS.

Retrieved from *https://www.casas.org/docs/default-source/institute/casas-reading-standards-2016.pdf?sfvrsn=6?Status=Master.*

CASAS (2018). *Reading GOALS.* San Diego, CA: CASAS. Retrieved from *https://www.casas.org/product-overviews/curriculum-management-instruction/sample-test-items/reading-goals.*

Casner-Lotto, J., & Barrington, L. (2006). *Are They Really Ready to Work? Employers' Perspectives on the Basic Knowledge and Applied Skills of New Entrants to the 21st-Century U.S. Workforce.* New York, NY: Conference Board. Retrieved from *http://www.p21.org/storage/documents/FINAL_REPORT_PDF09-29-06.pdf.*

CAST (2018). *Universal Design for Learning Guidelines Version 2.2*. Wakefield, MA: National Center for Universal Design for Learning. Retrieved from *http://udlguidelines.cast.org.*

Casey, L. (2016). The Casey review: A review into opportunity and integration, London: Department for Communities and Local Government. Retrieved from *https://www.gov.uk/government/publications/the-casey-review-a-review-into-opportunity-and-integration.*

Celce-Murcia, M., Brinton, D., Goodwin, J. & Griner, B. (2010). *Teaching Pronunciation, 2nd edition.* Cambridge: Cambridge University Press.

Center for Postsecondary and Economic Success (2017). Defining on-Ramps to adult career pathways: Issue brief. CLASP. Retrieved from *https://www.clasp.org/sites/default/files/publications/2017/04/Minnesota-Career-Pathways-On-Ramps.pdf.*

Centre for Canadian Language Benchmarks (2017). *PBLA Emerging Practices Guidelines*. Ottawa, Ontario: Centre for Canadian Language Benchmarks. Retrieved from *http://pblaepg.language.ca/.*

Chisman, F. & Crandall, J. (2007). *Passing the torch: Strategies for innovation in community college ESL.* New York, NY: Council for Advancement of Adult Literacy. Retrieved from *https://files.eric.ed.gov/fulltext/ED506584.pdf.*

Chomsky, N. (1959). Review of Verbal Behavior by B.F. Skinner. *Language 35/1*: 26–58.

Chong, W. & Kong, C. (2012). Teacher collaborative learning and teacher self-efficacy: The case of lesson study. *The Journal of Experimental Education*, *80*(3), 263–283.

Chowdhury, M. R. (2003). International TESOL training and EFL contexts: The cultural disillusionment factor. *Australian Journal of Education 47*(3), 283–302.

Ciampa, K. & Gallagher, T. (2016). Teacher collaborative inquiry in the context of literacy education: Examining the effects on teacher self-efficacy, instructional and assessment practices. *Teachers and Teaching 22*(7), 858–878.

Clymer, C., Toso, B., Grinder, E. & Sauder, R. (2017). Changing the course of family literacy. Policy Paper. Goodling Institute for Research in Family Literacy. Retrieved from *https://ed.psu.edu/goodling-institute/policy/changing-the-course-of-family-literacy.*

Cohen, A. D. & Griffiths, C. (2015). Revisiting LLS research 40 years later. *TESOL Quarterly*, *49*(1) 414–429.

Comings, J. (2007) Persistence: Helping adult education students reach their goals. Review of adult literacy, Volume 7. NCSALL. Retrieved from *http://www.ncsall.net/fileadmin/resources/ann_rev/comings-02.pdf.*

Comings, J., Parrella, A. & Soricone, L. (1999). Persistence Among Adult Basic Education Students in Pre-GED Classes. NCSALL Reports 12. Cambridge, MA: National Center for the Study of Adult Learning and Literacy.

Commonwealth of Australia (2012). *Australian Core Skills Framework*. Retrieved from *https://www.education.gov.au/australian-core-skills-framework.*

Condelli, L. & Wrigley, H. (2008). The what works study: Instruction, literacy and language learning for adult ESL literacy students. In S. Reder and J. Bynner (Eds.) *Tracking Adult Literacy and Numeracy Skills: Findings from Longitudinal Research.* London & New York: Routledge.

Condelli, L. & Zaidi, A. (2003). Using NRS data for program management and improvement. U.S. Department of Education, Washington, D.C.: American Institutes for Research. Retrieved from *http://www.hed.state.nm.us/uploads/FileLinks/123fc5bf8f824bfbb304398ec7e190a2/Data_Use_Guidebook_1.pdf.*

Conklin, L. (2011). *What's Next? Book 1.* Syracuse, NY: New Readers Press.

Cooke, M. (2006). "When I wake up I dream of electricity:" The lives, aspirations and "needs" of Adult ESOL learners. *Linguistics and Education 17*, 56–73.

Council of Europe (2001). *Common European Framework of Reference for Languages: Learning, Teaching, Assessment (CEFR).* Cambridge: Cambridge University Press. Retrieved from *https://www.coe.int/en/web/common-european-framework-reference-languages.*

Coxhead, A. (2000). A New Academic Word List. *TESOL Quarterly, 34*(2), 213–238.

Crandall, J. & Finn Miller, S. (2014). Effective professional development for language teachers. In M. Celce-Murcia, D. Brinton, D. & M. Snow (Eds.) *Teaching English as a Second or Foreign Language, 4th edition* (pp. 630–648). Boston: National Geographic Cengage Learning.

Cummins, J. (2000). *Language, Power and Pedagogy: Bilingual Children in the Crossfire.* Clevedon, England: Multilingual Matters.

Dao, P., & McDonough (2017). The effect of task role on Vietnamese EFL learners' collaboration in mixed proficiency dyads. *System, 65*, 15 –24.

Darkenwald, G. (1986). Adult literacy education: A review of the research and priorities for future inquiry. New York: Literacy Assistance Center.

Daly, A. (2009). Teaching prosody through reader's theatre. *School of Education Student Capstone Theses and Dissertations.* Retrieved from *https://digitalcommons.hamline.edu/hse_all/394.*

Derwing, T. (2003). What do ESL students say about their accents? *Canadian Modern Language Review, 59*(4), 547–66.

Derwing, T. & Munro, M. (2014). Once you have been speaking a second language for years, it's too late to change your pronunciation. In L. Grant (Ed.), *Pronunciation Myths* (pp. 34–55). Ann Arbor, MI: University of Michigan Press.

Derwing, T. M., & Munro, M. J. (2005). Second language accent and pronunciation teaching: A research-based approach. *TESOL Quarterly, 39*(3), 379–397.

Di Tommaso, K. (2005). Strategies to facilitate reading comprehension in college transition students. *Research to Practice Brief (5),* National College Transition Network. Retrieved from *http://www.collegetransition.org/promising/rp5.html.*

Dörnyei, Z. (2013). Communicative language teaching in the twenty-first century: The "principled communicative approach." In J. Arnold & T. Murphey (Eds.), *Meaningful Action: Earl Stevick's Influence on Language Teaching* (pp. 161–171). Cambridge: Cambridge University Press.

Dörnyei, Z., & Ushioda, E. (2011). *Teaching and Researching Motivation, 2nd edition.* Harlow: Longman.

Dow, H. (2011). The acculturation processes: The strategies and factors affecting the degree of acculturation. *Home Health Care Management & Practice 23*(3), 221–227.

Duff, P. (2012). Identity, agency, and SLA. In A. Mackey & S. Gass (Eds.), *Handbook of Second Language Acquisition* (pp. 410–426). London, UK: Routledge.

Dutro, S., & Kinsella, K. (2010). English language development: Issues and implementation in grades 6–12. In *Improving Education for English Learners: Research-Based Approaches.* California Department of Education.

Dyck, S., Battell, E., Isserlis, J. & Nonesuch, K. (1996). Women and work. In *Making Connections: A Literacy and EAL Curriculum from a Feminist Perspective*. Toronto: Canadian Congress for Learning Opportunities for Women.

Eckersley, N. (2017). Digital literacy: Consume, create, curate! EdTech Center Inspirations and ideas blog post. Boston, MA: World Education. Retrieved from *https://edtech.worlded.org/digital-literacy-consume-create-curate/.*

Ediger, A. (2014). Teaching second/foreign language literacy to school-age learners. In M. Celce-Murcia, D. Brinton, D. & M. Snow (Eds.) *Teaching English as a Second or Foreign Language, 4th edition* (pp. 154–169). Boston: National Geographic Cengage Learning.

EdTech (2013). Helping English language learners select alternative phrases. *EdTech Inspirations and Ideas web page*. Retrieved from *https://edtech.worlded.org/helping-ells-select-alternative-phrases/*.

EEOC (2016). Notice 915.005 EEOC Enforcement Guidance on National Origin Discrimination. Retrieved from *https://www.eeoc.gov/laws/guidance/national-origin-guidance.cfm#_Toc451518822*.

Egan, P. & Parrish, B. (2019). Oral language as a bridge to academic writing, in K. Schaetzel, J. K. Kreeft Peyton, J. & R. Fernandez (Eds). *Teaching Academic Writing to Adults Learning English*. Ann Arbor, MI: University of Michigan Press.

Ellis, R. (2008). *The Study of Second Language Acquisition, 2nd edition*. Oxford: Oxford University Press.

Ewert, D. (2014). Content-learning tasks for adult ESL learners: Promoting literacy for work or school. *TESOL Journal, 5*(2), 265–287.

Ewert, D. (2013). The effects of extensive reading on adult reading behavior and proficiency in an intensive English program. *Extensive Reading World Congress Proceedings, 1*, 141–144. Retrieved May 1, 2017 from *http://erfoundation.org/proceedings/erwc1-Ewert.pdf*.

Fernandez, R., Peyton, J.K., & Schaetzel, K. (2017). A survey of writing instruction in adult ESL programs: Are teaching practices meeting adult learner needs? *Journal of Research and Practice for Adult Literacy, Secondary, and Basic Education, 6*(2), 5–20. Retrieved from *https://static1.squarespace.com/static/55a158b4e4b0796a90f7c371/t/59782f28e58c62b0e4b701cc/1501048703128/Summer+Journal+Interactive+FINAL.pdf*.

Finn Miller, S. (2010). Promoting learner engagement when working with adult English language learners (Network Brief). Center for Adult English Language Acquisition (CAELA). Washington, DC: Center for Applied Linguistics. Retrieved from *https://lincs.ed.gov/ professional-development/resource-collections/pro le-421*.

Flege, J. (1981). The phonological basis of foreign accent: A hypothesis. *TESOL Quarterly, 15*(4), 443–455.

Foner, N. & Dreby, J. (2011). Relations between the generations in immigrant families. *Annual Review of Sociology 37(1)*, 545–564.

Ford, K. (2014). Competency-based education: History, opportunities, and challenges. Center for Innovation in Learning and Student Success. University of Maryland University College. Retrieved from *http://files.eric.ed.gov/fulltext/ED114384.pdf*.

Foster, D. & Bolton, P. (2018) Adult ESOL in England. Briefing Paper Number 7905. House of Commons. London, UK. Retrieved from *http://researchbriefings.files.parliament.uk/documents/CBP-7905/CBP-7905.pdf*.

Foster, M., Strawn, J., & Duke-Benfield, A. E. (2011). Beyond basic skills: State strategies to connect low-skilled students to an employer-valued postsecondary education. Washington, DC: CLASP Center for Postsecondary and Economic Success. Retrieved from *https://www.clasp.org/publications/report/brief/beyond-basic-skills-state-strategies-connect-low-skilled-students-employer*.

Gaer, S. (1998). Using software in the adult ESL classroom. ERIC Digest. Washington, D.C.: National Center for ESL Literacy Education (EDRS No. ED 418 607)

Gaer, S. (2011). Cell phones in the classroom? Yes! *Adult Basic Education and Literacy Journal, 5*(3) 176–180.

García, O. (2013). Theorizing and enacting translanguaging for social justice. In A. Blackledge and A. Creese (Eds.), *Heteroglossia as Practice and Pedagogy* (pp. 199–216). New York, NY: Springer.

Gardner, H. (1993). *Frames of Mind: The Theory of Multiple Intelligences, 10th anniversary edition*. New York: Basic Books.

Garvey, J. (2018). *Promoting Adult English Language Learner Reading Practices Through Sustained Silent Reading*. Unpublished MA Capstone, Hamline University, St. Paul, MN.

Gatbonton, E., Trofimovich, P. & Magid, M. (2005). Learners' ethnic group affiliation and L2 pronunciation accuracy: A sociolinguistic investigation. *TESOL Quarterly 39*(3), 489–511.

Gibbons, P. (2009). *English Learners' Academic Literacy and Thinking*. Portsmouth, NH: Heinemann.

Gibbons, P. (2015). *Scaffolding Learning Scaffolding Language, 2nd edition*. Portsmouth, NH: Heinemann.

Gibb, T. (2015). Literacy and language education: The quantification of learning. *New Direction for Adult and Community Education, Special Issue: Transnational Migration, Social Inclusion, and Adult Education Volume 2015, Issue 146*, 53–63.

Gilbert, J. (2012). *Clear Speech, 4th edition.* New York: Cambridge University Press.

Grabe, W. (2009). *Reading in a Second Language: Moving from Theory to Practice.* New York, NY: Cambridge University Press.

Grabe, W. & Stoller, F. (2014). Teaching reading for academic purposes. In M. Celce-Murcia, D. Brinton, D. & M. Snow (Eds.) *Teaching English as a Second or Foreign Language, 4th edition* (pp. 189–205). Boston: National Geographic Cengage Learning.

Graff, G. & Birkenstein, C. (2014). *They Say, I Say: The Moves That Matter in Academic Writing, 3rd edition.* New York, NY: W.W. Norton and Company, Inc.

Graham, C. (2000). *Jazz Chants.* New York, NY: Oxford University Press.

Graves, K. (2001). *Designing Language Courses.* Boston, MA: Heinle and Heinle.

Griffiths, C. (2012). Learning styles: Traversing the quagmire. In S. Mercer, S. Ryan, M. Williams (Eds.). *Psychology for Language Learning: Insights from Research, Theory and Practice.* London: Palgrave Macmillan.

Guskey, T. R. (2000). *Evaluating Professional Development.* Thousand Oaks, CA: Corwin.

Hamayan, E., Marlerm, B., Damico, J. & Sanchez-Lopez, C. (2013). *Special Education Considerations for English Language Learners: Delivering a Continuum of Services, 2nd edition.* Philadelphia, PA: Caslon Publishing.

Hanh, L. (2004). Primary Stress and Intelligibility: Research to motivate the teaching of suprasegmentals. *TESOL Quarterly, 38*(2), 201–223.

Harmer, J. (2015). *The Practice of English Language Teaching, 5th edition.* London: Longman.

Harris, K. (2015a). Integrating digital literacy into English language instruction: Issue brief. LINCS ESL Pro Project. Washington, D.C.: U.S. Department of Education, Office of Career, Technical and Adult Education. Retrieved from *https://lincs.ed.gov/programs/eslpro*.

Harris, K. (2015b). *Integrating Digital Literacy into English Language Instruction: Professional Development Module.* Washington, D.C.: U.S. Department of Education, Office of Career, Technical and Adult Education. Retrieved from *https://lincs.ed.gov/programs/eslpro.*

Healey, D. & Johnson, N. (2002). A place to start in selecting software. *CAELL Journal* 8:1.

Hinkel, E. (2014) Culture and pragmatics in language teaching and learning. In M. Celce-Murcia, D. Brinton, D. & M. Snow (Eds.) *Teaching English as a Second or Foreign Language, 4th edition* (pp. 394–408). Boston: National Geographic Cengage Learning.

Hoose, S. (2017). *The Effectiveness of Project-Based Learning in Teaching Adult ESL Students How to Cite Evidence from Texts.* Unpublished MA Capstone, Hamline University, St. Paul, MN.

Horton, B. & Hall, J. (2005). *Accommodating Adults with Disabilities in Adult Education, 2nd edition.* Lawrence, KA: University of Kansas Center for Research on Learning. Retrieved from *http://das.kucrl. org/projects/accommodating-adults-with-disabilities-in-adult-education-programs.*

Hymes, D. (1971). On linguistic theory, communicative competence, and the education of disadvantaged children. In M.L. Wax, S.A. Diamond & F. Gearing (Eds.), *Anthropological Perspectives on Education* (pp. 51–66). New York: Basic Books.

Isserlis, J. (2009). Trauma and learning: What do we know, what can we learn? *In Proceedings of the Fifth LESLLA Symposium*, Banff, Canada. Retrieved from *http://www.leslla.org/files/resources/Conference_ Proceedings_FINAL_Aug12.pdf.*

Isserlis, J. (2000). Trauma and the adult English language learner. ERIC Digest. Washington, D.C.: National Center for ESL Literacy Education (EDO-LE-00-02). Retrieved from *http://www.cal.org/ncle/digests/ trauma2.htm.*

Isserlis, J. (1996a). Dialogue journal writing as part of a learner-centered curriculum. In Peyton, J.K. & Staton, J. (Eds.) *Writing Our Lives.* McHenry, IL: Delta Systems & Center for Applied Linguistics.

Isserlis, J. (1996b). Women at the centre of the curriculum. In K. Nonesuch (Ed.), *Making Connections: Literacy and EAL Curriculum from a Feminist Perspective* (pp. 13–14). Toronto, Canada: Canadian Congress for Learning Opportunities for Women.

Jacobs, B. (1988). Differentiation of primary and secondary language acquisition. *Studies in Second Language Acquisition, 10*(3), 303–337.

Jiang, X., & Grabe, W. (2007). Graphic organizers in reading instruction: Research findings and issues. *Reading in a Foreign Language, 19*, 34–55.

Johnson, K. & Parrish, B. (2010). Aligning instructional practices to meet the academic needs of adult ESL students. *TESOL Quarterly, 44*(3), 618–628.

Kagan, S. & Kagan, M. (2009). *Kagan Cooperative Learning.* San Clemente, CA: Kagan.

Kim, Y. (2009). The effects of task complexity on learner–learner interaction. *System 37*(2), 254–268. Retrieved 5/20/28 from *https://www.sciencedirect.com/journal/system/vol/37/issue/2.*

Kinsella, K. (2012). Cutting to the Common Core: Disrupting Discourse. *Language Magazine.* Retrieved from *http://languagemagazine.com/?page_id=5114.*

Kirschner, P. (2017). Stop propagating the learning styles myth. *Computers & Education, 106*, 166–171.

Klas, K. & Kreil, J. (2017). *#Iam ABE Online Curriculum.* Minneapolis, MN. Retrieved from *https://sites.google.com/view/iamabe/about-iamabe.*

Klingner, J. (2015). Distinguishing language acquisition from learning disabilities. New York City Department of Education; Division of English Language Learners and Student Support. Retrieved from *http://schools.nyc.gov/NR/rdonlyres/DABEF55A-D155-43E1-B6CB-B689FBC9803A/0/LanguageAcquisitionJanetteKlingnerBrief_73015.pdf%20Resource.*

Kolb, D. (1984). *Experiential Learning,* Englewood Cliffs, NJ.: Prentice Hall.

Kolb, D. & Kolb, A. (2017). *The Experiential Educator.* Kaunakakai, HI: Experience Based Learning Systems Inc.

Krashen, S. (1982). *Principles and Practice in Second Language Acquisition.* Oxford: Pergamon.

Krashen, S. (1985). *The Input Hypothesis.* London: Longman.

Krashen, S. & Terrell, T. (1983). The Natural Approach: Language Acquisition in the Classroom. Oxford: Pergamon Press.

Kunnan, A. & Grabowski, K. (2014). Large scale second language assessment. In M. Celce-Murcia et al. (Eds.), *Teaching English as a Second or Foreign Language, 4th edition* (pp. 304–319). New York, NY: Heinle/Cengage.

Ladousse, G.P. (1987). *Role Play.* Oxford: Oxford University Press.

Learner Web (2017). What is learner web? Retrieved from *http://www.learnerweb.org/infosite/.*

Leu, D. J., Kinzer, C. K., Coiro, J., Castek, J., & Henry, L. A. (2013). New literacies: A dual-level theory of the changing nature of literacy, instruction and assessment. In D. E. Alvermann, N. J. Unrau, & R. B. Ruddell (Eds.), *Theoretical Models and Processes of Reading 6th edition*, (pp. 1150–1181). Newark, DE: International Reading Association.

Leu, D. J., McVerry, J. G., O'Byrne, W. L., Kiili, C., Zawilinski, L., Everett-Cacopardo, H., and Forzani, E. (2011). The new literacies of online reading comprehension: Expanding the literacy and learning curriculum. *Journal of Adolescent and Adult Literacy, 55*(1), 5–14.

Levis, J. (1999). Intonation in theory and practice, revisited. *TESOL Quarterly 33*(1), 37–63.

Liden, A., Poulos, A., & Vinogradov, P. (2008). Building literacy in emergent adult readers. Pre-Convention Institute presented at TESOL Convention. New York City, NY.

Lightbown, P. & Spada, N. (2013). *How Languages Are Learned.* Oxford: Oxford University Press.

Long, M. (1983). Native speaker/non-native speaker conversation and the negotiation of comprehensible input. *Applied Linguistics 4*: 126–41.

Lyster, R. & Saito, K. (2010). The role of oral and written corrective feedback in SLA. *Studies in Second Language Acquisition 32*(2), 265–302.

Magy, R. (2017). *Road to Work.* Syracuse, NY: New Readers Press.

Magy, R. & Price, D. (2011). ESL in the 21st century: Workforce transitions, materials and policy. Presented at the International TESOL Convention, New Orleans, LA.

Malan, S.P.T. (2000). The "new paradigm" of outcomes-based education in perspective. *Journal of Family Ecology and Consumer Science, 28,* 22–28.

Marzano, R. (2009). When students track their progress. *Educational Leadership, 67*(4), 86–87.

McKay, S. (2013). Authenticity in the language teaching curriculum. In C.A. Chapelle (Ed.), *The Encyclopedia of Applied Linguistics* (pp. 1–6). London, UK: Blackwell.

McKay, H. & Tom, H. (2000). *Teaching Adult Second Language Learners.* Cambridge: Cambridge University Press.

Migration Policy Institute's National Center on Immigrant Integration Policy (2015). *Overcoming WIOA's Barriers to Immigrant and Refugee Adult Learners.* Webinar offered through MPI National Center on Immigrant Integration Policy September 28, 2015.

Moll, L., Amanti, C., Neff, D. & Gonzalez, N. (1992). Funds of knowledge for teaching: Using a qualitative approach to connect homes and classrooms. *Theory into Practice, 31*(2), 132–141.

Mollica, R. (2006). *Healing Invisible Wounds: Paths to Hope and Recovery in a Violent World.* Harcourt, New York.

Morley, J. (1991). The pronunciation component in teaching English to speakers of other languages. *TESOL Quarterly 25*(3), 481–518.

Moustafa, M., & Maldonado-Colon, E. (1999). Whole-to-parts phonics instruction: Building on what children know to help them know more. *The Reading Teacher, 52*(5), 448–458. Retrieved from *http://www.jstor.org/stable/20202102.*

Moyer, A. (1999). Ultimate attainment in L2 phonology: The critical factors of age, motivation and instruction. *Studies in Second Language Acquisition, 21,* 81–108.

Muñoz, C., & Singleton, D. (2011). A critical review of age-related research on L2 ultimate attainment. *Language Teaching, 44*(1), 1–35.

Munro, M. (2003). A primer on accent discrimination in the Canadian context. *TESL Canada Review 20*(2), 38–51.

Murray, D. E. (2005). ESL in adult education. In E. Hinkel (Ed.), *Handbook of Research in Second Language Teaching and Learning* (pp. 65–84). Mahwah, N.J.: Lawrence Erlbaum Associates.

Murray, K., Davidson, G., & Schweitzer, R. (2010). Review of refugee mental health interventions following resettlement: best practices and recommendations. *The American Journal of Orthopsychiatry, 80*(4), 576–85.

Nash, A. & Hewett, E. (2017). *Integrated Education and Training: Implementing Programs in Diverse Contexts.* Boston: World Education. Retrieved from *http://www.collegetransition.org/docs/IET_Guide.pdf.*

Nash, A. & Kallenbach, S. (2009). *Making It Worth the Stay: Findings from the New England Adult Learner Persistence Project.* Boston, MA: The New England Literacy Resource Center at World Education. Retrieved from *https://nelrc.org/persist/report09.pdf.*

Nash, A. (2001). *Civic Participation and Community Action Sourcebook.* Boston, MA: New England Literacy Resource Center.

Nation, P. (2007). The four strands. *Innovation in Language Learning and Teaching, 1,* 2–13. National Center for ESL Literacy Education (EDRS No. ED 418 607).

National Commission on Adult Literacy (2008). Reach higher, America: Overcoming crisis in the U.S. workforce. Report of the National Commission on Adult Literacy. New York, NY: Center for Advancement of Adult Literacy.

National Joint Commission on Learning Disabilities (2016). National Joint Committee on Learning Disabilities definition of learning disabilities. National Joint Commission on Learning Disabilities website. Retrieved from *http://www.ldonline.org/about/partners/njcld.*

National Reporting System (2017). *Technical Assistance Guide for Performance Accountability Under the Workforce Innovation and Opportunity Act.* Washington, D.C.: Office of Career, Technical, and Adult

Education U.S. Department of Education. Retrieved from *https://nrsweb.org/sites/default/files/NRS-TA-January-2018-508.pdf.*

Neri, R., Lozano, M., Chang, S. & Herman, J. (2016). High-leverage principles of effective instruction for English learners. The Center for Standards & Assessment Implementation, UCLA.

New English Literary Resource Center. (N.D.) Managing Stress to Improve Learning. Boston MA: World Learning. Retrieved from *https://nelrc.org/managingstress/program_background.html.*

Newman, A., Rosbash, T., & Sarkisian, L. (2015). *Learning for Life: The Opportunity for Technology to Transform Adult Education.* Chicago, IL: The Joyce Foundation. Retrieved from *http://tytonpartners.com/library/learning-for-life-the-opportunity-for-technology-to-transform-adult-education/.*

Newton, P. M. (2015). The learning styles myth is thriving in higher education. *Frontiers in Psychology 6,* Article 1908. Retrieved from *https://www.frontiersin.org/articles/10.3389/fpsyg.2015.01908/full.*

Northstar Digital Literacy Standards (N.D.). Northstar Digital Literacy Project. St. Paul MN: St. Paul Public Library. Access at *https://www.digitalliteracyassessment.org/.*

Norton, B. (2013). *Identity and Language Learning: Extending the Conversation, 2nd edition.* Bristol, UK: Multilingual Matters.

Norton, B. (2000). Identity and Language Learning: Gender, Ethnicity and Educational Change. Harlow, UK: Longman.

Nunan, D. (2014). Task-based learning and teaching. In M. Celce-Murcia, D. Brinton, D. & M. Snow (Eds.) *Teaching English as a Second or Foreign Language, 4th edition* (pp. 455–470). Boston: National Geographic Cengage Learning.

Nunan, D. and Bailey, K. (2009). *Exploring Second Language Classroom Research: A Comprehensive Guide.* Boston MA: Heinle ELT.

OECD (2016), Skills for a digital world: Policy brief on the future of work, OECD Publishing, Paris. Retrieved from *https://www.oecd.org/els/emp/Skills-for-a-Digital-World.pdf.*

Olsen, L. (1988). *Crossing the Schoolhouse Border: Immigrant Students and the California Public Schools.* Oakland, CA: A California Tomorrow Report.

Olsen, R., & Kagan, S. (1992). About cooperative learning. In C. Kessler (Ed.), *Cooperative Language Learning: A Teacher's Resource Book* (pp. 1–30). Englewood Cliffs, NJ: Prentice Hall.

O'Malley, J.M., and Chamot, A. (1990). *Learning Strategies in Second Language Acquisition.* Cambridge: Cambridge University Press.

Oxford, R. (2016). *Teaching and Researching Language Learning Strategies: Self-Regulation in Context, 2nd Edition.* New York, NY: Routledge.

Oxford, R. (1990). *Language Learning Strategies: What Every Teacher Should Know.* New York: Newbury House.

PANDA (N.D.). Minnesota Adult Basic Education Disability Specialists web page. *http://mn.abedisabilities.org/.*

Parrino, A. (2001). The politics of pronunciation and the adult learner. In T. Smoke (Ed.): *Adult ESL: Politics, Pedagogy, and Participation in Classroom and Community Programs.* Mahwah, NJ: Lawrence Erlbaum Associates.

Parrish, B. (2015a). Meeting the language needs of today's adult English language learner: Issue brief. *LINCS ESL Pro Project.* Washington, D.C.: U.S. Department of Education, Office of Career, Technical and Adult Education *https://lincs.ed.gov/programs/eslpro.*

Parrish, B. (2015b). Meeting the language needs of today's adult English language learner: Online Module. *LINCS ESL Pro Project.* Washington, D.C.: U.S. Department of Education, Office of Career, Technical and Adult Education *https://lincs.ed.gov/programs/eslpro.*

Parrish, B. & Pecoraro, D. (2002). EL civics: Taking learning outside of the classroom. Presentation at Minnesota ABE Summer Intensive. Breezy Point. Brainerd, MN.

Parrish, B., & Johnson, K. (2010). *Promoting Learner Transitions to Postsecondary Education and Work: Developing Academic Readiness from the Beginning.* CAELA Network Brief. Washington, D.C.: Center for Applied Linguistics. Retrieved from *http://www.cal.org/caelanetwork/resources/transitions.html.*

Peterson, L. (2018). Converting a lesson to integrate technology. EdTech Lesson Plans and Classroom Activities. Boston, MA: World Education. Retrieved from *https://edtech.worlded.org/converting-lesson-integrate-technology/*.

Peyton, J. (1993). Listening to students' voices: Publishing students' writing for other students to read. In J. Crandall and J. Peyton (Eds.) *Approaches to Adult ESL Literacy*. McHenry, IL: Delta Systems & Center for Applied Linguistics.

PIACC (2009). PIAAC problem-solving in technology-rich environments: A conceptual framework. OECD Education Working Paper No. 36. Paris: OECD. Retrieved from *https://files.eric.ed.gov/fulltext/ED530714.pdf*.

Pimentel, S. (2013). *College and Career Readiness Standards for Adult Education*. Washington, D.C.: U.S. Department of Education, Office of Vocational and Adult Education. Retrieved from *http://lincs.ed.gov/publications/pdf/CCRStandardsAdultEd.pdf*.

Porter, K., Cuban, S., & Comings, J. (2005). *One day I will make it*. New York: MDRC.

Purcell-Gates, V., Anderson, J., Gagne, M., Jang, K., Lenters, K. & McTavish, M. (2012). Measuring situated literacy activity: Challenges and promises. *Journal of Literacy Research 44*(4), 396–425.

Purcell-Gates, V., Degener, S., Jacobson, E., & Soler, M. (2002). Impact of authentic adult literacy instruction on adult literacy practices. *Reading Research Quarterly, 37*, 70–92. doi:10.1598/RRQ.37.1.3.

Ramirez, S. (2001). Noncredit ESL managed enrollment pilot. MiraCosta College Report. (*http://www.miracosta.edu/instruction/continuingeducation/esl/managedenrollment.html*).

Reimer, J. (2008). Learning strategies and low-literacy Hmong adult students. *Minne/WITESOL Journal, 25*. Retrieved from *http:// minnetesol.org/journal/vol25_html_pages/6_Reimer.htm reluctant adult ESL students. Journal of Adult Education, 44(2), 15–20*.

Reimer, J. (1998). *Learning to observe learning: The role of peer interaction in a practicum*. Unpublished MA Project. Vermont: School for International Training.

Richards, J. (2013). Curriculum approaches in language teaching: Forward, central, and backward design. *RELC Journal 44*(1), 5–33.

Richards, J. & Rogers, T. (2014). *Approaches and Methods in Language Teaching, 3rd Edition*. Cambridge: Cambridge University Press.

Ritchhart, R., Church, M. & Morrison, K. (2011). *Making Thinking Visible: How to Promote Engagement, Understanding, and Independence for All Learner*. San Francisco, CA: Jossey-Bass.

Rosa, J. & Nelson, F. (2017). Do you hear what I hear? Raciolinguistic ideologies and culturally sustaining pedagogies. In D. Paris & S. Alim (Eds.), *Culturally Sustaining Pedagogies: Teaching and Learning for Social Justice in a Changing World*. New York, NY: Teachers College Press.

Rosen, D. J. and Vanek, J. B. (2017). Technology for innovation and change in adult basic skills education. *New Directions for Adult and Continuing Education*, 51–60. doi:10.1002/ace.20240.

Rothstein, D., & Santana, L. (2011). Teaching students to ask their own questions. *Harvard Education Letter, 27*(5), 1–2. Retrieved from *http://hepg.org/hel-home/issues/27_5/helarticle/teaching-students-to-ask-their-own-questions_507*.

Rowe, M. B. (1986). Wait time: Slowing down may be a way of speeding up! *Journal of Teacher Education, 37*, 43–50.

Rubin, D. (2012). The power of prejudice in accent perception: Reverse linguistic stereotyping and its impact on listener judgments and decisions. In. J. Levis & K. LeVelle (Eds.). *Proceedings of the Third Pronunciation in Second Language Learning and Teaching Conference*, Sept. 2011. (pp. 11–17). Ames, IA: Iowa State University.

Rudling, J. (2012). *Improve Spelling with Look, Say, Cover, Write*. How to Spell [video file]. Retrieved from *https://howtospell.co.uk/LSCWvideo.php*.

Savage, K.L. (1993). Literacy through a competency-based educational approach. In *Approaches to Adult Literacy Instruction*. J. Crandall and J. Peyton (Eds.) McHenry, IL: Center for Applied Linguistics and Delta Systems, Inc.

Scarcella, R. (1990). *Teaching Language Minority Students in the Multicultural Classroom.* Upper Saddle River, NJ: Prentice Hall.

Scarcella, R. (2003). *Accelerating Academic English: A Focus on the English Learner*. Oakland, CA: Regents of the University of California.

Schalge, S. & Soga, K. (2008). "Then I stop coming to school": Understanding absenteeism in an adult English as a second language program. *Adult Basic Education and Literacy Journal 2*(3), 151–61.

Schrock, K. (2001–2016). The five Ws of website evaluation. *Kathy Schrock's Guide to Everything*. Retrieved from *http://www.schrockguide.net/critical-evaluation.html.*

Schumann, J. (1986). Research on the acculturation model for second language acquisition. *Journal of Multilingual and Multicultural Development. 7,* 379–392.

Schwarz, R. (2009). Issues in identifying learning disabilities for English language learners. In J. M. Taymans (Ed.), Learning to Achieve: A Review of the Research on Serving Adults with Learning Disabilities (pp. 73–117). Washington, D.C.: National Institute for Literacy.

Scogins, J., Thompson, J. & Reabe, L. (2008). Illinois Adult Education Enrollment Study. Chicago, IL: Center for Adult Learning Leadership. Retrieved from *https://education.illinoisstate.edu/downloads/casei/ FullEnrollmentStudy.pdf.*

Scrivener, J. (2011). *Learning Teaching, 3rd edition.* London: Macmillan Heinemann.

Shank, C. & Terrill, L. (1997). Multilevel literacy planning and development. *Focus on Basics,* 1(C).

Shiring, B. (2017). Connect, relax, and refocus: Using technology to alleviate anxiety for language learners. EdTech Center tech tips blog post. Boston, MA: World Education. Retrieved from *https:// edtech.worlded.org/connect-relax-refocus/.*

Simons Loustalet, A. (1999). Teaching ESL among adults with learning disabilities. Training materials for facilitators and participants CAEPA Conference Fall 1999. Retrieved from *http://www.coloradoadulted. org/ld/esl-ld.html.*

Singleton, D. & L. Ryan (2004). *Language Acquisition: The Age Factor, 2nd edition.* Clevedon: Multilingual Matters.

Skinner, B. F. (1957). *Verbal Learning.* New York, NY: Appleton-Century-Crofts.

Smith, C. (2010). The great dilemma of improving teacher quality in adult learning and literacy. *Adult Basic Education and Literacy*, *4*(2), 67. Retrieved from *http://scholarworks.umass.edu/cie_faculty_pubs/36.*

Snow, C. E., & Uccelli, P. (2009). The challenge of academic language. In D.R. Olson and N. Torrance (Eds.), *The Cambridge Handbook of Literacy* (pp. 112–133). Cambridge: Cambridge University Press.

Spencer, D. (1993). The Freirean approach to adult literacy education. In J. Crandall and J. Peyton (Eds.) *Approaches to Adult Literacy Instruction*. McHenry, IL: Center for Applied Linguistics and Delta Systems, Inc.

Stanley, N. & Dillingham, B. (2017). Making learners click with digital storytelling. *Language Magazine.* Retrieved from *https://www.languagemagazine.com/making-learners-click-with-digital-storytelling/.*

Sticht, T. (1982). *Evaluation of the reading potential concept for marginally illiterate adults*. Alexandria, VA: Human Resources Research Organization.

Street, B. (1995). *Social Literacies: Critical approaches to literacy in development, ethnography and education.* New York, NY: Routledge.

Swain, M., & Lapkin, S. (1998). Interaction and second language learning: Two adolescent French immersion students working together. *Modern Language Journal, 82,* 320–337.

Swartz, T. (2009). Intergenerational family relations in adulthood: patterns, variations, and implications in the contemporary United States. *Annual Review of Sociology 35(1),* 191–212.

Tarone, E., & Bigelow, M. (2005). Impact of literacy on oral language processing: Implications for SLA research. *Annual Review of Applied Linguistics, 25,* 77–97.

Tarone, E. & Parrish, B. (1994). Task related variation in interlanguage: The case for articles. In H.D. Brown (Ed.) *Readings on Second Language Acquisition*, Englewood Cliffs, NJ: Prentice Hall.

Taylor, K., and Thompson, S. (1999). The color vowel chart. Santa Fe, NM: English Language Training Solutions. *https://www.colorvowelchart.org.*

TEAL (2010). TEAL Center fact sheet # 2: Universal Design for Learning. *Teaching Excellence in Adult Literacy Center*. American Institutes for Research. Retrieved from *https://lincs.ed.gov/sites/default/ files/2_TEAL_UDL.pdf.*

TEAL (2013). Deeper learning through questioning. *Teaching Excellence in Adult Literacy Center*. American Institutes for Research. Retrieved from *https://lincs.ed.gov/professional-development/resource-collections/profile-759.*

TESOL (2018). *The Six Principles of Exemplary Teaching. http://www.tesol.org/the-6-principles/.*

The Teaching Center (2009). Establishing classroom ground rules to promote an environment of inclusion and respect for all contributions. Washington University of St. Louis. Retrieved from *http:// teachingcenter.wustl.edu/resources/inclusive-teaching-learning/establishing-ground-rules/.*

Tomlinson, C. (2014). *The Differentiated Classroom: Responding to the Needs of All Learners, 2nd edition.* Alexandria: ASCD.

Tomlinson, C., & Imbeau, M. (2010). *Leading and Managing a Differentiated Classroom.* Alexandria: ASCD.

Trilling, B., & Fabel, C. (2009). *21st-Century Skills: Learning for Life in Our Times.* Hoboken, NJ: Wiley.

Trupke-Bastidas, J., & Poulos, A. (2007). Improving literacy of L1-non- literate and L1-literate adult English as a second language learners. *Minne/WITESOL Journal, 25.* Retrieved from *http://minnetesol .org/ journal/articles/improvingliteracy.html.*

Tsui, A. (2001). *Classroom Interaction.* In the *Cambridge Guide to Teaching English to Speakers of Other Languages.* 120–125. 10.1017/CBO9780511667206.018.

Tsui, A. (2009). Teaching expertise: Approaches, perspectives, and characteristics. In A.Burns and J. Richards (Eds.). *Cambridge Guide to Second Language Teacher Education,* (pp. 190-197). New York, NY: Cambridge University Press.

Tyton Partners (2016). *Learning For Life: The Opportunity For Technology To Transform Adult Education.* Chicago, IL: The Joyce Foundation.

U.S. Committee for Refugees and Immigrants (2007). *Resource Guide for Serving Refugees with Disabilities.* Washington DC: USCRI. Retrieved from *https://refugees.org/wp-content/uploads/2015/12/Serving-Refugees-with-Disabilities.pdf.*

U.S. Department of Education, Office of Career, Technical, and Adult Education (2016a). *Implementation guidelines: Measures and methods for the National Reporting System for Adult Education.* Washington, D.C.: Author. Retrieved from *http://www.nrsweb.org/docs/ NRS_Implementation_Guidelines_ February2016.pdf.*

U.S. Department of Education, Office of Career, Technical and Adult Education (2016b). *Adult English Language Proficiency Standards for Adult Education.* Washington, D.C. Retrieved from *https://lincs. ed.gov/publications/pdf/elp-standards-adult-ed.pdf.*

U.S. Department of Education Office of Career, Technical, and Adult Education (2015). *Workforce Innovation and Opportunity Act: Integrating Technology in WIOA. Fact S*heet. Retrieved from *https:// www2.ed.gov/about/offices/list/ovae/pi/AdultEd/integrating-technology.pdf.*

U.S. Department of Education, Office of Vocational and Adult Education (2013). College and Career Readiness Standards for Adult Education. Washington, D.C. Retrieved from *https://www.vrae.org/ images/customer-files/ccrstandardsadulted.pdf.*

UNESCO (2005). *Literacy for life.* Paris: United Nations Educational, Scientific and Cultural Organization. Retrieved from *http://unesdoc.unesco.org/images/0014/001416/141639e.pdf.*

Ur, P. (2009). *Grammar Practice Activities 2nd edition.* Cambridge: Cambridge University Press.

Van de Craats, I., Kurvers J., & Young-Scholten, M. (2006). Research on low-educated second language and literacy acquisition. In I. van de Craats, J. Kurvers, and M. Young-Scholten (Eds.), *Low-Educated Adult Second Language and Literacy Acquisition: Proceedings of the Inaugural Symposium Tilburg 2005* (pp. 7–23). Utrecht: LOT.

VanDerWerf, S. (2017). Stand and talks: The best thing I ever did to get students talking to one another. VDW Blog. Retrieved from *https://saravanderwerf.com/2017/08/09/stand-talks-the-best-thing-i-ever-did-to-get-students-talking-to-one-another/*.

Van Dyke-Kao, R. & Yanuaria, C. (2017). The translanguaging project: A multilingual pedagogy for student advocacy. Presented at the CATESOL Conference, Santa Clara, CA, October 2017.

Vanek, J., Simpson, D., Johnston, J. & Petty, L. (2016). *IDEAL Distance Education and Blended Learning Handbook, 5th edition.* Boston, MA: IDEAL Consortium. EdTech Center at World Education.

Velasco, P. & García, O. (2014). Translanguaging and the writing of bilingual learners. *The Bilingual Research Journal, 37*(1), 6–23.

Vesely, C., Goodman, R. & Scurlock, S. (2014). Turning points and transitions: The role of family in women's immigration experiences. *International Journal of Child, Youth and Family Studies 5*(2):308–331.

Vinogradov, P. (2016). *Meeting the Language Demands of Today's Adult English Language Learner: Companion Learning Resource.* LINCS ESL Pro Project. Washington, D.C.: US Department of Education, Office of Career, Technical and Adult Education *https://lincs.ed.gov/programs/eslpro*.

Vinogradov, P. (2009). Balancing top and bottom: Learner-generated texts for teaching phonics. *Low Educated Second Language and Literacy Acquisition Proceedings of the Fifth Symposium.*

Vinogradov, P. (2008). "Maestra! The letters speak." Adult ESL students learning to read for the first time. *Minne/WITESOL Journal, 25.* Retrieved from *http://minnetesol.org/blog1/minnetesol- 2008-journal/2008-journal/vinogradov_ nal/*.

Vuorikari, R. Punie, Y., Carretero, S. & Van den Brande, L. (2016). *DigComp 2.0: The Digital Competence Framework for Citizens. Update Phase 1: The Conceptual Reference Model.* Luxembourg Publication Office of the European Union. EUR 27948 EN. doi:10.2791/11517.

Vygotsky, L. (1986). *Thought and Language.* Edition edited by A. Kozulin. Cambridge, MA: MIT Press.

Vygotsky, L. S. (1978). Mind in society: The development of higher psychological processes. In Cole, M., John-Steiner, V., Scribner, S., and Souberman, E., (Eds.). Cambridge, MA: Harvard University Press.

Wallerstein, N. and Auerbach, E. (2004). *Problem-Posing at Work: Popular Educator's Guide.* Edmonton, Canada: Grass Roots Press.

Weigle, S. (2014). Considerations for teaching second language writing. In M. Celce-Murcia, D. Brinton, D. & M. Snow (Eds.) *Teaching English as a Second or Foreign Language, 4th edition* (pp. 222–237). Boston: National Geographic Cengage Learning.

Wenger, E. (1998). *Communities of Practice: Learning, Meaning, and Identity.* Cambridge, UK: Cambridge University Press.

Wiggins, G. & McTigue, J. (2005). *Understanding by Design, Expanded 2nd Edition.* Association for Supervision and Curriculum Development.

Willis, D. & Willis, J. (2007). *Doing Task-Based Teaching.* Oxford: Oxford University Press.

Workforce Innovation and Opportunity Act. (2014). Pub L. No. 113–128, Stat. 1425 2014.

Wrigley, H. (2017). English innovations: Learning English with digital literacy and community engagement. *EdTech Updates from the Field.* World Education. Retrieved from *https://edtech.worlded.org/english-innovations/*.

Wrigley, H. (2015). Preparing English learners for work and career pathways: Issue brief LINCS ESL Pro Project. Washington, D.C.: U.S. Department of Education, Office of Career, Technical and Adult Education *https://lincs.ed.gov/programs/eslpro*.

Wrigley, H. (2008). Capturing what counts: Language and literacy assessments for adult English language learners. In K.M. Rivera and A. Huerta-Macias (Eds.), *Adult Biliteracy: Sociocultural and Programmatic Responses.* Mahwah, NJ: Lawrence Erlbaum.

Wrigley, H. S. (2007). Beyond the lifeboat: Improving language, citizenship, and training services for immigrants and refugees. In A. Belzer (Ed.), *Toward Defining and Improving Quality in Adult Basic Education: Issues and Challenges* (pp. 221–240). Mahwah, NJ: Erlbaum.

Wrigley, H. (1998). Knowledge in action: The promise of project-based learning. *Focus on Basics, 2* (D), 13–18.

Young, R. (2011). Interactional competence in language learning, teaching, and testing. In E. Hinkel (Ed.) *Handbook of Research in Second Language Teaching and Learning, 2nd edition* (pp. 426–443) London: Routledge.

Zoshak, R. (2016). "Tiny talks" between colleagues: Brief narratives in teacher development. *Language Teaching Research, 20*(2), 209–222.

Zwiers, J. (2014). *Building Academic Language, 2nd edition*. San Francisco, CA: Jossey-Bass.

Zwiers, J., & Crawford, M. (2011). *Academic Conversations: Classroom Talk That Fosters Critical Thinking and Content Understandings.* Portland, ME: Stenhouse.

Index

Canada, standards frameworks 322, 325, 331
Canadian Center for Victims of Tortures
    (CCVT) 243–4
can-do statements 218
career pathways/career-focused
    programming 50–3
Cell-Ed 280–1
central design 188
chain activities 83–4
checking learner understanding 200–2, 211
    see also assessment; correcting learner
        language
checklists for assessment 299–300, 307–8
children of adult learners 11
Chomsky, N. 19
citizenship
    teaching approaches 40
    teaching programs 49
civics education (CE) programs 49
class field trips 263–7
class sizes 231–2
    see also multilevel classes
class web pages 281
classroom practice
    communicatively-based approaches 37–8
    content-based instruction 40
    learner-centered 11–12, 26–7
    and standards 326–30
    task-based learning 39–40
    see also learning environments; teaching
        approaches
classroom volunteers 230–1
Cognitive Academic Language Proficiency
    (CALP) 21–2
cognitive strategies 206
collaborative dialogue 21
collaborative professional development 310
College and Career Readiness Standards
    (CCRS) 66, 68, 322, 329, 331, 333–5
color vowel approach 129
communicative competence 16–18
    see also language acquisition
communicative language teaching
    pronunciation 123
    teaching approaches 34, 36–8
communicative pronunciation practice 131
communicatively-based approaches 37–8

Communities of Practice (CoPs) 312
community events 266
community services 46–7
compensation strategies 205, 206
competency-based education 35–6
comprehensible input 20
computer-assisted language learning (CALL)
    268
computer labs 229–30
concentric circles 237
content standards 319
content words 128
content-based instruction 40
content-based textbooks 254
contextualized teaching approach 59–60: see
    integrated and contextualised teaching
    approach
continuous professional development: see
    professional development
cooperative language learning 38
cooperative learning
    and assessment 300–1
    digital resources 277
    paired reading 160, 277
    pairing/grouping students 234–7
cooperative professional development 310
core series textbooks 253
correcting learner language
    checking learner understanding 200–2, 211
    dialogue journals 175
    integrated and contextualised teaching
        approach 89–95, 99
    writing skills 176–7
    see also teacher talk
corrective feedback 91–4
course design 185
    see also lesson plans
critical thinking
    integrated and contextualised teaching
        approach 62
    lesson plans 188
    teacher talk 202–4
cultural adjustment
    beyond basic skills 21–2
    factors affecting 7–10
    learner-centered classrooms 11, 26–7
cultural background (multilevel classes) 215

language demands of today's world 12–14
  speaking, listening, reading and writing 62
  transitions level 49
  see also listening skills; reading skills;
    speaking skills; writing skills
skill-specific textbooks 254
social context 66–7
social interaction 18
social media for professional development
  309
social strategies 206
software for learning 281–2
  see also digital learning
speaking skills
  fluency as goal 114, 135–6
  modes of communication 62
  practice activities 115–22
  pronunciation factors affecting 125
  pronunciation in your curriculum 123–5,
    136
  pronunciation teaching 126–32
  standards frameworks 329
standardized tests 291–5, 333–5
  see also assessment
standards 319–21, 338
  and accountability 319, 321, 322
  and assessment 333–5
  in the classroom 326–30
  in context 323–5
  and emergent learner needs 330–3
  frameworks and reporting 321–3
stress (pronunciation) 126–8, 129–30
study circles 312
summative assessment 295
suprasegmentals 126, 128
survey activities 266
survival literacy 143

task-based learning 38–40, 326
teacher resource books 254
teacher talk 197
  checking learner understanding 200–2
  giving directions 199–200, 204, 211
  maximizing learner involvement 198
  promoting critical thinking 202–4
teacher-directed classes 12
teaching approaches 31–2, 33–4, 56

audiolingual method 34
citizenship 40
collaboration 2
communicative language teaching 34, 36–8
competency-based education 35–6
content-based instruction 40
cooperative language learning 38
language experience approach 34
multi-faceted 32–3, 44
natural approach 34–5
participatory 41–2
project-based learning 42–4
pronunciation 126–32
task-based learning 38–40
whole language approach 34
  see also assessing teaching effectiveness;
    integrated and contextualised teaching
    approach
teaching programs 45–6, 57
  career pathways/career-focused
    programming 50–3
  citizenship 49
  distance education 53–4
  English language acquisition programs
    48–9
  family and intergenerational literacy 50
  integrated English literacy/civics education
    49
  literacy tutoring 50
  to promote learner persistence and success
    46–8
technology integration 268–9
  see also digital learning
TESOL, Six Principles for Exemplary Teaching
    of English Learners 314
testing 290–1
  see also assessment
textbooks
  adaptation and supplementation 259–61,
    284
  selection 254–7, 284
  sources for listening passages 113
  standards-based 329–30
  types 253–4
top-down processing 107–9, 145
topic choices 188–9
torture victims 243–5

total physical response method 82–3
transactional dialogue 114
transition skills 49
translanguaging 230
trauma victims 243–5

unemployment rates 11
United Kingdom, standards frameworks 322, 324
United States, standards frameworks 322–3, 324
universal design for learning 241–2, 243

validity, assessment 290
vanishing letters 167–8
video recordings 302
videos as resources 261
visual literacy 144
vocabulary, learning strategies 208–9
volunteers 230–1
Vygotsky, L. 21

web searches 275–6
   see also digital learning
web pages, for the class 281

whole language approach 34, 148–9, 165
whole-part-whole approach 149–50
word association activities 131
word search activities 128–9
work samples 302
workplace ESL programs 52
Wrigley, H. 42, 54
writing skills
   dialogue journals 174–5
   extensive writing tasks 169–73
   graphic organizers 173–4
   integrated and contextualized teaching approach 87–8
   learners with limited literacy 146–51
   literacy types 143–4
   modes of communication 62
   product-oriented tasks 165–9
   promoting strategies development 154–7
   responding to learner writing 176–7
   situated skills development 141–2
   social construction of literacy 142–3
   standards frameworks 329
   and technology 175–6
   text types 153–4
   types of writing task 165–7